Unity 3D Game Develop

Designed for passionate game developers—
Engineered to build professional games

Anthony Davis
Travis Baptiste
Russell Craig
Ryan Stunkel

<packt>
BIRMINGHAM—MUMBAI

Unity 3D Game Development

Copyright © 2022 Packt Publishing

All rights reserved. No part of this book may be reproduced, stored in a retrieval system, or transmitted in any form or by any means, without the prior written permission of the publisher, except in the case of brief quotations embedded in critical articles or reviews.

Every effort has been made in the preparation of this book to ensure the accuracy of the information presented. However, the information contained in this book is sold without warranty, either express or implied. Neither the authors, nor Packt Publishing or its dealers and distributors, will be held liable for any damages caused or alleged to have been caused directly or indirectly by this book.

Packt Publishing has endeavored to provide trademark information about all of the companies and products mentioned in this book by the appropriate use of capitals. However, Packt Publishing cannot guarantee the accuracy of this information.

Senior Publishing Product Manager: Manish Nainani
Acquisition Editor – Peer Reviews: Saby Dsilva
Project Editor: Rianna Rodrigues
Content Development Editor: Grey Murtagh
Copy Editor: Safis Editing
Technical Editor: Srishty Bhardwaj
Proofreader: Safis Editing
Indexer: Subalakshmi Govindhan
Presentation Designer: Rajesh Shirsath

First published: August 2022

Production reference: 3300822

Published by Packt Publishing Ltd.
Livery Place
35 Livery Street
Birmingham
B3 2PB, UK.

ISBN 978-1-80107-614-2

www.packt.com

Contributors

About the authors

Anthony Davis is a Senior Technical Artist with Accelerate Solutions, living in Orlando, Florida. Before working with Unity, he worked in several verticals, ranging from being a military veteran and a gymnastics coach to starting an indie game development studio, and a few things in between. His work in independent and freelance work lent to a great many hats learning all facets of game development. In his free time, he plays Dungeons and Dragons, attempts art, and plans for his next project.

I'd like to thank my entire family for allowing space to work on this. Tica, thank you for keeping everything moving forward. Jehryn and Kember, thank you for understanding that sometimes I had to work on this instead of playing games with you. Mohss, I thought about you the whole time making this. I hope this serves you well for your own game projects.

Travis Baptiste: Artist, life-long learner, and recreational gamer are a few of the terms that can be used to describe Travis. After his time in the military, Travis attended Full Sail University, where he studied Game Art. Since graduating in 2015, he has worked as a freelance 3D modeler while homeschooling his two children. Between servicing clients and personal projects, Travis has kept his 3D talents sharp across multiple programs.

My family, thank you for your understanding at the times I have to work. To my sons, I hope that this experience can further inspire you both to pursue your own goals in spite of hardships. To my wife, Almira, thank you for the support. The late nights of work were much easier with the help you have provided with the kids. Thank you, David Nguyen, for the life guidance and being in my corner. Thank you, Anthony, for the opportunity. I am grateful that I had the chance to work with you on this.

Russell Craig is a Senior Software Engineer at Unity Technologies. At the time of writing, he has 10 years of professional Unity simulation experience in the areas of application development, product hardware/firmware simulation, sensor simulation, medical training simulation, and AR/VR development. A speaker at Unite and jack of all trades in all things Unity, Russell spends his free time with his wife and children, building computers, playing video games, and modifying cars.

I would like to thank my family, friends, and coworkers for putting up with my hectic schedule.

Ryan Stunkel is a professional sound designer for video games who runs his contracting studio, Blipsounds, out of Austin, Texas. In addition to Blipsounds, Ryan is a teacher and mentor to a community of sound designers through the Blipsounds YouTube channel. He has traveled the world sharing his knowledge on video game sound design for Google, PAX, and Schools.

About the reviewers

Ģirts Ķesteris is the Studio Lead @HyperVR Games and also freelance XR/Unity software engineer at Ubiquity Inc. He is a lecturer in the development of 3D interactive environments (also covering Unity game engine) at Vidzemes Augstskola / Vidzeme University of Applied Sciences (part-time), and an indie game developer at NYAARGH! (self-employed). He has extensive experience with Unity at multiple companies.

Thanks to my wife for her patience and support!

Montica "Tica" Sansook (she/her) is a Asian-American serial entrepreneur, speaker, game artist, and content creator. Tica serves as the Co-Founder of Defy Esports Bar, an esports nightlife venue, and Defy Games, an indie game development studio. She has graduated twice from Full Sail University with Entertainment Business Masters of Science and Game Art Bachelors of Science. Her vast and varied career experiences have ranged from creative brand and business development within gaming to community management of content creators and professional esports organizations. Tica takes great joy and fulfillment from supporting others through mentorship, diversity advocacy, and consulting. She loves encouraging people to explore their potential and spotlighting her colleagues' accomplishments. On her journey, she wishes to be a positive influence in nurturing the ecosystem of the gaming industry for the better.

Table of Contents

Preface xix

Chapter 1: A Primer to the Third Dimension 1

Goal of this book 2

Coming around to 3D 3

Coordinate systems • 4

Vectors • 6

Cameras • 6

Faces, edges, vertices, and meshes • 6

Materials, textures, and shaders • 7

Rigidbody physics • 9

Collision detection • 10

The Unity interface 11

Scene view and hierarchy • 11

Inspector • 13

The Project window • 14

Game view • 15

Package Manager • 16

Essential Unity concepts 18

Assets • 18

Scenes • 18

GameObjects • 18

Components • 18

Scripts • 19

Prefabs • 20

Packages • 20

Summary 20

Chapter 2: Design and Prototype — 21

Game design fundamentals 21

Game design document • 22

Deliberate decisions • 23

Iterative production • 24

Concepting • 26

Your first Unity project 28

Unity Hub • 28

Choosing a version • 28

Choosing a template • 29

Scriptable rendering pipeline • 30

Built-In Rendering • 30

Universal Rendering • 30

High-Definition Rendering • 31

Prototyping 31

Wireframing or paper creation • 31

Grayboxing • 32

Proof of Concept (PoC) • 33

Minimum Viable Product (MVP) • 34

Vertical slice • 34

Summary 35

Table of Contents

Chapter 3: Programming — 37

Setting up the environment 37

   The Unity environment • 38

Fundamentals 40

   Variables • 41

   Data types • 41

     Int • 42

     Float • 43

     String • 43

     GameObject • 44

   Programming logic • 44

     If statements • 45

     While loops • 46

     For loops • 47

     Choosing between for and while • 48

   Methods • 48

Summary 51

Chapter 4: Characters — 53

Design and concept 54

   Asking why • 54

   Concept time! • 54

Rigging 58

   Animation-first thinking • 58

   Deformation • 59

   Hierarchy • 60

   Bones or joints • 61

   Forward Kinematics/Inverse Kinematics • 62

    Constraints • 62

    Deformers • 64

    Controls • 64

    Physics-based animation • 66

    Human Inverse Kinematics (HIK) system • 66

    Animation • 66

Character controllers 67

    Built-in character controller • 68

    Rigidbody character controller • 68

Scripting your character's movement 68

    Initial setup in Unity • 69

    Idling • 75

    Code entry point • 77

    RequireComponent • 78

    Update code • 78

    Methods • 80

Summary 83

Join us on Discord! 84

Chapter 5: Environment   85

    Sketching • 86

    Mood boards • 88

    Staging • 89

Blocking it out 90

    Unity terrain • 90

        Creating a terrain • 91

        Terrain settings • 92

        Terrain painting • 94

        Painting trees • 102

Painting details • 104

3D geometry • 104

ProBuilder • 105

Premade basic shapes • 115

Summary 117

Chapter 6: Interactions and Mechanics — 119

Game loops 119

Mechanics toolbox 121

Resource management • 122

Risk versus reward • 122

Spatial awareness • 122

Collection • 123

Research • 123

Limitations • 123

Design and implementation 124

Our project 125

The stairs • 126

Design • 126

Implementation • 128

The rings • 132

Design • 133

Implementation • 134

Tight spaces • 140

Design • 140

Implementation • 141

Interactive volumes • 142

Design • 142

Implementation • 142

Summary 143

Chapter 7: Rigid Bodies and Physics Interaction — 145

The Rigidbody component — 145

Mass • 146

Angular Drag • 146

Use Gravity boolean • 147

Is Kinematic boolean • 147

Interpolate • 148

Collision detection • 149

Continuous • 150

Continuous Speculative • 150

Constraints • 151

Info • 151

Telekinesis and physics interaction — 152

Rocks Falling • 153

Design • 153

Implementation • 153

The Broken Pedestal • 153

Design • 154

Implementation • 154

The Final Puzzle • 154

Design • 155

Implementation • 155

Summary — 165

Chapter 8: User Interface and Menus — 167

User interface — 168

Diegetic – Narrative Yes, Internal Yes • 169

Non-diegetic – Narrative No, Internal No • 171

Spatial – Narrative No, Internal Yes • 171

Meta – Narrative Yes, Internal No • 172

Table of Contents xiii

UI elements 173

   Main menu • 174

   Inventory systems • 174

   Health representation • 175

   Item interaction system • 175

UI in our project 175

   Main menu • 176

   Escape menu • 177

   Spatial tooltip • 178

Unity UI 179

   Unity canvas system • 179

     Rect transform • 180

     Canvas component • 182

     Canvas Scaler • 185

     Graphic Raycaster Component • 187

   Unity UI objects • 188

   Implementation • 192

     Main menu implementation • 192

     Journal implementation • 194

     Interaction UI implementation • 195

Summary 197

Chapter 9: Visual Effects   199

Visual effects overview 200

Shader Graph 201

   Setup • 201

   Creation • 202

     Lit Shader Graph • 203

     Sprite Lit Shader Graph • 204

     Sprite Unlit Shader Graph • 204

     Unlit Shader Graph • 204

Shader Graph interface • 204

  Master Stack • 205

  Blackboard • 213

  Graph Inspector • 214

  Main Preview • 215

  Nodes • 216

Commonly used nodes • 217

  Add • 218

  Color • 218

  Lerp • 219

  Multiply • 219

  Sample Texture 2D • 220

  Saturate • 221

  Split • 221

  UV • 222

  Vectors • 222

Particle Systems 223

Shuriken • 223

VFX Graph • 224

  Nodes • 229

Summary 229

Chapter 10: Sound Effects — 231

Sound... design? 232

The five elements of sound design 232

Source • 232

Envelopes • 233

  Attack • 234

  Release • 235

Pitch • 235

Frequency • 236

Table of Contents   xv

    Layering • 238

Designing for scale **238**

Our project's sound design and implementation **239**

    Getting our first sound to play • 239

        Organization • 240

        Music • 240

    2D sounds • 241

    3D sounds • 242

        Using 3D sounds • 242

        Audio listener part I • 243

    3D sound settings • 243

        Audio listener part II • 246

        Adding 3D ambient sounds to the game • 249

        Filling out our ambient sounds • 251

        2D ambience • 251

Triggering sound through player interaction **251**

    Triggering sound through Unity events • 252

    Rotating puzzle sounds • 254

    Tree puzzle • 255

Summary **255**

Chapter 11: Build and Test   257

Building with Unity **257**

    Target platform • 259

    Architecture • 259

    Server Build • 259

    Copy PDB files • 259

    Create Visual Studio Solution • 259

    Development Build • 259

    Autoconnect Profiler • 260

    Deep Profiling Support • 260

Script Debugging • 260

Scripts Only Build • 261

Compression Method • 261

Testing 261

Functional testing • 262

Performance testing • 263

Unity profiler • 264

Memory Profiler • 265

Frame debugger • 267

Physics debugger and Profiler module • 267

Playtesting • 269

Soak testing • 270

Localization testing • 270

User experience, or UX 271

Branding • 271

Design • 271

Usability • 271

Initial problem • 272

First puzzle • 272

Introduction to a secondary mechanic • 273

Final puzzle • 274

Summary 275

Chapter 12: Finishing Touches 277

Overview 277

Asset finalization 278

Stylized pass on assets • 279

Detail normals • 280

Architecture cleanup • 283

Texture blending • 284

Environment clutter • 286

Detail meshes • 287

Effects • 287

   Stair blocker • 287

   Shuriken system – stair blocker particles layer • 292

   VFX Graph – Myvari's telekinesis • 296

Cinematics • 304

Secondary animation • 305

Lighting 305

3D form • 305

Providing mood • 305

Gameplay design • 305

Unity lighting • 306

   Mixed lighting • 306

   Light probes • 310

   Reflection probe • 312

Sound polish 314

Triggering sound through animation events • 314

Tagging animations with events for sound • 316

   Randomized sounds • 319

   Randomized pitch • 321

Summary 322

Chapter 13: Bonus: Other Unity Tools!   323

Unity Gaming Services 323

Multiplayer tools • 323

   Creation • 324

   Connection • 324

   Communication • 325

XR plugin • 326

Machine Learning Agents • 326

Bolt visual scripting • 327

Flow Graphs • 327

State Graphs • 327

Live Editing • 327

Debugging and Analysis • 327

Codebase Compatibility • 327

Summary 328

Other Books You May Enjoy   331

Index   335

Preface

This book is a thorough run through the design and development of a 3D environment puzzle game made in Unity. We go through the design, creation, and implementation of characters, environment, UI, sound, and game mechanics.

Who is this book for?

This book is especially good for anyone who has an interest in making 3D games but hasn't started their journey yet. We cover the fundamentals all the way up to some advanced topics.

Secondarily, this book would help anyone who has already started their journey and wants to learn other parts of game development as we cover a broad range of skills and knowledge throughout the book.

What this book covers

Part 1 — Plan and Design

Chapter 1, *A Primer to the Third Dimension*, takes a ride through 3D terminology and the initial jargon of what the book will go through.

Chapter 2, *Design and Prototype*, starts the user down the design rabbit hole and ends with installing Unity to create your first project.

Chapter 3, *Programming*, lays down the foundation of programming. This chapter leans in on the power of C# (C Sharp) by explaining the basics of logic and the initial use of Visual Studio.

Part 2 — Build

Chapter 4, *Characters*, goes over designing 3D characters while thinking about how they will be used for rigging and animations.

Chapter 5, *Environment*, walks you through thinking about the environment for your game as well as what we did to design and build our environment.

Chapter 6, *Interactions and Mechanics*, takes the time to break down how mechanics need to be thought about and what interaction is for the user, while also covering the programming needed for the interactions in our project.

Chapter 7, *Rigid Bodies and Physics Interactions*, adds complexity to the interaction with physics and more advanced programming concepts.

Chapter 8, *User Interface and Menus*, goes over Unity's canvas component and how the overall game interface is developed on any project.

Part 3 – Polish and Refine

Chapter 9, *Visual Effects*, dives into how the visual effects systems can be worked with to add a further emotional connection to your world. This is done by explaining the foundation of rendering and the systems surrounding it.

Chapter 10, *Sound Effects*, blasts in with explaining the sound systems within Unity as well as setting a solid foundation of sound design.

Chapter 11, *Build and Test*, teaches you how Unity builds a final executable game and explains testing methods to root out bugs that you can squash to make a better product.

Chapter 12, *Finishing Touches*, looks to be a toolbox of utility for making your game as polished as it can be. We go over what we used to polish our project. This is including specific particle systems, lighting, art defining, and advanced sound polish.

Bonus Chapter, *Other Unity Tools!*, is a chapter going over some of the services Unity has to offer just in case this book inspires you to work on a project that we haven't been able to cover, such as multiplayer or mixed-reality requirements.

To get the most out of this book

- Pay attention to this book not as a tutorial but as many tools being used to develop a 3D game. We're only going over a few simple examples. Take the logic out as something to apply to your projects as much as possible.
- Be prepared to take your own notes on the topics that are being covered. We ramp up the difficulty in programming quite a bit during the physics portion.

- Ask questions in the Discord, which is attached to the book through a QR code.

Download the example code files

The code bundle for the book is hosted on GitHub at https://github.com/PacktPublishing/Unity-3D-Game-Development. We also have other code bundles from our rich catalog of books and videos available at https://github.com/PacktPublishing/. Check them out!

Download the color images

We also provide a PDF file that has color images of the screenshots/diagrams used in this book. You can download it here: https://static.packt-cdn.com/downloads/9781801076142_ColorImages.pdf.

Conventions used

There are a number of text conventions used throughout this book.

CodeInText: Indicates code words in text, database table names, folder names, filenames, file extensions, pathnames, dummy URLs, user input, and Twitter handles. For example: "Mount the downloaded WebStorm-10*.dmg disk image file as another disk in your system."

A block of code is set as follows:

```
void OnStartGameButtonPressed()
    {
        SetPlayerEnabled(true);
        Cursor.lockState = CursorLockMode.Locked;
        Cursor.visible = false;
        this.gameObject.SetActive(false);
    }
```

Bold: Indicates a new term, an important word, or words that you see on the screen. For instance, words in menus or dialog boxes, also appear in the text like this. For example: "Select **System info** from the **Administration** panel."

> Warnings or important notes appear like this.

> Tips and tricks appear like this.

Get in touch

Feedback from our readers is always welcome.

General feedback: Email `feedback@packtpub.com` and mention the book's title in the subject of your message. If you have questions about any aspect of this book, please email us at `questions@packtpub.com`.

Errata: Although we have taken every care to ensure the accuracy of our content, mistakes do happen. If you have found a mistake in this book, we would be grateful if you reported this to us. Please visit `http://www.packtpub.com/submit-errata`, click **Submit Errata**, and fill in the form.

Piracy: If you come across any illegal copies of our works in any form on the internet, we would be grateful if you would provide us with the location address or website name. Please contact us at `copyright@packtpub.com` with a link to the material.

If you are interested in becoming an author: If there is a topic that you have expertise in and you are interested in either writing or contributing to a book, please visit `http://authors.packtpub.com`.

Share your thoughts

Once you've read *Unity 3D Game Development*, we'd love to hear your thoughts! Scan the QR code below to go straight to the Amazon review page for this book and share your feedback.

https://packt.link/r/1801076146

Your review is important to us and the tech community and will help us make sure we're delivering excellent quality content.

1
A Primer to the Third Dimension

Welcome!

It's a pleasure to have you join us on this journey to learn the fundamentals of 3D game development. Firstly, we will introduce you to the team who wrote this book.

- **Travis Bapiste** (3D Artist) directed the art, modeled every model in the game, rigged the character, and helped define the design of the story.
- **Russell Craig** (Sr. Software Engineer) created the scripts for the mechanics.
- **Ryan Stunkel** (Sound designer) created and implemented all the sounds throughout the project.
- **Anthony Davis** (Sr. Technical Artist) wrote the book, managed the project, built effects and shaders, and polished the project.

Ensuring we brought out the best of our collective experience of over 50 years (with 4 brains behind every page in this book) was a roller-coaster (and too much fun!) each day. We've spent over six months and two revisions to the entire book (as well as hundreds of GIFs that we have exchanged during the process) to include the most suitable use-cases that explain new concepts and, most importantly, offer a teaching approach that works. In the end, we believe we've successfully created a book that would have shaped the trajectory of our careers in game development and pushed us ahead by at least 3-5 years.

This book will equip you with all the tools you'll need to start building; however, you might need more support and advice en-route to turn your ideas into creations.

That's where our Discord server comes into play. It introduces the element of interactivity for us to connect, read the book together and have a conversation about your 3D game projects. I am available on Discord more than ever to ensure you get through with the book with ease, so please feel free to come say hi and ask any questions!

Don't forget to drop in your quick intro in the channel *#introduce-yourself* when you join in: `https://packt.link/unity3dgamedev`

Well, let's get started!

Goal of this book

Our goal with this book is to enable every reader to build the right mindset to think about 3D games, and then show them all the steps we took to create ours. An absolute beginner is welcome to work through this book, however the topics may ramp up in difficulty quite quickly. Though difficult, if you stick with it, you will have taken multiple steps towards mastery in game development. The main target audience for this book is those with some prior knowledge in game development, though regardless of your experience, we hope to create an enjoyable learning journey for you. The concepts we will cover soon become complex with characters, programming, design patterns, and more that we'll learn.

To make the best use of the book, I'd recommend you follow the approach below:

- Read through the chapters, deliberately taking breaks to think about the concepts.
- When something is brand new, check our project in GitHub to see if viewing it in action can help explain it further. If it doesn't, take to Google to do your own research on it.
- If something isn't available in the project, send me a message over Discord or seek help from peers in the community server—the link is shared above.
- Move on to the next section and repeat!

This approach will allow you to take ownership over the areas you struggle with; once you have gone through the process, you can seek help from peers. The problems that you encounter may also be encountered by others. Solving them and bringing them to the Discord or having your peers help with the solution emboldens the overall knowledge of the community.

This book is designed for you to read through our approach and then look into the project to understand all the underpinnings. It's more important to understand the design of why we did what we did first. We take time to go over fundamentals of the Unity interface as well, but tech can be learned over time with plenty of resources online.

Some things you will not find in here are how to model characters, rig, or animate them. We speak very little about this process as that is its own training. We *do* go over why we designed our character the way we did, to help you on your journey to do the same. The project has all the animations and cinematics in it, so the final products are available to see the results of our work. This approach is a strong way to learn, and we teach you why things are done the way that they are. This way, you get to see the end result, and you're allowed to be creative and give your own thought to design, as well as work through the process on your own with new tools while working your way through the chapters.

Lastly, before we sink our teeth into the content, we'd like to advise you to open the GitHub repo, navigate to the Builds folder, and play it for yourself. This will help you to see what our small team put together in its complete form. After playing it through, you can visualize what we went through while building this project from the start.

Let's dive into what topics we will cover in this chapter:

- Coming around to 3D
- Essential Unity concepts
- The Unity interface

Let's get started by familiarizing ourselves with the basic components of 3D game development.

Coming around to 3D

We will be going over a basic understanding of 3D work within this section. From coordinate systems to the makeup of how the 3D model is rendered, we will only go surface-level to ensure that you fully understand the foundations as you progress through this journey. By reading through this, you will gain a strong understanding of how Unity displays items.

Coordinate systems

3D coordinate systems are not all the same in each 3D application! As is demonstrated in *Figure 1.1*, Unity is a left-handed world coordinate system with *+y* facing upward. Looking at *Figure 1.1*, you can visualize the difference between left-handed and right-handed systems.

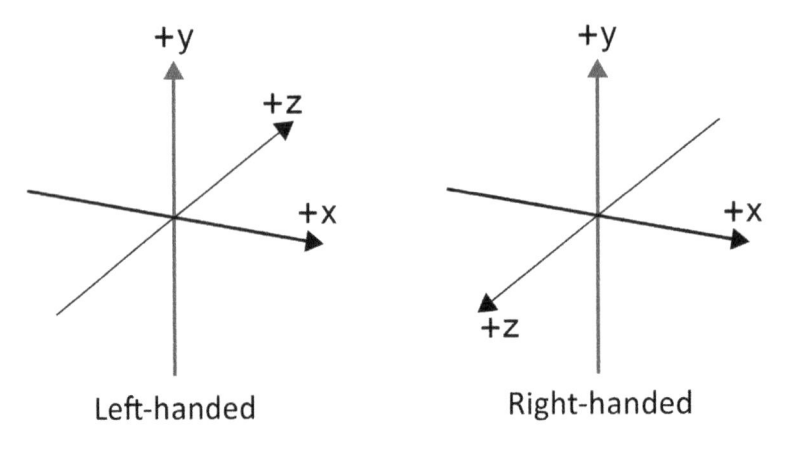

Figure 1.1: Coordinate systems

While we work within these coordinate systems, you will see the positions of objects represented in an array of three values within parentheses as follows:

(0, 100, 0)

This represents *(x, y, z)* respectively. This is a good habit to get into as programming utilizes very similar syntax when writing positions within scripts. When we talk about position, it is commonly referred to as the `transform` inside whichever **Digital Content Creator** (**DCC**) you're using. In Unity, the transform holds position, rotation, and scale.

Now we understand the world coordinates, *(x, y, z)*, and that those coordinates each start at 0, represented by *(0, 0, 0)*. In *Figure 1.2* below, where the colored lines meet is *(0, 0, 0)* in the world. The cube has its own `transform`, which encompasses that object's `transform`, rotation, and scale. Keep in mind that `transform` holds the local position, rotation, and scale. World `transforms` are calculated from this following their hierarchy.

Chapter 1 5

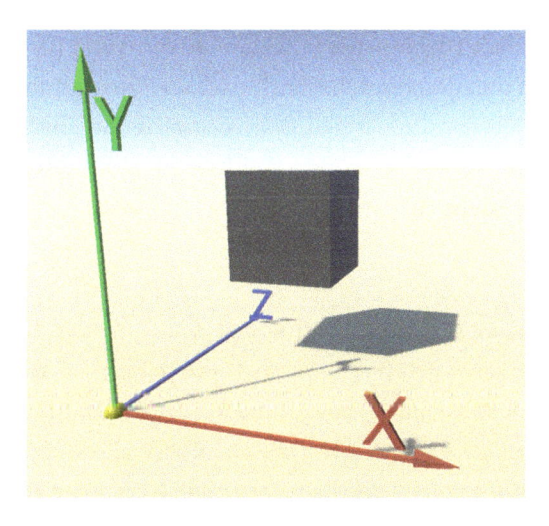

Figure 1.2: 3D coordinate system

The cube in *Figure 1.2* is at *(1, 1.5, 2)*. This is called **world space** as the item's `transform` is being represented through the world's coordinates starting from *(0, 0, 0)*.

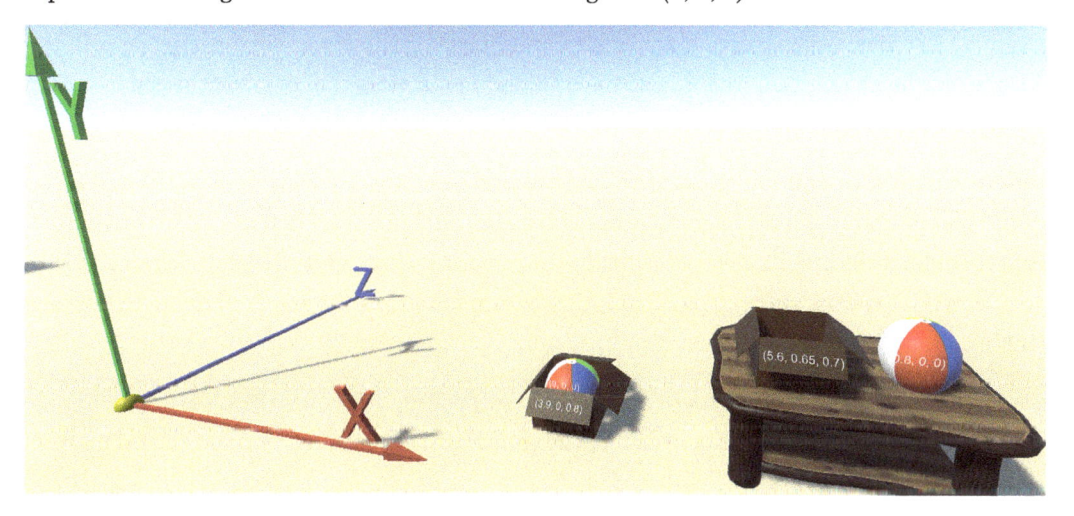

Figure 1.3: World space vs local space

Now that we know the cube's transform is in relation to the world *(0, 0, 0)*, we will go over the parent-child relationship that describes the local space. In *Figure 1.3* above, the sphere is a child of the cube. The sphere's local position is *(0, 1, 0)* in relation to the cube. Interestingly, if you now move the cube, the sphere will follow as it's only offset from the cube and its transforms will remain *(0, 1, 0)* in relation to the cube.

Vectors

Traditionally, a vector is a unit that has more than one element with a direction. In a 3D setting, a Vector3 will look very similar to what we've worked with so far. *(0, 0, 0)* is a Vector3! Vectors are used in very many solutions for game elements and logic. Usually, the developer will normalize vectors so, that way, the magnitude will always equal 1. This allows the developer to work with the data very easily as 0 is the start, 0.5 is halfway, and 1 is the end of the vector.

Cameras

Cameras are incredibly useful components! They humbly show us their perspective, which allows our players to experience what we are trying to convey to them. As you may have guessed, a camera also has a transform, just like all GameObjects (which we will describe later in the chapter) in the hierarchy. Cameras also have several parameters that can be changed to obtain different visual effects.

Different game elements and genres use cameras in different ways. For example, the game *Resident Evil* uses static cameras to give a sense of tension, not knowing what's outside the window or around the corner, while *Tomb Raider* pulls the camera in close while the player character Lara goes through caverns, giving a sense of intimacy and emotional understanding, with her face looking uncomfortable in tight spaces.

Cameras are essential to the experience you will be creating for your users. Take time to play with them and learn compositional concepts to maximize the push of emotions in the player's experience.

Faces, edges, vertices, and meshes

3D objects are made up of multiple parts, as seen in *Figure 1.4*. Vertices, represented by the green circles, are points in space relative to the world *(0, 0, 0)*. Each object has a list of these vertices and their corresponding connections.

Two vertices connected make an edge, represented by a red line. A face is made when either three or four edges connect to make a triangle or a quad. Sometimes quads are called a plane when not connected to any other faces. When all of these parts are together, you have a mesh.

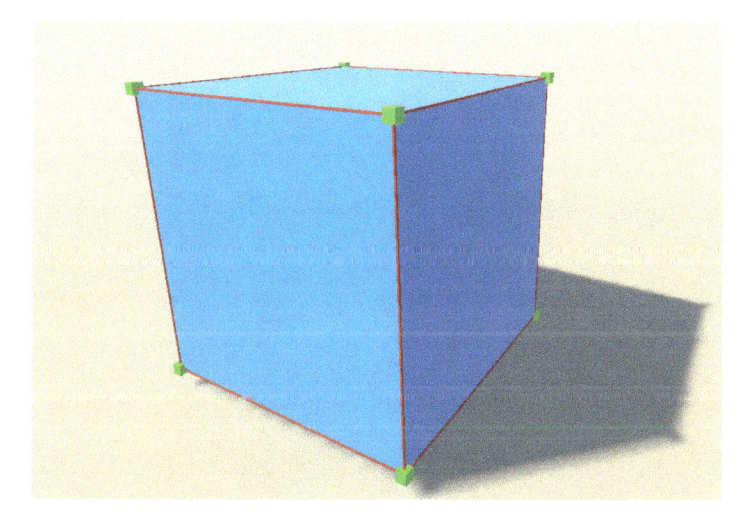

Figure 1.4: Vertices, edges, faces, and meshes

Materials, textures, and shaders

Now that you know what a mesh is comprised of in all DCC tools, let's look into how Unity displays that mesh to you. At the base level is a shader. Shaders can be thought of as small programs, which have their own language and run on the GPU, so Unity can render the objects in your scene on your screen. You can think of the shader as a large template for materials to be created.

The next level up is materials. A material is a set of attributes that are defined by the shader to be manipulated, which helps show what the object looks like. Each rendering pipeline will have separate shaders: **Built-in**, **Universal Rendering Pipeline (URP)**, or **High Definition Rendering Pipeline**. For this book, we are using the second option, which is also the most widely used: URP.

Figure 1.5 shows an example of a material using the URP's **Standard Lit** shader. This allows us to manipulate surface options, inputs for that surface, and some advanced options. For now, let's just talk about **Base Map**, the first item in the **Surface Inputs** section. The term **Base Map** is being used here as a combination of the **Diffuse/Albedo** and **Tint**. **Diffuse/Albedo** is used to define the base color (red) that will be applied to the surface—in this case, white.

If you placed a texture into this map by either dragging a texture onto the square (green) to the left of the base map or clicking on the circle (blue) in between the box and the name, after that, you can tint the surface with the color if there need to be any adjustments.

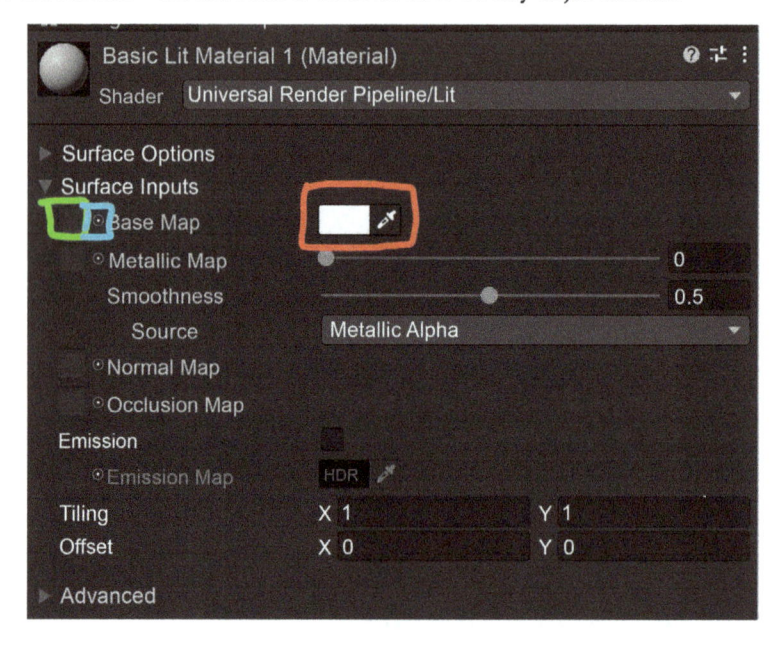

Figure 1.5: Base material attributes

Figure 1.6 shows a simple example of what a cube would look like with a tint, texture, and the same texture with the tint changed. As we progress through the book, we will unlock more and more functions of materials, shaders, and textures.

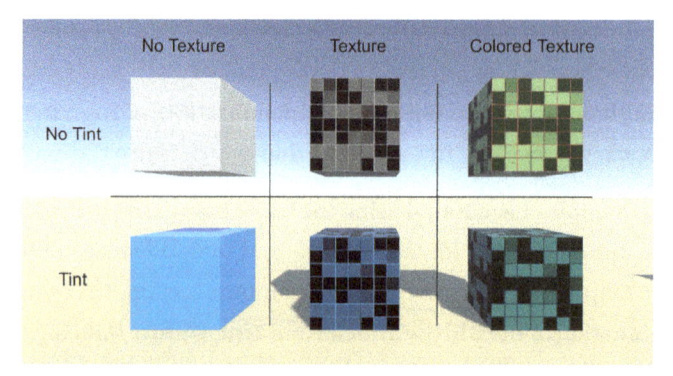

Figure 1.6: Tint and texture base color

Textures can provide incredible detail for your 3D model.

Chapter 1

When creating a texture, the resolution is an important consideration. The first part of the resolution that needs to be understood is "power of 2" sizes. Powers of 2 are as follows:

2, 4, 8, 16, 32, 64, 128, 256, 512, 1024, 2048, 4096, etc.

These numbers represent the pixel size for both width and height. There are cases where you may need to mix the sizes as long as they fit the power of 2 scale. Examples are:

- 256×256
- 1024×1024
- 256×1024 (this is less common to see, but is valid)

The second consideration regarding resolution is the size itself. The easiest way to work through this consideration is by thinking about how large the 3D object will be on your screen. If you have a 1920x1080 screen resolution, that is 1920 pixels wide by 1080 pixels tall. If the object in question is only going to take up 10% of the screen and will rarely be seen any closer, you may consider a 256x256 texture. By contrast, if you are making an emotional, character-driven game where emotions and facial expressions matter, you may want a 4096x4096 or 4K texture on just the face during those cutscenes.

Rigidbody physics

Unity assumes that every GameObject does not need to be evaluated every frame for physics. Unity uses Nvidia's PhysX engine for its physics simulations. To get any calculated physics responses, the GameObject needs a Rigidbody component added.

By adding the Rigidbody component to the GameObject, you are then adding some properties to the GameObject seen in the inspector in *Figure 1.7* below.

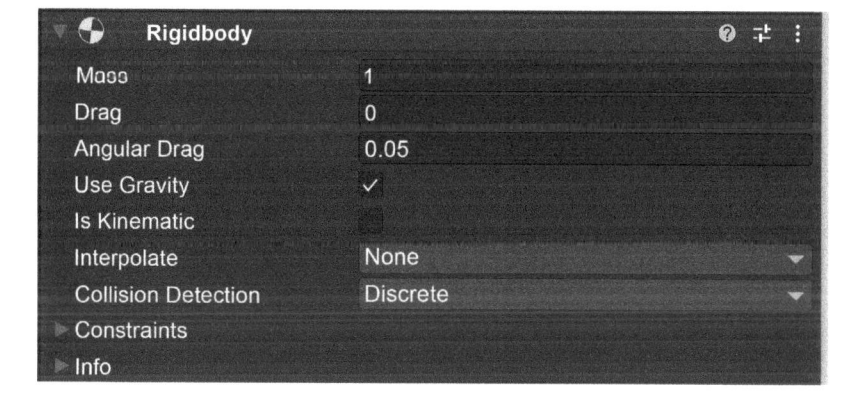

Figure 1.7: Rigidbody

One Unity unit of mass is equal to 1 kg of mass. This affects the physics decisions upon collisions. **Drag** units add friction, reducing the velocity over time. **Angular drag** is similar but constrained to only rotation speed. **Use Gravity** either turns gravity on or off, equal to standard Earth gravity *(0, -9.81, 0)* so the mass makes sense! Sometimes you may not want to use Earth gravity, so you can change the physics settings to make the gravity what you would like.

A thorough explanation of Rigidbody will be worked through in *Chapter 7, Rigidbodies and Physics Interaction*. We will be using Rigidbodies in the creation of characters as well as environments and interactive gameplay.

Collision detection

A GameObject with a Rigidbody without any colliders will not fully utilize the physics and with gravity turned on will just fall through the world. There are quite a few colliders to play with to best suit your games' needs. In *Figure 1.8* below, you can see that there are separate colliders for 2D. These use a different physics system from 3D. If you are using 2D only for your game, make sure to run with the 2D colliders.

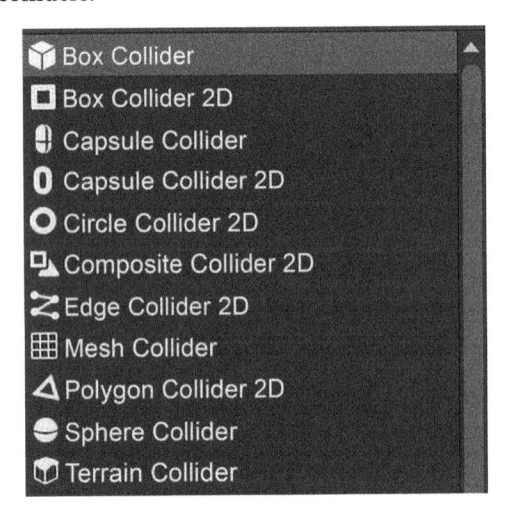

Figure 1.8: Collider component options

You are also welcome to add multiple colliders—with the basic options seen in *Figure 1.8* above—to an object to best suit the shape of the GameObject. It is very common to see colliders on empty GameObjects that are children of the primary object, to allow the easy transformation of the colliders. We will see this in practice in *Chapter 4, Characters*, and *Chapter 5, Environment*.

Chapter 1 11

The Unity interface

The interface for Unity is separated into several major components. In *Figure 1.9* below, we will go over the scene (red) and the items within its interface as well as how to manipulate their properties in the inspector (orange). Then we will go into items that aren't active in the scene but are available to add in the project window (yellow). Finally, we will go over the game view (green) and the package manager (separate from *Figure 1.9*).

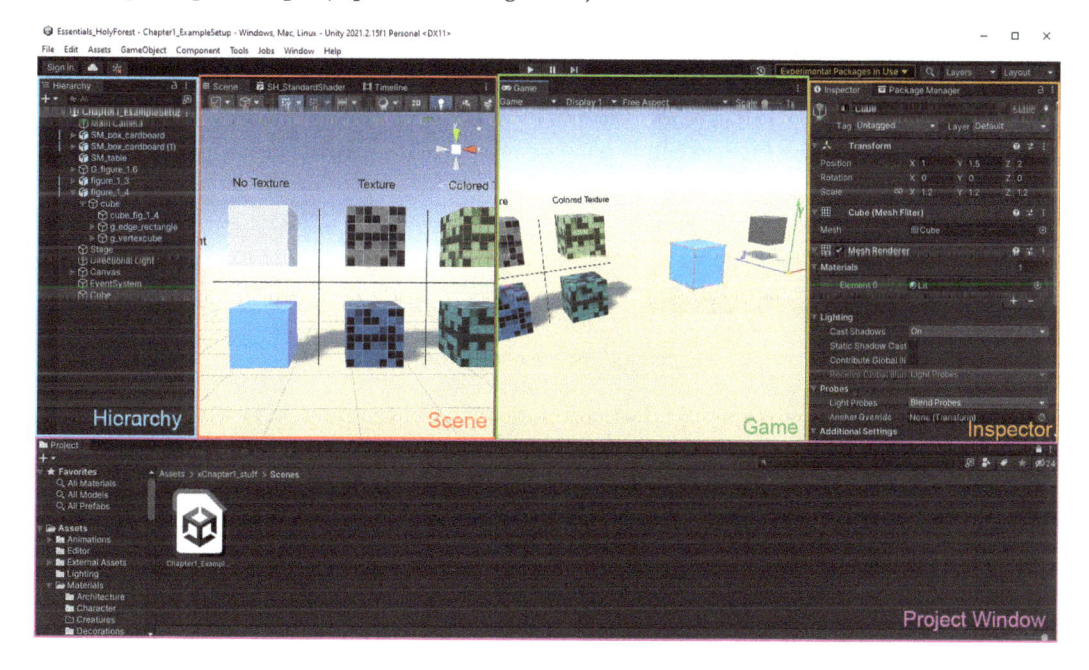

Figure 1.9: Overall interface

Scene view and hierarchy

The scene view and hierarchy work in tandem. The hierarchy is how the scene will be rendered when the game is played. The scene view allows you to manipulate the GameObjects and their values in real time. Furthermore, when the editor is in **Play** mode, the game can make changes to the GameObjects in the hierarchy.

> When the GameObjects are being manipulated in **Play** mode, to include if you change them yourself in the scene view, after you stop the game, the GameObjects will revert to their original state before play has started.

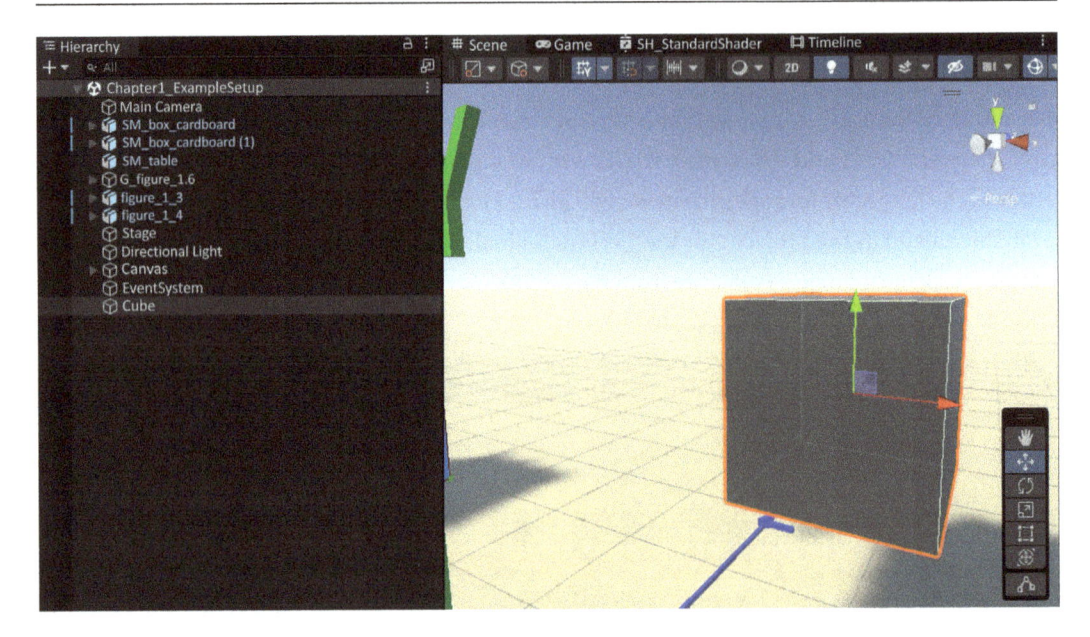

Figure 1.10: Scene and hierarchy

In *Figure 1.10* above, there is a lot of information that can be seen right away. On the left, in the hierarchy, you can see that there are objects in the scene. These objects all have a transform, which places them in the world. If you double-click on an item or click on an item, put your mouse in the scene view, and then press *f*, you will then focus on that GameObject, which puts the item centered on the scene's viewport.

When you have an item selected, you can see that at the object's pivot point—usually the center of the object—there is a tool showing colored arrows. The tool allows you to position the GameObject in space. You can also position the object on a plane by selecting the little square in between two axes.

In the upper right of *Figure 1.10*, you will see a camera gizmo. This little gizmo will allow you easily orient the viewport camera to the front, sides, top, bottom, or change it to an isometric camera or perspective with a single click.

Now that you have seen the item in the scene, selected by left-clicking in the scene or the hierarchy, you may want to change some properties or add components to that GameObject. This is where the inspector comes into play.

Inspector

To manipulate a GameObject's value, when you select the GameObject in the scene or hierarchy, the inspector will update to show you the viable options to change per GameObject.

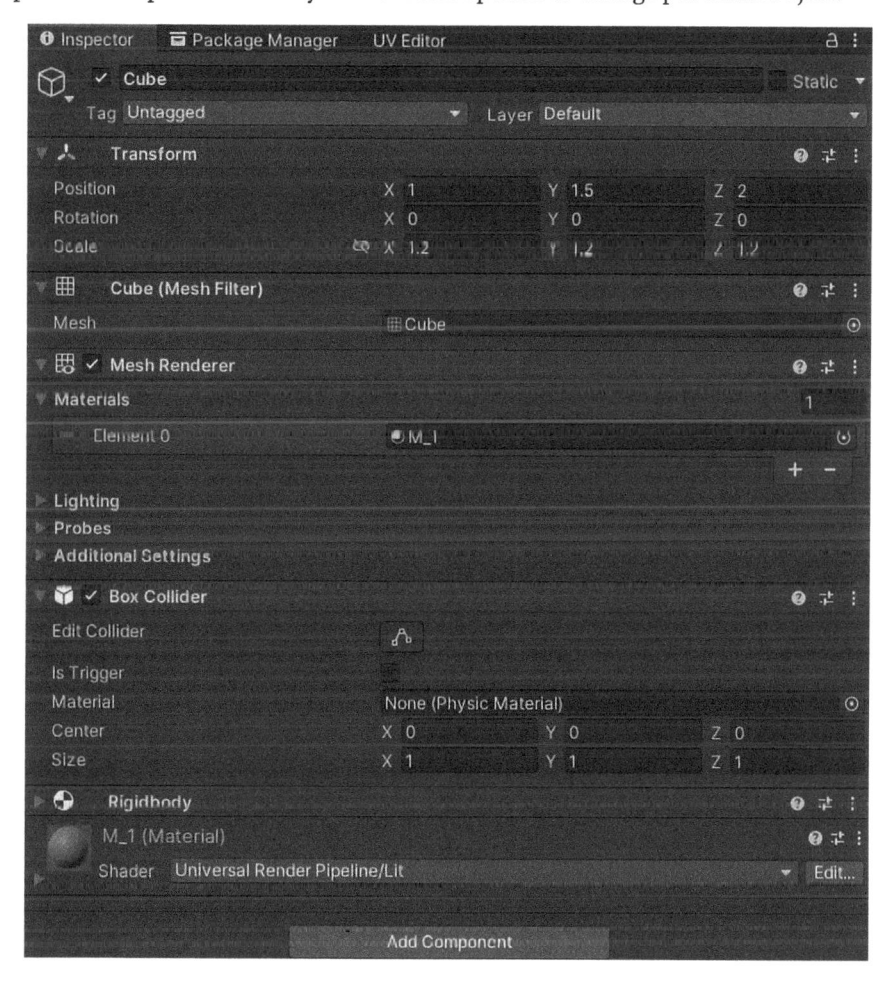

Figure 1.11: Inspector window

The inspector window in *Figure 1.11* shows that a good amount of this item has been chosen. At the top, the name is **Cube** and the blue cube to the left denotes a prefab data type. You are able to make changes to the prefab itself by clicking the **Open** button just below the name. This will create a new scene view that shows the prefab only. When you make changes to the prefab, it will make a change to all instanced prefabs in any scene that is referencing it.

The **transform** component shows the position, rotation, and scale of the prefab in the scene.

The **mesh filter** shows the vertices, edges, and faces that make up that polygon.

Below that is the **mesh renderer**. This component will allow the rendering of the mesh rendered in the mesh filter component. We can set the material here and other options that pertain to this item's specific lighting and probes, which we will cover in *Chapter 12, Final Touches*.

Now, below this is a collider and a Rigidbody. These work in tandem and help this object to react to physics in real time, according to the settings on the components.

We've talked a lot about items in the scene and their properties, but where are they housed outside of the scene if they're only referenced items? The **Project** window will answer this question.

The Project window

Here you will find assets that will be instanced in the scene or used as a component to fully realize the game you are building.

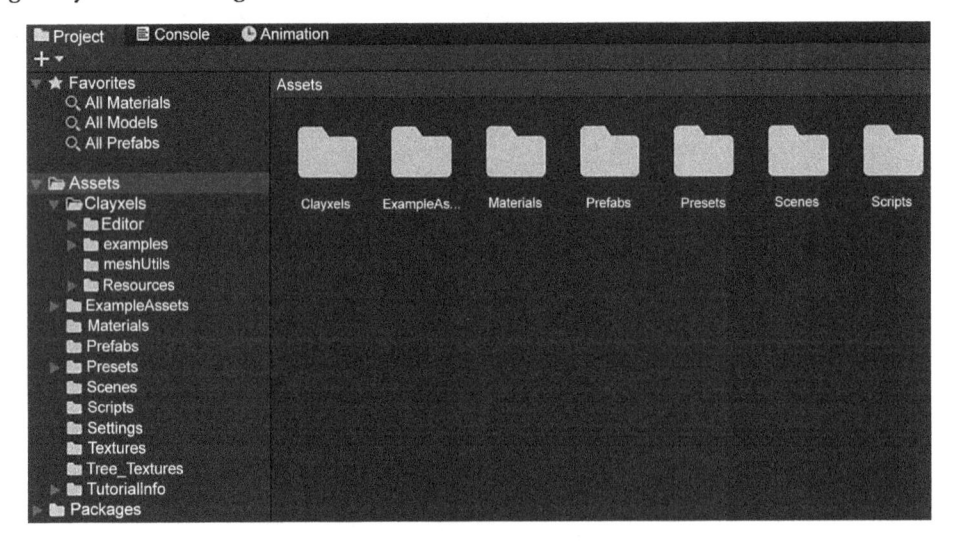

Figure 1.12: Project window

This window is the physical representation of the GameObjects that are referenced. All of the items in the assets folder seen in *Figure 1.12* are physically on your hard drive. Unity makes meta files that house all of the properties of the items.

The interesting thing about having the raw files in the **Project** window is that you can make changes to the items and when you focus on the Unity project (click on the Unity app), it will readjust the meta files and reload the items in the scene. This makes it so that, you can iterate on scripts and art faster!

We've looked at the GameObjects in the scene, placed them by manipulating the transforms, and know where the GameObjects were referenced from. Now we should look at the game view to know how the game itself looks.

Game view

The game view is similar to the scene view; however, it follows the rules that are built in the scene view. The game will automatically render scene content through the main camera unless you define a different camera to render through.

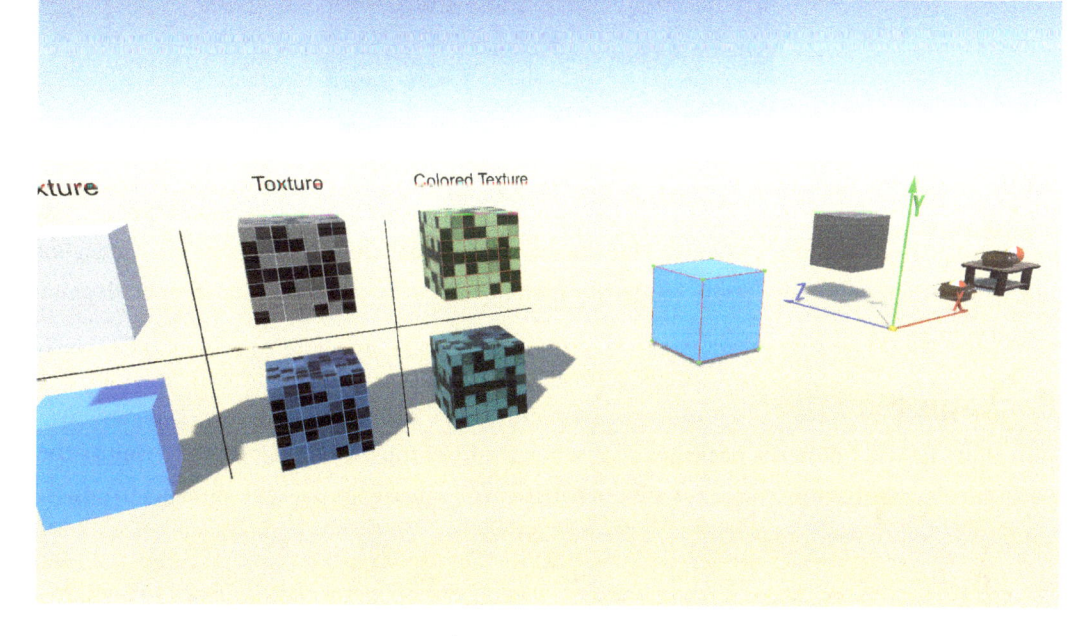

Figure 1.13: Game view

You can see that this looks very similar to the scene window, but the top has different options. At the top left, we can see the **Display** dropdown. This allows us to change cameras if we have multiple in the scene. The ratio is to the right of that, which is helpful to look at so you can target certain devices. **Scale**, to the right of the screen ratio, is helpful to quickly make the window larger or zoom in for debugging. **Maximize On Play** will maximize the screen on play to take advantage of the full screen. **Mute Audio** mutes the game's audio. **Stats** will give a small overview of the stats in the game view.

Later on in this project, during optimization, we will go through profiling for a much more indepth way to look at what may be causing issues within the gameplay in terms of memory usage and other optimization opportunities.

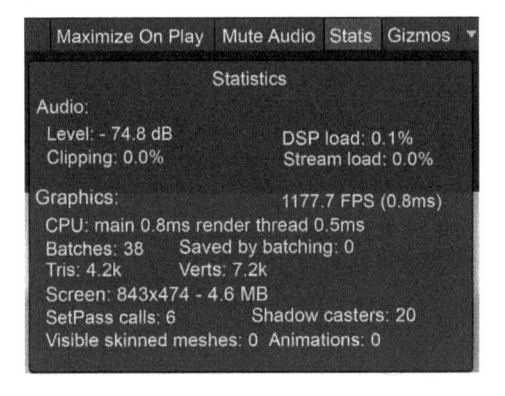

Figure 1.14: Game statistics

Continuing on to the right is **Gizmos**. This is a set of items that show in the game view in *Figure 1.14*, which you might now want to see. In this menu, you are able to turn them off or on depending on your needs.

Package Manager

Your Unity ID will house the packages you've bought from the Unity Asset Store as well as the packages you may have on your hard drive or GitHub! You can use the package manager to import the packages into your project.

You can get to these packages under **Window > Package Manager** as seen in *Figure 1.15* below.

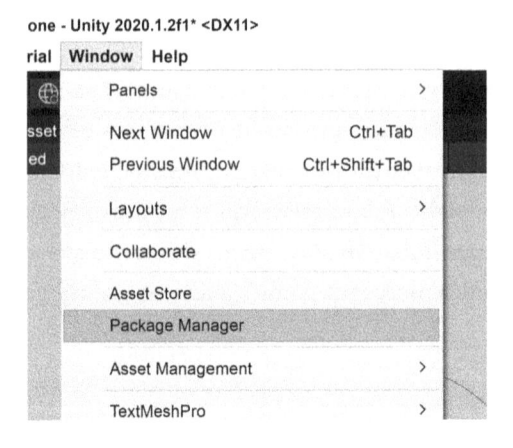

Figure 1.15: Package Manager path

Chapter 1

After you open the package manager, you will initially be shown what packages are in the project. You can change the top-left dropdown to see what is standard in Unity or what packages you have bought in the Unity Asset Store.

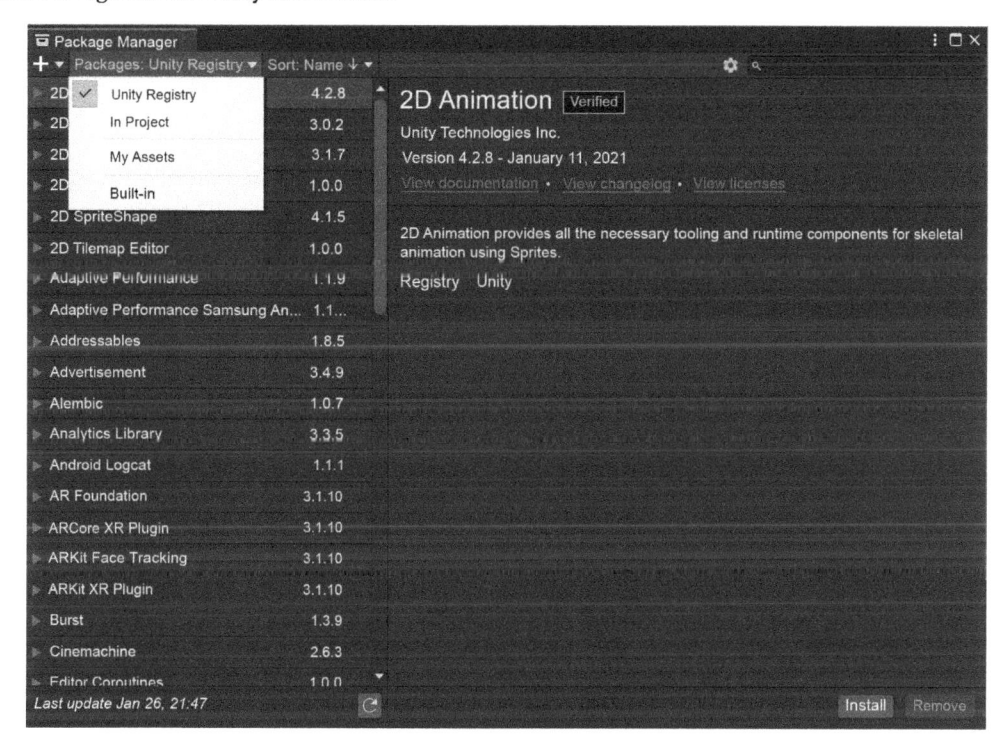

Figure 1.16: Package Manager

By choosing **Unity Registry**, you'll see a list of the Unity tested packages that come free and are part of the Unity platform, available if you need them. You can read up on every package in the documents that are provided via the link on the right-hand side labeled **View documentation** when you click on a package on the left.

If you select **In Project**, it will show you what packages are already installed with the current project that is loaded. This is helpful when you want to uninstall a package that may not be needed.

My Assets are the assets that you've bought or the project you are on and those associated with your Unity ID as paid for previously.

Built-in is standard with any project. You may need to enable or disable a built-in package depending on what your needs are. Explore them and disable what is not needed; a tidy project now leads to less optimization later.

Essential Unity concepts

In the first section, we already went over some Unity concepts. We will go over them in a bit more detail here as you've read previously where several of these might be used. Unity houses a very modular focus on the items that are housed within the game development environment.

Assets

Unity treats every file as an asset; everything including a 3D model, a texture file, a sprite, a particle system, and so on. In your project, you will have an **Assets** folder as the base folder to house all of your project items. These could be textures, 3D models, particle systems, materials, shaders, animations, sprites, and the list goes on. As we add more to our project, the **Assets** folder should be organized and ready to grow. It is strongly recommended to keep your folder structure organized so that you or your team aren't wasting time trying to find that one texture item that was left in a random folder by accident.

Scenes

A scene houses all of the gameplay logic, GameObjects, cinematics, and everything else that your game will reference to render or interact with.

Scenes are also used to cut up gameplay sections to bring down the load times. If you imagine trying to load every single asset on a modern game every time you loaded it up, it would take way too much precious gaming time.

GameObjects

Most assets that are referenced in a scene will be a **GameObject (GO)**. There are some instances in which an asset can only be a component of a GO. The one common factor that you will see with all GOs is that they have the **Transform** component. As we read at the beginning of this chapter, a transform holds the local position, rotation, and scale. World transforms are calculated from this following their hierarchy. GOs can have a long list of components connected to give functionality or data to be used in scripts for mechanics to grow.

Components

GOs have the ability to house multiple pieces of functionality attached as "components." Each component has its own unique properties. The entire list of components you can add is fairly extensive, as you can see in *Figure 1.17* below.

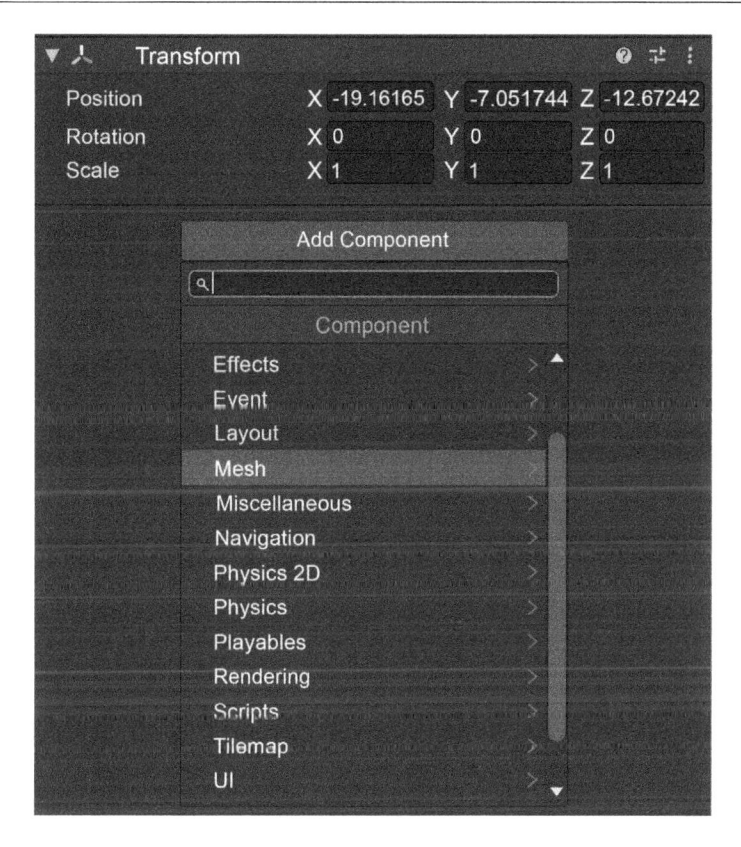

Figure 1.17: Component list

Each of these sections has smaller subsections. We will go over quite a few of them in this book. When you add an asset to the scene hierarchy that requires components, Unity will add them by default. An example of this default action happening is when you drag a 3D mesh into the hierarchy, the GOs will have a mesh renderer component attached to the object automatically.

Scripts

One component that is often used on a GameObject is a script. This is where all of the logic and mechanics will be built onto your GameObjects. Whether you want to change the color, jump, change the time of day, or collect an item, you will need to add that logic in a script on the object.

In Unity, the primary language is **C#** (pronounced "C sharp"). This is a strongly typed programming language, meaning that there must be a type assigned to any variable that is being manipulated.

We will be using scripts in a multitude of ways and I know you are excited to get right into coding, but first, we need to get into other Unity standard processes.

Prefabs

Utilizing the modular and strong object-oriented nature of Unity, we can put together a grouping of items with default values set on their components, which can be instanced in the scene at any time and house their own values.

To make a prefab, you drag a GameObject from the hierarchy in the scene to the asset browser. It will create a new prefab as well as turning that GameObject into the newly created prefab. It will also turn blue by default in the hierarchy as seen in *Figure 1.18*.

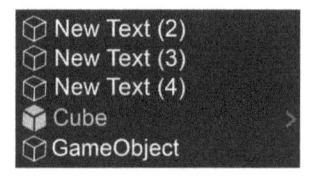

Figure 1.18: Prefab in hierarchy

Packages

To take the modular components to a whole new level, Unity can take a package with all of its dependencies and export them out so you can bring them into other projects! Even better, you can sell your packages to other game developers from the Unity Asset Store!

Now that you have a solid foundation in 3D and Unity terms, let's open it up and go over the interface itself. The next section will be a look into all of the most common interface pieces of Unity.

Summary

Together, we went over several key areas to begin your journey in game development. In this chapter, we laid the foundation for what is to come by going over some fundamental features of three primary topics. For the third dimension, we went over the coordinate system, vectors, cameras, 3D meshes, and the basics of Rigidbody physics and collision detection. This was enough of the basics to allow us to get into Unity concepts, such as assets and GameObjects, followed by scripting in C# and prefab basics. To end this chapter, we went through a virtual tour of the Unity interface—scenes, the hierarchy, inspectors, and the package manager.

In the next chapter, we will be going over design and prototyping fundamentals. This will allow you to follow along while we describe our thought processes for the project being created throughout this book. It will also lay the foundational knowledge for you to follow when you make your own projects, following your completion of this book.

2
Design and Prototype

Now that we have worked through all of the primary lingo of game development and have a stronger understanding of 3D spaces, we need to talk through the game itself. In this book, we are building a vertical slice—a fully-functional portion of the game. For this chapter, we're going to go into the beginnings of getting the project going. The main topics include:

- Game design fundamentals
- Your first Unity project
- Prototyping

To begin, let's start from the top and go over the game design fundamentals in greater detail. Take your time reading through this portion as it's dense with knowledge nuggets that will take your game to the next level.

Game design fundamentals

Game design is a young art. With any art, there are some very basic fundamentals that must be thought about before you can explore. We will go through ways in which developers like to capture their thoughts in a "document." Then, we will start with a micro-lecture on how each decision should be deliberately as granular as possible. Then, we will build on those decisions with iteration. Finally, we will go through an explanation of concepting. Let's get started with a discussion of design documents.

Game design document

There was a time where our team had some downtime between our development sprints in which we wanted to all jump on board with a new tool. Our project management was using the Atlassian stack (*Jira*, *Confluence*, etc.), but we wanted to see what would be better, so we looked through several different software. This included *Hack N' Plan*, *Trello*, *Notion*, and several other tools. We used all these tools to see which ones would end up getting used after our break. In the end, we found out we liked *Jira* for the project management and tasking, but for everything else we stuck with *Miro*. *Miro* ended up being our concepting boards and design/workflow brainstorming tool. This happened organically through other tools just not being used by the majority of the team.

No matter how small it seems your game is going to be, there will be some sort of documentation that will need to take place. There are strong organizational reasons behind making a document, but the strongest reason is that when we put something down on paper or draw it out in a collaborative space, we tend to take time to more seriously consider its merits. This pause is sometimes referred to as heuristic design. This can be done alone or in collaboration.

Some designers wish to draw up a beautifully written, well-outlined document in a word processor or an online collaboration tool. This gives a neat outline and the ability to write each detail exactly. When the scope of the game is going to be larger, this works out well. The writers tend to be technical writers and well-versed in the art of documenting processes. The approach is to have a single source of truth for any part of the game that anyone can refer to while developing, but to go to this extent may not be the best method for you or your team.

Another option for game design documents is done through collaborative brainstorming software. This allows users to work together to make flowcharts, draw, and outline in a creative manner. This manner is the direct opposite of the curated form of the aforementioned written document approach, but serves a different need. The creative form tends to be more intimate and art-focused. Some pre-concept art sketches are done, flowcharts are drawn up quickly to draw out questions about the gameplay elements, and ideas can be swiftly drawn upon and tossed away or kept. This way of designing wouldn't work well for a large-scale team as there is no real organization of sorts. New members would have a hard time onboarding in these situations.

Chapter 2 23

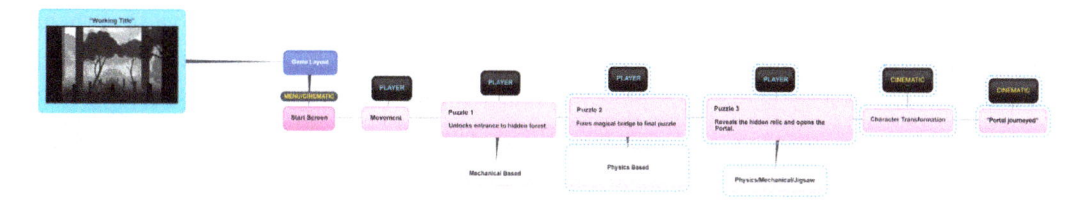

Figure 2.1: Example of a flowchart

Neither of these options is the magic pill to make a game design document, but rest assured, your team needs to have some sort of document to keep your ideas written down. Ideas are fleeting on the mind and some of the best ideas slip into the ether if they aren't written down to keep. Experiment with your team to find the option that best suits them. There is a saying in design groups: "The best tool is the tool your team will actually use".

We've gone over quite a few options for game design documents and shown that they have pros and cons. Even though there isn't a perfect way right off the bat, a great starting point would be to start with a more visual and collaborative approach. If you are together, this could be a dry erase board with sticky notes. The dry erase board allows for non-permanent thoughts, while the sticky notes would be tasks that need completing. Place them on the left side for "need to be completed," and move them to the right side when they are complete.

I recommend you spend some time over in our GitHub repo created for this book. I've added a `GDD images` folder in there for you to take a look at a large scale of examples to see what we'll work through in the next set of chapters.

`https://github.com/PacktPublishing/Unity-3D-Game-Development`

Now that we have started documenting our game design, we need to take our thoughts and make deliberate choices with them to make them concrete.

Deliberate decisions

Although this part of the chapter may be slightly shorter than others, take this section to heart: being a designer means building an immersive world that makes sense, even when it doesn't make sense. The player subconsciously makes observations at an alarming rate. The more that the player can see non-congruent pieces to the puzzle that is the game environment or character, the more immersion is broken. The best way to fix any immersion-breaking issue is deliberate decisions.

To give a very simple explanation of this, take the example of door handles. You've seen them your whole life and used them intuitively. In fact, when you have to deal with a poorly designed door handle is when your actual, real-life immersion breaking happens. If you have ever grabbed a handle to a door and tried to pull inward, only to find out the door was designed to be pushed, you've encountered this issue. If the door was designed to only be allowed to move in one direction, the correct design for an exit is a flat panel where the door handle would be. This immediately implies "push."

Every level, mesh, texture, concept, and feeling needs to be deliberately thought about with an attempt to implement. Only after you have a strong reason to place something in a certain way without giving in to clichés is when you then can explore other unique aspects to build something truly unique.

The project you will be making and playing with in this book has undergone prolonged and deliberate thought. To emphasize this, in each section, you will see a set of questions that are answered in as much detail as needed in a concise manner.

Iterative production

Game development has an interesting need for immersion to be at the forefront of play. To get this immersion as complete as we can get it, the development team needs to continuously ask whether the direction it is going in works well. Very often, the game that you began developing is not what you will ultimately end up with. This cycle is called an iterative design or production.

There are a multitude of patterns you can use when you undertake iterative design. The approach that will be described here is not the only definitive approach to completing a design, but it is a good starting point from where your team can branch off as it sees fit.

Iteration needs to happen often and early for a game to grow in terms of how easy it is to understand. There is a concept called **MVP**, or **Minimum Viable Product**, where game developers make the minimum amount of gameplay elements required to give the game to testers. This should take very little time and the feedback is invaluable. When you hand this off to the testers, there will be feedback that you and your team could not have seen as you are very close to the product. Make sure to listen to the feedback carefully with an open mind as their experience could be common among your players. We're working toward a deliberately designed experience for as many players as possible. This feedback forces you and your team to iterate on the design, and possibly cut or add game mechanics, to respond to the main testing feedback.

Figure 2.2 a, b: Examples of iterations in level design

After having iterations resolve major holes in your design, you then move into a vertical slice (which will be covered in the *Vertical slice* section of this chapter) of the game. This should be an iteration where you are comfortable with the basics of the movement and primary game mechanics. Your team will want to make a full game loop from start to finish with a single level that houses a win and lose condition. Then, you guessed it, test again, but this time with new testers that have never seen this game. Ask similar questions and some new ones that have surfaced during internal playtesting.

The loop for development should seem repetitive, and it is:

1. Think and test
2. Create and test
3. Update and test

Then, continue this approach until you are at number of iterations until it's a shippable product. The most important portion of each step is the testing. Make sure to take feedback from testing as strong indications of where improvement is required. We will begin this cycle with conceptualization.

Concepting

You need to make a game and you have a group ready to go. You are comfortable with deliberately making granular decisions and know the iterative process. Now you need to get a concept started.

The first step to getting a project going is to explore what emotion you and your team want your players to experience. With our art form being so young and malleable, we can pursue this emotion any way we like. This is the power of the game developer. Once you know what emotions you are focused on as regards the experience players will have, start thinking about how you can create it as a gameplay experience.

If the emotion is fear, you could have the player deal with spaces that are dark, with just a flashlight as their primary defense tool. This may lead you to explore sound design as your development focus since vision will not be the primary experience tool.

If the emotion is grieving, then you may work through a narrative focus, where you play a child who has lost a family member and the players work through a narrative-driven gameplay in a dream world. This pushes storytelling and pacing, with a tight understanding of color theory as well as the stages of grief through a child's perspective.

We could go on for a while regarding concepts as there is an infinite number of scenarios. Choose what your primary goal is and then work toward it. After this, you may want to put some of these ideas to paper to get an idea of what the feelings of the immersion will be, from an artistic viewpoint. This could potentially be silhouettes of character concepts. It could also be architectural designs.

It could also be a collection of pictures you've saved that gave you a feeling of the emotion you want to evoke that you can draw ideas from.

Figure 2.3 a, b, c: Concepts used in project

Either way, the prominent action is to get the ideas started visually. After you have some art panels drawn up and you have a visual idea of how this may be built, we then make a Unity project.

Your first Unity project

You've put together a concept that you want to develop, and now we need to get Unity and create a project. To do this, we need to get the Unity Hub and then choose a version, followed by a template to start with.

Unity Hub

Unity Hub is a small application that holds all of the projects in a centralized location so all of your projects are easily accessible as well as the versions of Unity you have installed. To acquire Unity Hub, you need to go to unity.com and create a **UnityID**. After you create an account, click the blue button named **Get Started**. Follow the prompts that best make sense for your needs and operating system. Download and install **Unity Hub** and let's get creating!

Choosing a version

Unity runs multiple versions at once. There are **Alpha**, **Beta**, **Official**, and **LTS** releases.

Alpha versions have experimental features that may not be fully complete or production-ready and are not recommended for builds as there may be features causing build-breaking bugs. Studios and enthusiasts may use this for testing mechanics, engine features, or packages. They are generally one release ahead of official releases. Beta is similar to Alpha versions; however, they are experimental versions of the most current official release. Official releases are stable current releases. LTS means **Long-Term Support**. These are the final releases of a version with minor hotfixes if bugs are found.

An easy way to see the versions is through the **Unity Hub**. An example of what this may look like can be seen in *Figure 2.4*:

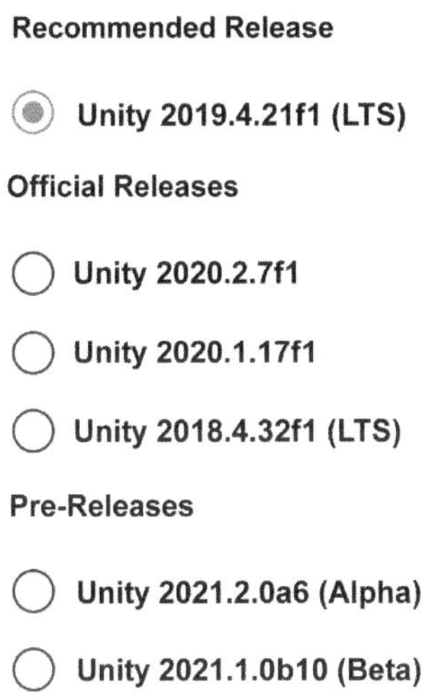

Recommended Release

⦿ Unity 2019.4.21f1 (LTS)

Official Releases

○ Unity 2020.2.7f1

○ Unity 2020.1.17f1

○ Unity 2018.4.32f1 (LTS)

Pre-Releases

○ Unity 2021.2.0a6 (Alpha)

○ Unity 2021.1.0b10 (Beta)

Figure 2.4: Example list of Unity versions

LTS releases are recommended for a production application. If your team is experimenting or looking to prototype with new features, it would only be possible in prerelease versions. After choosing a version for your project to be built in, you need to choose a template from Unity's options as you make a new project.

This book, however, is version independent. If you've bought this book after 2022, the book is still as relevant as it can be. The screenshots may have slight UI changes, but the foundations still remain intact.

Choosing a template

Unity presents you with a few template choices when you press the **New** button on the projects tab. This gives you the options of **2D**, **3D**, **Universal Rendering Pipeline (URP)**, and **High-Definition Rendering Pipeline (HDRP)**. There are large rendering differences as well as some functionality that might be interesting to you and your team to work with. These differences between these templates, arose when the **Scriptable Rendering Pipeline (SRP)** came to life!

Scriptable rendering pipeline

Rendering and computer graphics are a detailed subject that you could get a PhD in, so we will scratch the surface of what is possible through a rendering pipeline. The top level of the pipeline entails three tasks: **Culling**, **Rendering**, and **Post-Processing**. In each of these categories, many tasks are taking place in certain orders and to certain degrees of accuracy. The primary function of all of this is to optimize the view to the end user for a high frame rate as well as maintain the art style that is required for the experience you are wanting for the user.

With the advent of the SRP, these templates split into three main categories: **Built-in**, **Universal**, and **High Definition**. To get an idea of these three templates, let's break them out into their respective groups and dive in a little bit further. For our project, we will be using Universal Rendering as we will be utilizing several features inside this rendering pipeline.

Built-In Rendering

This is an older pipeline that doesn't use scriptable pipelines. There are a great many applications for the built-in renderer. Both of the 2D and 3D templates run Built-In Rendering systems. This is also the standard for which most of the assets in the asset store were built before the SRP came out. You can think of "Built-in" as the base experience in Unity. There are several reasons why you may not want to use the Built-In Renderer. If you are looking to use volumetric lighting, GPU particles, or ray tracing you would want to look into the scriptable render pipelines below.

Universal Rendering

The Universal Rendering pipeline is aptly named as it has the most features available with a scriptable rendering pipeline available. If you are looking to make a 2D game, this is the best option to choose as it has built-in, pixel-perfect rendering, 2D lights, and 2D shadows. For the 3D option, this is also a fantastic choice. There are two graphs available to both URP and HDRP, which are ShaderGraph and VFXGraph. ShaderGraph is a visual shader creation tool that allows for complex shaders to be written visually. VFXGraph's primary function is to be a particle system focused on GPU particles, allowing you to create millions of particles on screen at the same time for stunning visuals.

We would like to use GPU-based particles, in our project which VFXGraph is responsible for handling, as well as show the use of ShaderGraph. With these requirements, we chose to work within URP as our rendering pipeline.

If you are looking for more of a physically accurate rendering system with ray tracing and volumetric clouds, then HDRP is what you are looking for.

High-Definition Rendering

This rendering pipeline has one major purpose: to give the best-looking output while remaining as optimized as possible. Whether to use HDRP or not is a widely discussed topic. There are several main reasons why HDRP would be the option for you. This is if you are looking for a physical-based sky with cloud layers, volumetric clouds, multiple directional lights, highly customizable shadow options, and ray tracing to include raytraced reflections, volumetrics, and multiple high-level shader outputs. There are many other high-level rendering options that HDRP only can provide. These concepts are deep topics in the computer graphics world and we implore you to look them up to see the beautiful work of what real-time rendering is becoming.

Prototyping

Now that you have a project, you can start putting together the assets that will create the game. In this book, we have worked through how we are going to build this game out so that way, we can section off each major chunk into chapters. Prototyping can happen in a multitude of ways. We can't go over every way in which every studio will prototype as each business has its own manner of creation. We will talk about major progression patterns that are common within the industry as a whole. Breaking down the life cycle of any task that is built upon iteration, there needs to be a cycle to pull out the impurities. This is commonly regarded as analyze, design, implement, and test, and then iterate again until complete. The prototyping phase goes through all of these steps as well. Take a look at them all and work through each portion that makes sense to you or the group building your game.

Wireframing or paper creation

In this form of prototyping, the creator breaks the video game down into phases in a physical or digital system to go through each game loop or experience the player will feel throughout your game. Sometimes, this could be creating a paper board game to run through the rules. Sometimes, this may involve digitally drawing game wireframes through the user interface to intuition for the gameplay experience.

Grayboxing

This name is what you think it means! A bunch of untextured shapes, generally gray boxes, that line out your environment to ensure that the storytelling of the environment through its silhouette can be defined. This version of prototyping is particularly useful if you need a very direct camera angle you need to display, and do not have assets to set up the environment. This can also be useful in the development of concept art as you can push the composition to the concept artists for quicker turnarounds.

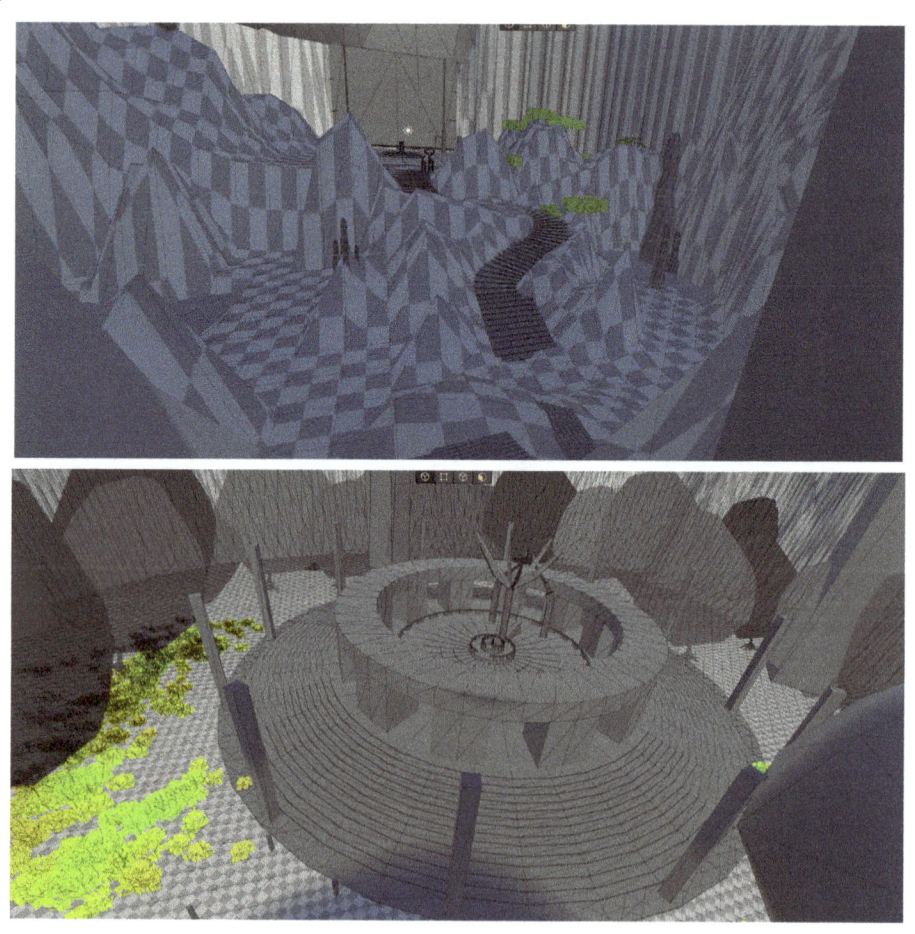

Figure 2.5 a, b: Greyboxing examples in project

From *Figure 2.5* above, you can see how a concept artist could take these and draw over them to get a rendered concept in order to provide more design ideas for the space, even if this means changing the environment, since this was a quick mock-up of the space to get things started.

Proof of Concept (PoC)

The naming is fairly accurate. This is where you are getting very specific about your testing. Maybe you need to tune a camera to get a very specific feel for the gameplay. This might take several iterations in itself and multiple people taking a crack at it if you have a team.

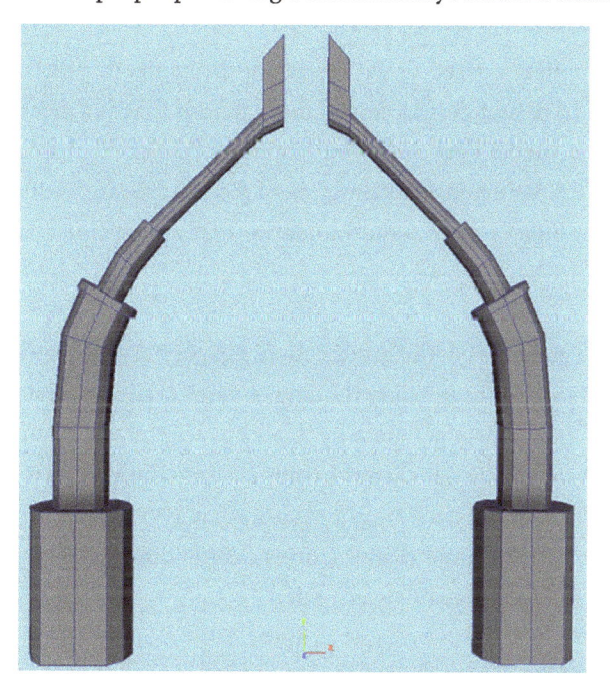

Figure 2.6 a, b: An example of iterating on a game asset

Figures 2.6 a and *b* above show the iteration of some architecture. We started with a simple archway that had a feeling of fantasy just to start. After we put it in the level, we had more time to think about the styling and add more appealing parts to the archway. This is a helpful concept to understand that your assets can be perfect in the beginning. To get to an MVP, you have to start somewhere and work toward greatness!

Minimum Viable Product (MVP)

This is as the name implies: a pared-down version of the game. In a platformer, there must be jumping. Perhaps you have swinging as your game demands that as a mechanic, this will not get cut no matter how much funding you have? You do not need polished art assets or even animations. The purpose of an MVP is to demonstrate the gameplay's features are within an acceptable range to ensure that anything built on top has the foundation of the MVP's mechanics working properly.

Vertical slice

Sometimes you have a good idea of the art direction, the primary mechanics, and narrative, but need to gather some feedback or possibly funding. A vertical slice is when you take a very thin slice of the game and polish it to generate hype and a sense of the end product. Demos are a similar concept to a vertical slice. This is more complex than the MVP as there is a level of polish to the art, animations, mechanics, lighting, and so on that MVPs aren't expected to have, which can take a significant amount of time as well as an understanding of the final product, which may not have been available when the MVP was made.

This style of prototyping is the best use case for our project needs within this book. We are developing a small portion of the game to get a strong understanding of what the entire game could be. This is our best option.

While making prototypes, your game may need to go through all of these to get to proper gameplay that feels good to play. You may also not need all of them. This varies greatly within each development group.

Summary

Within this chapter, we went over some deep topics—game design, what options to choose for your first project, and prototyping fundamentals. We went over how you and your team could collaborate in a Word document or a more visual flowchart to bring your game together. The idea here is to make the design's ideas a reality. Once you've done this, you should dig into your first Unity project, choosing which template to work with and utilizing effects that follow the setting of your game concept, such as GPU particles. Finally, we covered prototyping to get your project started and get a sense of whether it conveys the experience to the user that you want it to convey.

In the next chapter, we will begin to look at programming, helping you to bring all your game ideas to life.

3

Programming

Welcome to Chapter 3! We are going to cover all the basics of C# and how to use it in Unity. We'll go over the primary chunk of programming knowledge required for most projects. This chapter should serve as a referenceable chapter throughout the rest of the book when we get into scripting in each future chapter. We will first need to begin by ensuring that your computer's environment is set up to start programming with Unity and then flow into the fundamentals of programming. This chapter will serve as a foundational lynchpin to your Unity projects. Topics include:

- Setting up the environment
- Variables
- Data types
- Programming logic
- Methods

Setting up the environment

Programming environment specifically refers to the **Integrated Development Environment (IDE)** that you will use, and the dependencies associated with it. C# is part of .NET Framework from Microsoft, which needs to be installed on your machine to work. Luckily for us, many of the IDEs in the world will install that for you when you start working in C#. Even more luckily for us, Visual Studio, if installed from Unity Hub, is preconfigured and you can get right to developing your project straight away! Let's go through the steps to see how you can set up your environment.

The Unity environment

Microsoft Visual Studio is free, directly connects to Unity, and comes with tools to help you right off the bat! This is like needing to work on your car and someone just hands you the right tool for what you need as you put your hand in the engine bay.

There are some steps to ensure that every application is talking to each other. Let's walk through them together so we can ensure we're on the same page moving through the book as well as the rest of this chapter; we will work through small snippets of code right away. No need to check the water's temperature, let's dive in!

1. Install Unity Hub by googling `Unity Hub` and selecting the top link. This will take you to the official Unity webpage where you can download Unity Hub. After installing the hub, you will need to install a version of Unity to use.

   As the previous chapter explained the version of Unity, we are going to recommend production using the latest LTS version. In Unity Hub, when you're installing a version of Unity and if you do not have Visual Studio installed, there will be an option to install it for you preconfigured. In *Figure 3.1* below, you can see that we already have Visual Studio installed, however, if you do not, there will be a checkbox next to it to select it. It will then install the application for you ready to go!

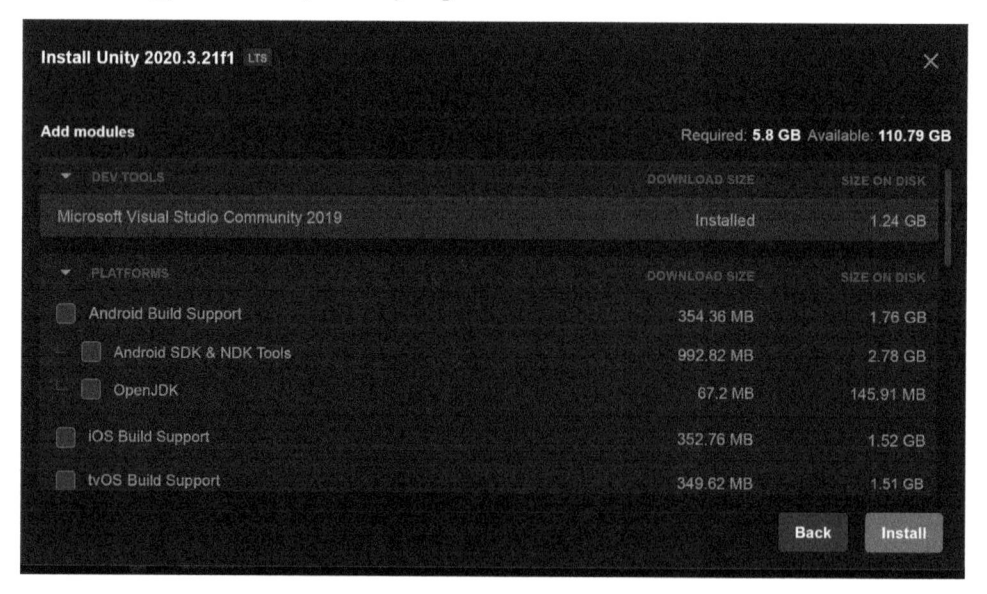

   Figure 3.1: Unity Hub Install Unity modal

Chapter 3 39

2. If you didn't have Visual Studio installed, then this will take care of configuring Unity and Visual Studio for you. If you did already have it installed, you will need to check to ensure the connection between the programs is ready for them to work together. Let's connect Unity to it and start learning.

To begin, close Visual Studio and open the Unity project we created in the previous chapter. If you didn't make one, no better time than now.

Navigate to these respective menus to connect Visual Studio to Unity:

Mac: **Unity (Top left of the screen) -> Preferences -> External Tools tab**

PC: **Edit -> Preferences -> External Tools tab**

In the external scripting tool dropdown, choose **Visual Studio**. After this has been selected, go to your **Assets** folder in the project window and right-click in the gray open space. Following *Figure 3.2*, you can create a script by choosing: **Create -> C# Script**. Name it ScriptingLesson and double-click it to open it. This should open Visual Studio with the proper hooks from Unity. This means that Visual Studio will read in the project file and Unity will keep it up to date with any changes.

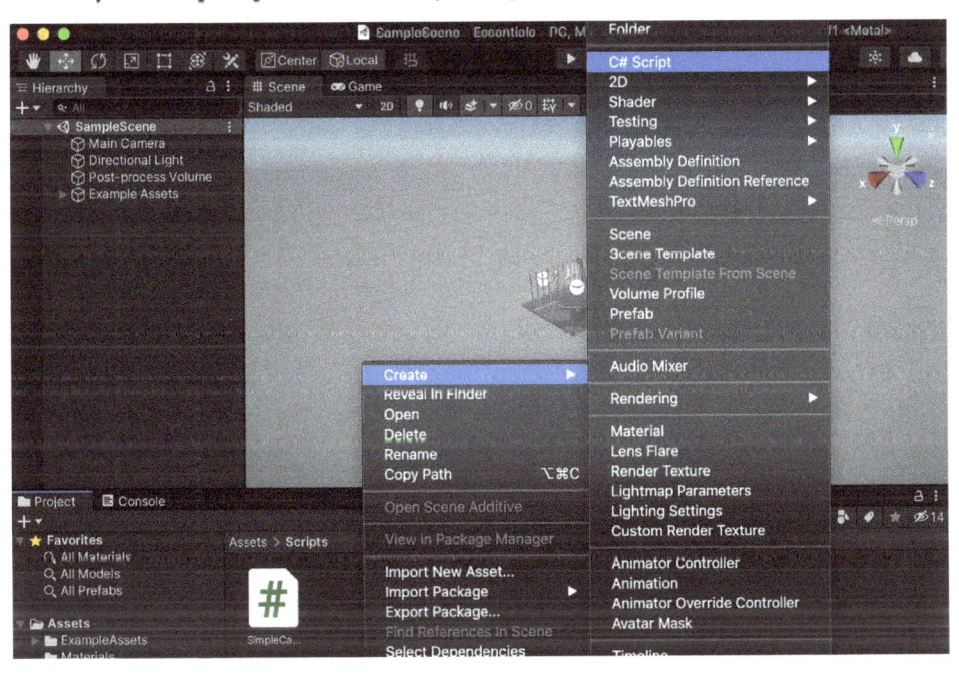

Figure 3.2: Creating a C# script in the editor

Now we can get started on scripting! In the next sections, we will be working through the fundamentals. These will stick with you and be part of every project that you work on in the future. This would be a good section to put a sticky note in to come back to for reference.

Before we get too far, we wanted to make a point here. There may be a spot this and other chapters where the code will get unruly. Your script may not work due to a single line difference or a forgotten semicolon. This happens very often. There is no need to worry; we will have all the scripts in the project safely set up for you to recover from. However, a note is that we have heavily commented on the lines for readability. This may result in different lines being stated in the chapters than you see in the code. We will try to be as accurate in the book as possible, but sometimes a single line comment can cause this. Be flexible with us as a comment can make the difference in understanding the entire script's inner workings and is more important than a single line number being accurate.

Fundamentals

With Visual Studio installed and connected to Unity's editor, we should go over the basics. In this section, we will talk about data types, variables, logic or code flow, methods, classes, and MonoBehaviour. There is a lot of knowledge in this section of the chapter, but it is meant to be referenced. If you have a sticky note, it might be a good idea to place it in this chapter to easily be referenced. When you open the file, there will be autopopulated C# that we will not need for this part. For now, delete the extra parts so that it looks like this:

```csharp
using UnityEngine;

public class ScriptingLesson : MonoBehaviour
{
// Data and Variables
// Logic and Flow
// Methods
}
```

The code here is doing two primary tasks. The first line imports the UnityEngine library so that we can use types and methods from the UnityEngine namespace for our game. This is called the "using directive". Inside the UnityEngine namespace, we have access to all of our game types, such as GameObject. Since we will be working in the editor to manipulate these GameObjects, we should be using this namespace in our class.

The next portion is a class named `ScriptingLesson` that inherits from `MonoBehaviour`. Inheritance is part of **Object Oriented Programing**. This class needs to inherit from `MonoBehaviour` as it's directly affecting objects in the game. During the *Programming* logic portion below we will explain how we utilize inheriting from `MonoBehaviour`.

The `//` means comment. Anything on that line will not be compiled by the IDE. You can use this to help yourself out with pseudocode or by adding some defining words to your code to help other programmers that may work with your code. We're using it for organization purposes.

After you make the change to the script, save it by pressing *Cmd + s* or *Ctrl + s*.

If you then go back to Unity, you will see that Unity will compile the scripts. Every time we make a significant change to the script, we will go back to Unity and check on how we are doing. There will be times that the Unity Editor will not like the code we are working with, but Visual Studio doesn't get these editor warnings or errors.

In the **Scene**, add an empty **GameObject**. Name it `Scripting Lesson` and then select it. In the **Inspector**, click **Add Component** and type `scriptinglesson` in the search bar. Left-click the script to add it to the empty GameObject. There is another way to add the component. If you have the scripting lesson selected, you can also click and drag the script onto the inspector to add the script onto the component section of the GameObject. Both ways are commonly used. Smaller projects may drag more than larger projects. Where there are many scripts and you know exactly what you're looking to add, you may use the **Add component** button and type in the script name to add it. Now, when we make changes, you will see them on this GameObject.

Before we get into any data types, we should have a small discussion about variables.

Variables

Just like in algebra, variables are named containers for something. C# is a strongly-typed programming language. This means that each variable needs to have its own data type associated with it when it is declared. There are guidelines on how to name your variables and which data type to use for certain situations. We will go into detail on this within each section. Naming conventions are case sensitive, and each type of naming has its own set of rules that need to be followed.

Data types

There are 10 Unity data types that are utilized in C#, however, in Unity, we will primarily need to know 4 well. They are **bool**, **int**, **float**, and **string**. We will be creating each of these data types in the `ScriptingLesson.cs` file that we created.

Bool

This stands for the Boolean data type, which is designed for either true or false variables. These values are also represented by a 1 (True) or 0 (False).

As an example, this could be used when your character enters an area that they shouldn't have to trigger something to happen, like a SPIKE TRAP!

On line 5 add:

```
public bool isActive;
```

There are four parts to this line and all of them have specific purposes:

- `public` allows Unity to access the item we are creating for use in the editor.
- `bool` is the data type of the item we are creating.
- `isActive` is the name of the `bool` data we are creating. It will default to `false` as a value.
- The semicolon (;) is being used here to denote that it's the end of the instruction.

If you save and go back into the Unity Editor, you will now see there is a checkbox in the inspector named **Is Active**. It should look similar to this:

Figure 3.3: "Is Active" checkbox visible

Int

An integer, or int, is a whole number such as 1, 100, 200, -234571, or 0. It cannot take decimal places. This is used, for example, if you have a discrete value needed to count up or down. How many points are gathered in a play session is a great place to use ints.

On line 6 add:

```
public int myInt;
```

This is very similar to the `bool`. We are declaring that `myInt` is a publicly accessible integer data type variable. When you save and go back to the Unity Editor, you will now notice a text input to the right of a variable named `myInt`. Since it is an integer, you cannot put a period (.) in there to make a decimal as it's an int and only whole numbers are allowed.

Float

You might be asking, how can I get decimal places in my numbers? The answer you seek is the almighty float! With a float, you can get decimal places such as 1.3 or 100.454.

There is a small unique factor to the float. When you are scripting, you must put a small f after the value to help the compiler know the value is a float. C# assumes that any number without f at the end, such as 3.14, is a type of double. We won't be using a double for our scripting, so we need to remember to add the little f after our floats.

On line 7 add:

```
public float myFloat = 3.14;
```

When you tried to enter this, there was an issue with the number and there was a red line underneath the **3.14**, right? If you hover over the red-underlined area, you will get an error. It might look something like *Figure 3.4*:

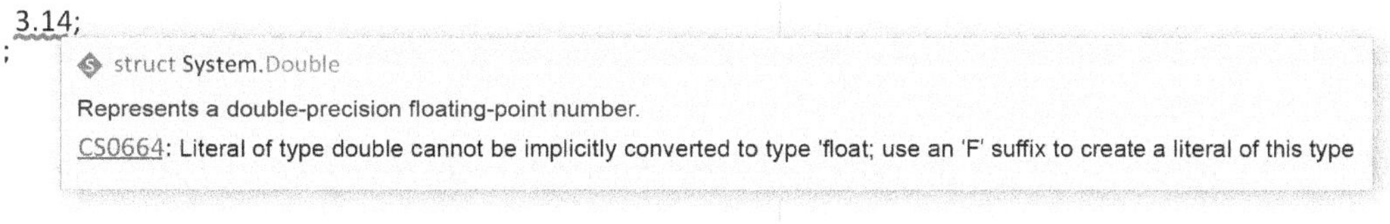

```
3.14;
;
    struct System.Double
    Represents a double-precision floating-point number.
    CS0664: Literal of type double cannot be implicitly converted to type 'float'; use an 'F' suffix to create a literal of this type
```

Figure 3.4: CS0664 error display

Visual Studio is trying to tell you that the number you entered will be thought of as a double, so let's make a bit of a change to help the IDE.

Change line 7 to:

```
public float myFloat = 3.14f;
```

There we go. Now we have a float declared and initialized. We declared it as myFloat and initialized the value as 3.14. The default float is 0, but when you tell it to assign a value as you are declaring it, the IDE overwrites that default 0 with the value you set it to. When you go into Unity and look at the inspector, you will now see the value starts out as **3.14**.

String

We've been working with numbers this whole time. Now it's time for letters to shine. Strings hold the values of characters. An example of this could be the character's display name.

On line 8 add:

```
public string mystring = "Myvari";
```

This looks the same as well, but now you can add letters! The interesting point to be made here is that these public values' inputs all look the same, so we need to make sure our variable names are unique.

GameObject

This is an interesting data type as it's unique to Unity. Its reference is to a GameObject that you place in it from the scene or prefab. This is extremely powerful as the item you place in here has components and we can access them from the script to do a great many things.

On line 8 add:

```
public GameObject myGameObject;
```

Save your code and head back into the editor. You will notice this time, instead of an input field, it is wanting a GameObject to be placed here. In our scene, there is a directional light. Let's drag that light from the hierarchy and into that spot. You now have a reference to a scene GameObject! Let's continue a bit further to logic and flow to see what we can do with our initial variables.

Programming logic

We've created some amazing variables filled with such fantastic data. The only problem is that we aren't doing anything with it. Why don't we start working some logic into our little script to start making some connection as to why we would need to program in the first place? For this, we are going to go into **if statements** and **while loops**.

Before we get to do some runtime work, we need to add MonoBehaviour to our class. The term for the actions we're about to take is inheritance. We will derive our class from MonoBehaviour, which will give us access to its class by inheriting them! To do this is very simple.

Remembering line 3:

```
public class ScriptingLesson : MonoBehaviour
```

We are inheriting properly by adding : MonoBehaviour after our class name, and now we have access to any of the methods inside the MonoBehaviour class. There are quite a few methods we are able to use from MonoBehaviour. For now, we will use the Start() and Update() methods that are inherited from MonoBehaviour.

If statements

We're now going to set up some simple code to turn a GameObject off and on according to the state of the isActive bool we've defined. To do this, we will need to check it on an update method, which is part of MonoBehaviour.

Starting with line 13, we made these changes:

```
private void Start()
{
    isActive = true;
}

private void Update()
{
        if (myGameObject != null)
        {
            if (isActive)
            {
                myGameObject.SetActive(isActive);
            }
            else
            {
                myGameObject.SetActive(isActive);
            }
        }
}
```

Inside the Start method from MonoBehaviour, we are setting isActive to true. This was added here to set the Boolean to be considered regardless of what was set in the editor.

After that, there is an update method. The update method from MonoBehaviour will do a check of the entire code inside the curly braces in every frame. Initially, we check out the GameObject we defined by comparing it to a **null**. This is a validity check. Null is a special keyword that denotes the lack of type or data. If you do not perform these checks, your editor will not be able to play as there will be a null exception. An example of this is if you have a public GameObject that isn't assigned in the inspector, this will throw a null exception as the GameObject is null!

Inside the validity check, we have an if/else statement. It's currently saying if the isActive variable is true, then set myGameObject to active. For anything other than true, set myGameObject to inactive.

If you save and press play, you will be able to select the scripting lesson GameObject and then uncheck the isActive boolean checkbox. It will turn off the light. Since this is checking every frame, you can do this forever and it will turn on and off until your heart's content.

Before we move on to while loops, we wanted to do a bit of a refactor of our block above. This is a good time to learn about this as well. We went through this if block to learn the syntax, but we could've made it better! We are running this check every frame, so the if block isn't needed here as we have a Boolean to compare it with. You could instead write the following code to refactor this down, saving compute time:

```
private void Update()
{
        if (myGameObject != null)
        {
            myGameObject.SetActive(isActive);
        }
}
```

How this can be read is, every frame, if myGameObject isn't null, set its active state to either true or false depending on what the Boolean is set to. We don't have to ask it if it's true or not since the data type only has two states! This is awesome.

Let's move on to while loops for a take on looping code.

While loops

An if statement is a simple branching pattern checking for a true or false to execute something. while loops will continually run code until the statement is true or false. This can cause issues – as you can imagine, some tasks could go on forever. This is called an infinite loop and can hang your application indefinitely or until it's forced to close. For the most part, we catch infinite loops quickly and they don't cause much of a fuss. We should still pay attention to our criteria when creating a while loop.

On line 32, add these lines to the update method:

```
while (MyInt > 0)
        {
            Debug.Log($"MyInt should be less than zero. It's currently at: {MyInt}");
            MyInt--;
        }
```

There are several new things we're doing here in this `while` loop. We are doing a **debug log**, **string interpolation**, and a **decrementer**. Let's go through those.

Debug log

`Debug.Log` allows us to pass in a string and it will be written out in the console inside Unity. This is very helpful if there are strange things happening and you want to get some runtime information out to the console.

String interpolation

Inside the log, we are performing an action called string interpolation. This is a very handy way to add your variables into a string. This is started off with a **$** followed by double quotes. Inside this is a string that you want to write out. It is a literal string to include spaces. The interesting thing is that there are curly braces **{}** inside the string! If you place the variable name inside the curly braces, you will get the data passed into the string. In the `while` loop just slightly above you can see us performing this in the `Debug` line.

Decrementer

The next line is a decrementer. This is an efficient way to write this line:

```
MyInt = Myint - 1;
```

If you save this and then run it, there will be nothing in the console. This is because we haven't set `MyInt` to anything, so it defaults to 0. The `while` loop will not run because `MyInt` is not greater than 0 – it is 0. Let's make this change:

On line 16, add this:

```
MyInt = 10;
```

Save and run the game. Now if you look at the console, it will quickly decrement `MyInt` down to 0 and print out the line letting you know its current value. If you look in the inspector, you will see that `MyInt` is showing 0 as well.

Now that we have an idea about programming logic, let's add some functionality.

For loops

Like `while` loops, `for` loops are an iteration over a set number of items. `for` loops are most used if there is an idea of how many times the iteration will need to run. We will do a simple `for` loop to show the syntax of it and go over it below:

First, let's comment out line 35 as we don't need the while loop debug log cluttering up our for loop debug lines.

Then, on line 39, add this block of code:

```
for (int i = 0; i < 10; i++)
    {
            Debug.Log($"For Loop number: {i}");
    }
```

for loops tend to be more common, but let's go over a bit of reasoning as to why you would want to use one or the other.

Choosing between for and while

for and while loops are similar in function. They are designed to iterate over some set of items. The rules on this aren't written in stone. They are interchangeable technically, but there is some nuance to readability. The for loop reads as if there is a set number to iterate over. This value doesn't need to be known to the for loop, but an example of this is a group of GameObjects. If you needed to iterate over all of them and perform logic on all of them, you wouldn't need to code the number of items to iterate over as the grouping has a count. You can iterate over this count. We will see an example of this in *Chapter 6, Interactions and Mechanics*.

The difference between this and the while loop is that the while loop reads as follows: Do something until a condition is set to true. It doesn't matter how many items need to be iterated on as it will go until the other condition is met. while loops have an inherent issue in them for making infinite loops. If you don't 100% understand what you are looping over or accidentally use the wrong symbol (< instead of >) for your condition, you can run into that infinite loop explained in the while loop section. while loops aren't used as much as for loops, but they do have a good place in programming.

Methods

If logic is the butter of programming, this is the bread. The purpose of a method is to perform actions in a concise manner. A very simple example of a method is a basic calculator function called Add. To perform this function, we will do three things: Create some public variables to add with, have a way to trigger the method, and the method itself. We decided to use the input system for all our inputs. To get this working, there are a few new concepts to add here as well. Previously, we asked you to insert code into specific lines. We will now just ask you to insert the code into the specific sections instead.

At the top, we need to let the program know we want to use the input system. To do this, we will add a using statement:

```
using UnityEngine;
using UnityEngine.InputSystem;
```

In the class's variable section, add these lines:

```
public int addA;
public int addB;
public int totalAdd;
private InputAction testInput = new InputAction("Test", binding:
"<Keyboard>/b");
```

We're making the int variables public so we can make changes to them and see that they are able to be changed during runtime when we run the method. The input system is private as it doesn't need to be affected by any other scripts. This is a good practice to think about when writing your code. If a variable will not be changed from another script, then keep it as a private variable. Though it may not adversely influence the current working environment on a small project, there could be conflicts later on when projects get more fleshed out. We want to keep the code clean from the beginning.

InputSystem requires the input to have listeners turned on and disabled when not being used. We will create two methods that are native to MonoBehaviour; OnEnable and OnDisable.

```
private void OnEnable()
    {
        testInput.performed += OnTestInput;
        testInput.Enable();
    }

private void OnDisable()
    {
        testInput.performed -= OnTestInput;
        testInput.Disable();
    }
```

These methods automatically fire during runtime. OnEnable is directly after Awake on initialization. Do not worry if this is a little bit much, we will go over them multiple times throughout this book for different perspectives.

For now, the reason these methods are here is to add the method OnTestInput when testInput is performed. We bound the letter **B** to our input in the variable portion, now we're adding a method to be performed when it's pressed.

Below and outside the update method let's add our addition method.

```
private int IntAdd(int a, int b)
{
    totalAdd = a + b;
    return totalAdd;
}
```

This is a method that is private, which means outside of this class, we can't access this method. This is going to return an int and its name is intAdd. Inside the parenthesis after the name are arguments for the method. We have two ints: **a** and **b**. We need to define their data types and their names. When the method is running, our method makes two ints with the values at that time and assigns them to variable **a** and **b**. We made totalAdd equal to it so we could show the values change in the inspector as well as in the console to debug it even further.

To bring this all together, we need to create the OnTestInput method. This method has new terms, but for this instance, we will give them to you to get the test going for a simple button press. Later on, in the mechanics portion of the book, we will need to have more logic involved with our input. Having this system set up early allows for quick iteration and scalability with new input schemes, such as controllers.

Create a new method below the intAdd method:

```
private void OnTestInput(InputAction.CallbackContext actionContext)
{
    // If the action was performed (pressed) this frame
    if (actionContext.performed)
    {
        Debug.Log(IntAdd(addA, addB));
    }
}
```

The magic here is that this method is placed on the `performed` of the `testInput` we enable in this script. This script gets called with the action assigned to that input. Currently, we are only running simple logic to allow for the debug log to print out if the `actionContext` is performed.

In our case, this will be true when the method is called. If we needed other logic, such as if a cooldown for a skill wasn't completed yet, we could tell the user they can't perform that skill within this method. This is a very powerful system that can be built to be extremely robust.

Back in Unity, click on the script in the hierarchy and then put some values in the `addA` and `addB` variables in the inspector. Start the game and press **b**. You should see `totalAdd` change as well as the console print out the number from the `Debug` line.

Summary

This may have been your first time reading anything about programming. Going through these small examples is going to provide you with strong fundamentals. Take your time to fully understand what we went over in this chapter as it will be the glue holding together the rest of the chapters. We will be using all these features when programming later as well as adding new libraries and different implementations of classes. These are the foundations of programming; we will build upon them thoroughly throughout the book. If you ever get lost, refer to GitHub where you'll find these scripts in their completed form, which you can reference if something isn't working correctly.

This is the end of the foundations that we will build upon greatly over the next five chapters. *Part 2: Build and Design* will add onto everything you've learned so far, answer even more questions about building the design of our prototype, and show you how Unity can help you create games with as much ease as possible. Let's move on to building out the character and put some of these programming skills together to get Myvari moving around with input.

4
Characters

In *Chapter 2*, *Design and Prototype*, we discussed that this book will be utilizing a vertical slice method for our model. Being a vertical slice, the project is a simplification of the game. It is similar to a demo, but it has all of the main mechanics the game would contain, just in a simpler form. It is meant to give investors a strong example of what could be an entire game experience. We will be showing the character's behavior to draw the player in and then lead into a small portion of the story with mechanics driven by environment puzzles while learning about the main character's past.

We will start with the concepts related to the main character; we will then model the character out and make changes as we see fit by working through their mechanics and movement. We will make a rig for them so they can be animated. After this, we will put them in Unity and test out how it feels moving them around in the engine. This chapter will be packed with a lot of information, and we will be going over many different production concepts to create our character and get them properly moving:

- Design and concept
- Rigging
- Character controllers
- Scripting your character's movement

Let's start with the conception phase for Myvari, the main character of our small story.

Design and concept

To make a character, there can be many dimensions. We want to make sure that the hero character of this vertical slice, Myvari, is as fleshed out as possible. One of the best tools for this is asking "why" for aspects of the character.

Asking why

We are building an adventure-based puzzle game. The first question that comes to mind is: why is the character on this adventure? In this case, we answered that question with: "She is seeking to find answers about her race's past that aren't in the stories being told or the books she's read." Now we've defined a few things, but there are still more questions.

To give an idea of the questions that came up from this initial answer, look at this list:

- What race is she and why does this matter to the story?
- Why female?
- Why is her history hidden?
- What is her clothing like?
- What does the race look like?
- Is she humanoid?

As you can see, this can go on for a while, and it should. All of these answers should bring more questions. Take them down to their lowest possible components. This may seem tedious, but when you are done, you will know how this character acts when they are confronted, their facial expressions, behaviors, inside jokes, family backstory, and everything in between.

Concept time!

Now that we have a strong idea of Myvari and who she is, we can draw up concept art. We first start out with some proportion work and sketch work to find her basic appearance.

On the left in *Figure 4.1*, we also drew up a behavioral take. This gives us a visual idea of how she may act in an **idle break** animation. An idle break is an animation that occurs when your character remains still for some time. We felt that her character would be studious and inquisitive, so she would pull out a book and just start studying on the spot.

Chapter 4

Figure 4.1: Initial Myvari sketches

After we have drawn up the sketches of what she may look like, including giving a sense of her personality, we need to get a feel for the colors to finalize the design. The color scheme shown in *Figure 4.2* was chosen after answering all the previous questions.

Myvari's overall color themes give the sense of royalty, curiosity, and safety. These are depicted through regal clothing with gold lines denoting royalty. Blue evokes a sense of safety—a psychological and physical effect, as seeing this color lowers our blood pressure. Using blue draws the player slightly more into her character, curious about this bright blue amongst the rest of her neutrally colored outfit.

Her most unique accessory is her necklace, which has a mechanical purpose. It will be the key for the puzzles that she will have to interact with. For this reason, the necklace has a color that stands out from the rest of Myvari. This color will also be unique in the environment utilizing a concept known as **user guidance**, which we will talk about in *Chapter 5, Environment, Chapter 6, Interactions and Mechanics, Chapter 7, Rigid Bodies and Physics Interaction*, and *Chapter 12, Final Touches*. We will need to use this color continuously in the environment, the mechanics, as well as the polishing of the entire vertical slice.

Figure 4.2: Myvari's color scheme

Once we have a strong idea about the character's personality and colors, we need to move into the 3D versions of concepting. This is less creating and more defining a character. The following image depicts the character's facial features using a **sculpting** tool. Our team has a strong background in the use of Pixologic's ZBrush, which allowed us to create the sculpt you see in *Figure 4.3*. 3DCoat and Blender also offer sculpting tools.

After we've worked through enough iterations with the sculpts, we will use this as a beginning high-resolution model.

Now that we've defined our primary high-res sculpt, we can move on to getting a low-res model out of ZBrush.

Figure 4.3: Myvari's high-resolution head sculpt

The low-res model will be our scale bias for everything in the game, as seen below in *Figure 4.4*. When you are creating buildings, flora, fauna, or characters, this model will act as the universal **scale** for them. There are multiple ways to work through scale, however, I know that this character is the main creature in this game; all of the items will be environmental or props, which will all be scaled off her size as the base scale.

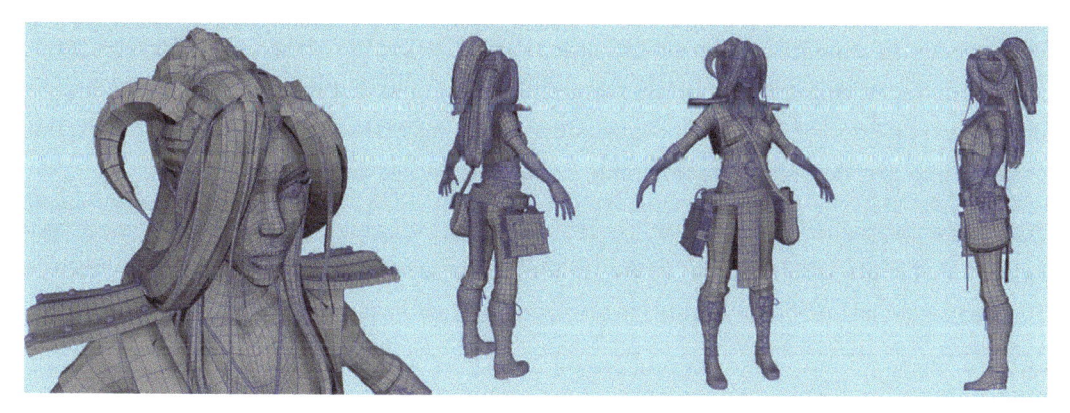

Figure 4.4: Myvari's low-resolution head sculpt

Some other ways scaling can be done is by building to scale. Unity's units are centimeters. If you build to a meter and then export from your Digital Content Creation (**DCC**) as a centimeter, everything will follow a single unit scale. This is a great way to build if you are building a large game with many teams working around the world. You could also build the game around the environment itself. An example of this could be a top-down game using squares for environment creation, so it all clicks together. The squares may be a 10th of the screen. From this information, you would take a screenshot at the resolution expected, then draw the character concepts on that picture to fit the scale. Look at your project and look through what the single point of scale that you can build off is. This will ultimately save you time down the road.

You could potentially just build whatever you can and scale the item in-game after it's imported. However, what will happen with that is the mechanics may not work properly. Think about games like Tomb Raider or Assassin's Creed, where the main character must climb onto walls. This requires the character to have a very specific height and a large amount of conditioning to ensure they are in the right spot at the right time for the animation.

Rigging

After working through this whole concepting phase, we need to work on getting some bones into the character so we can animate her. We will be using Autodesk's Maya 2022 to rig our character. The points we will go over will be principles, not technical details. Depending on your DCC tool, you may encounter slightly different terminology, however, the following terms will generally apply to any of the major DCCs in use for game development.

Animation-first thinking

When beginning the rigging task, the most efficient way to work is by having a detailed conversation about the animations themselves with the artists who will be responsible for them. Even if you're doing the animations yourself, successful rigs are ones that ensure the animator doesn't need an explanation of what each control does. There may be some technical attributes, but overall if a control doesn't need something, it should be locked and hidden.

When the animator moves a control that oversees the hand, they may expect all the finger controls to be on that control. This is intuitive but it shouldn't be assumed that the animator needs this. They may want all individual controls to be placed on their own control.

Chapter 4

Deformation

This is the ability for a mesh to be able to bend in a predetermined way, such as the elbows or knees. Since you know how they will be bending, you can plan your mesh for that deformation to be possible with a proper **edge flow** in your model. Edge flow is an art form all on its own, ensuring that there is enough geometry to keep the shape when deforming. An example edge flow can be seen in *Figure 4.5*. Take your time working through other AAA model examples and learn how each body structure may bend.

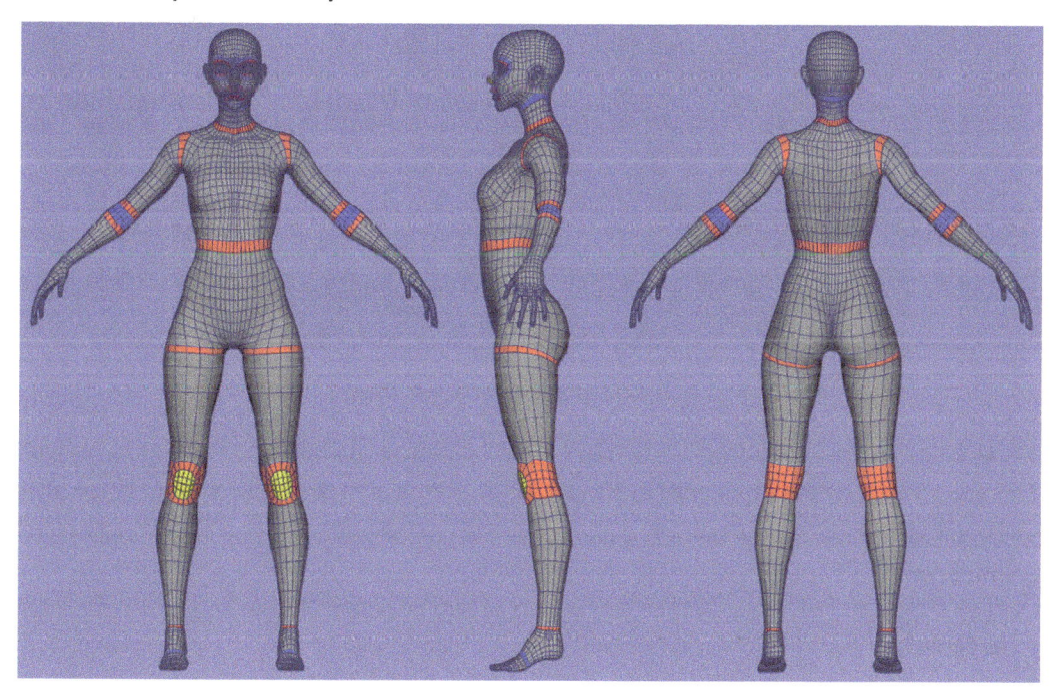

Figure 4.5: Example of edge flow on a humanoid

Facial deformation is by far the most specific deformation. If you are planning on having any facial deformation when you start rigging, look for some videos explaining how to set up the character for this. Facial expressions are intricate and hard to do correctly.

A small example of edge flow and separation can be seen in *Figure 4.6*.

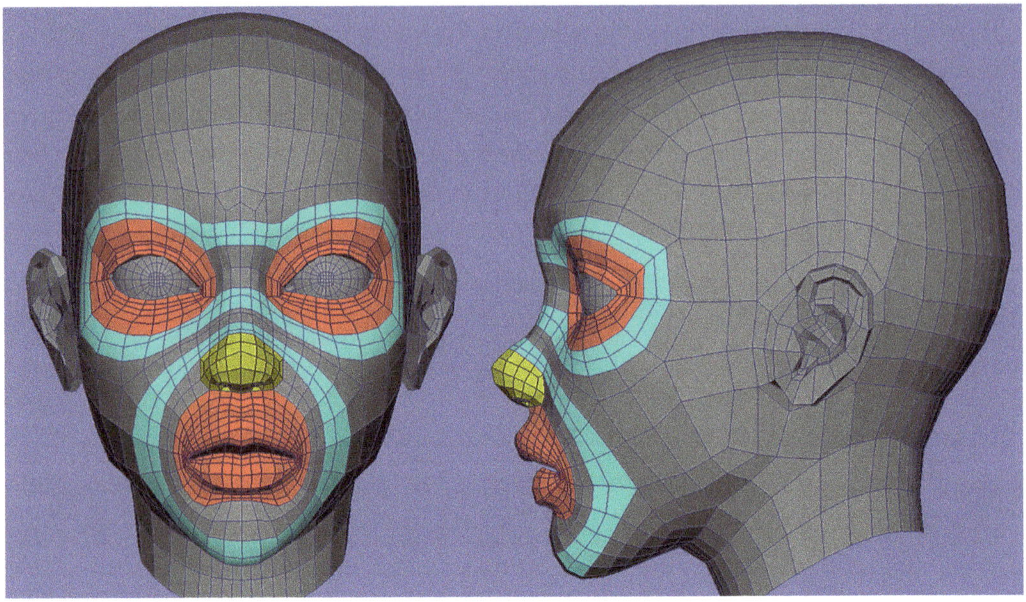

Figure 4.6: Example of facial edge flow

Facial deformation done correctly will result in your character producing relatable expressions. This can accentuate the experience by bolstering the immersion through emotion. If you plan on having close-ups of your character, it's a good idea to take the time to work through facial deformation.

Hierarchy

Hierarchy and parenting are an integral part of rigging knowledge. When Unity imports a skeletal mesh, there may be transforms that your DCC had in place. This can sometimes be a grouping or hierarchical change that has its own transform. Unity would see these items as GameObjects and place them in the same spot in the Hierarchy of the skeleton. Every application may be slightly different. An example of this is with Maya: if your hierarchy has a group node as a parent of your rig, Unity will think this is a transform of its own and import it as such. This may not cause an issue in the beginning with no logic on the GameObject, but it's always best to be as clean as possible. If you are using Maya, we recommend that you don't have any parent nodes on the skeleton you will be binding.

Chapter 4

This brings up a topic that is interesting to work with: the **control rig**. The most customizable rig that we've worked with was a binding rig, which was bound to all the vertices on the character. This was then driven directly by a duplicate rig, which we called a control rig. This allowed for the bind rig to only worry about the inputs of a single entity. This is important as sometimes you may want to have multiple deforming tools moving around the rig. You might want a separate squash control and twist control. All this logic on the control rig will drive the bind rig without worrying about breaking the binding on the character.

Bones or joints

Bones and joints are terms used interchangeably in rigging. The bind skeleton consists only of bones or joints in its own Hierarchy from the root, through the spine, arms, legs, neck, and head. These bones can be seen in *Figure 4.7* below.

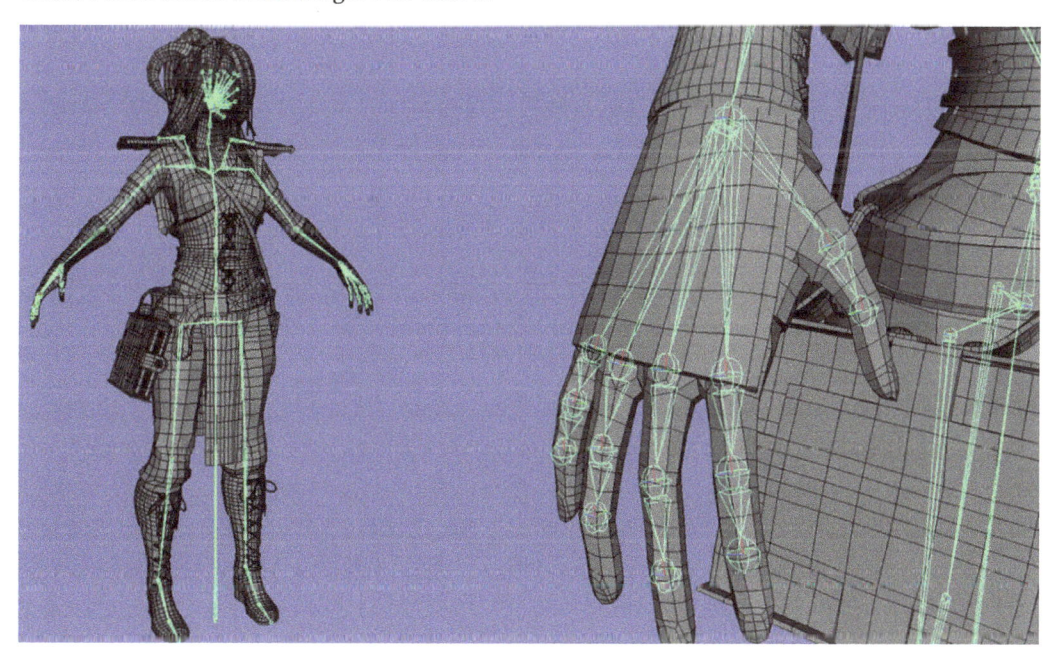

Figure 4.7: Examples of joints of character inside DCC

After you've laid out your bones, you then need to plan out the next level by constraining systems that will drive the bones' structure. If you are using a control rig on top, these constraints would instead drive the control rig bones.

Forward Kinematics/Inverse Kinematics

Forward Kinematics (FK) and **Inverse Kinematics (IK)** are two major forms of animation for arms and legs. FK is a technique where the animator will manually rotate every joint individually. If you are animating an arm, you would start from the shoulder, then the elbow, then the wrist, etc. It's called "forward" as you are going forward down the Hierarchy for animation. On the contrary, IK is where you would animate the hand, and the shoulder and elbow would follow from the guidance of a rotate plane. There is a debate on whether to use one or the other, however, they are tools. If you work with one and it makes your job easier, then use that style. It is very common to see FK/IK switches on character rigs as both have their places in certain animation workflows.

Further, the primary concern about IK is that you can keep the hand in the same position or to the space where it was last placed. Imagine standing up and putting a hand in the air, then moving your hips up and down while keeping your hand in the air in the same place. This would be extremely tedious to animate with an FK-only setup as you would have to key the shoulder, elbow, and wrist separately to all the hip motions. With IK, you would be able to key the wrist in the spot where it would be and then just animate the hips. IK would handle the shoulder and elbow for you. However, a walk cycle where gravity is working on the hand and it's mostly just making an arc with the momentum of the movement is better suited for FK.

As previously mentioned, these are tools that can potentially produce the same result. As you build experience with your tools, it will provide you with insight into your animation style.

Constraints

Constraining is a simple action. Using visual objects, we want the animators to understand the control's purpose straight away. A concise example would be a **NURBS (non-uniform rational basis spline**—a point in space that creates something visual) curve that will point to each finger in a rigged hand to help with making a fist. *Figure 4.8* below shows how we did this with Myvari's rig.

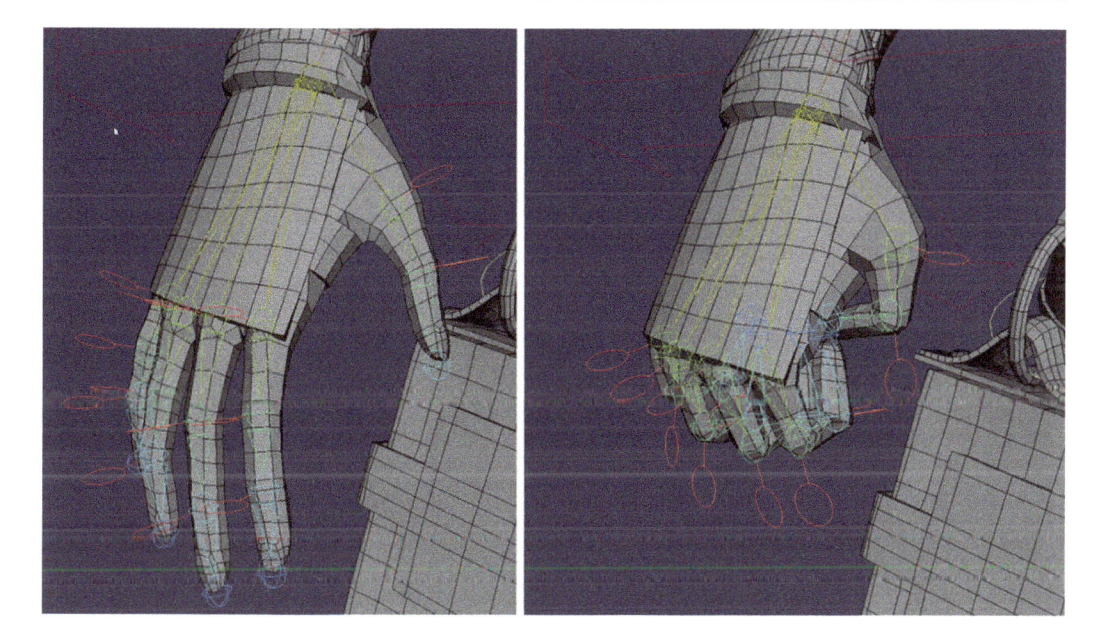

Figure 4.8: Myvari's hand controls

These are called controls simply because they allow the animators to control certain aspects of the character. Reading this may sound similar to another term we introduced in *Chapter 1, A Primer to the Third Dimension*: **parenting**. It is true that there is a similarity between constraining and parenting, however, we are allowed to be specific in what we want to constrain with constraints. In Maya, this is separated into translation, rotation, and scale constraining. You can also constrain individual components of each of these, such as "rotate x" only. This allows the rigger to be able to restrict the animator a bit. The above example with the head control may only need a rotational constraint. This makes it so the translation of the box would not affect the bones. With parenting, you wouldn't be able to separate these. Parents affect all transforms of the child object.

Deformers

The deforming tools will be unique to each DCC. The primary function of a deformer is to control the top-level hierarchy in certain ways. An example of this may be a twist deformer, which could allow a nice twist of the controls to make it easier for the animator to build a twist animation.

Some advanced animations use the deformers on another mesh that is controlling the bones, which is sometimes called a ribbon rig, which is seen below in *Figure 4.9*. This image shows the ribbon on the left and the deformers that control the underlying joints of the necklace. The right side shows what the animator sees by hiding the underlying ribbon control.

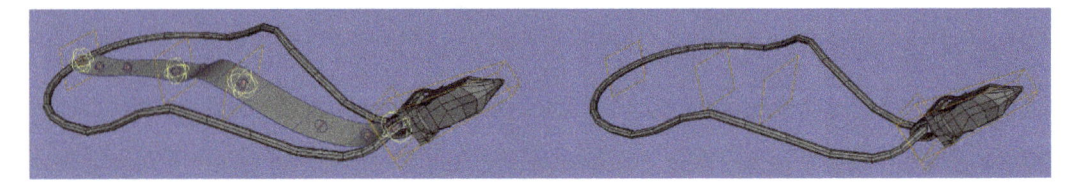

Figure 4.9: Examples of a ribbon rig for Myvari's necklace

Controls

Animators have the unique job in the 3D world of working with representations of the items they need to move in real time. Whether this is a box surrounding the hand or head, each shape gives the animator control. Each character will have controls unique to their needs. Myvari will have standard controls for a biped and extra controls for her clothing and trinkets.

Below in *Figure 4.10* is our character's controls for her whole body.

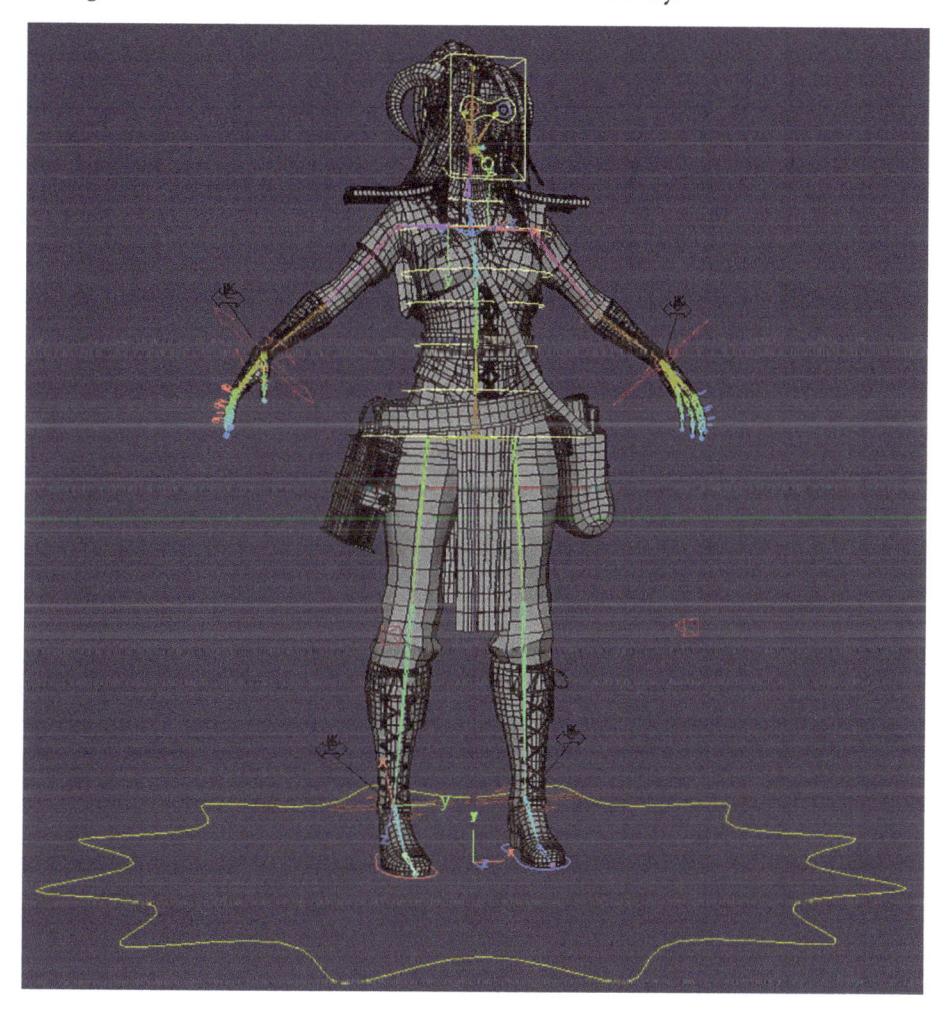

Figure 4.10: Myvari's whole-body controls

Physics-based animation

Some animation can be done through a simulation. There should be a bone attached to the mesh, but the DCC will perform physics movements that would be slightly constrained. These are very good to work with for chains, necklaces, and basically anything springy or dangly. These things are notoriously difficult to animate by hand, so it's best to let the application handle it for you. In some cases, the game engine can handle all the physics-based animation and doesn't need to be keyed by the animators. This means that the physics animation would be independent of the animation file itself, which would allow for a much smoother blending of animations.

Human Inverse Kinematics (HIK) system

Autodesk has created a biped rigging system to integrate multiple software easily. This is needed primarily for motion capture work where the animations are created through separate technologies. Motion capture is done through suits, facial capture devices, as well as specialized gloves.

The primary purpose of a **Human Inverse Kinematics (HIK)** rig is to gather animation data for the biped's head, spine, arms, and legs. There is an advanced version that allows for fingers as well as more features on the arms and legs, such as twists. To gather more information about HIK skeletons, Autodesk has published documentation about how best to use it. For our demonstrations, we will not be using the HIK system. With Myvari, we will be doing all hand-keyed animations and no mocap work. In knowing this, we decided to stick to just keeping a custom rig and control system.

Animation

We have now designed, modeled, and rigged a character with controls. Now we can use our animation skills in our DCC to give some life to the character. When you are deciding what animations to make, be sure to give good thought to what personality the character has. Since we spent a good amount of time asking all the hard questions about our character's motivations and desires, we should honor that with the correct movements expected of someone with that personality.

A strong way to work through animations is the same way that you would work through any art form. First, we will work with a blocking phase to get the timing right by working with just key poses. While you are doing this, get the key posing as strong as possible. Every keyframe should have a personality in it. If you look at the keyframe and cannot get a sense of the character, then it would not be considered "key" to the character. After you have blocked in some keyframes and moved them to get a sense of timing, this is when you would then add in-betweens.

These are keyframes in between the key poses in timing. These keys will help sell the movement within each key pose.

Once you get to this point, it can be a good idea to add it into the game engine to get a sense of actual movement with the character controller to see if what you see in the DCC translates into the game's movement. Doing this at this stage is smart as you will have a good amount of time near the end of the project to polish all your animations after you learn how to move your character.

Character controllers

Now that we have put together a character design, model, and rig, we need to set up a **controller** to have them react to inputs. There are two general methods for character controllers. The built-in character controller that Unity provides will allow you to have a character walk around, up stairs, and easily build in further functions of interaction, but it has its limits. The largest limitation is that it is not used as a physics object. If you need your character to get pushed around by physics, there is a second option available. The second option is using a Rigidbody and collision capsule with a character script using these as restrictions to the physics engine. Just as you may have come to expect by now, to choose the correct option here we need to ask questions! The following are some examples:

- What are the primary mechanics?
- Do I need physics for movements?
- How many other limitations will there be for my character?

After some time, you may learn to ask these questions very early when you start seeing what architecture may be needed to pull off the gameplay you want within Unity. This will only happen after leaving these questions unanswered and missing the mark slightly. Do not get discouraged by this. This is the best way of learning: failing fast and failing often. The options available to you are not always obvious.

An example of this is asking yourself what the primary mechanics are. Looking at your game, you may try to push crafting weapons in the game, but the combat mechanics are more fun during production. After finding this out, you may cut most of the crafting and put more effort into polishing the combat mechanics. What this does is place more emphasis on the character controller over UI or interactive crafting work.

In our game, we decided to take a simple approach to the character movement. We only need movement, and all other interactions will mostly be through mouse position and camera work. With that in mind, we will investigate the character controller foundation to build upon.

Built-in character controller

Unity has a built-in character controller component that can be added to your character. This will give you solid foundations to work with. It is simply a capsule collider that allows simple movement for a first-person or third-person game. The interesting portion of this is that it does not use physics or Rigidbodies for physics. Unity documentation explains this the best as a "Doom-style" controller: moving very fast and when you let go of the thumbstick, it stops immediately. This is sometimes desirable, but not often. An example of when this could be desirable is when you're making a game where extremely tight controls are needed. Metroid uses this to flip the character left and right immediately. If you had to slow to a stop before turning, the game wouldn't feel as good as it does.

The best part of this is that it is fast and easy to throw it on your character to get moving if you want to just test something simple. If you want to add jumping, floating, swimming, flying, or anything dealing with physics, this application will not work without a good amount of work.

We will be using the built-in character controller for this tutorial, as Myvari only needs to explore on the ground without jumping or sliding and none of her interactions use any focused physics.

Rigidbody character controller

This option for a component starts with coding in mind but offers a large amount of flexibility that the built-in character controller can't provide for many purposes. The initial reasoning for using a Rigidbody is if you are looking to have different physics materials in your game. If your game is planning on utilizing physics in multiple ways, then it would be better to plan on working with the Rigidbody and collision components as your choice for physics on your character controller.

Scripting your character's movement

When you're scripting your character, it's a good idea to have as many movement-related design conversations as you can to know what to architect out. For Myvari, we wanted to have a few movement-related specifics in the environment because this game is an environmental puzzle game. We should have the environment interact with her as she traverses it. Here is a list of what we went over:

- Idling
- Walking:

- On the ground
- In water
- On ledges
- Rotation

There are two movement-related scripts that we, at this time, haven't fully decided on implementing. These are running and jumping. The reason we aren't going to implement these currently is that we do not know for certain that we need them. As we move through the level currently, it feels good walking through it, and we want the player to pay attention to the environment as well. We will set up the character controller to accept a running movement if we think it's needed later. Jumping is similar, but we have no mechanics that require jumping up or over. You would only implement this to satisfy the need for jumping around in an environment. We may find that this is needed after some QA passes are done and player feedback states that they need to jump around. If this is a strong enough case, we can add it in.

Initial setup in Unity

To begin with, to get Myvari set up to even accept scripts for movement, we should set it up in Unity. We should already have Myvari imported into the Unity project. Just so you are aware, the way to go about this is just a simple drag and drop onto the project's folder you want her to be in. If you select SM_Myvari in the Character folder, the Inspector will show the imported settings on the model, as shown in *Figure 4.11*. The default settings that are in use here are good for our needs.

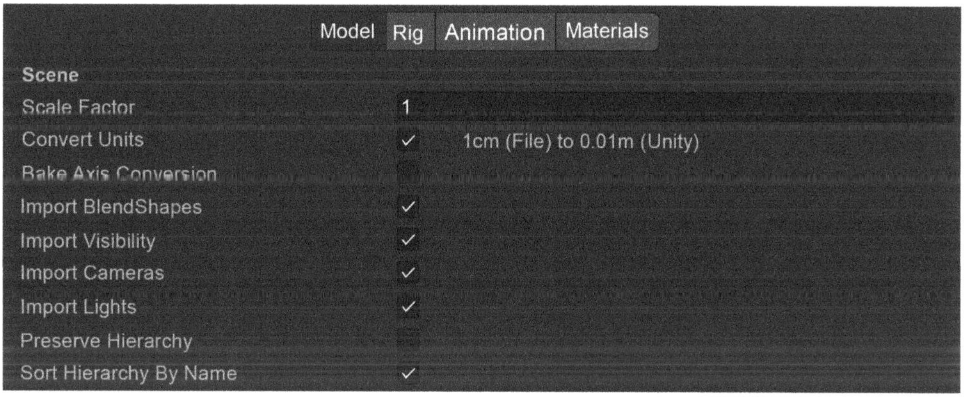

Figure 4.11: Import settings Model tab

We need to move over to the **Rig** tab and set up our rig. In *Figure 4.12*, we have a couple of options to go over. We want to make sure that **Animation Type** is set to **Humanoid**. We also want to create an avatar from this model and then configure it. This will open another window to set up the bones in the humanoid structure.

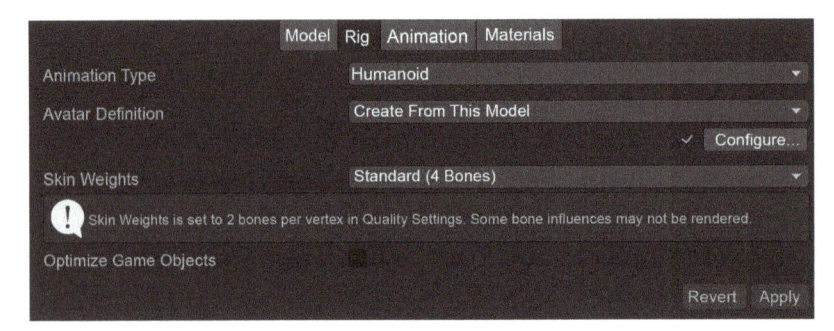

Figure 4.12: Import settings Rig tab

This window will default to the body portion, though we're showing the head section in *Figure 4.13*. It's best to go through every portion of the body as the avatar system will do its best to align the joints to the right location, but sometimes it doesn't work out. If it isn't set up properly, just select the correct joint to fill the slot properly.

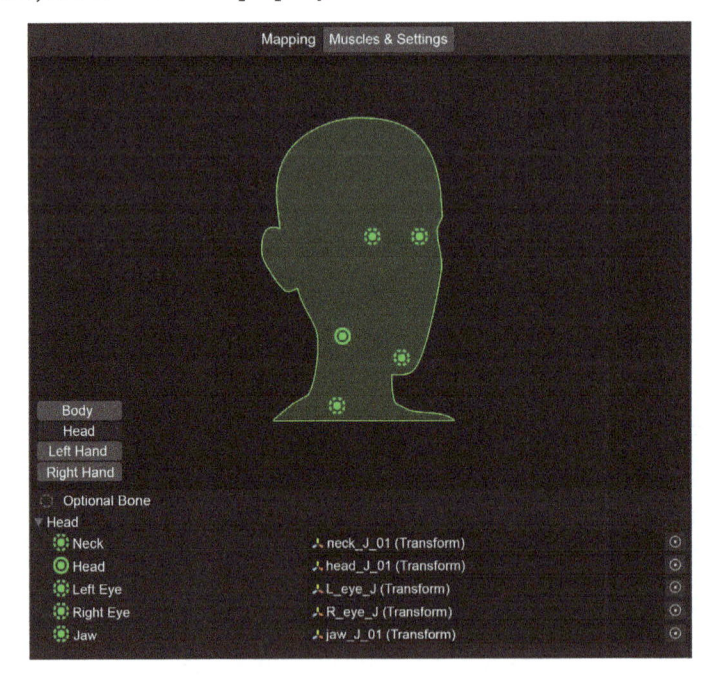

Figure 4.13: Import settings Rig, configure head portion

Before we set up the controller, we should have a chat about our decisions on how the game will be played. We have a third-person, over-the-shoulder play style. This means we must add a camera to the character. As such, we should make a **Prefab** with our character and our camera. To set this up, we make a Hierarchy that will allow for independent camera movement but keep the camera and character together. In *Figure 4.14* you can see the way we set up the Prefab.

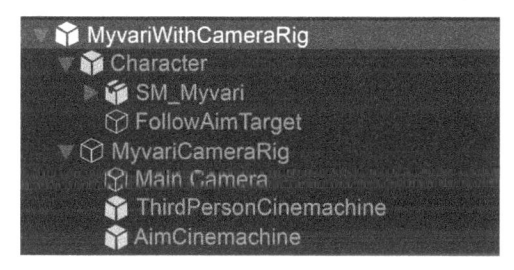

Figure 4.14: Character prefab hierarchy

The reason we set it up this way was that we wanted a container to hold both the camera and the character. The character GameObject holds all the scripts needed for the character. The mesh will hold the animator and avatar. The camera rig will house the camera as well as the scripts needed to maintain the camera in the position we want. Later in the book, when we get into the mechanics in *Chapter 6, Interactions and Mechanics*, we will be going over **Cinemachine** quite heavily as there are parts of the game where we will need to put the camera in a location for a cinematic.

For the rest of this chapter, we will go over just the basics of setting the character up for movement. On the character GameObject, let's set up the components to get her moving around. As shown in *Figure 4.15*, we will add four more components. These are the character controller, our movement script, a Rigidbody component, and a player input system.

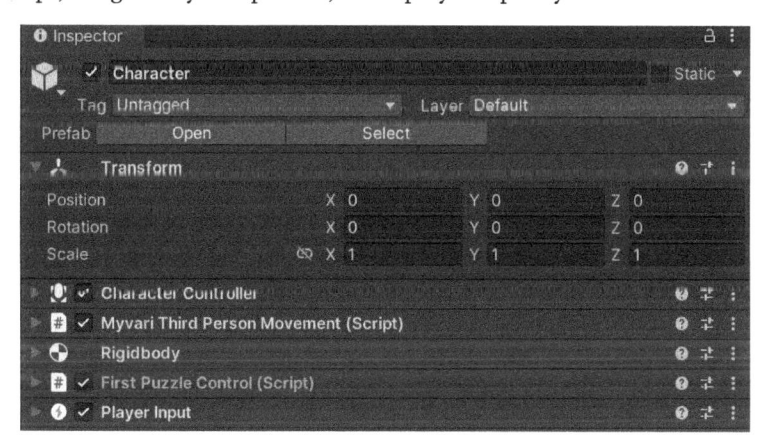

Figure 4.15: Character GameObject components

As stated previously, we will be using the base character controller. These settings are subjective, and we haven't finalized them, but this is what we have so far. One note we should add here regards the **center attribute**. This is where the character controller thinks the center of the character is. It defaults to being on the ground, but you need to move it up so the capsule is closer to the center and slightly off the ground. We try to put it near the pelvis and then use the radius and height to encompass the general body of the character. We do this because the pelvis controls the overall height as the human structure has its center of mass in the belly button.

We're going to skip over the movement script for now. The Rigidbody here is to help with future mechanics needs and physics-based work. We will cover this in *Chapter 5, Environment*, and *Chapter 6, Interactions and Mechanics*.

PlayerInput is a Unity system that sets up modular inputs to easily add different input systems without needing to change the code. Firstly, open your **Package Manager** and see if the **Input System** is installed. It would be part of the **Unity Registry**. If it's not installed, install it! If it is, then we need to make an input system for us to work with.

This can be done by adding a new asset called **Input Actions**, as shown in *Figure 4.16*.

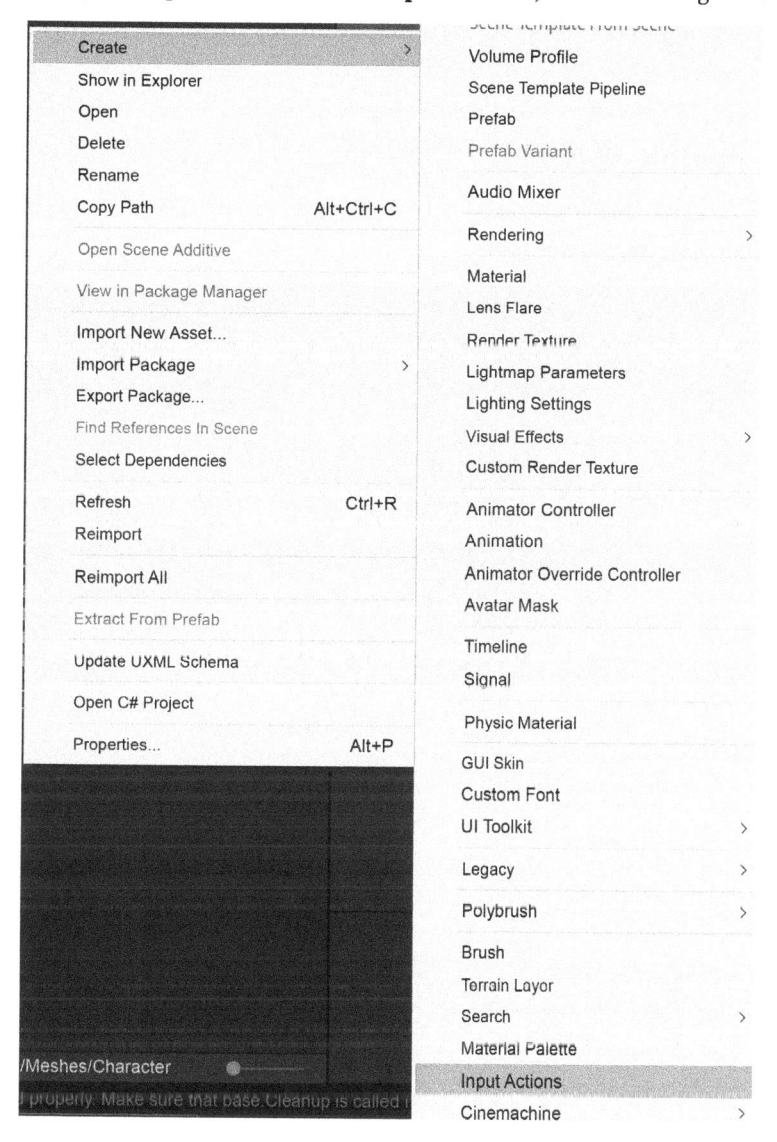

Figure 4.16: Adding an Input Actions asset

After you create the input action, name it according to your needs. We are naming ours `Player Actions`. We are going to use this grouping of input actions specifically for any player actions needed. You may need other actions besides characters in your future projects. At this point, you will need to double-click the asset to open the **Input Actions** window. Here, we will design the input options for use as currently needed for Myvari.

Figure 4.17 shows a completed input system as we need it currently. We may add more inputs as the vertical slice continues to develop.

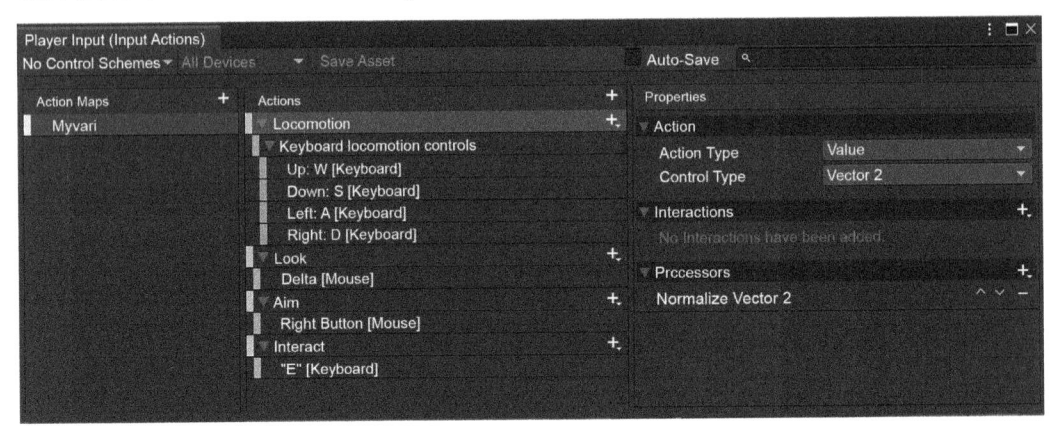

Figure 4.17: Input Actions

Action Maps are groupings that have their own set of actions that can be called upon. Properties are details and options for the selected action. For this case, we only need inputs for Myvari, so we created a Myvari Action Mapping. Notice the capitalization of the **Action Mapping** name, as it will be used in scripting once we get into the movement script.

In **Actions**, the green sections are the actions themselves, the blue are the bindings, and the light red are the binding parts. For **Locomotion** we only need to worry about a composite of vectors. When adding a new binding, if you press the plus (+) symbol on the right of the action, you have two options. These are **Binding** or **2D Vector Composite**. When you click **2D Vector Composite**, it automatically adds the **Up**, **Down**, **Left**, and **Right** composite parts. We are defining them as keyboard inputs currently to stick with a certain input system. There is a very interesting and useful tool when setting an action, called the **Listen** button. Looking at *Figure 4.18*, you can see that it's pressed and is listening for input. For us, being able to press the assumed button that may be pressed gives us a sense of immediate player feedback. If it feels odd at this point to assign a keystroke to an action, then it won't feel much better during gameplay.

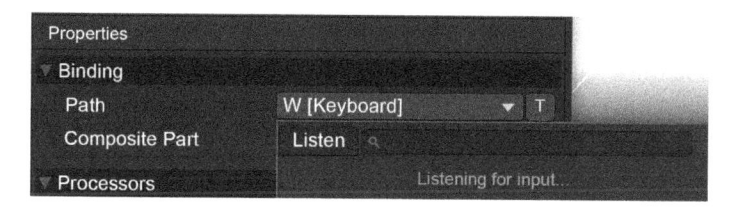

Figure 4.18: Listening for input

The **Look** input is for camera movement, and we are using **Delta** for mouse movement. Our **Aim** action is meant for when you're holding down the right mouse button for precision. This is choosing the **Action Type** as a **button** and expecting a right mouse button input. Finally, we have an **Interact** button. This is the same as **Aim** but designed for the *E* key to be hit at certain times. Those times will be defined in, *Environment*, and , *Interactions and Mechanics*.

We now have a setup for the inputs we as players put into the game. Even if we wrote scripts to work with this input system, it wouldn't affect anything. So, before we start scripting, we need to put together the basics of the animation setup for Myvari. Let's look at the animations we will need. For now, we only need **Idle** and **Walk** for animation transitioning. We do not need to set up **Interact** just yet here as we do not currently have a use for it. In *Chapter 5, Environment*, we will be looking at the use of **Interact**.

Idling

Myvari may have to stand still for a time as the player looks around. Most of the time, there is no scripting involved when idling as this should be the standard state in your animation controller. When you bring the character into your Scene, you will need to add an **Animator** component. See *Figure 4.19* for a correct configuration.

Figure 4.19: Animator component

Controller and **Avatar** will be empty. We need to create the controller by creating a new asset and going to **Create > Animator Controller**. The controller is an interface between the code and visuals to move the skeletal mesh we want to animate.

With **Idle**, we will make a default state and name it Idle. You can see this in *Figure 4.20*. In the **Characters > Animations** folder within the project, there are animations we've set up with Myvari. Select the **Idle** state and drag the idle animation from that folder onto the **Motion** parameter in the inspector, as shown in *Figure 4.21* below.

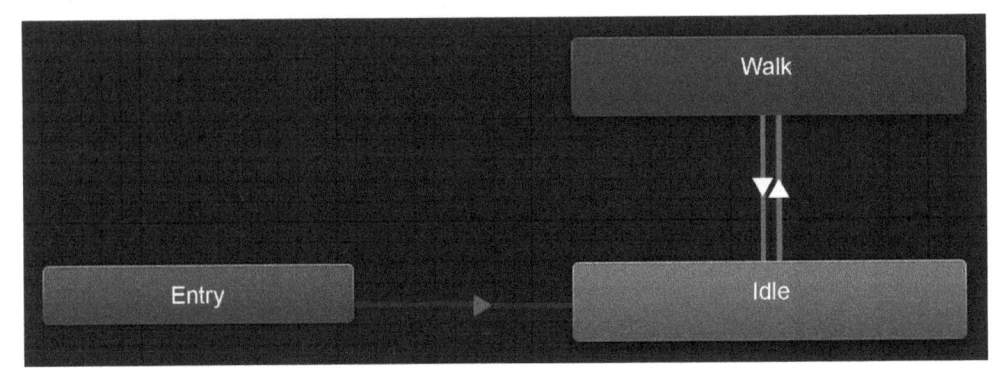

Figure 4.20: Controller state machine

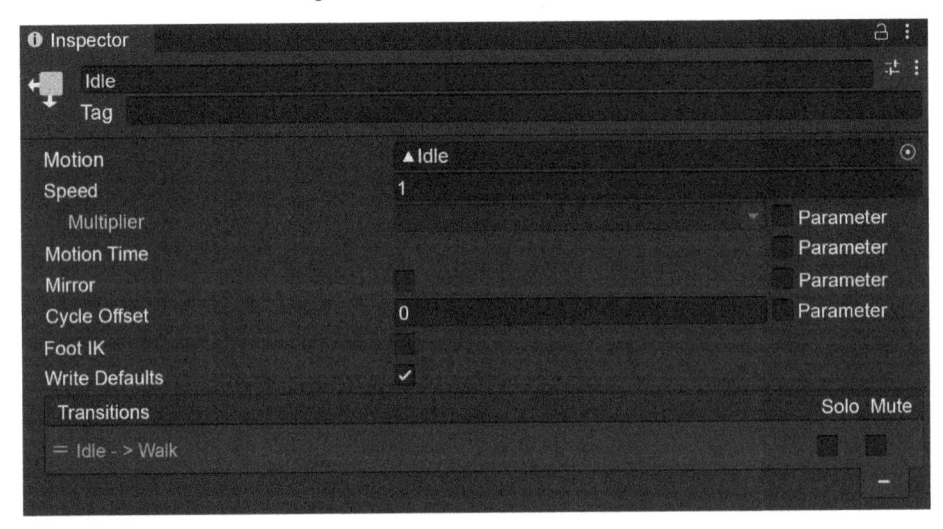

Figure 4.21: Idle animation state inspector

When you have the idle animation in place, when you press **Play**, the character will enter idle mode and loop that animation forever!

We also want to have a walk animation though. To add this, in an empty space, right-click and choose **Create State** and then choose **Empty**.

Name it Walk. Select it and add the walking animation. After that, right-click on **Idle** and choose **Make Transition**, then left-click on the **Walk** state.

Chapter 4   77

This will make a transition from **Idle** to **Walk**. Do the same thing from the **Walk** state back to **Idle**. This allows us to set up parameters to transition to and from **Idle** and **Walk**. We will now add a parameter of `isWalking` to the controller, as seen in *Figure 4.22*.

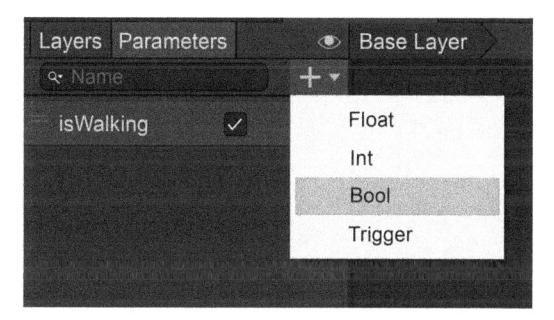

Figure 4.22 Controller parameters

The **Parameters** section is found on the upper left of the controller. We want to make a bool and name it `isWalking`. We will be using this parameter in the transition points. If you select the transition from the **Idle** to **Walk** states, you will see the transition from one animation to the other in the inspector. At the bottom of the inspector are conditions. Let's add a condition and set it to **isWalking is True**. The animation state of **Idle** will change to **Walk** when `isWalking` is true. You can then do the opposite to revert to **Idle**.

We now have inputs and animations in place with a transition ready to listen to the character logic. We now need to get in there and get the movement script working. Let's dive into the code!

Code entry point

We wanted to add a small section here explaining how we will go over the code. In *Chapter 3*, *Programming*, we went step by step through every line to go over the basics of code. What we plan on doing here is having the script in its entirety available to you, with full comments so you can read it if you're more comfortable with code. In the rest of this chapter, we will be going over small parts we haven't been over previously and explaining them as tools. We encourage you to build your own scripts and work with the tools we go over to build your own character movement scripts.

We are going to be working through the `MyvariThirdPersonMovement.cs` file. We have some simple work here as well as a complicated function. While we are going through this, know that it is OK not to fully grasp everything that is discussed. By noticing the hard parts and working through them, you are solidifying that knowledge and understanding how to work as a developer in Unity.

RequireComponent

When you see a `RequireComponent` above the class definition, this is saying that the GameObject that this script is attached to is required to have something. In our case, we want `MyvariThirdPersonMovement.cs` on the character, and we need to ensure it has a character controller. Something that is very helpful is that if Unity sees that the GameObject you attach this to doesn't have the required component, it will just attach it to the GameObject for you! Isn't that nice? We think so.

```
[RequireComponent(typeof(CharacterController))]
```

Update code

We're going to go through this part in a bit of detail as each line goes in-depth about the previous information and it's difficult to explain a single line at the end without showing the context. For the first part, we want to ensure that if the character is grounded and their velocity isn't above 0, it is set to 0. Sometimes GameObjects will move in small increments in the *y* direction. This isn't a common occurrence, however sometimes in 3D applications, rotations and movement causing rounding to happen for values and velocity can increment when it shouldn't. This can be prevented by using these few lines of code.

```
if (controller.isGrounded && playerVelocity.y < 0)
    {
        playerVelocity.y = 0f;
    }
```

In the next section we are breaking down the code we've written to ensure a thorough explanation leading up to the character movement script assignment in the Editor.

If you recall at the start of the *Scripting your character movement* section of this chapter, walking through water was one of the movements we wanted to have set up. We need to check if the character is in water to know how to set up that logic. We will be using a method from the **Physics** library called **Raycast**, which takes arguments, as seen in the helper tooltip in *Figure 4.23* below.

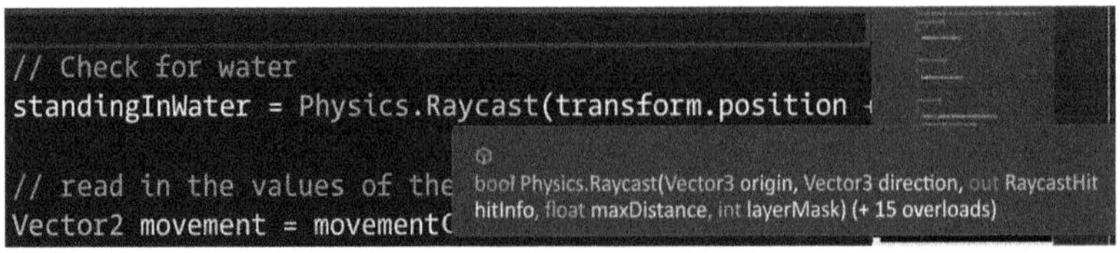

Figure 4.23: Physics.Raycast arguments

When a Raycast is used, its arguments are as follows: **origin**, **direction**, **hitInfo**, **maxDistance**, and **layerMask**:

- We define **origin** as this GameObject's position plus one unit in the up direction
- **direction** is the down direction
- **hitInfo** is being saved as a `RayCastHit` named `hit`
- **maxDistance** is set to 2 units
- **layerMask** is set to `waterLayer`

To test this, make a cube and select **Water** for its layer value in the inspector. We will call for this waterLayer check during the controller.Move portion at the bottom.

```
// Check for water
standingInWater = Physics.Raycast(transform.position + Vector3.up,
Vector3.down, out RayCastHit hit, 2f, waterLayer);
```

This next part is where the **Input System** is reading the value of the locomotion we put together. The **movement** variable is a Vector2, or *x* and *y* only. So, we will need to manipulate this to make sure it makes sense for a 3D movement.

```
// read in the values of the input action assigned to this script
Vector2 movement = movementControl.action.ReadValue<Vector2>();
```

We make a Vector3 and place the *x* and *y* from the read value while keeping the *y* of the Vector3 as 0.

```
// Use the values from the inputs and put them into a vector3, leaving up
blank
Vector3 move = new Vector3(movement.x, 0, movement.y);
```

We now need to think about the character and camera coordination. We have a move variable that has the movement we need to move toward, but the camera may be looking in another direction other than straight forward relative to your character. So, let's take that into account before moving.

```
// take into account the camera's forward as this needs to be relative to
the view of the camera
move = cameraMainTransform.forward * move.z + cameraMainTransform.right *
move.x;
```

Then we again just zero out that *y* value. If we were to implement jumping sometime later, we would need to change this from *0* to different values depending on the jump.

```
// zero out that y value just in case ;)
move.y = 0.0f;
```

Here we go. Now it's time to move the character. We've thought about all the possible problems we could have with the camera, character, and type of terrain. The standard Unity character controller has a method named **Move**. This method takes a single argument, a Vector3. This tells the character which way to go. We need to take advantage of a few things. How fast are they moving? Are they in water? Something new we are using here is something called a **ternary**.

Let's give a slight explanation before we get into the next line of code. This is the ternary function. What is being said here is this:

```
If standingInWater is true, this value is whatever the value of
waterSlowFactor is. Otherwise, this will be 1f.
(standingInWater ? waterSlowFactor : 1f)
```

This is handy! We can slow the character down by a tunable value easily and if we aren't in water, she moves at the regular rate we have already designed.

```
controller.Move(move * Time.deltaTime * playerSpeed * (standingInWater ?
waterSlowFactor : 1f));
```

We have gravity defined at the top of this class, and we set the velocity to that gravity value multiplied by the change in time to account for framerate. This will not be accounted for unless Myvari is not grounded due to the `if` statement on top of the update function, which sets the velocity.y to *0* if it's less than *0* and isGrounded.

```
playerVelocity.y += gravityValue * Time.deltaTime;
controller.Move(playerVelocity * Time.deltaTime);
```

Here we are calling two methods to handle rotation and animation states.

```
HandleRotation(movement);
HandleAnimation(movement);
```

Methods

In an effort to keep the update loop as clean as possible, we refactored out handling the rotation and animation from the Update function.

Refactoring is the process of restructuring existing code to make it more readable. It's running in the update, but it's only called one line per method. The initial method we'd like to go over is the HandleAnimation method. This takes a Vector2 as an input, which is the direct input to the Vector2 reading from the input system. We are only worried about the single animation parameter isWalking.

We first get the value of the bool at its current state and store it in a local variable. Then we check if either of the vectors in the input movement is nonzero as well as if isWalking is currently false. If so, we set the animator bool to true. Otherwise, we set it to false. When this bool changes, it will update in the controller and set the animations to the appropriate state.

```
void HandleAnimation(Vector2 movement)
    {
        bool isWalking = animator.GetBool("isWalking");

        if (movement != Vector2.zero && !isWalking)
        {
            animator.SetBool("isWalking", true);
        }

        else if (!(movement != Vector2.zero) && isWalking)
        {
            animator.SetBool("isWalking", false);
        }
    }
```

This is the most advanced method we have going on here. We think it's a smart idea to get out of our comfort zones as often as possible to continue growth. We will walk through this and if it's not making sense right now, let it sink in and your brain will work through it. There are three actions taking place here. We need to find the angle we want to rotate to, get a rotation value, and then rotate!

Firstly, targetAngle is doing a Mathf method called Atan2. Atan2 is an arctangent method that allows you to find the angle given the target position of where you want to rotate to. It's an interesting method that is very useful in games for character rotations in 3D applications. The problem is that we need to also account for the camera again. Atan2 returns radians, so we need to multiply it by the radians-to-degrees constant and then add the camera's y angle. This is the offset from the character's angle.

Next, we then take that target angle and create a quaternion from it in the current camera angle on the *y* axis. This will allow us to get an angle we will need to go to without worrying about **gimbal locking** occurring. Gimbal locking is when two axes get stuck in rotation due to one axis being 90 degrees off center. Quaternions are not susceptible to gimbal locking, which is why we transfer to quaternions in the end from the Euler angles.

By definition, Euler angles are oriented with respect to a fixed coordinate system. This is how we represent the angle we are at in the game where the reference is from *0, 0, 0* in rotation on import. If you rotate the character 90 degrees on the *y* axis, it is represented as *0, 90, 0* in the rotational fields of the transform of that GameObject. These values are Euler angles.

Finally, we need to transition to that rotation value. We do this through a **Slerp**. This stands for a **spherical lerp**. When working with rotations, it's best to use the Slerp method. The arguments are our current rotation, the new rotation we just made, and then how long it should take to rotate to that new position. We made this rotation speed publicly available so we could change it on the fly to get the variable that feels best.

```
Void HandleRotation(Vector2 movement)
    {
        if (movement != Vector2.zero)
        {
            float targetAngle = Mathf.Atan2(movement.x, movement.y) * Mathf.Rad2Deg + cameraMainTransform.eulerAngles.y;
            Quaternion rotation = Quaternion.Euler(0.0f, targetAngle, 0.0f);
            transform.rotation = Quaternion.Slerp(transform.rotation, rotation, rotFactorPerFrame * Time.deltaTime);
        }
    }
```

After this is done, your character now has movement and rotation. This is a great first step to building out an environmental, narrative-driven exploration game. Let's finish up with a summary of what the whole chapter covered.

Summary

In this chapter, we covered a large amount of character information. We went through design, modeling and rigging, character controllers, rigid bodies, working in Unity, and scripting a movement controller.

Design will always be boiled down to the question of "why?" You should've taken away from this chapter that the why of your character and their motivations will help secure a unique character that can be relatable. Modeling and rigging are heavily dependent on the type of modeling you will need to do. We went over some key methods to help guide your modeling to think of animation first. This also applies to rigging. Animation will be the final stage, and the easier it is to properly animate, the easier you and your players will find a better overall experience. Animations tend to be continually worked on until very close to release. Take the design of the rig seriously, as making changes after animations start could end up requiring a remake of animations.

We realized that Unity built-in character controller makes the most sense to us as we don't need Myvari to be tossed around by physics, such as ragdolling. We then went into Unity and imported Myvari and went over the components needed to get input as well as animations for her. Finally, we finished going over a character script for movement and rotations.

In the next chapter, we will look at the environment, the terrain, and a tool called ProBuilder.

Join us on Discord!

At the time of writing this book, we had over 200 Unity professionals on the Unity server and we are constantly adapting to add new channels to facilitate conversations on key topics such as C# programming, game mechanics, game UI, animations, 3D games, sound and effects, and a dedicated channel for Packt authors to connect with the book's readers.

Tell us about your progress made so far and the game idea you have in mind to build alongside this book. You never know—you might end up collaborating with someone on the server to build your mini-team today.

https://packt.link/unity3dgamedev

5
Environment

When a player enters a game where the narrative is mostly driven by the environment, you need to ensure that most of the questions they may ask are answered. We will spend time in three major structures of environmental development – environmental design, blocking, and iteration. This should sound familiar from the character work we did previously in *Chapter 4*! Fortunately, there are differences involved in the environment regarding characters that we will cover quite extensively in this chapter. By the end of this chapter, you will have worked through enough environment questions to know how we designed our narrative, but also to work on your own. Let's break down the topics so that you can get a glimpse of the chapter:

- Design – sketching, mood boards, and staging
- Blocking out – Mesh Blocking, Unity Terrain, Unity Probuilder
- Working through the iteration process
- Environmental design

The environment in a game is just as important as the character. We need to think deeply about our choices in terms of how the environment is in keeping with the theme and narrative of the gameplay. This is where we sit down with concept artists and designers to ask the difficult questions. Work through as much detail as possible to develop the purpose for the pieces of the environment.

Conceptualizing an environment needs to start somewhere. We started with sketching. We had an idea of what we wanted the environment to feel like from the beginning, so we decided to sketch up some quick concepts. After sketching, we put together some mood boards for a better definition of the style.

Once we are happy with the style and general concept, we then want to work in the following three stages to set the tone for the key points:

- Sketching
- Mood boards
- Staging

Let's look at these stages in detail, starting with sketching.

Sketching

You may have some strong ideas on what you want the environment to look like. Just as in the other concept phases, you need to spend a large amount of time asking "why?". This question will help define the context of your environment, so the experience fits together.

To perform sketching, you could employ several methods. Pen and paper work great for this to get sketches out quickly. Someone might have a great idea and draw on some napkins at a restaurant! If you're in front of a computer, you can use Photoshop if you have a subscription, or try alternatives such as Krita or GIMP for free. Take some time to sketch out the architecture, broad shapes, and feeling. Each sketch will give you a closer look at what the final product could be. After each quick sketch, have a small conversation with yourself or the team to determine whether you need to ask more "why" questions in relation to the environment. The amount of sketching required will vary depending on how confident you are with conveying the emotion you want the player to experience. If you cannot fully describe the reasoning for each piece, then continue sketching and continue asking "why?". Over time, the granularity will be enough to move on.

Below, in *Figure 5.1*, is a series of images, and I will briefly explain what they brought to the design of the environment for our vertical slice of the game. We really wanted to paint broad strokes of the environment type, meaning we're developing without worrying about the subtle definitions. We were not looking for the architecture of the ruins or the flora of the environment. Initially, we were 100% certain of how we would put together a ruin in the mountains, but we needed to search through our sketches to figure out what felt right. We discovered that we wanted a remote mountainous region that was overgrown far enough that it almost felt cave-like in nature the entire time. This built up to a feeling that you weren't actually on Earth, but on a planet similar enough to Earth to feel comfort in the shapes of nature.

Chapter 5

Figure 5.1: Examples of sketches

While you are working your way through the tutorial, we wanted the last section when you reveal Myvari's past to come with a drastic change to the feel of the area. This is initially shown in the bottom-right concept sketch in *Figure 5.1*. From this point, we knew we needed to push the architecture question and get the medium shapes defined.

Figure 5.2: Last puzzle area

By furthering the development of the last section, we knew we would need to have a stark contrast in terms of thematic visuals when the world shifted into Myvari's realm. Looking at the differences in the images in the preceding *Figure 5.2*, the major difference is daytime versus nighttime. That's a large change in itself, but we also wanted to make the ground and trees disappear while growing the architecture back to its old glory and bringing up reflective still water that reflects the stars in the sky, thereby really opening up this place as a new dimension.

After you get to a good point of sketching out your environment concepts, you want to then take what you've learned from the sketches and build out a **mood board**. Here, you can solidify references for the creation of your pieces in the future.

Mood boards

A **mood board** is a collage of images that draw out the style and mood of an area. There are hundreds of thousands of images on the internet that people have drawn, rendered, sketched, or even photographed that may be close enough to your style and tone that you can pull them together to inspire a little bit more of the experience you're looking to provide to the player.

If you have definitive sketches, then this is your time to shine with mood boards. Take some time to search out similar features and feelings of architecture to make a collage of what the environment mood should feel like. This will define the palette of colors for you to work with on the modeling portion of this environment journey.

For our project, we had several major requirements. We wanted a mountainous jungle that brought an ancient magical fantasy civilization feeling to the game. Even if you were to search for "magical fantasy ancient jungle ruin," there is a large chance that you wouldn't be able to find exactly what you needed by way of reference. Instead, you break down the primary functions of each area and come up with a mood board. For our two examples, we will go over the cave and ruins mood boards.

Figure 5.3: Cave mood board example

Chapter 5

In *Figure 5.3* above, we focused on the primary function of the caves. What does it feel like to be small? What are the atmospheric tendencies for fog and lighting? This gives that sense of an alien environment even though you are still on Earth, perhaps in an unexplored area of our Earth.

Figure 5.4: Ruins mood board example

In *Figure 5.4*, we wanted to break down the function of ruins in a magical, fantastical civilization. What shapes would a nature-focused magical being want to strive for? How do the colors blend with one another?

Mood boards need to answer for mood and tone. You will know when you've completed your searching for mood when each of your key areas has a collage that best suits the mood that area needs to convey. In our case, we needed to feel out the caves versus the ruins. You'll notice that both are drastically different in mood without even seeing all the finer details of the images.

Starting this after sketching makes sense if you can get questions answered through that step. However, if you find that sketching is only raising more questions overall, and muddling up the style that you want instead of defining it, then mood boards should come first. Searching for imagery of architecture tends to add a lot of clarity in terms of what is conceived.

Staging

After quickly sketching ideas and feelings to define the questions of "why," you then built a mood board to further solidify the feeling of the environment. The next step is to take the previously defined shaping and mood and use it to push your narrative and mechanics into the stages of the game. The first location you bring your players to needs to answer a lot of questions rather quickly. Luckily, you took the time to answer as many questions as possible before this stage. You can now stage your narrative design with confidence. For our project, we knew we would need to explain as much of Myvari's past as possible in each area you progress through.

When you're building a stage, place yourself on the stage as best you can. Take your time going through the stage and ensure your primary questions were answered the way you expected in previous sections. Now, let's try a new experiment: imagine the experience you've created through the lens of a new player. Try to feel what they might feel as a new player of 3D games. Are there enough hints to describe the experience for them? Then look at it from the point of view of an experienced player; would adding anything else take away from these power users?

This could take several iterations. Be patient with this step, and go through the stage to make sure you can explain the character's assumed movements.

This is a good time to show someone else your designs and see what unprompted questions they have to offer you as well; it is amazing what we answer for ourselves without giving it much thought. Having a fresh set of eyes at each stage will reveal areas where a little more detail is required.

After some time, a picture of what you need at each stage will be clearer, and you can then take your stages into a blocking-out phase.

Blocking it out

Now that you have worked through as many of the concepts as you can, you should have a very strong idea of what would make your environment appropriate to the narrative and the characters. At this point, the next step would be to work through **"blocking out"** as much as possible; the point of blocking out is to put all the pieces together within Unity to fulfill the experience we worked so hard to define in the previous stages.

Now that you are aware of, and comfortable with, what goes into each portion of the entire level, you can speak to the mood and tone in each portion and become attuned to the general shaping from the concepts. To block a level out, we will use a few of the tools at our disposal; Unity Terrain, Basic Shapes, and Unity Probuilder will set us up to put down the basic environment pieces.

Unity terrain

Working with the **Terrain** tool in Unity is empowering. It's very easy to get going and make a beautiful landscape quickly. To get started, let's create a terrain entity. After creating the terrain entity, we will go through the settings, painting, and foliage that Unity provides us with as tools to create the terrain.

Creating a terrain

The first step to working with terrain is to create one. There are two main methods for doing so.

One way is to click on the **GameObject** menu, then **3D Object**, and then **Terrain**, as shown in *Figure 5.5*.

Another way to start is by right-clicking an open area in the hierarchy and then selecting **3D Object**, followed by **Terrain**.

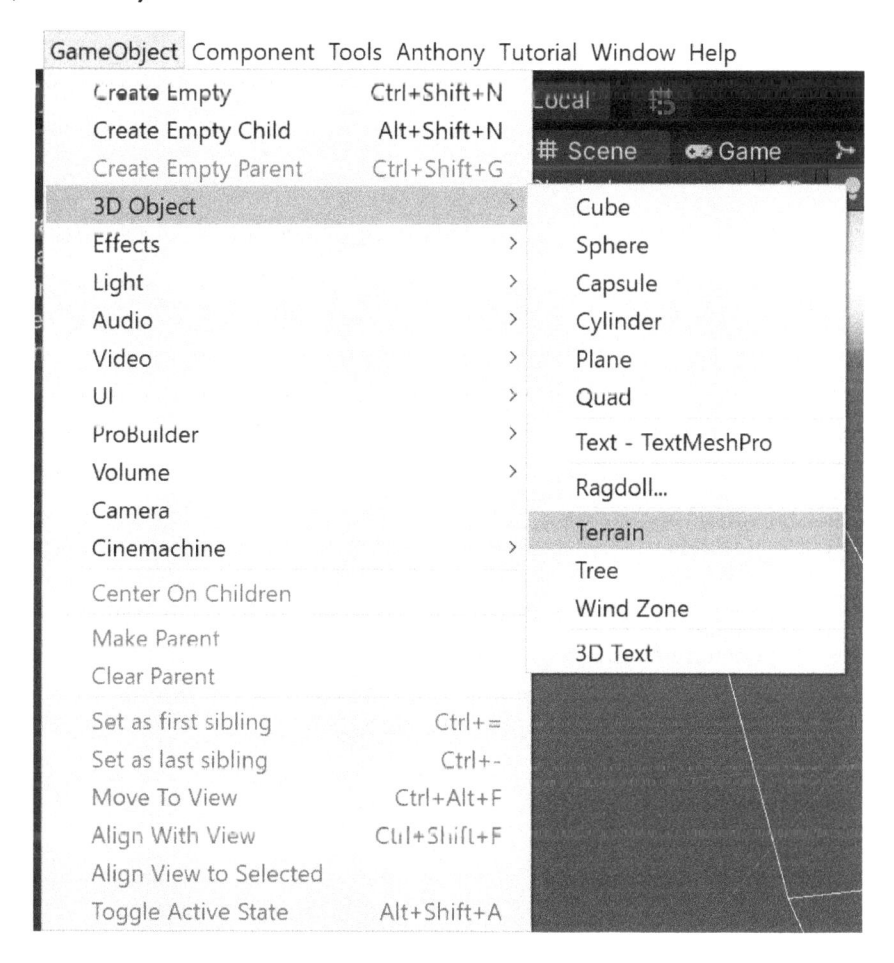

Figure 5.5: Creating a terrain entity

Either of these options will create a terrain GameObject in the scene at the global coordinates of *0, 0, 0*, sprawling positively in the *x* and *z* planes by 1,000 units, each by default. This value may not be what you need, so let's go over the terrain settings.

Terrain settings

In our vertical slice, we will be using the default units as these are what we ended up needing for a sense of scale. This may not be the case for your game. One nice thing about the terrain is that it can be connected to neighboring terrain tiles easily.

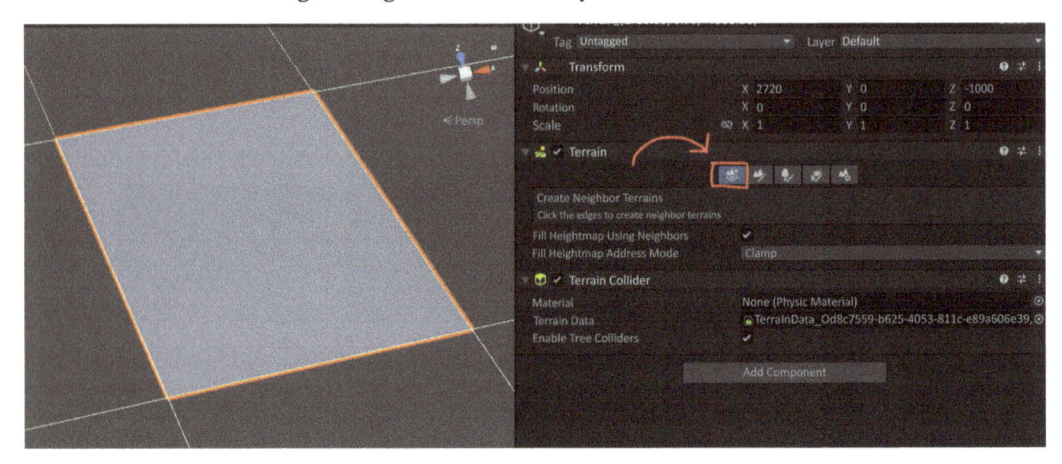

Figure 5.6: Creating a neighboring terrain

The first option in the **Terrain** component is the **Create Neighboring Terrain** button. When this is selected, you will see an outline of the adjacent tiles, as seen in *Figure 5.6*. If you were to click on any of these squares, the terrain will create a new terrain asset that is linked to the primary terrain asset.

Now that you understand how the **Terrain** tool can connect to other terrains quite easily, you can now think about your terrain settings in terms of the size of each tile. It may be the case that your terrain only ever needs to be 500 units in length, and 200 in width. A common denominator of those is 100 units, so you could set your settings as in *Figure 5.7* below.

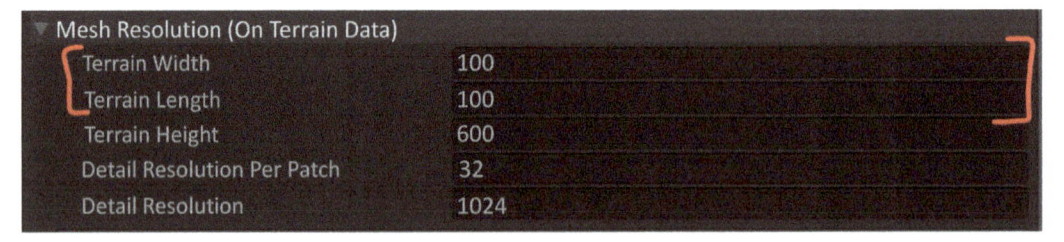

Figure 5.7: Mesh resolution settings

If you plan on using grass or details on your terrain, make sure your terrain is square. If the width is different from the length, the **Details Brush** will have a hard time placing the billboards in an orderly way.

Clicking on the open squares will fill them in with another terrain tile. Clicking several may result in a terrain that looks similar to *Figure 5.8*.

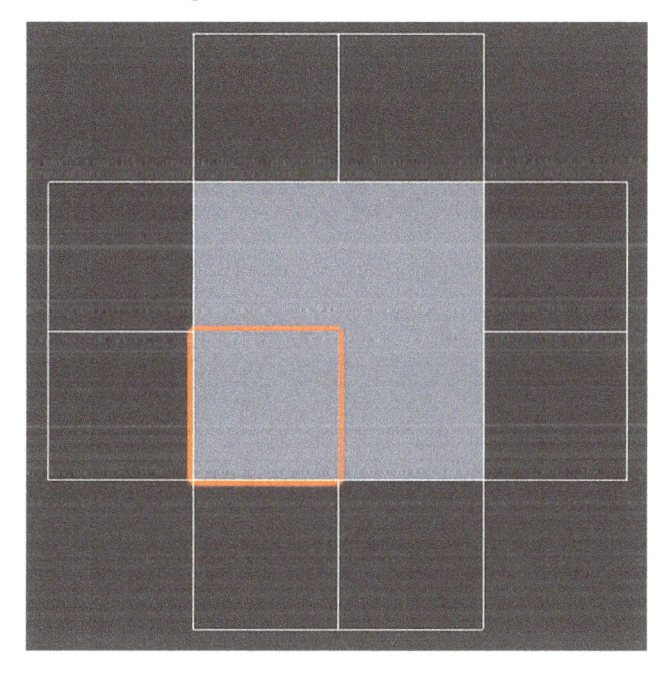

Figure 5.8: Adding neighboring tiles

This gives you the freedom to add small offshoots that aren't too large if you only need a little bit more terrain where you didn't expect to need it.

In our case, we knew we only needed one block of 1000x1000, so we stuck with the default sizing. Our entire vertical slice will take place in a single scene with this default size for ease of setup.

Once you have your terrain scaled and set to the sizing that you will need, you may then need to add some detail to your terrain. Even though a stretching plane of infinite flatness is interesting in its own way, there is a good chance that your concept does have some hills or mountains in it. Let's get to painting those in there.

Terrain painting

To get all those beautiful mountains and hills, we need to affect the terrain's geometry. The **Paint Terrain** tool allows just this. You can find the tool button in the second available option in the **Terrain Objects** Inspector, which is shown in *Figure 5.9*.

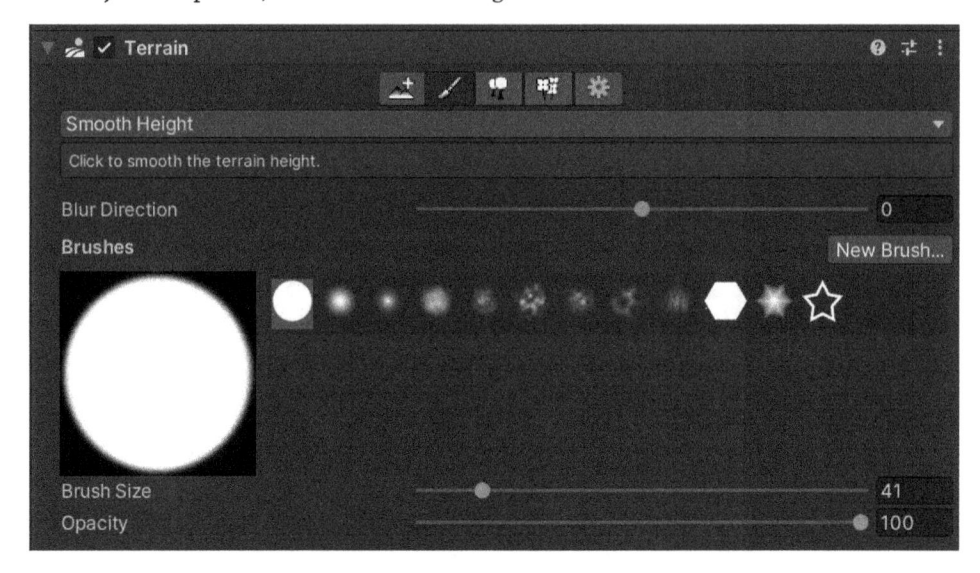

Figure 5.9: Brush options

Your **Brush** option, which is located directly under the **Tool** options, is a dropdown that will change the functionality of the brush. To look at a list of brush options, click the dropdown as seen in *Figure 5.10*.

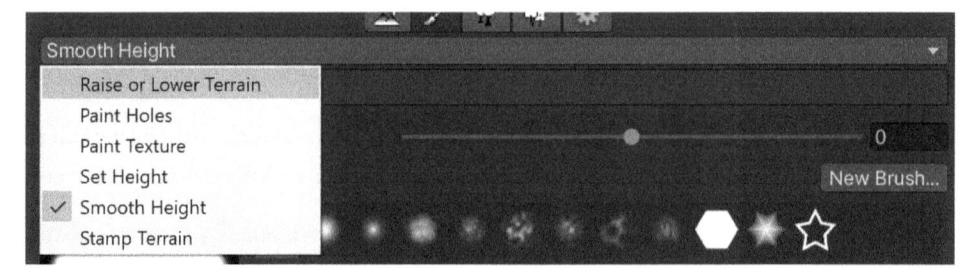

Figure 5.10: Painting options

We will go over their exact functions, but I suggest you take a bit of time to make a terrain you're comfortable with by playing with the different brushes. There's nothing like experience to get a feel for how they act on the terrain.

Raising or lowering the terrain

This tool will be your bread and butter while making a terrain. Depending on the size of your terrain and the scale that you need to make changes to the terrain, your brush size will be unique to your needs. Fortunately, there is a nice indicator, shown in *Figure 5.11*, to let you know the size and shape of your changes before you commit to the change and click.

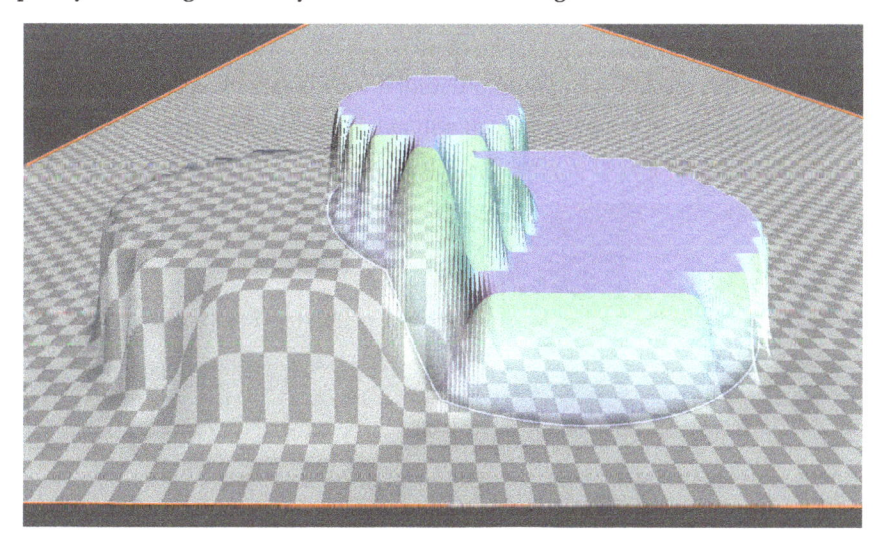

Figure 5.11: Visualization of brush on different heights

When you select the **Raising or Lowering Terrain** brush, it shows a description box that explains if you click on the terrain, the brush will raise the terrain according to your brush shape, and if you hold down the *Shift* key while clicking the brush, this will lower the terrain according to your brush shape. If you attempt to lower your terrain on the flat parts, you'll notice that it will not go below 0. This could be a problem if you're planning on making indentions in the terrain to possibly put water in; there is a way to work around this, which we will go over later in the *Setting the Height* section.

Paint holes

After selecting the **Paint Holes** tool and taking a moment to click around with paint holes, this tool may not jump out as the most useful tool relating to terrain as it just erases the terrain. In addition to it just making a hole, it makes jagged edges, which don't fit well with the rest of the terrain being nice and smooth!

But all is not lost! This tool is fantastic for you if you need to have a cave built as a terrain that is not designed to deal with concave shapes that would force an overlap in the terrain vertex.

It is common to design 3D meshes that encompass your needed cave system and then place it below the terrain and cut a hole in the terrain to access it.

> We'll cover 3D meshes in more detail in a later section, but here's a rough and ready explanation: a 3D mesh is a set of vertices, creating polygons, that we use to visualize a 3D space.

The terrain is just a flat section being manipulated; it isn't ground you can just dig into with a shovel. If you want a cave in the ground, you will need to make a hole, and then build a mesh below the terrain. This will leave some jagged edges, which you can see in *Figure 5.12*.

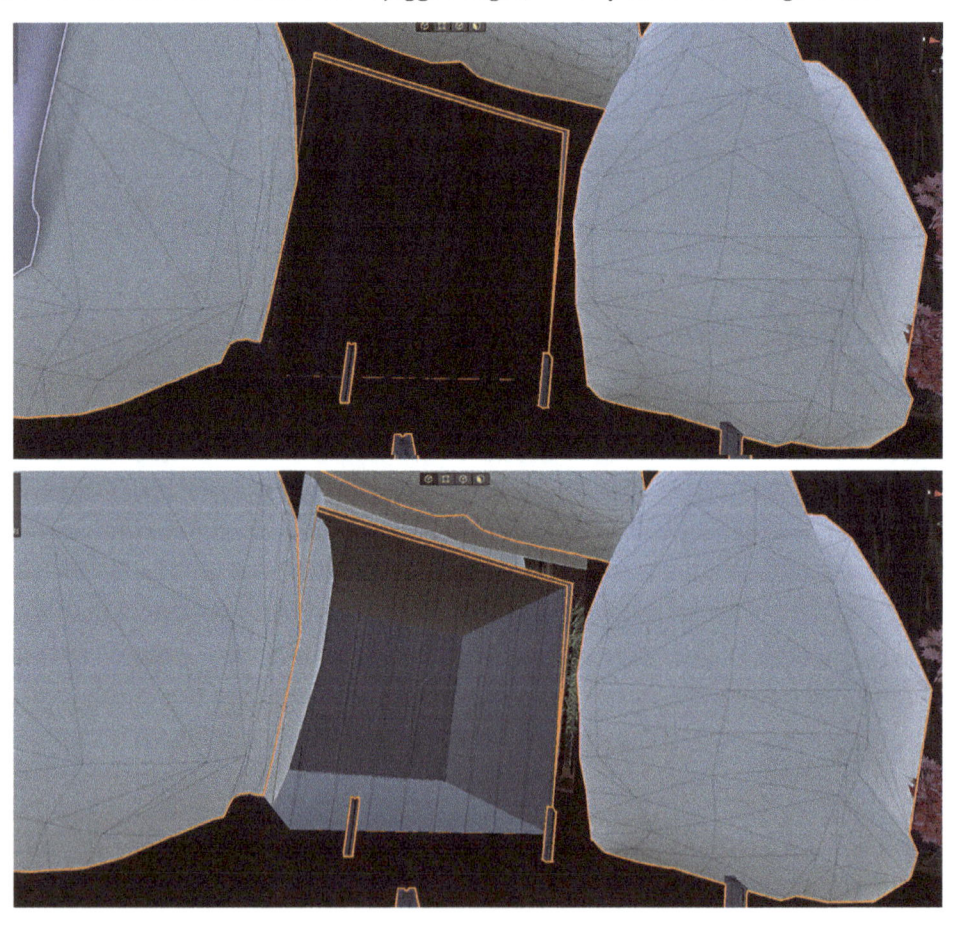

Figure 5.12: Example of paint holes before and after in the terrain

You can cover up those jagged edges with rocks, or other meshes that lead into the cave system.

Paint texture

Now you have most likely played enough that you have some hills, plateaus, and other various gray terrain-related material. You may want some color in your life, and luckily, there is an easy way to add some! You can search for a tileable texture online, or you can use one of the textures provided in the project to set this up.

When you first select the paint textures tool, there is nothing to paint as you need to create layers to paint with. Your terrain layers will be blank until you create one, so let's do that first.

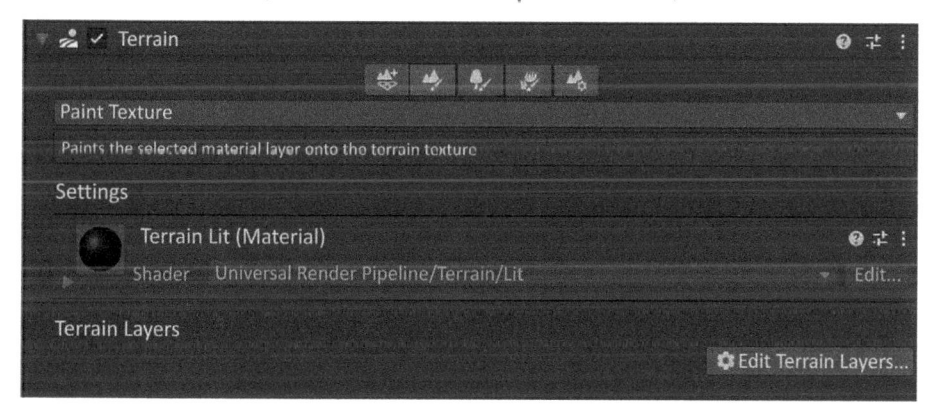

Figure 5.13: Editing terrain layers for painting

On the bottom right of the terrain layers, seen in *Figure 5.13*, there is a button labeled **Edit Terrain Layers**. If you select this, you can either create or add a layer. If you haven't made a layer previously, you can click on the **Add Layer** option, but there will not be any options to fill that. Instead, let's click on **Create Layer**. This will bring up a dialog box to select a texture. A tip here would be to name your texture something that you can search for easily, just in case you have a large number of textures to sift through. An example of this could be to name your terrain textures with a prefix of TT , such as TT_Grass for grass. Then, when the dialog box is up, you can type TT in the search bar and it will only show the terrain textures. This trick can be used all over the project as there are search bars in most available options to select an asset to fill a role.

When you choose your texture, it will create a **Terrain Layer** asset that contains the texture you chose and some material options.

Figure 5.14 shows an example of a **Terrain Layer**.

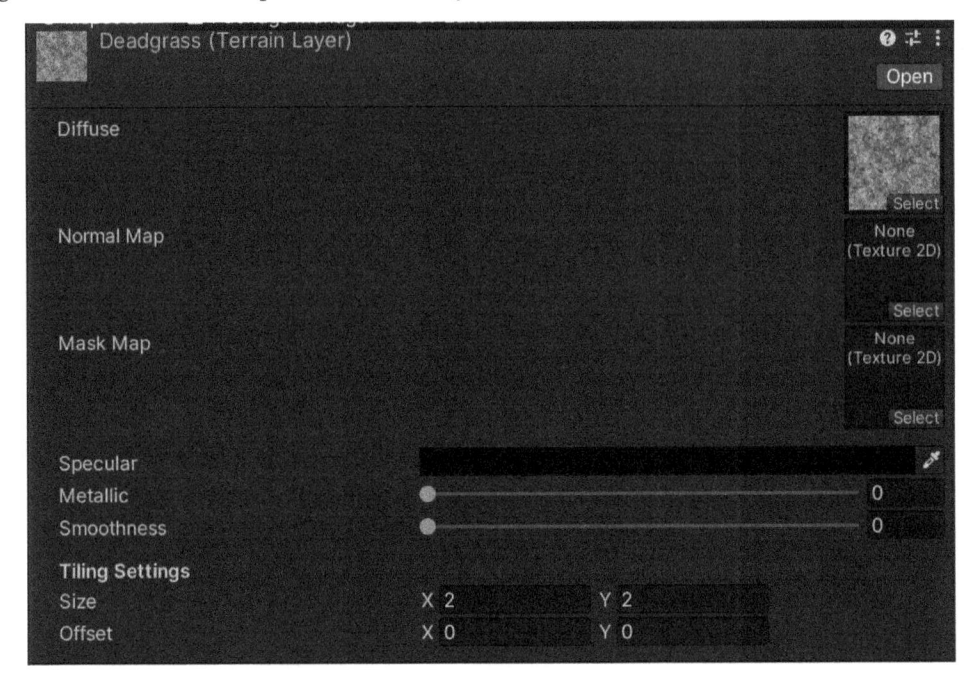

Figure 5.14: Terrain Layer example

The primary property you will want to see here is the **Tiling Settings**. Depending on the scale of the game, you may need to increase or decrease the scaling to avoid seeing the tiles of the texture. If you look below at *Figure 5.15*, you can see where the texture tiles over and over. This looks bad from the camera's current location, but in-game, it will be much closer, which allows us to prevent tiling from being as visible. The most interesting part of this is that it's not connected to the terrain, so if you make a change to the layer asset, it will update the terrain right away. This makes it nice in terms of working quickly and getting an idea of what you want the terrain to look like while you can add normal maps and the metallic or smoothness elements later on.

The second thing that will happen is that the entire terrain will be painted with this texture. When you add another layer, you will then be able to utilize the same brush shapes and sizes to paint other layers onto the terrain.

Technically Interesting!

The way that terrain layers work is that Unity creates a texture map for each texture painted on the terrain. If you have four layers, each layer corresponds to the four channels in a texture: **Red (R)**, **Green (G)**, **Blue (B)**, and **Alpha (A)**. If you have five, the terrain gains a new texture, and it adds it to another R channel of another texture. Since this is the case, limit each tile to four textures for reasons of performance!

After you get the hang of working through the layers, it's good to test small sections with your character to ensure that the scaling on the layer makes sense for the game scale itself, while keeping in mind that there will be other noisy factors to break up the texture tiling, such as grass, rocks, trees, or anything else that will be placed in your environment.

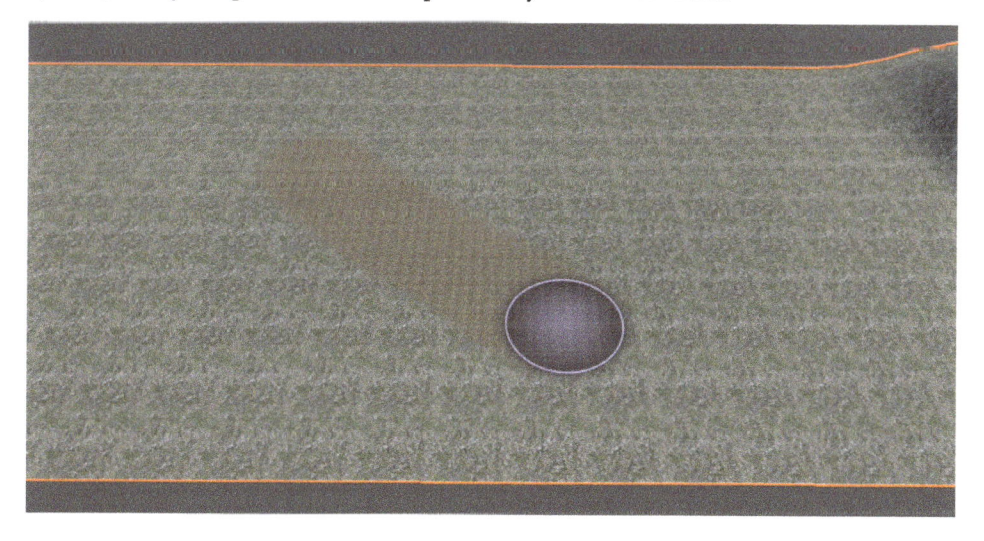

Figure 5.15: Testing brush strength when painting

If the character looks good at this point regarding the textures in respect to scale, let's move on to the next option.

Setting the height

When working with the lower height tool, you may have noticed that it doesn't go below the zero point. If you know you will be working below zero, which is very common, then the workflow to start is: before making any changes, set the height of the terrain to what might seem appropriate for the height you would need to go below zero in units.

Do you need to go 200 units down? If so, set the terrain GameObject to *-200* in the position *y*, *Figure 5.16* highlighted as step *1* in red. Then select the **Paint Terrain** option while also selecting the **Set Height** dropdown as shown in *Figure 5.16* marked as *2* in red. After that, the value will be -200, so set it to 0, then flatten it with the **Flatten** button in *Figure 5.16* marked as red *3*.

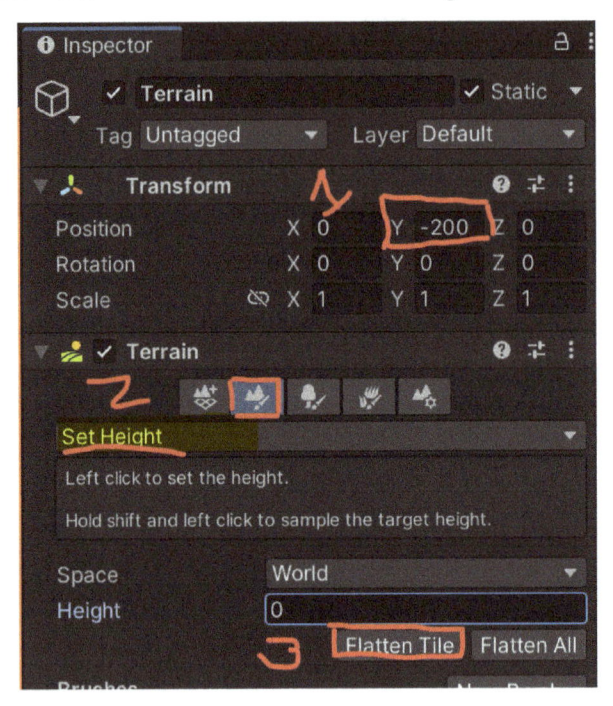

Figure 5.16: Setting Height to allow for lower than world 0

This will set the terrain visually back to *0, 0, 0* as its location and keep the offset in place so that you can lower the terrain below that mark. This is very effective for making swamps, caverns, and rivers.

Smoothing the height

Smoothing is a straightforward tool. Sometimes, you may need to just smooth out the terrain slightly as the noise placed on it could have gotten out of hand, or you needed to smooth a path for the player character to walk on to help guide the character's movement.

As a simple example, look at *Figure 5.17* below.

Figure 5.17: Smoothed terrain

This is a somewhat extreme version of smoothing, but both looked the same prior to smoothing. You can also apply smoothing with a noisy brush to smooth in a non-uniform way to give a look of erosion to the terrain.

Stamping the terrain

The **stamp** tool is used as a 3D stamp! If you need a specific terrain feature, you author a height map to stamp the terrain with. You add the heightmap to the brushes and then you use it on the terrain.

One of the main use cases for this tool is that you can get pre-authored heightmaps that have already been proven to look good on terrain. If you want to find nice mountains and hills, you can search for them in the asset store and there will be examples for you to start with. This will speed up the process drastically. It may not be what you need exactly, but every step is progress.

Painting trees

When you select the **Paint Trees** tool, it will have the options as seen in *Figure 5.18*.

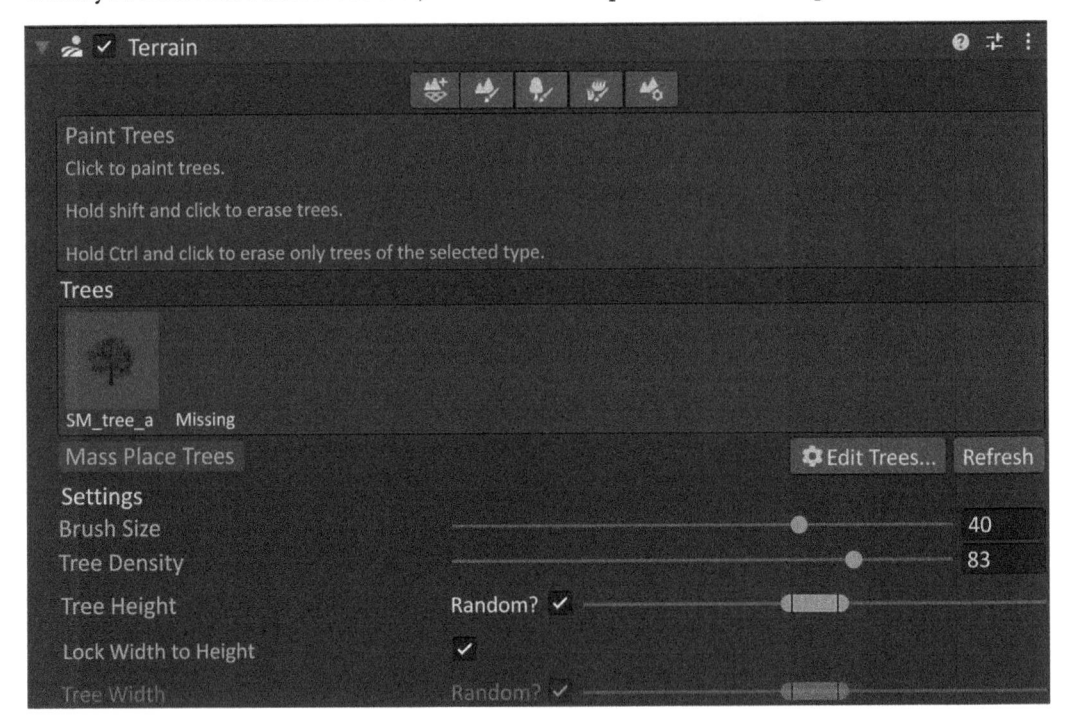

Figure 5.18: Paint Trees terrain mode

To get started, click the **Edit Trees** button, and add trees. You'll be able to add whatever mesh you like even if it isn't a tree! There is a warning, seen in *Figure 5.19*, that pops up if your mesh isn't built correctly for the tree placement on the terrain. It looks like this:

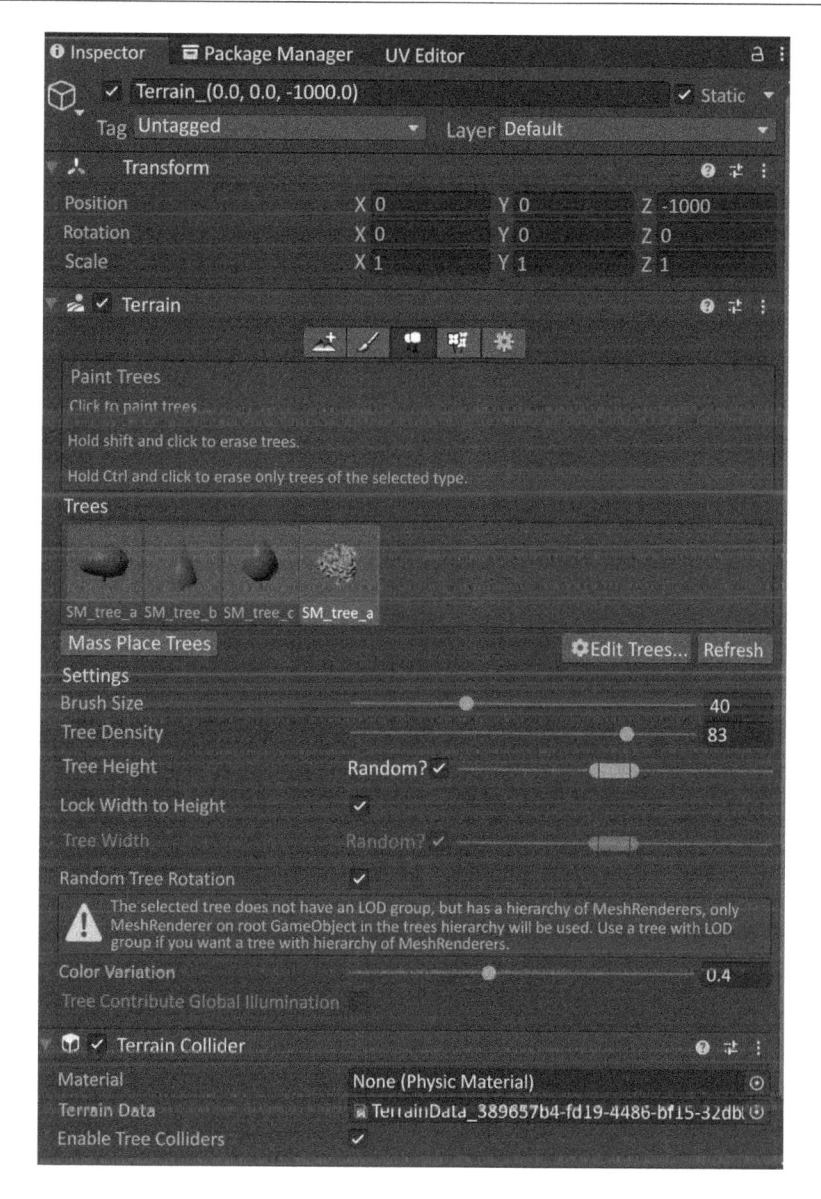

Figure 5.19: Defined Tree and LOD group warning

Luckily, there is a free asset on the asset store by *SpeedTree* that you can download to get a great example of how to properly put together a tree for the **Paint Tree** tool.

Painting details

Lastly, we have painting details. Here, you can either add a detail texture, which will get rendered on a quad, or you can use a detail mesh to create your own mesh. Here is an example of a simple grass texture being used and painted on a flat terrain:

Figure 5.20: Grass as a detail

Painting details such as grass helps to break up the ground texture, shown above in *Figure 5.20*. These items can also be affected by **wind zones**, which are another component that could be added to the terrain object. If you wish to push this further, please investigate *Chapter 10*, *Sound Effects*, where we will add ambient sounds and other small polishing details, and *Chapter 12*, *Finishing Touches*, to breathe life into the terrain.

3D geometry

Now that you've set up your terrain, you will need to augment the terrain for architecture or building out a cave system. You will need to utilize a **3D Digital Content Creation (3D DCC)** tool to build out the meshes for your environment. There is another option to build out the blockout phase, which is Unity's ProBuilder. In our case, we will be using both ProBuilder as well as creating our own geometry for custom shape definition to denote specific architectural portions of the environment.

Let's dig into what ProBuilder and custom meshes mean for your environment blockout.

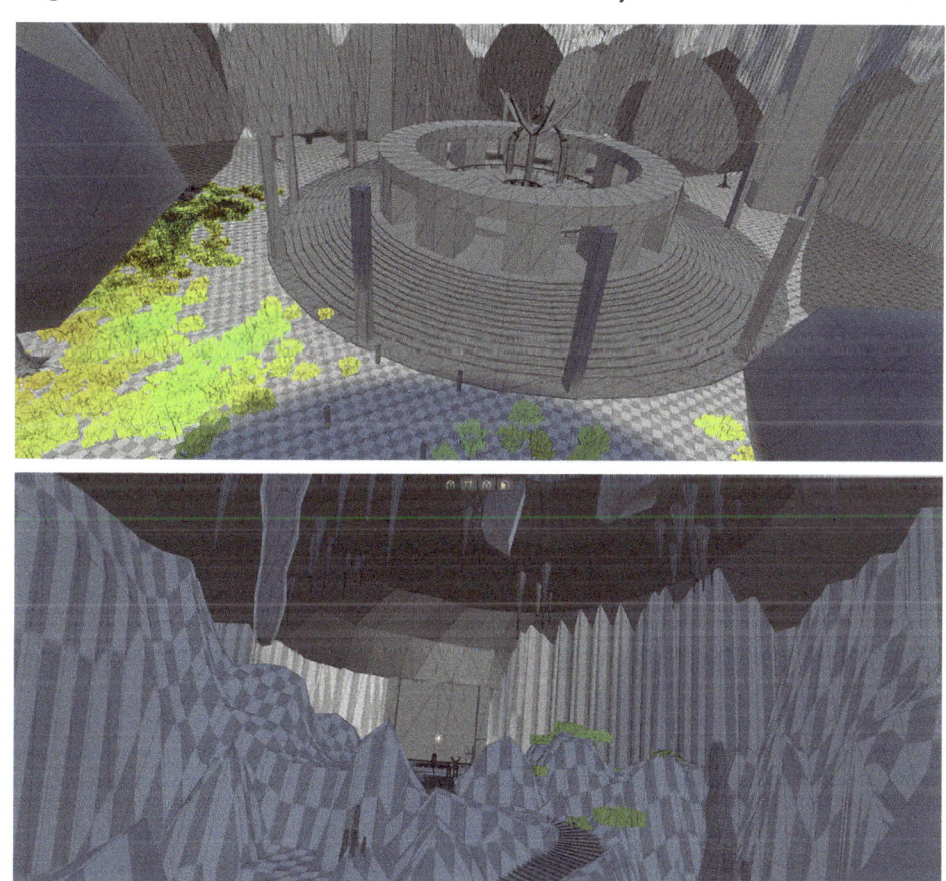

Figure 5.21: Examples of Unity's ProBuilder and custom meshes from our 3D DCC

ProBuilder

From the Unity documentation, ProBuilder is defined as follows:

> *You can build, edit, and texture custom geometry in Unity with the actions and tools available in the ProBuilder package. You can also use ProBuilder to help with in-scene level design, prototyping, collision meshes, and play-testing.*

ProBuilder can quickly set up your scene with collidable surfaces to quickly visualize your environment with ease. To get started with the tool, we will go over some starting steps where you can create your own scene for ease of familiarity. We will go over the installation, creation of the ProBuilder shapes, editing, and then some commonly used tools in ProBuilder.

Installing ProBuilder

To install ProBuilder, open the package manager and go to the **Unity Registry**, shown in *Figure 5.22*. Select **ProBuilder**, and then download and install it.

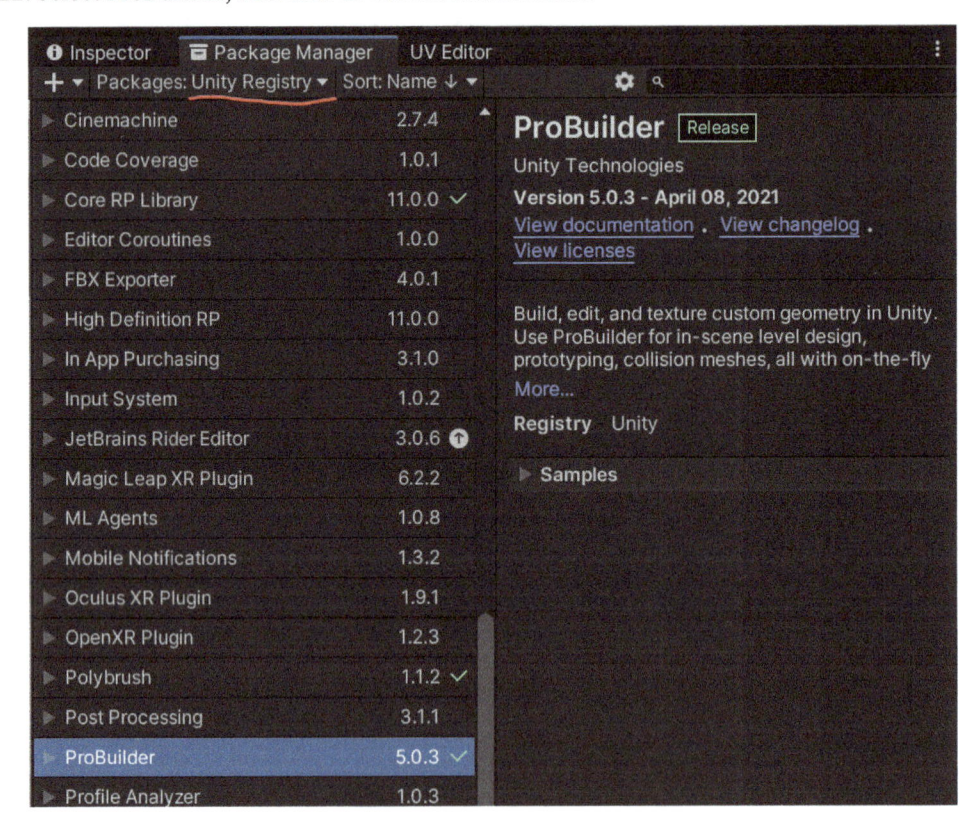

Figure 5.22: Unity Registry Package Manager

Chapter 5												107

After you install it, you will need to access the **Tools** menu to open the **ProBuilder Window**, as seen in *Figure 5.23* below.

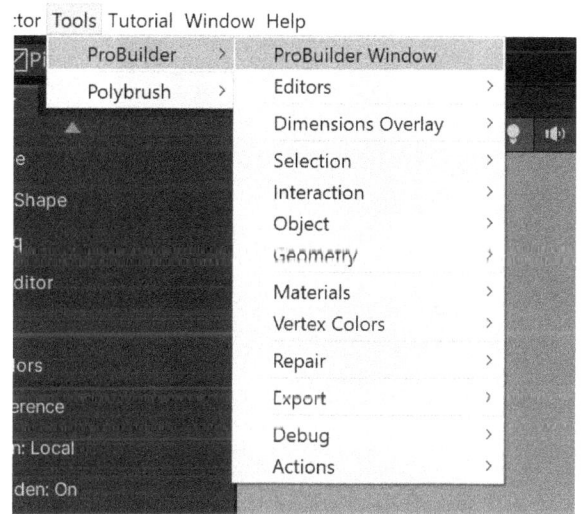

Figure 5.23: Probuilder Window path

This will open a floating window with a lot of options. To get started, let's dock the window to the left of the scene window. This is a personal preference, but we like to be able to work with ProBuilder and still be able to select the items in the hierarchy with ease. Now that we're set up, let's go over the colors in the menu.

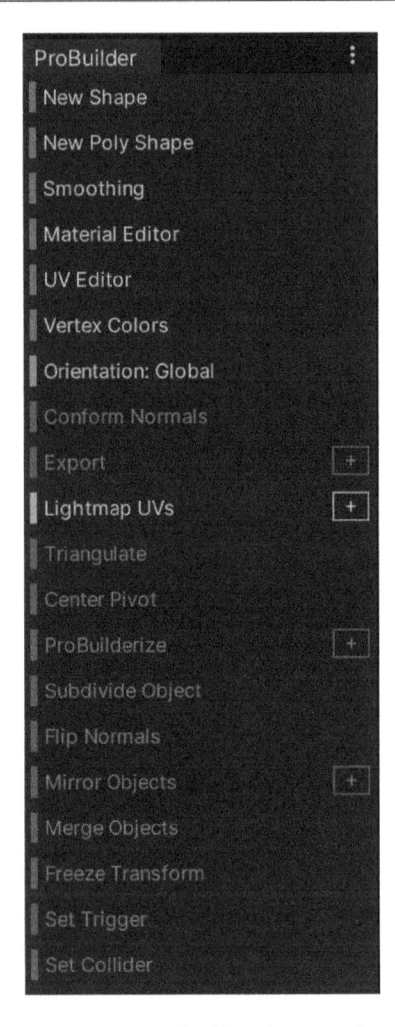

Figure 5.24: Probuilder Object mode

In *Figure 5.24* above, we are currently looking at the **Object** mode of ProBuilder and there are only three colors available in this menu, but there is a fourth color, which we will go over in the *Common ProBuilder Tools* section. The three colors we currently see are used in specific ways to help work through all the options easily. They work like this:

- **Orange**: Object and windowed tools
- **Blue**: Selection-based functions

Chapter 5   109

- **Green**: Mesh editing tools that affect the entire shape that's selected

Now that we have an idea of what these are for, let's get to building our first shape.

Creation of ProBuilder shapes

Open a new scene and let's create a new shape from the ProBuilder menu. This will reveal a small window in the bottom right of the **Scene** viewport, seen in *Figure 5.23*. You will have several options in terms of the type of shape you want to create. We're going to select the **Plane** option so that we can have something for our shapes to attach to. You can find this located in *Figure 5.25* below.

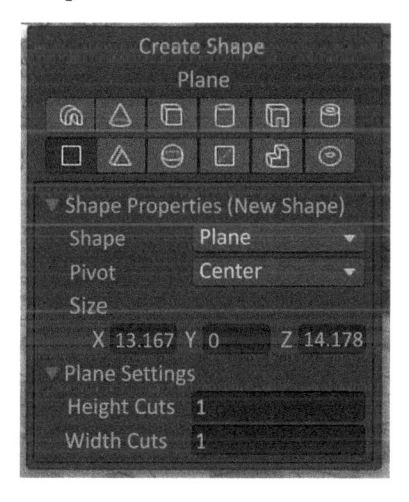

Figure 5.25: Create Shape submenu

After you select the plane, left-click and drag in the scene to create a plane. Don't worry about the size of it for the time being; just create the plane and we will make edits next.

Now, in the hierarchy, if the plane isn't selected, go ahead and select it. In the Inspector, let's set the transform to *0, 0, 0* so it is centered in our scene at *0*. Then, go down to the ProBuilder script and change the size to *80, 0, 80*. This will give us a sufficient size to play with whatever shape we want to in the scene. The Inspector should look similar to *Figure 5.26* when you've finished these steps.

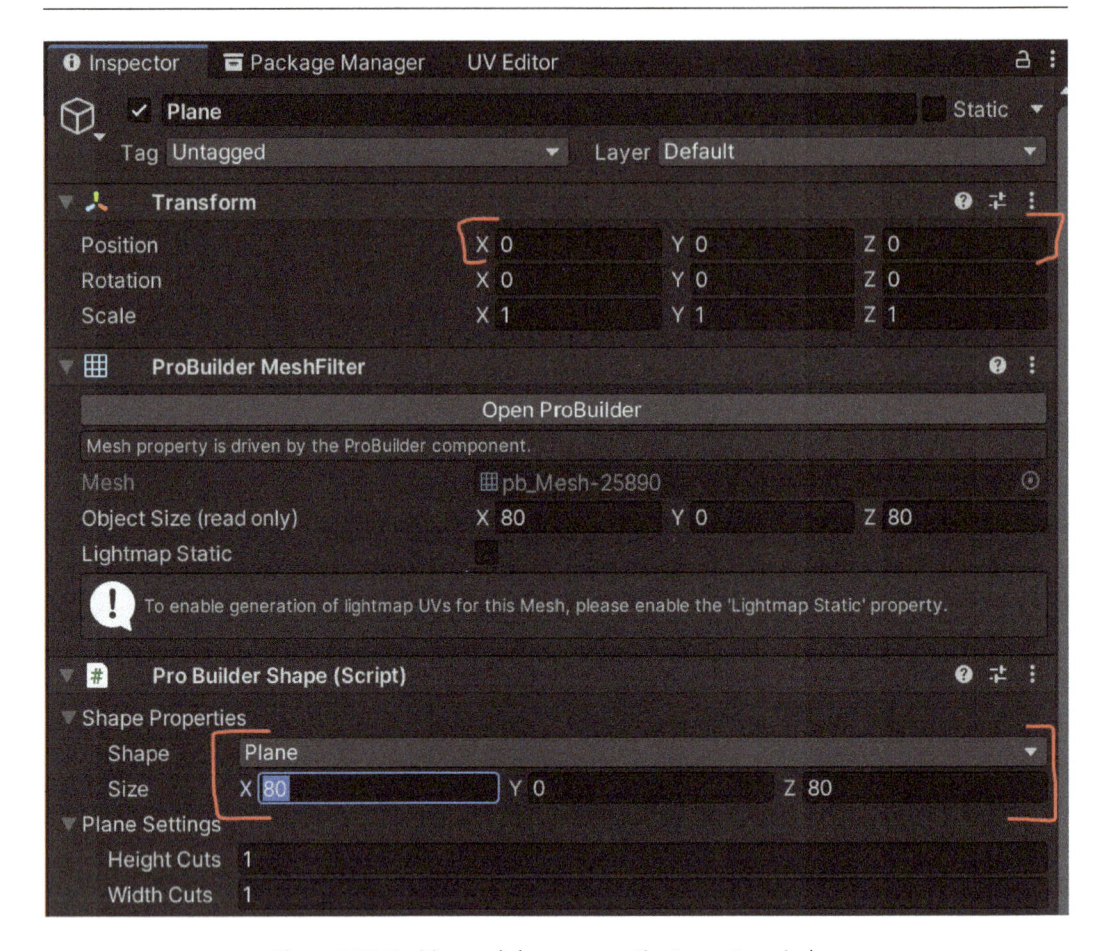

Figure 5.26: Position and shape properties Inspector window

After the plane is created, let's make a cube. Create a new shape and choose a cube shape in the interactive tool in the scene. Left-click and drag to make the base whatever shape you wish. Release the left-click and then you will be able to drag up to give the cube its height. Finish making the cube by clicking again at the height you'd like it to be for now. Once you have that, let's add one more shape, stairs, to the cube. The goal is to make a set of stairs that would allow a character to be able to climb up to the top of your cube. If your stairs turn out strange, don't worry; just delete them and try again until you get it close enough. Don't worry about getting it perfect; we will go into the editing of shapes next.

Chapter 5   111

Editing the shapes

It's possible that when you made your stairs, they turned out something like *Figure 5.27* below.

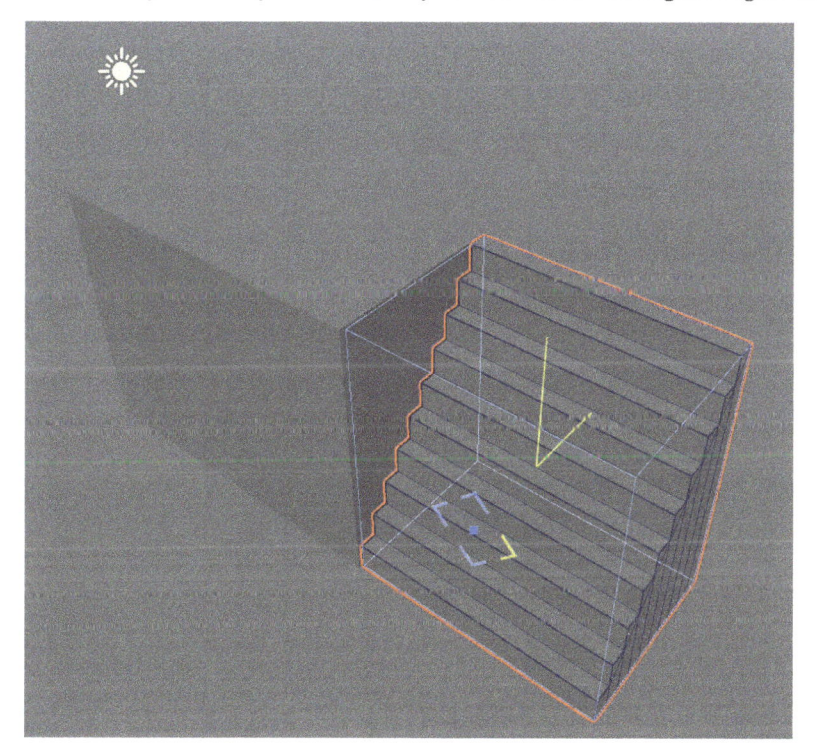

Figure 5.27: Stair placement problem

Not that you wanted that, but it just turned out this way. Luckily, the editing portion of Pro-Builder is very strong. If you hover your mouse over the face of the stairs, there should be a blue arrow facing up, down, left, and right respective to the center square of that face, as shown in the preceding figure.

If you do not have this when you hover over, this means that you may have deselected the stairs and ProBuilder thinks you don't need to edit the base shape anymore. This can easily be fixed by selecting another item in the scene and then reselecting the stairs. Then, in the Inspector and the ProBuilder script, there is an **Edit Shape** button. Selecting this will give you access to the basic editing features again.

Clicking and dragging the middle square will allow you to move that face of the shape. Clicking the arrow will reorient the entire shape. This is very useful for our stairs. The yellow arrow highlighted in *Figure 5.27* will orient the shape to the back of the stairs, which will make the topmost stair be against the cube. This is what we wanted, so we selected it and then used the middle squares to redefine the shape to how we thought the stairs would look the best in this example.

Even though these tools are quite powerful for blocking out, we can go a bit further and talk about the component manipulation tools.

Common ProBuilder tools

We've created some shapes and edited their overall state and shape to get the basic building blocks of a structure. To get some more medium shapes, we need to work on the components of these shapes. Looking back to *Chapter 1, A Primer to the Third Dimension*, the component structure of 3D objects are the vertex, edge, and face. These are denoted by a small icon shape at the top of the scene viewport when ProBuilder is installed, seen in *Figure 5.28*.

Figure 5.28: Component Selection tool

From the left to the right, we have **Object**, **Vertices**, **Edges**, and then finally, the **Faces** selection. If you select one of them, you will then be able to select those component types of the ProBuilder shape that you have selected in the hierarchy. This will also change the available options in the ProBuilder toolset. Compare this to *Figure 5.29*, with the options from *Figure 5.24*, and you will see we added red to our available options and the other colors have had changes in their options as well.

Chapter 5   113

Figure 5.29: Component Menu options

The red options that are available are per component. In this case, we've selected the vertices manipulator; the options for component tools relate to the vertices. The same would be true regarding the selection of edges or faces. Take some time and cycle through them to see the available options for each component. When you get to faces, let's stop for a moment as there is one tool that is used very often – the **Extrude** tool.

Extruding a face will duplicate the vertices and keep the faces connected to extrude your geometry out from the selected faces. This is an incredibly powerful and fast tool to build many shapes or add detail. We will perform two versions of this to give an idea of how this works. These are **extrusions** and **insets**.

To make an **extrusion**, select the **face** component option at the top of the scene window, and then select a face of the box we have next to the stairs. Press the *W* key to get to the transform tool. While holding the *Shift* key, left-click and drag the arrow facing up. You should get an extrusion going up! It should look like *Figure 5.30* below.

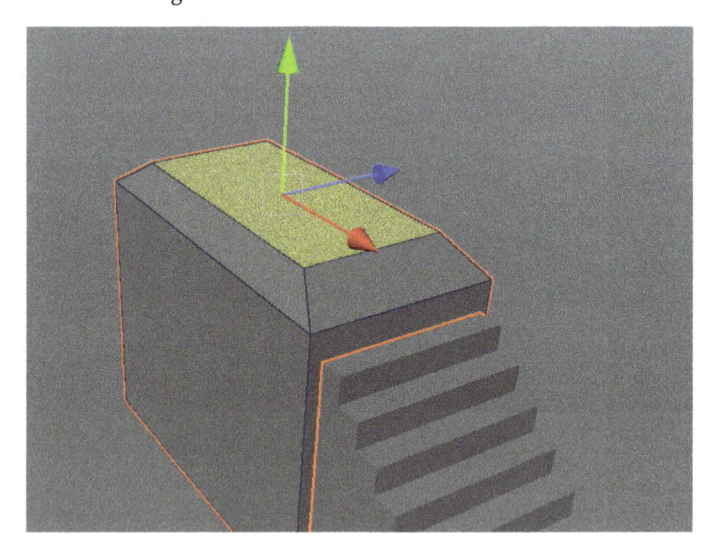

Figure 5.30: Extrude tool

The extrusion is the top box that was pulled out from the selected face. You can now manipulate the face to make it into any shape you would like. We aren't big fans of all 90-degree angles, so we pressed *R* and scaled it in from the middle to give it a little bit of personality.

Now, **insets** are interesting as they are a specific set of extrusion to bring the face back into the current shape. This is great for adding quick details. How we are going to perform this is by selecting the face that is on the side of the box facing the camera, hitting the letter *R* for the scale tool, and, while holding down the *Shift* key, left-clicking the gray box in the center to scale from all sides. After doing that, we will hit the *W* key to get back to the transform tool, and, while holding the shift key down again, pull the blue arrow to bring in the inset. *Figure 5.31* below includes both steps for creating the inset on the same face as suggested.

Chapter 5 115

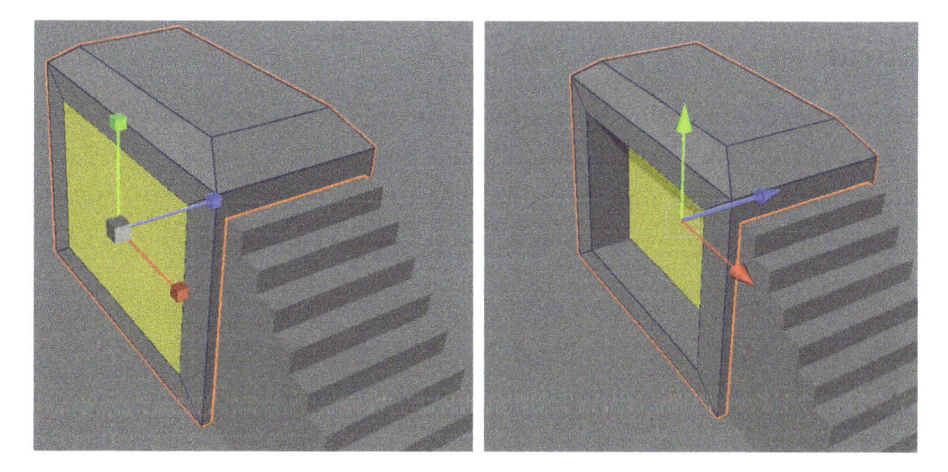

Figure 5.31: Inset example

Play around with the tools for each of the components. You will find that they are there to help speed up the workflow so you can get to blocking out as much as possible, as quickly as possible. There may be a time when you know a specific shape is needed, but you cannot achieve it with ProBuilder tools. In this case, you may need to get into an external tool such as Autodesk Maya or Blender to achieve the look that is needed. We tend to call these objects **premade shapes**.

Premade basic shapes

If you have a good idea of the shaping that you need for your environment, you may already have set up environment pieces that link together at the right scale. ProBuilder is very good with basic shapes, but you may need some architecture that is specific to your game. If you have the availability, it may be easier to just create that and use the mesh instead of using ProBuilder.

In some cases, you may have shapes already created previously that would work just as well as ProBuilder, and all you would need to do is import them into Unity and place them where you'd like. This could prove useful for speeding up the block-out phase.

In our scenes, you will see that we use all three (Terrain, ProBuilder, and premade shapes) to put together a cohesive integrated scene. This is primarily due to the speed at which our artist could create certain models in a DCC versus ProBuilder. Sometimes, however, a basic block that's been extruded is all we need to make the scene make sense for blocking in.

Iteration

The process of **iteration** is looping through portions of the work to get to a refined enough state to move on to other parts of the game. We will follow *Figure 5.32* below as a simple track. This is a high level of the process and after you go through it a few times, you will create more steps for yourself and your team to follow. For now, let's work through the highlights.

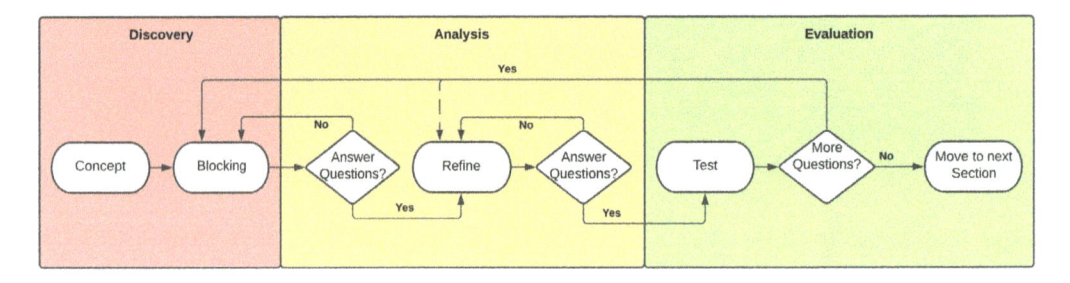

Figure 5.32: Iteration process

We've already gone through several blocks in the process above, such as conceiving and blocking. We just need to go through refining and testing. Refining is the action you take to get as close to answering an action as you can on a granular level. An example of this in relation to our project is asking how close to Myvari's culture each puzzle is. We needed to refine this from blocks to architecture and ensure the puzzle itself makes sense to the style in mechanics, which we will go over in *Chapter 6, Interactions and Mechanics*. If the granular level answer makes sense, extend your scope to testing. In testing, you will take a broad stroke of the game. If you can, test the feel of the game by walking around and see whether there are any other questions on a high level that may have emerged through the refinement process.

This is where time can easily go out the window. You will need to have a firm grasp of what "good enough" means for your game. One of the hardest parts of game development is where you must realize that shipping the game is more important than making everything perfect. Be vigilant in your cause to release and get it looking and feeling good enough, and then move on. You have a lot more to get through!

We've only talked about the block-out phase in this environment chapter. This is because of how important it is to block it out and take some time to feel it through play. Fail fast and make changes according to your feedback from either you playing the game yourself or one of your friends playing it. After you get to the point where you think each section is good enough, then you can start importing final meshes that are in the shape or in the place that you've decided was the correct space. Once this is complete, make another run with the game as you may see changes from the final meshes coming in that weren't apparent previously with the block-out meshes.

Moving around the level and throughout multiple parts of the scene, look carefully at cohesion. Once moving around the level feels good, then you need to push more into the mechanics of the game itself and get into more development, beyond just the art. There will be more questions that pop up in the future. Taking these iterations seriously first will lay a strong foundation to work through when you get into the next portions of your game.

Summary

We've gone through a large number of Unity tools in this chapter. Take your time to work through the Terrain tools and the ProBuilder tools to get a good understanding of how they work.

From this chapter, you gained knowledge of multiple tools to build out an environment. We took time to explain how to iterate through this whole process to gain a strong sense of structure in your environment. You learned how to start with design thinking to build out a concept. Then, you took the concept and started staging each section of the concept, before finally putting the environment together and iterating on it to get a clear view holistically.

Next up, we will go over the mechanics of your game to fit it within your environment. Keep this chapter in mind when placing the interactions for the mechanics as there will be more iteration throughout the development process.

6

Interactions and Mechanics

Now that we have a character with basic locomotion and an environment to work with, let's take a look at how this character should interact with this environment. Unity allows us to use C# to build logic around GameObjects that the player can interact with. This is the basis of game design and helps tell the story or experience through actual interaction.

You'll learn more about the specific interactions and mechanics that can be implemented with Unity in this chapter. We will cover:

- Game loops
- Mechanics toolbox
- Interactions within our project
- Stairs
- Rings puzzles
- Tight spaces
- Interactive volumes
- Design and implementation

Game loops

Video games have a unique concept called a **game loop**. As you might be able to guess, it's a loop of mechanics that are performed throughout the experience. The game loop itself could be very short, such as Call of Duty's multiplayer team deathmatch. The loop looks something like this, where the goal is to kill more enemies than the number of times you die:

1. Kill enemies

2. Die and respawn

There's more to it than that, and if you are a professional Call of Duty player, you may think this is an over-generalization of the gameplay. Ultimately, however, it really is the case 90% of the time. Now let's look at Minecraft's game loop:

1. Gather resources in the day
2. Build in the day
3. Survive at night

We are going to simplify this: there are specific circumstances that fall outside this loop, such as creepers in the day and rainfall, which reduces light levels such that it essentially becomes night. Let's assume those two factors aren't part of this study. This is interesting, as this loop is particularly complex. By this, I mean that surviving doesn't always happen in this loop. The majority of the game is 1, then 2. Only at night does 3, **Survive at night**, become a large portion of the gameplay, visually represented in *Figure 6.1*. The core game loop needs to be as concise as it can possibly be.

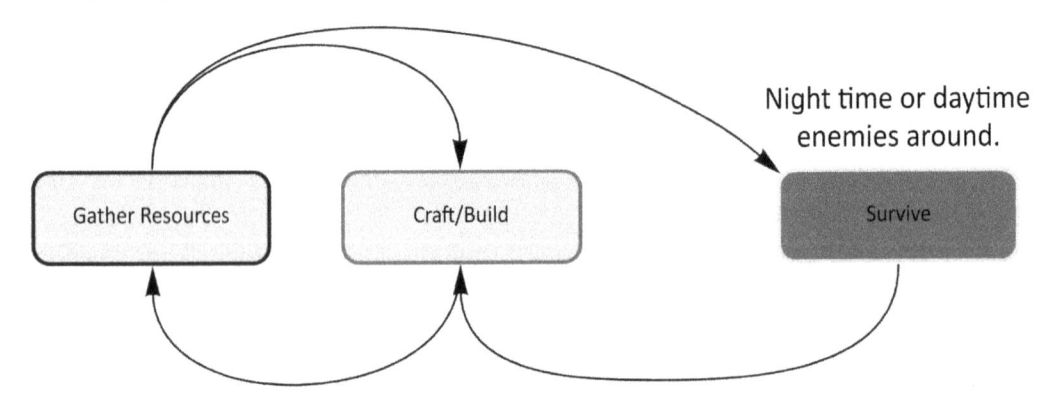

Figure 6.1: Minecraft game loop

Take a look at your favorite games and break down their main game loops. You may find that there are layers of game loops. Sometimes this is called **meta-progression**. In the game Hades, the game loops are as follows:

1. (Optional) Talk to NPCs
2. (In lobby) Choose skills to upgrade
3. (In lobby) Choose weapon for the next run
4. (In game) Fight

5. (In game) Earn currency for in-lobby upgrades
6. (In game) Upgrades to strengthen this playthrough
7. Die and respawn in lobby

The meta-progression takes place at step 2. Base health and damage upgrades make it slightly easier to progress further. This is a common factor in rogue-like genres where the game's experiences are focused on skill mastery and game progression through death.

You'll notice that in the Call of Duty loop we didn't mention meta-progression, even though there is heavy meta-progression in that game. This is because meta-progression is essentially **cosmetic**. You do not have to change anything between matches in Call of Duty. Any equipment that is gained in Call of Duty will be the same as another player's equipment with the same mods. If you put a player that has played 1000 hours against a player with the same exact loadout, it would only come down to skill. In Hades, however, you have to spend points on upgrades to actually complete the game.

These loops are interesting, but we should take some time to go deeper into the interactions that make up these loops. In the next section, we will cover a broad set of game mechanics individually.

Mechanics toolbox

An interaction is an action taken using a mechanic. For example, the mechanic of Use Item could be used to pull a lever, push a button, or use a phone. Those three examples are interactions; the mechanic allows the player to interact with the items through a button press. If we only had the ability to interact with something in this way, we would have very few genres to play with. Luckily for us, there is a broad world of mechanics available for us to use to make interactions. Using interactions, we can design amazing experiences!

To begin this chapter, we thought it would be a good idea to provide a list of mechanics and some interactions that come from those mechanics. We will not be able to go through every mechanic, but we will be going over some primary concepts to get a good feel for the mechanics landscape.

What we will be providing here is an understanding of mechanics and how they can be viewed. If this interests you, take some time to read through several different authors on the subject, as their views on the mechanics may differ from our explanations. Our way of seeing mechanics is that they are layers of experiential movement. There are core concepts that can be layered on top of each other to form an interaction. These include:

- Resource management

- Risk versus reward
- Spatial awareness
- Collection
- Research
- Limitations

Read on to get an understanding of these modular core concepts of game design.

Resource management

You may know of this as a primary mechanic of **real-time strategy** games, or **RTSs**. Starcraft, Age of Empires, and Total Annihilation are examples of popular resource management-focused games. The concept here is that there are finite resources that you need to gather and spend on something that can help you win. This could be soldiers for an army or experiments to make your soldiers stronger. A non-combat-related scenario is a city builder. You need to monitor the people of your city and build things to make them happy, and you manage the money coming in from them.

Risk versus reward

This mechanic is used in many combat-oriented games. It's usually given in the form of cooldowns. Do you want to use your ultimate right now, to take an example from the popular title League of Legends? It could take out an enemy and give you a major advantage. However, it could also potentially put you at a disadvantage if you miss, because the enemy will know you have one less power to use. This is the risk vs. reward concept. The simplest form of this is in Super Mario Bros. Should you try for those coins that are hard to reach? You want those points for an extra life, but at the same time, there is a pit that you might fall into if you don't jump just right.

Spatial awareness

It is common to find this in first-person shooters. Call of Duty and Overwatch utilize this in several ways. First, you have spatial awareness of the enemy on the screen. You need to be able to place your cursor where they are on the screen to shoot at them. Secondly, there is spatial awareness of the entire map. If you are not spatially aware of the map, you can easily get caught unawares. This is the core of platforming games as well. Understanding your position in space in 2D and being able to maneuver deftly is the name of the game in any action platformer. Celeste takes full advantage of this by giving the player tight control schemes that move as you expect every time. The movement is so well put together that when you make a mistake, you feel as though it's your fault.

This is interesting: if you have loose controls in a game that needs tight controls, the player can feel cheated by the game and may stop playing. This is undesirable!

Collection

Any CCG gamers out there? It's in the name! Collectable Card Game. Magic: The Gathering, Hearthstone, Yu-Gi-Oh!, and Pokémon are just a few examples. Although this mechanic is not flashy, the concept of collection is used in all sorts of games.

Skills can be collected, as well as weapons, codex entries, armor, and the list can go on forever. Humans enjoy collecting stuff. It could be that you want every card in the season to unlock an achievement. This is double collecting, as you want the cards, but you also want to collect those achievements. It could be that you want to collect all the codices in a game, such as in Mass Effect, where the lore of the game comes from interacting with as many unique things as possible and your journal updates a codex, which holds information on unique items, characters, races, history, etc.

Research

Research is the ability to engage in investigation to establish facts and rules to your surroundings. We can use the concept of research in a few unique ways. One thought is that the player should be the one doing the research, rather than the character. Meaning the player sees the environment for the character. Because of this, the player can learn about subjects and things that may be outside of the character's knowledge. We as designers can utilize this knowledge and relay information easier to the player by outlining interactable objects or by making climbable ledges a specific color.

On the other hand, the concept of research could refer to the character themselves. The character in-game researches and concludes something new to them in their world and becomes stronger while expanding their awareness both physically and mentally. This may seem similar to collection and resource management; however, if it involves knowledge transfer from the character to the player or things being inherently learned from play, it should be considered research.

Limitations

Pressure makes diamonds. Rather than being a mechanic in and of itself, limitations can be seen as modifiers of other/all mechanics, but we like to break it out as its own mechanic, as not every interaction requires there to be heavy limitations. There can be overarching limitations that affect the overall gameplay. For example, adding a timer to the game as a whole is a limitation. Another is giving the player only 3 lives before ending the play session. In a CCG, you may see there is a hard cap to the decks. This limits the number of turns that can be taken.

When you take the time to figure out how these mechanics fit together to build interactions and make and experience, you've designed a complete mechanic. How all these pieces fit together is the crux of mechanics and interaction design. Let's take some time to go over some of the nuances involved.

Design and implementation

In good design fashion, we need to break down the reasons for the mechanics and interactions that we are going to use. In general, you want to minimize the number of mechanics in a game while spreading their use to many unique interactions. Mega Man is a great example of minimal mechanics with elegant use for slight variations. Locomotion, jumping, and shooting are the only things you have to worry about. After defeating the enemies, you gain different shooting abilities or skills, but you will still use the same button to engage the shooting mechanic. This mechanic is kept to a single button press all the way up until Mega Man 4; when the character is able to charge up his weapon and the button designation changes to adapt to the skill change.

This is an interesting thought: the gameplay involves a very limited number of changes to the mechanics, instead just changing graphics and narrative. When you begin designing this portion of your game, think about the smallest action your player should take to progress and break it down to its smallest components.

If you're thinking about designing a game that is heavily combat-driven, you need to ask yourself some questions:

- What type of combat style is it?
- Does the combat style match the historical theme of the surrounding environment?
- Does the combat style align with the character or contrast their morals?

How do the answers to all of the above questions align with the emotional experience you are asking the player to feel? These questions aren't exhaustive by any means. Each of the questions should lead to a further clarification of the game mechanics and shape the experience you want for your players.

It is all too easy to look at the game you are making and fall into the trap of comfort, just falling into line with other games from the genre that you're developing for. If you find yourself designing something and thinking to yourself, "This is how it's always been done," you need to evaluate that interaction. **First-person shooters** (**FPSs**) are a great example of this because of the restrictions of the first-person viewpoint.

There is one major unique outlier that did very well in the FPS space: Half Life. Valve created an FPS with physics-based puzzle mechanics and a heavy emphasis on narrative. This was highly unique compared to the run-and-gun hyper-destruction that was the focus of previous FPS games.

Since we are talking about interactions and mechanics through the design lens, we need to talk about the game Undertale. Undertale is a game that begins as a low-graphical-fidelity role-playing game. The gameplay narrative feels normal at first; then combat happens! You quickly learn the combative mechanics you need to win and combat gameplay feels great. However, hurting things isn't always what you want to focus on. There is a subversion of the players' expectations, where the game sees you asking the character to hurt people that the character may have an emotional tie to in the game. That emotional difference is being brought into view to show the use of what is standard in a way that turns the players' expectations on their head. This is only available if you, the designer, study and know game design intimately.

This entire chapter could easily be spent talking about the design of other games' mechanics and interactions. Instead of breaking down loads of games, let's work through our own project and investigate some simple examples of mechanics and interactions to use within them.

Throughout the sections, we will also be looking at the implementation of various game designs. Metaphorically speaking, our hope here is that we will break down the puzzle pieces from top to bottom in interaction, to show you that developing a game is all about breaking down each piece while keeping the whole picture in mind.

One piece of advice while reading through these sections is that the implementations of these game interactions are not set in stone, nor are they the only way to use these interactions. They are just examples of our approach. Try to imagine how you might change the design of each piece.

Our project

We are building a 3D puzzle adventure game. Our initial mechanics will be using research as the primary component. Later in the book, in *Chapter 7, Rigid Bodies and Physics Interaction*, regarding our design of telekinesis, we will layer spatial awareness on top of this. With this understanding, we will build out our game loop. To make an experience worth playing, we can define the game loop as follows:

1. Search environment for clues
2. Solve puzzles from clues

With the game loop defined and the understanding that we are focusing on research as a primary mechanic, we now need to build interactions to make an experience.

To get started on our interactions, we are going to work through a couple of simple non-physics-focused actions. The character, Myvari, needs to be able to interact with the environment to complete puzzles and enter areas to get to her destination. Thematically the environments are ruins from her race's past. Through our demonstrative vertical slice, Myvari will encounter multiple environmental puzzles where she will need to take in her surroundings and overcome obstacles. The player of this game, leading Myvari with their controller, is to pay attention to the detail of the environment and learn how to work through the environmental puzzles. The first interaction the character will face is the stairs. Let's dive into the design of that to get a real sense of what the rest of the interactions will need in terms of definition.

The stairs

In this demonstrative level, there exists a set of stairs woven within the environment for the character to traverse. Understanding what these stairs convey to the player helps to establish a foundational sense of early interaction affordance, meaning that your environment will be the primary guiding factor for players navigating the level. Let's work through designing this initial interaction, as it is the first experience the player truly gets to be part of.

Design

When the player enters the game, Myvari will enter from the woods into a cave that seems normal. Moving into the cave brings you into a small hallway that leads to an opening with a steep slope that's too steep to walk up. There are two pools, one on each side of this slope. There are levers on each side. All that needs to happen is that each level needs to be interacted with. *Figure 6.2* shows the blockout of how this will flow.

Figure 6.2: Overview of initial interaction, the stairs

In the first open space encounter, you can get a sense of wonderment. Here is a cave with man-made features. In the distance, there is a semblance of a door and a path leading to it. Making your way toward the door, you will notice the path ahead becoming very steep. Walking around, you research the area and find levers. These levers bring stairs to the path so you can climb to the door surrounded by what looks to be ruins.

Simple environment design needs to be in place here with "light pooling." This is when you add lighting to an area to draw the attention of the player. We tend to go to areas with more light. Therefore we need the players to interact with particular models within the scene. To make it noticable to the player, you add player affordances to these designated models. For example when you get close enough to the levers, they will become highlighted slightly. Suddenly, a tooltip will be displayed to show you which button to press to interact with it.

Interacting with both levers creates a clicking noise. Moving away from your current camera, a small cinematic will play showing the stairs rising and moving into place. From this point, you may move up the stairs onto the Rings area. The Rings will be the initial puzzle with environmental research at play. We have a sense of how this should be played out, but implementation always throws us a few kinks. We need to put things into practice to see if the design works. Let's get into Unity and see how it feels!

Implementation

First things first, we need something that we can interact with. Let's break this down just a little bit. There are 3 points to this implementation. We need an interaction block, a stair blocker, and a manager to work with these two elements.

Interaction block

We know we have two interaction points that both need to be interacted with to satisfy the success of the stairs. This means we should build a trigger that we can use more than once. This cube needs to have a box collider on it, as we will be using collision to help with setting the states.

We're now going to look at some code. As with *Chapter 4, Characters*, we won't be going over each and every line of code – we'll only look closer at code if we haven't gone over it before or if, for some reason, we make a change to previously explained code. We are going over `InteractionTrigger.cs`, which can be found in the *Assets/Scripts* folder of the project's GitHub. If you haven't set up GitHub yet, please refer to the start of this book for instructions on how to do so. When implementing something for the first time, there may be some key areas that you couldn't design for, so it's a good idea to work through some visual debugging code to make it easier for you. We want to implement a simple cube that, when you enter it, you can interact with. unclear wording and noticing when we interact with it. The way we do this is by using some colors.

```
public Color idleColor = new Color(1f, 0f, 0f, 0.5f);
public Color occupiedColor = new Color(1f, 1f, 0f, 0.5f);
public Color interactColor = new Color(0f, 1f, 0f, 0.5f);
```

We define these in the beginning so we can reference them when we define the states a bit later. We are using the input action `interact` from the input system we defined in *Chapter 4, Characters*. In this case, we need to pay attention to that input, so we put it on `Update`.

```
void Update()
    {
```

```
        interactPressed = interactInput.action.ReadValue<float>() > 0f;
    }
```

The input here is either 0 or 1, but we want to use it as a bool. This allows us to make simple `if` checks when we want to change the state. To do this, we ask if the value is above 0. If the assigned interaction button is being pressed, the value is 1, which sets `interactPressed` to `true`; otherwise, it's set to `false`.

In the next sections, we are going to use some MonoBehaviour methods that we haven't gone over yet. These are `OnTriggerEnter`, `OnTriggerStay`, and `OnTriggerLeave`. As the names suggest, these methods are useful for dealing with collision states for when something enters, stays, or leaves a collision box.

We will start with `OnTriggerEnter`. We are only using this to set the color of the box so that we can see that we have entered it. This isn't mechanically useful, but it is visually helpful. Maybe later on during the polishing stage, we may want to spawn some particles or change some lights to show the player that they are in an area that can be interacted with. For now, let's just change the color of the cube's material for the visual debugging.

```
    void OnTriggerEnter(Collider other)
    {
        MyvariThirdPersonMovement player = other.GetComponent<MyvariThirdPersonMovement>();
        if (player != null)
        {
            mat.SetColor("_BaseColor", occupiedColor);
        }
    }
```

What's happening here is that when the player collides with the box's collision box, we are looking to see if the other component that made the collision has `MyvariThirdPersonMovement` script. Since no other item that can collide should have that component, this is a good check. We assign that to the `player` variable and then do a small check asking if the `player` value isn't `null`, then change the color to the occupied color. Now we need to work through `OnTriggerStay`, which will be where we allow the player to interact with this previously collided-with object.

```
    void OnTriggerStay(Collider other)
        {
            MyvariThirdPersonMovement player = other.
```

```
            GetComponent<MyvariThirdPersonMovement>();
        if (player != null)
        {
            if (interactPressed)
            {
                mat.SetColor("_BaseColor", interactColor);
                OnInteract?.Invoke();

                Debug.Log($"Interacted with {gameObject.name}");

                if (disableOnInteract)
                {
                    this.enabled = false;
                    this.GetComponent<BoxCollider>().enabled = false;
                }
            }
        }
    }
```

This should all look similar to the enter trigger until we get to the `if` block that is waiting for the interact button to be pressed. When the interact button is pressed, we do a few things:

1. Set the color to an interact color
2. Invoke an action
3. Log it out for another debug check
4. Disable it so we can't interact with it again

We've already set a color previously, so this should seem familiar. We are using the interact color instead here, which also makes sense!

The next portion is invoking an action. This has a bit of a two-part explanation. Our manager will be listening for the action to be invoked. When we get to our manager, we will go over how this works fully. For now, understand that another item will be waiting for a signal to enact the action fully.

We set debugging to the console so we can see what is happening in the logic. When we remove the debugging color, the console debug will be our guide if there is a bug in the future.

Chapter 6

The last part is to disable it so we can't interact with it again. We need to disable both the object and the collider. We're doing this as this interaction only needs to be pressed once per side.

That's it! We now need to go over the stair blocker before we get into the manager.

Stair blocker

We know that there will be an effect to blocking the stairs beyond, but we have finished up the look of this blocking mechanism. For now, it is a debugging red block with a collider. This isn't a problem, as we know how we want the experience to play out, so we need to make a blocker that just doesn't allow the player through to the stairs yet. We will add the visual portion of that later in *Chapter 12*, *Final Touches*. This could be in the form of the stairs being flat so that the player can't walk up to them, and we make it look slippery, or maybe there can be a rock obstructing the stairs that disappears after the right interaction.

There isn't any scripting to be done here. We will be offloading any logic for this onto the manager. One of the reasons why we need to have this manager is that we cannot have a script on the stairs themselves to turn themselves on or off. If you have a GameObject that is disabled, the scripts won't be able to be activated without some outside object with its reference to the disabled GameObject enabling it. So we need to do this with the manager. Let's do that now.

Interaction manager

Stitching together scripts is much easier if you have a parent object for interactive items in a manager of sorts. In the editor, this is often done by creating a prefab that the parent prefab houses a script to hold the state of the interaction. What we are doing here is making sure that the stairs cannot be turned on without both buttons being pressed. It would be difficult for this to be done without a GameObject knowing the state of each item. Getting into the code, we define our public variables and class variables to set up as we normally do, and then we get into the second part of the events we talked about in the *Interaction block* section. In the Awake and OnDestroy sections, we need to handle the events listening.

```
void Awake()
{
    leftTrigger.OnInteract.AddListener(OnLeftTriggerInteract);
    rightTrigger.OnInteract.AddListener(OnRightTriggerInteract);
}

void OnDestroy()
```

```
    {
        leftTrigger.OnInteract.RemoveListener(OnLeftTriggerInteract);
        rightTrigger.OnInteract.RemoveListener(OnRightTriggerInteract);
    }
```

We defined each of our triggers publically and they both have their own events. On Awake, we listen to the OnInteract event, and if it's invoked, we will then run the function that is the argument of the listener. In this case, it's OnLeftTriggerInteract for the left side. The one for the right side is similarly named. We're only going to look in detail at the left side as the right side is very similar.

```
    void OnLeftTriggerInteract()
    {
        leftTriggerFired = true;
        if (rightTriggerFired)
        {
            stairsRaised = true;
            OnStairsRaised?.Invoke();
            stairsBlocker.SetActive(false);
            Debug.Log("RAISE STAIRS HERE");
        }
    }
```

If the left side gets triggered, we immediately set leftTriggerFired to true. That checks if the right side has been triggered already. If it hasn't been, then nothing happens. If it has, then we will set stairsRaised to true, invoke another action, set the stair blocker GameObject to not active, and log out a string to help with later debugging.

The OnStairsRaised UnityAction will fire, but there isn't anything attached to this yet. After we finish up this area and finalize what exactly we need, we will add more to this action.

Interestingly, this setup allows the player to start from the left or the right without problems. It also sets us up for future development. We don't need to have everything laid out, but we do need to have an understanding of what the general idea is so we can write the architecture accordingly.

This completes the current implementation of the stairs puzzle. Now that Myvari is up the stairs, we need to work through our first main puzzle, the rings.

The rings

Passing through the stairs, we're now faced with a door and rings.

Chapter 6									133

The door signifies the first narrative-driven answer to the puzzle versus lighting drawing them to an area. The puzzle will only be able to be figured out if you pay attention to the image on the door and correlate it to the puzzle rings. Let's break down the design of the Rings puzzle.

Design

The first puzzle the player will need to work through is the rings. When you get onto the platform of the puzzle, your necklace will animate in front of you and both the necklace and the middle pillar will glow a soft blue before fading. On the door, there will be a time-worn inscription of what the pillars should look like if manipulated properly.

What the player needs to do is push the pillars in the rings to match an image of the celestial bodies found on the door. This allows for multiple levels of research and interaction within a small scene. The player already knows that there is interaction within the environment from the hints given previously, and a small outline will indicate the button to press to interact with the pillars. The new information gathering would be the shape of the imagery in the door to fit the shape of the ground. *Figure 6.3* shows a concept of the area. The big blank area at the back is the door. The pillars are within the circles outside the middle pillar. There are three rings in all.

Figure 6.3: The Rings and environmental research puzzle

Working through this puzzle will open the door, but time has not been kind to this door or the area surrounding the ruins in general. When it tries to open, there is debris that collapses within the hallways leading further into the cave. We will take this opportunity to work through another simple interaction, which is navigating tight spaces.

Implementation

We thought a lot about how we would put this one together. Two pillars on either side of each ring. Three rings in total. We needed a certain configuration to end with that would fit our design ideas of a constellation as well. Another problem with this is how to deal with Myvari moving these things. At first, we thought of pushing and pulling, but to make things simpler, we went with pushing only. This allowed us to only worry about rotating in one direction as well as cutting out an animation. Myvari isn't a large character and pulling might not make much sense. We need to come up with two scripts. The first script will look similar to the one for visual volumes we worked with previously. We will use this to tell which side of a pillar Myvari is on. This tells us which way to rotate it. After we have it rotated to the correct position, we need to have a puzzle manager to know where to initially place the pillars, what the victory rotation value looks like, and how to deal with the ending of the puzzle. Let's run through the easy one first and look at the puzzle trigger volumes.

Puzzle triggers

This item is simple. We need a box that we will change colors for debugging, just as previously had for the stairs, and then we need to have a few choices that are properties in the inspector that we get to choose before the game starts. These choices (outer, middle, and inner) will be which ring they are located on and which direction they should move. The direction is counterclockwise or clockwise.

Even though we've seen it before, in this implementation of color changing, we did something a little bit different that involves the puzzle accessing a method of this class.

```
public void SetColor(Color color)
{
    meshRenderer.material.color = color;
}
```

Something to notice here is the public access modifier. It takes in a color. Remember this when we go over the manager of the puzzle script right after this. Next, there are two defined enums. We will put them both below: `FirstPuzzleTriggerType` and `FirstPuzzleTriggerDirection`.

```
public enum FirstPuzzleTriggerType
{
    Outer = 0,
    Middle,
    Inner
}
public enum FirstPuzzleTriggerDirection
{
    Clockwise = 0,
    CounterClockwise
}
```

We've made public enums in the top portion of this class and here we are defining them. These definitions will allow us to choose the ring and direction for each trigger. Look below at *Figure 6.4* to see an example of what the enum looks like in the inspector.

Figure 6.4: Display of a public enum in the inspector

If you were to select either of these, they would display the options that are seen in the code above. One more small detail in the code is the first value in the enum, which we are assigning as 0. This will happen by default; however, making it explicit may be a good habit to get into. When someone looks at this code, they know for sure that the enum value will start at 0.

The Puzzle pieces

Open the `FirstPuzzle.cs` file that is in the `scripts` folder and attached to the `FirstPuzzle` GameObject in the hierarchy. We start as we always do by defining the variables we want to use. For this puzzle manager, it needs to have a reference to each transform of the pillar sections, the center pillar, which takes care of finalizing the puzzle, and the properties of the puzzle's timing. Directly after the public variables that we will assign in the inspector, we have quite a few variables that are not public but are assigned and used within the class' logic. Take a few moments to read over the comments on them. We will be referencing those class variables throughout the rest of this section.

Though we've seen this a few times, this is a larger piece of the definition than we've seen previously. We will pull in the whole initialization and go over each piece.

```
void Start()
    {
        // Cache references to the trigger volumes and the player
        triggers = GetComponentsInChildren<FirstPuzzleTrigger>();
        playerController = FindObjectOfType<CharacterController>();

        // Random starting positions
        outerPillars.eulerAngles = new Vector3(0f, Random.Range(-180f, 180f), 0f);
        middlePillars.eulerAngles = new Vector3(0f, Random.Range(-180f, 180f), 0f);
        innerPillars.eulerAngles = new Vector3(0f, Random.Range(-180f, 180f), 0f);

        // Starting center spire position
        centerSpire.position = new Vector3(centerSpire.position.x, centerSpireStartHeight, centerSpire.position.z);
    }
```

Regarding the MonoBehaviour class we're inheriting from, we are using the Start method to initialize the cache references and starting positions of the pillars when the game starts. First off, we need to cache the references to each trigger volume. We are using a UnityEngine.Component method that we have available due to us having a using UnityEngine; directive at the top of this file. This is GetComponentsInChildren<FirstPuzzleTrigger>();. The type that is used in this is called a generic type. You could place any type in the place of FirstPuzzleTrigger, in the code above. This could be Image or Transform. In this case, we only want to grab each trigger. We will clarify why we need them in this manner shortly. Just know that they are all in a bucket waiting to be called.

Next, we need to use FindObjectOfType, which is another UnityEngine method, but it's on the Object class. It's part of the UnityEngine library and we're already requesting access to its methods. It's going to find the character controller and return it to the playerController variable.

The next three lines are for setting the rotation of the rings. We wanted them to be unique, so if someone played the game more than once, it would be a little bit different each time.

Finally, we have the position of the puzzle being set. We are using this line to set the height of the center spire. After the puzzle is completed, the center spire will raise up to be interacted with. This will move you on to the next section. We wanted this to be animated as you completed the puzzle to reveal the way forward.

We're going to now move on to the Update method. This is again from MonoBehaviour. The interesting thing about this puzzle is that there are a lot of points where we don't do much. We mostly just need to wait until the character moves the pillars into the right positions. The way that we are running the update section is like a lock system in a waterway. You must finish the first step to get to the next step. We have a very simplified logic flow for this system. You can see it in *Figure 6.5*.

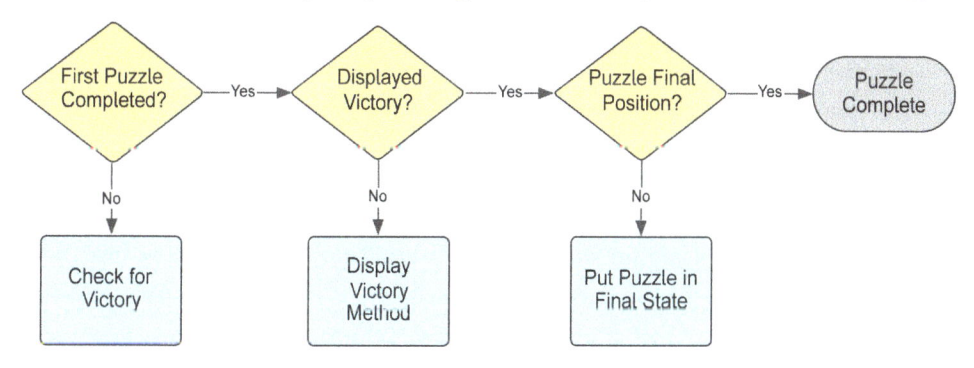

Figure 6.5: Basic lock flow for the puzzle manager

Let's keep *Figure 6.5* in mind while we finish up the puzzle manager. The first step here is to check for victory. Let's dig into that process block. Victory is dependent on all three pillars being closely enough aligned to the desired rotation values.

```
outerAligned = CheckAlignment(outerPillars, correctRotationOuter);
```

We're checking every frame for the right alignment. Because we are checking the alignment for three separate items, we shouldn't write the code on all three rings. Let's write it once and then ask it to refer to a method for each pillar instead. This is called refactoring. Digging in even further, we should break down how it checks for alignment.

```
bool CheckAlignment(Transform pillarGroup, float correctRotation)
{
    return Mathf.Abs(pillarGroup.eulerAngles.y - correctRotation) < correctThreshold;
}
```

First, we need it to return a bool. This is very helpful when you want to run a conditional against the response. We're asking for the current pillar and the correct rotation value. We look at the absolute value of the current rotation in the *y* value minus the correct rotation. We take that value and check if it's less than the threshold we're allowing for "closeness." If it is, then outerAligned will return true. If all three pillars are returning true, then CheckForVictory will return true, which allows us to move on to the next block in our lock.

The next block is displaying victory. This seems like an innocent block that is just a display for debug; however, there is one small bit of logic in here that helps us with the end block.

```
victoryStartTime = Time.time;
outerStartVictory = outerPillars.eulerAngles;
middleStartVictory = middlePillars.eulerAngles;
innerStartVictory = innerPillars.eulerAngles;
```

These four values being set are important. We need to have set the values before we move on to the next block. We could potentially have this done in the final block; however, sometimes it's a good idea to set up each bit of logic in a lock so that you can debug easily and know exactly where you are and what the data is that you need at that exact point in the logic. To finish the last block, we know that we need to record what the pillars' current information is. We have tolerance as to where we need to place the pillars, so this doesn't mean the puzzle's solution is always the same. Now that we've stored values of the pillars and displayed our victory in the console for debug, we can move on to the final block.

The final block is in the PerformVictoryLerp method. Take your time looking over the whole method. We will break down a single Lerp below. Interestingly, this method is mostly just animating some environmental items for a final piece and allowing us to finish the block, so we don't check for rotations in this puzzle anymore.

```
outerPillars.eulerAngles = Vector3.Lerp(outerStartVictory,
outerEndVictory, lerpVal);
```

We've seen something similar in the character with using the Slerp method. That one was better for spherical needs. The Lerp is a linear interpolation. You're transforming a value to another value of the same type over a period. In this case, it's the rotational values of the pillars to the predetermined end victory rotational values we need to get the pillars to, because there is a small amount of leeway we give to each section. It may feel daunting to work through this method. If you are feeling overwhelmed, just look at a single line and slowly work through it. Each line has a task and it's providing context for the Lerp time, or it's lerping itself to another value over that time.

We also have at the end a `PrintDebug` method outside of our lock system. This allows us to check for what's going on in the puzzle at any given moment. Take some time to go over this method and surmise what it might show you, and then run the game to see if your assumptions are correct. Did something print in the console you didn't expect? See if you can find it in the code by following the game's logic and identifying when you saw the console message arrive.

The next questions that might come to mind are, "That's a great way to do it, but how do we *actually* control it? Also, why didn't we cover the `RotatePillar` method?" These are great questions! Let's explore them in the next section.

Puzzle control

Should we have put the control on the puzzle trigger volume? Our thinking is that all control mechanisms should be on the object that's containing the control. We made another script called `FirstPuzzleControl.cs` in the `scripts` folder, which will be attached to the Character GameObjects. This script is responsible for setting up the color of the trigger volume as well as calling the rotate from the `FirstPuzzle` class. We wrote it in this manner as we wanted to ensure the manager of the puzzle would oversee the rotation of each ring. Even if the character is the object initiating the `RotatePillar` method with input, the puzzle manager needs to rotate whichever pillar section the player is interacting with, as it owns those GameObjects. Thinking about it this way is a little unique. Try to imagine a manager owning the GameObjects and telling them what to do. We have them already being referenced in this script; we should keep them in this script. The other option would be to also reference them in the control script that is on the character, and then you have multiple references, and could potentially cause a bug that you may not see. Attempt to centralize your GameObjects in a single script that manages them as much as possible.

The `RotatePillar` method is slightly tricky. In this method, we need to not only rotate the rings, but also need to push the character along with it as well. How are we doing this? Let's look into it.

```
public void RotatePillar(FirstPuzzleTrigger trigger)
{
    // Rotate pillars
    float rot = (trigger.triggerDirection == FirstPuzzleTriggerDirection.
Clockwise ? pushSpeed : -pushSpeed) * Time.deltaTime;
    trigger.transform.parent.parent.Rotate(Vector3.up, rot);

    // Keep player locked in trigger volume, facing the pillar. We need to
disable the CharacterController here
    // when setting a new position, otherwise it will overwrite the new
```

```
position with the player's current position
    playerController.enabled = false;
    float origY = playerController.transform.position.y;
    playerController.transform.position = new Vector3(trigger.transform.
position.x, origY, trigger.transform.position.z);
    playerController.transform.forward = trigger.transform.forward;
    playerController.enabled = true;
}
```

We first need to know how far we're going to rotate the pillar GameObjects. We're going to assign the rotation angle to a variable in the method's scope. We will use ternary to tell if it's clockwise or counterclockwise and multiply by `deltatime` to deal with framerate changes. Then we will rotate the item using `parent.parent.Rotate` along its up vector. The rotation angle and direction are decided on the line above, defined as `rot`.

One problem is that the character needs to move along with the pillar they are interacting with. The second problem is that the pillar rotates, so we need to face the character toward the pillar she's pushing. To do this, we will turn off the player's ability to move and then directly manipulate the character to the trigger's location and then keep her there while the interact button is held down. We will also point the character toward the pillar using the trigger volume's `forward` vector. In the end, we will transfer control back to the player. This makes it so that the character doesn't get stuck pushing the pillar forever.

That is it! We just made our first puzzle. What happens next after solving this puzzle is that the door tries to open, but it breaks a bit and only has a small space to move through. Let's take some time to break down why this might be useful.

Tight spaces

There are times when your game needs to load the next scene, but you may not want the loading screen to pull your player out of the immersion, or you may just want to add some environmental tension. Possibly you want to achieve both! Tight spaces is a common tool to use to achieve either of these situations. Let's go through how we're using tight spaces in our work.

Design

The concept of tight spaces is an interesting design use. We are using it in two ways. The first way is to add some tension to the exploration and movement. You have a character who must get through a space that is very narrow that she just watched collapse into place.

The second point is that this is a common design used for transitioning. Since we are only using this design concept on a small vertical of the game and we do not need to load multiple parts of the map, it isn't needed for that reason, but it is a good teaching point to you, the aspiring designer.

This helps with setting expectations for the player, letting them know that there will be slow-moving sections with tight animation and the camera close to the player to push up the intensity. While this longer animation and movement is happening, it will give time for the system to load into memory the next area without a loading screen. This trick is great as it doesn't hurt the immersion while allowing for detail to be retained. Nothing breaks the suspension of disbelief more than watching objects load into existence in front of you. After you finish working your way through the closed-off space, the rocks will fall naturally and close off the hallway. Not only does this stop any backward movement, but this also gives a feeling of necessity to move forward.

Implementation

The initial implementation of this is simple. We will make a Cinemachine camera move through the spaces to get the sense of timing needed for the cinematic while not allowing the player any inputs. We do this starting implementation through code as follows:

```
Void SetPlayerEnabled(bool enabled)
{
var cams = playerRoot.
GetComponentsInChildren<CinemachineVirtualCamera>(true);
   foreach(var cam in cams)
   {
      cam.gameObject.SetActive(enable);
   }
   playerRoot.GetComponentInChildren<MyvariThirdPersonMovement>().enabled
= enable;
}
```

We need to find the virtual cameras in the children and enable them while also disabling the player character. In *Chapter 12, Final Touches*, we will call this code when we trigger the cinematic. But instead of the virtual cameras that are in the children, we will call the camera made for the cinematic.

This implementation works very well for setting up the logic, without worrying about the nuance of each cinematic, which is very time- and animation-intensive.

Interactive volumes

This is the Swiss Army knife of mechanics. There are so many uses of interactive volumes that we can't cover them all in this book. This would also not make much sense as defining this takes away from the creativity that could be designed. This is not a tool that should be detailed in high granularity. Instead, let's go over how we will use it as well as some thoughts on it in general.

Design

As this is an adventure puzzle game, there will be points at which we need volumes where, when the character enters them, something happens. This definition is purposely broad. We are also using Cinemachine for our character's main camera. This allows us to link up virtual cameras in certain places when you trigger your volumes. Here are some examples of what we can perform with interactive volumes:

- Moving the camera over a cliff to give a sense of heightened anxiety
- Triggering rocks to fall
- Changing the walking animation to be slower when you walk through water
- Changing the lighting in an environment
- Spawning GameObjects

This list is not exhaustive by any means, as volumes are a creative tool to allow for interaction. We're using them in only a few ways, but the possibilities are endless. Let your imagination run wild while designing with interactive volumes.

This is powerful for many games to have, especially for us, with our environment-driven, research-focused mechanics. Our interactions require the environment to explain to the player what is going on and how to move forward. In the scripting section below, we will go through each interactive volume for this chapter. You can expect to see more volumes being used in future chapters, especially in the polishing phase as we can enhance the experience with many small interactions. This will help to make the environment and gameplay immersive.

Implementation

Luckily for us, you've seen two versions of interactive volumes. Look back up in the implementations of what we looked at earlier and pay close attention to the volumes. They are unique in their uses and can teach you some valuable lessons about developing in an environment without all the art assets being completed.

It may be a good idea to also think about some other ways we could've used interactive volumes so far. Were there any volumes you may have wanted to add?

Why don't we go over a bit of a summary of where we're using them in our game?

- We're using interactive volumes in any place where we can use an input action. An example of this might be the stairs buttons for accessing the stairs.
- We've added a volume to know the player is in the zone of the first puzzle. This allows the camera to move to a more advantageous position to understand the puzzle visually.
- Triggers on the puzzle pieces let you know you are close enough to interact with them.
- There is a volume for you to be able to tell you've entered the trigger point for entry into the tight spaces.
- Crossing the bridge, there is a small volume to change camera angles for a more cinematic shot.
- At the end of the bridge, there is a volume to trigger another tight space cinematic.
- While on a ledge, there is a trigger that unleashes a boulder to fall on you, whereupon you lift your arm up in defense. This will trigger you to discover a new power, which is a new mechanic.
- More triggers are used to open another door.
- There are triggers on items that you can interact with using your telekinetic powers.
- There are triggers on the final puzzle pieces.

This is a summary of all the triggers that are part of our core gameplay. There are a few others that deal with ambient flora and fauna, but they are simple collision triggers responsible for small changes or the simple movement of birds or deer. They are in random locations for cosmetic purposes.

Summary

In this chapter, we went over the design and implementation of interactions and mechanics. Even though the player's experiences and interactions seemed quite simple, the depth of design of player affordances allowed the player to know their limits and navigate the gameplay. We spent a good amount of time talking about interactions and mechanics. We defined the game loops and broke down parts of the mechanics toolbox. This was a very quick and short lesson into various game experiences. Finally, we broke down a bit of our game.

We broke down the stairs interaction and how that would be managed. We also went over why the stairs problem exists and where the solutions need to happen. Then, after that was completed, we went over the design of the first puzzle. After that was fully explained, we broke down our version of the implementation. Once this puzzle is completed, it's followed by a tight space segment, which could be used for loading the rest of the level, if we were on a larger scale project. Finally, there was a small section on how to use interactive volumes. As we used two different types of interactive volumes in our previous implementation, we went over them as well.

Overall, this chapter was very dense in information. Take some time to pause here and digest what you have just learned. Even if you feel like you could move on, let's just relax and let your brain process it all. In the next chapter, we will go over physics mechanics and interactions.

7

Rigid Bodies and Physics Interaction

In many game interactions, there needs to be physics. Whether you have items falling, bouncing, or just reacting to a collision in a procedural manner, you will most likely need to use Rigidbody components on your GameObjects. This component works with physics. We will first go through several use cases for the Rigidbody component. Once we've been through that, we will take some time to explain how we are using physics in our interactions for our project. Finally, we will show the scripting that is used to achieve these interactions in as much detail as possible. As always, the project files on GitHub will follow the structure in the *Readme* file. The topics in this chapter include:

- The Rigidbody component
- Collision detection
- Design and implementation
- Telekinesis and physics

The Rigidbody component

This powerful physics-focused component can be added to GameObjects to determine its position through physics. By default, just adding this component to a GameObject will put its motion under the influence of gravity. To understand how Unity uses physics, let's take some time to look at the component.

Figure 7.1 is a screenshot of the Rigidbody in Unity. There is a Rigidbody 2D component. Do not use this component for a 3D application. The primary problem with this is that the 2D and 3D versions of the physics steps do not interact with each other. It's best to choose one and stick with it! We will go through all the pieces to the **Rigidbody** component after the figure.

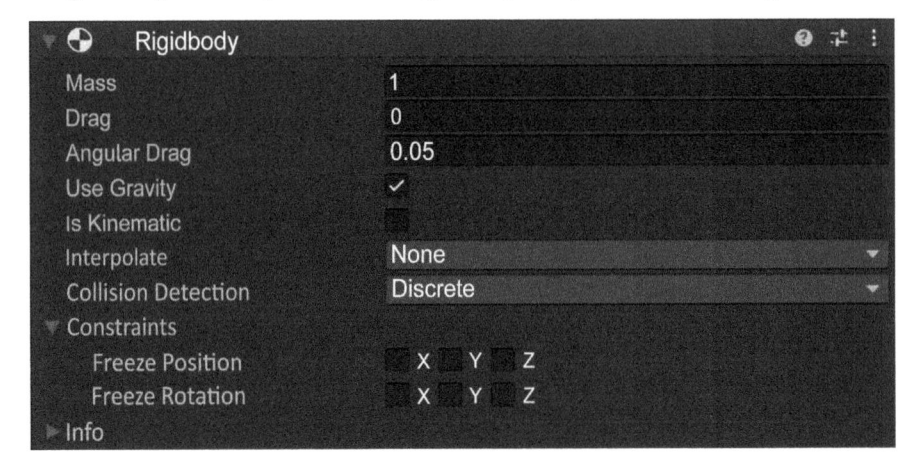

Figure 7.1: Rigidbody component

Mass

The **Mass** property of the Rigidbody refers to that object's relationship to other object's masses. This will not make gravity affect it differently, but it will affect collisions with other objects. For example, if two GameObjects that are identical except for their mass on the Rigidbody collide, the item with the larger mass will act as though it's heavier. Just as in the real world, mass doesn't cause items to fall faster. This is due to the drag of the objects.

Drag

Objects with **Drag** will decrease the rate at which it accelerates due to gravity. An example of this is a parachute. This object drastically decreases the acceleration of falling. For example, a skydiver has a very low drag, and when they open their parachute, the drag increases a lot. This is regardless of the rotation of the object.

Angular Drag

Angular Drag is the same concept as drag; however, it's specifically focused on rotation values. If you have a very small value for the angular drag, the object will rotate when bumped or collided with depending on the colliding object's oncoming angle. If you raise the value, it will rotate less.

Use Gravity boolean

The **Use Gravity** boolean simply allows gravity to affect the GameObject; the Rigidbody is a component of. As shown in *Figure 7.2*, in **Edit > Project Settings > Physics**, gravity is defined as -9.81, which is the same as Earth's gravity. Adjusting the **Y** axis gravity setting to -9.81 will be the most familiar to the players in emulating the likeness of Earth's gravity. If you are working with a game with less gravity and it's the same all the time, you can set it here. You can also set the gravity in code:

```
Physics.Gravity = Vector3(0, 0, 0,);
```

The 0s should be replaced with the values of gravity that are needed, generally in the *y* direction.

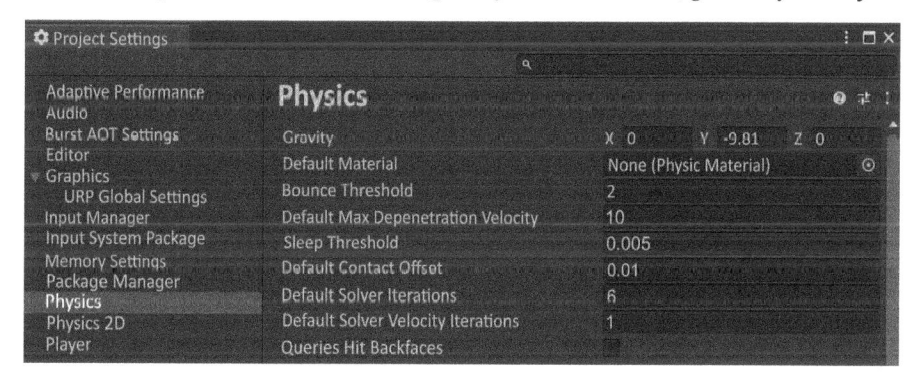

Figure 7.2: Project Settings – Physics settings

Is Kinematic boolean

When designing the level, there may be items that move around that need to affect the physics of another Rigidbody during runtime. A very simple example you could imagine is a sphere with a Rigidbody above a large cube. When you press play, the sphere would fall and hit the cube as expected. If you had the **Is Kinematic** boolean set to false and tried to rotate the cube, the sphere would stay put and clip through the cube. This is due to the cube not updating itself as a moving body after the sphere hit it and stopped. Setting this flag is helpful during an optimization pass, and it can be set for every known static item that still needs to have a Rigidbody component. Although, if you need to update the physics during runtime, set the ground to kinematic and when you rotate it, the sphere will react as expected and try to roll off the sloping downside of the cube.

This is a very common mistake when you start working with physics items. If during runtime your Rigidbody items aren't moving in a way you'd expect, check to see if they should be kinematic.

Interpolate

Interpolate means to place things in between other things. In our case, we need to know if interpolating is attempting to achieve one of three parameters in our physics update.

Those parameters are:

- **None**: Do not interpolate or extrapolate
- **Interpolate**: Place the object in between the current frame and the next frame
- **Extrapolate**: Assume the next location from the previous frames and put it where you think it might go

Figuring out the appropriate parameters to interpolate can be complicated to answer. The reason being is that there is more than one option when addressing interpolation, therefore, making the solution not as straightforward to resolve.

There are multiple variables to account for. These variables may contain these questions such as: How is the camera moving? Is the object moving quickly? Are you worried about the collision looking correct? Are you worried about the object moving incorrectly every time as the camera follows its motion? A simple answer is if your camera follows a character using a Rigidbody, then set it to **Interpolate** and everything else to **None**.

Diving into the physics system just a little bit, this system is calculated at a fixed interval, in contrast to graphics rendering. Graphics on a game can lag slightly and pop into place, where the physics will always calculate at a fixed interval. This can cause artifacts to visually occur, such as clipping into a wall. Clipping into a wall or other game objects within your scene would be seen if a fast-moving object is being followed closely by the camera and collides with the wall or surrounding GameObjects. The object would initially clip through the wall until the physics gets updated, and it would then update as though it bounced off the wall.

In this case, you would want to choose the **Interpolate** option because the physics system would interpolate the in-between values as the graphics are being rendered. This doesn't allow clipping while moving in a physics sense. It does cost some performance as it's calculating values in different intervals than it would normally.

Extrapolate does a good job of figuring out what the values will be in the future. This is helpful for simulating a flying object, but not good for collision detection as it will assume it's past a wall or object and clip at a higher framerate and movement. Movement being followed closely could use **Interpolate** or **Extrapolate**.

It's best to start with **Interpolate** and see if it feels good for the movement of your experience. If it feels slow, try **Extrapolate**. Weigh the pros and cons of each with a higher speed of movement in your action sequences to determine which interpolate method you need to use.

Understanding this will allow you to choose the best option for the physics values and the graphical representation of the items you are simulating with physics.

Collision detection

When using physics to determine the position of GameObject, there need to be collision checks to determine whether your object has collided with another object, regardless of if it's staying still or moving in the scene. This is an interesting dilemma now that you've learned that physics are fixed, and rendering is not fixed. The physics system can't assume what every object is using for collision types or interpolation. We need to have several options that would best suit each GameObject's physics needs from within the experience. There are four different collision detection types to consider: **Discrete**, **Continuous**, **Continuous Dynamic**, and **Continuous Speculative**. If you have a GameObject that is moving quickly, it may clip through GameObjects, meaning that it will not know that it has hit a collider and will keep moving through it as the physics is updated. This can be prevented through collision detection modes. Each mode has different implications on performance; however, the general guideline is that fast objects are set to **Continuous Dynamic** while the things they may collide with should be set to **Dynamic**. Other options are explained in the breakdown of each choice below.

Discrete

This collision detection mode is the best mode for performance, and it's aptly named **Discrete** as it's only checking the physics collision at fixed intervals, as mentioned previously. If you have a wall with a box collider and there is a ball moving quickly enough that its known location before the wall wasn't colliding with it and the next fixed update was past the wall, there is no collision! This can be frustrating at first as it looks like it's not working, or more frustratingly, it only happens intermittently as the ball may have collided with the wall when you ran the simulation a couple of times. It should be understood why this is happening so you can make different mode choices upon the needs of the physics simulation. The reason for this is that the physics update does not realize that the object was supposed to be affected by anything. The physics loop in **Discrete** mode will only check if the object needs to change trajectory once it's in the loop. If you have a fast-moving object, defined as an object moving more than its height or width in distance per frame, then there may be a point at which this object is past the other object and physics will not know to react to it.

If there are no fast-moving items, **Discrete** is a fantastic choice. If you are planning on having fast-moving objects, then **Continuous** is the answer, but please read about the rest of the options as they all don't interact with each other intuitively.

Continuous

If you choose **Continuous**, you may see that the object still clips through GameObjects you may not have expected it to. It is very important to understand that **Continuous** collision detection only checks if your GameObject is colliding with static objects. This mode is heavy on resources and should be used with caution.

> **Static objects** are GameObjects that are in the scene with collider components on them but no Rigidbody component. They are not updated with physics. Upon describing collision detection there will be modes that will only work with static GameObjects.

An example of an object that would use **Continuous** mode is fast moving GameObjects that need to collide with static items only. The simplest example of this is Pachinko. This is a game where a small metal ball gets dropped from the top of the screen and falls down, hitting static items, bouncing off them. All of the items on the field are static, so there will be no clipping.

Continuous Dynamic

This mode is very similar to the **Continuous** mode; however, it will also work with GameObjects that use a Rigidbody component. This is a common usage within game mechanics. As you can imagine, adding the ability to work with the Rigidbody component increases the cost of resources within a game. This is more resource-heavy than the standard continuous mode.

An example of continuous dynamic is a game you might have played, Smash Hit. This game is a mobile title in which you are a player on rails moving forward. When you tap the screen, a metal ball shoots out towards the location you tapped. If it collides with glass, it shatters. The glass is dynamic and interacts where the ball hits. Those broken pieces are also dynamic and interact with the environment when falling. If it wasn't dynamic, the ball would go right through the glass. This would make for a much less entertaining game!

Continuous Speculative

The word "speculative" suggests a sense of guessing. The system is speculating if the collision will happen.

This mode does what **Continuous Dynamic** does, and objects with this setting can collide with both static and dynamic GameObjects; however, it's cheaper. There is a bit of an accuracy cost, though. Two objects that are flying toward each other may end up bouncing away from each other without even touching if they both have **Continuous Speculative** set. This would happen because both objects are speculating where they will be in the next frame, which makes them think they should've bounced off each other.

An example of this is a game called Beat Saber. This is a game where you're in VR and you must hit blocks at certain angles to slice them properly. Having your saber's detection set to **Continuous Speculative** will allow you to know that you will hit the blocks that are moving at a high rate towards you.

Understanding all the modes for collision detection will help you create the right setup for physics-based work. Take time to play with these modes in your own project to get a good sense of how they all work together.

Constraints

Now that we've talked about some difficult questions, let's bring it back to a simpler topic: **Constraints**! This does exactly what you may think it does. If your item should not move or rotate on a specific axis, you may constrain it. An example of this is a platformer game that has moving platforms. You want them to move but maybe not along a specific axis. To ensure that the platform will not get nudged off course, you can constrain the GameObject in the x, y, or z direction so it will never update in that direction.

This was the last of the editable fields on the Rigidbody component. The last section is devoted to read-only fields for runtime debugging. Let's take a look at what information you can gain from these fields.

Info

The **Info** block of the Rigidbody component is essential for working with physics and debugging the strange behaviours that can come about. Every application may have unique problems that arise. Looking at the **Info** object when in play, you can debug what is going on with ease. This section has many values:

- **Speed**: Magnitude of the velocity
- **Velocity**: Rate of change of Rigidbody position
- **Angular Velocity**: Angular velocity vector of the Rigidbody measured in radians per second

- **Inertia Tensor**: Diagonal matrix in a reference frame positioned at this body's center of mass and rotated by **Inertia Tensor Rotation**
- **Inertia Tensor Rotation**: Rotation of the inertia tensor
- **Local Center of Mass**: Center of mass relative to the transform's origin
- **World Center of Mass**: Center of mass of the Rigidbody in world space
- **Sleep State**: Optimization strategy to not always account for every object, with two settings:
  - **Awake**: Physics is considering this Rigidbody
  - **Asleep**: Physics is not considering this Rigidbody

Each of these values above has its unique purposes depending on what you are trying to watch or debug during runtime. Working with the previously mentioned platformer, you may think that your platform should be in the alignment of your character, but something pushed it out of the way just enough to not allow the character to land on it. With the **Info** block, you can watch the movement or velocity. If there should be no velocity in the z direction, then looking at that value will let you know if it is working as intended.

We have a strong idea of how the Rigidbody 3D component works now and can refer to these pages if there are some confusing movements when building physics-focused interactions.

Design and implementation considerations

It is very easy to try to add physics to each of your GameObjects to get movement in your interactions. Not every item specifically needs a Rigidbody to complete its movement in a manner that your interactions need to provide a fantastic experience. At the end of the day, it's all about frames per second. Try to make any moving item without Rigidbody components, but if they're needed, then add them.

Telekinesis and physics interaction

For our game's first puzzle, we focused heavily on making the environment narrative the key interest point. From the moment you walk into the first room, your vision will be placed on the back door, which houses the puzzle's solution. In the final puzzle, we need to force the player to use more brainpower on figuring out the puzzle instead of finding the answers around them. To do this, we decided to give the player the power of telekinesis that Myvari, our character, realizes she has had within her the whole time. We have three steps to get the player to this point of understanding.

Rocks Falling

Telekinesis hasn't been seen in this game in any form yet. Some magic came from her necklace, but we need to provide some information to tell the player that she has something in her. A cinematic works well for this. We need to design the interaction.

Design

After finishing the first door puzzle, you encounter a large hallway with old statues of your past. This is a nice look into the culture of her race's past. There is nothing to solve here; there's just a nice walk. Behind the final statue is a tight space to walk through that leads to a cliff path. About halfway along the path, some rocks fall. This triggers a cinematic effect where Myvari defends herself from these falling rocks with her telekinesis. Looking confused, she needs to move forward to find out what is going on. Her adventurous side beckons her to push on.

Implementation

What needs to be implemented here is in two pieces. One large piece is the cinematic of the rocks and Myvari. Cinematics are when the user doesn't have power over the interaction. This is helpful for gaining knowledge but shouldn't be overused because the game can become like an interactive movie. Cinematics should be used with restraint. The second part is physics-based rocks as a secondary motion from the boulder falling.

The cinematic will be triggered in the same way as previously: we turn off the player's ability to manipulate Myvari or the camera and transition to the cinematics' animation while moving the camera to emphasize the object we want, in this case, the boulder. If you need a refresher for this, look at *Chapter 6, Interactions and Mechanics*, during the implementation of the tight spaces.

The physics-based rocks, however, we can't just animate. We want them to feel as though they fell on their own. It makes the larger boulder seem like it fell, which helps sell the immersion that this location might be real.

Even though this shows the telekinesis coming from Myvari, we need to have the player perform the interaction or else it's just an ability they can't use. We will go over the player's interaction next.

The Broken Pedestal

This is the first time the player gets to use Myvari's newfound power. We need to design this puzzle so it's impossible to miss because the player isn't used to using this power. This pedestal is a small version of the final puzzle.

In this micro-puzzle, you need to place the fallen piece onto the pedestal to fix it. We will need to be very careful with how we design this to ensure the player's experience explains how this works before they touch the interaction button. Let's run through the design together.

Design

After we make it along the cliff path and across a small crumbling bridge, the bridge then falls, and the way back is impassable. The only way to go is through a large door. When we walk up to it, it will start opening into a large open cavern, water pooled in the bottom, with ruins in the background and a fall to certain doom. Directly in front of Myvari is a pedestal that is broken, but the broken piece is on the ground close to it. Looking at it, we can see that it is outlined in the same color as the power that protected Myvari from the falling rocks. We will display a UI helper showing which button to press, which we will go over in *Chapter 8, User Interface and Menus*. This will make interaction with her ability tied to a button to provide the player agency. When we press the button, Myvari lifts the broken piece off the ground and fits it onto the pedestal, where it affixes itself and lights up. Pressing the interaction button will then transition the open space into a night scene and some water rises up from below to reveal a pathway to the ruins.

Implementation

We know that the mechanic we want to include here is a subset of the final puzzle. To do this, we don't want to write code just for this single item, so instead, we set it up to be a simple standalone using a public enum.

To keep this as easy to read as possible, we will ask you to take your time reading this section, which is about the final puzzle. We will be explaining some more advanced features and it all builds on itself up to the end. We are using some amazing Unity timing in this code, which will take some explanation, and breaking it up as we've done will help you to understand it. So, let's move on to the final puzzle design, and then we will break down all of the pieces of this and the final puzzle's implementation.

The Final Puzzle

We've made it to the big final puzzle. Luckily, we took the time to show the player what Myvari gained through stress from the boulder falling toward her. Then we learned how to use it to get here by fixing the broken pedestal. Now we have this puzzle slightly open, but allows the environment to teach the player what they need to do. Let's dive in to see how we design this last puzzle.

Design

Now that you've made it to the ruins, there is some architecture in the background that lights up some runes on the pillars. This corresponds with some cables on the ground that connect to all the pillars. The puzzle consists of six pillars that connect the power to the main tree, which is in the center of the ruins and has wires connected to it. The wires are only properly connected from three of the pillars. Myvari needs to use her telekinesis to connect the correct pillars following the wires on the ground. Bringing power to the tree opens a small compartment in the tree, which houses a tiara. The tiara is revealed through a cinematic and will end the gameplay of this vertical slice. Now that we have the general idea of what we need to do, let's move on to implementation.

Implementation

The implementation of this puzzle is the completion of the telekinesis mechanic. When we wrote this, we allowed ourselves to push into more advanced topics. To ensure this makes sense, we will go over all the topics here and break them down as much as possible. Ensure that you pay attention to the minutiae as there are bits of information here that will seem hidden or counter-intuitive at first.

Programming topics that we will be covering are:

- Execution order
- Static methods
- `UnityAction` (delegate)
- Coroutines

Let's first go over the execution order for Unity. We haven't spent any time talking about the nitty-gritty of how it works under the hood.

Execution order

There is an order to the execution of every frame when in runtime, or playing, inside the editor and opening a build. We would show you a screenshot of the flowchart, but it's a bit too large. Instead, we will place a link here as well as a Google search term for you to search online to find the website and see this flowchart. I will cover the higher-level topics here and the reason why they matter within each portion that they affect.

`https://docs.unity3d.com/Manual/ExecutionOrder.html`

Google search term: `Unity Execution Order`

The major concept here is that there has to be a hierarchy of execution of certain bits of information. We needed to have a strong think about this to have a baseline of what will be dealt with at each frame. The uncomfortable truth is that there is a lot to think about. Here is the list in chronological form with highest-level terminology for the execution order, with a small snippet of information on each of them:

- **Initialization**: This is for Awake and onEnable only.
- **Editor**: Reset when scripts are added and not in play mode.
- **Initialization**: The second part of initialization is for the Monobehaviour method Start only.
- **Physics**: This is where all physics updates will happen. It can potentially be run more than once per frame if the fixed time step is set higher than the frame update time.
- **Input Events**: Any non-update focused input, such as OnMouseDown.
- **Game Logic**: Update, coroutine logic and yielding, animation events, write properties, and LateUpdate run in here. These will be more apparent during implementation of the game logic further in the chapter.
- **Scene Rendering**: Many scene-rendering functions run here in every frame to deal with culling objects from the camera, visible objects, and post rendering. We will not be breaking this down heavily, if you are curious, please read into the execution order manual for more information.
- **Gizmo Rendering**: Specifically, the OnDrawGizmo method of the Unity Editor.
- **GUI Rendering**: The OnGui method, which can run multiple times per frame.
- **End of Frame**: Allows coroutines to be paused or yielded at the end of the frame, waiting for all of the rest to finish before starting again at the top of game logic section.
- **Pausing**: When the application has been paused; before the application is paused, a single frame is run.
- **Decommissioning**: Cleans up memory with OnApplicationQuit, OnDisable, and OnDestroy in that order.

Before we move on to the next section, there is something you need to make sure you understand. You do not, by any means, need to understand all of the preceding list. There is a lot to learn there, and if you go to the execution order documentation you will see every method that is listed in more detail. We will be showing portions of the execution and explaining what is affecting our code during the rest of this chapter.

The key takeaway from the chronological list of higher-level sections being listed is that Unity has an order. That's a relieving concept to wrap your head around as a developer. When you get confused about why something is happening the way it is, you can rely on this to see if it's an execution order problem that you might be running into.

During the next sections, we will have images of the section of the execution order we had to pay attention to. This will allow you to see how it can be used for your future development work.

Now that we've looked at the execution order, we should get into the code. We are using three scripts to make this work with the telekinesis mechanics:

- PhysicsPuzzleTrigger.cs
- PhysicsPuzzlePiece.cs
- FinalPuzzle.cs

PhysicsPuzzleTrigger.cs has two pieces of code that are important to know about first: the PhysicsPuzzleTrigger class and the PhysicsPuzzlePieceType enum. We will tackle the PhysicsPuzzlePieceType first as it's much easier to get into than the trigger. We have an enum that allows us to choose which puzzle piece type it is on the GameObject. We define this as follows:

```
public enum PhysicsPuzzlePieceType
{
    First = 0,
    Second,
    Third,
    Intro,
    Any
}
```

Then, in the PhysicsPuzzlePiece.cs script, we implement it as follows:

```
public class PhysicsPuzzlePiece : MonoBehaviour
{
    public PhysicsPuzzlePieceType pieceType;
}
```

When we add the PhysicsPuzzlePiece.cs script to any GameObject, we then get a dropdown to choose which type it is. This is very useful when you want explicit items to fit together. We're using this to use the same mechanics but allow for different puzzle types.

We said in *The Broken Pedestal* section above that we would explain it within the implementation of the entire mechanic. What we do is allow the Intro option to be aligned with this mechanic and be explicit for that action. Even though it's impossible to get the final puzzle pieces in that location, this is a great practice to ensure data is consistent with your code.

Let's get back into the PhysicsPuzzleTrigger.cs code. We start off by declaring the fields we're used to working with so far, but then on line 12, there is something unique that has two concepts we need to go over. This is the use of static and UnityAction:

```
public static UnityAction<PhysicsPuzzleTrigger, PhysicsPuzzlePiece> OnPieceSlotted;
```

We're going to break out of describing exactly what we're doing with this line to explain the context of what both static and UnityAction are. After we do that, we will then proceed to how we are using them in this code for this mechanism.

Static methods

A static method, field, property, or event is callable on any class that is within the namespace without needing the using directive or inheritance. Let's say you have one script that has a field as follows:

```
public class StaticTest
{
    public static int StaticInt = 10;
}
```

You could then have another script in the same project that, without specifically calling for that script when using or inheriting it, could access it like this:

```
public class UseStaticTest
{
    int BaseNumber = 0;
    int NewNumber = BaseNumber + StaticTest.StaticInt;
}
```

This may not look very useful by itself, but the concept is the important part to take away at this time. Static members of a class can be accessed by other classes by just using the class name before the required member.

An example of this being used commonly is keeping a count of something as the static field has only one instance. We're using it to store a UnityAction. We need to go over that next before we get into how we are using these directly.

UnityActions

A UnityAction is a Unity-specific delegate. A delegate in C# is a sort of generic concept of a method that has a parameter list which also returns a specific type. Interestingly, a UnityAction returns void by default. A common way of explaining delegates is through the concept of the subscribe model. This means that the delegate is looking for methods to be attached to it and when something uses the delegate, it will try to run the methods attached as long as the methods are returning the same type. This is a bit abstract, so let's look at an example. We will be using the UnityAction MathAction to add to how many times a button is pressed and then see if that new number is even or odd:

```
using UnityEngine.UI;

public class UnityActionTest : MonoBehaviour
{
    public Button AddButton;
    private UnityAction MathAction;
    float TimesClicked;

    void Start()
    {
        AddButton = GetComponent<Button>();

        MathAction += AddOne;
        MathAction += CheckEven;
        AddButton.onClick.AddListener(MathAction);
    }

    void AddOne()
    {
        TimesClicked++;
        Debug.Log("Clicked count : " + TimesClicked);
    }
```

```
    void CheckEven()
    {
        if (TimesClicked % 2 == 0)
        {
            Debug.Log("This click was even!");
        }
        else
        {
            Debug.Log("ThIs ClIcK WaS OdD.");
        }
    }
}
```

We're using the Button class, so ensure to import UnityEngine.UI so we can use buttons from that class. Following the lines down, we made a new UnityAction named MathAction. On Start, we grabbed the button so we could add logic to it. Then we attached the AddOne and CheckEven methods to UnityAction. The += that you see is MathAction attaching itself to those methods in order.

> Addition assignment operator – we're using a special "syntactic sugar" to make the code a bit cleaner to read and less redundant. The addition assignment operator looks like this:

```
MathAction += AddOne
```

> Written another way is:

```
MathAction = MathAction + AddOne;
```

You then see that we assigned UnityAction to the button's listener. When you press the button, both of these functions will be running because UnityAction is assigned to both of them.

Before we can go further into the code, we need to cover one more topic, coroutines.

Coroutines

A coroutine allows you to spread a task over multiple frames. This is not a form of multithreading. Every action is still being run on the main thread. The power of coroutines is that they allow directable pausing through a new term, yield. Taking a look at the execution order in the figure below, you may remember seeing **yield null** after **Update** in the **Game Logic** section. If you don't have the execution order up on a browser tab, look at *Figure 7.3*. The small note on the left says it nicely. If a coroutine previously yielded or paused, and it's due to resume, it will resume at that point in the execution order.

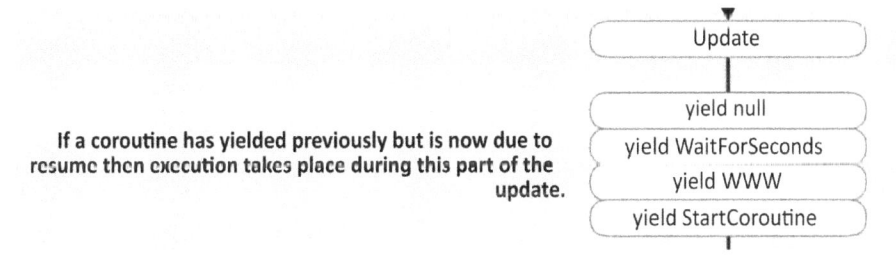

If a coroutine has yielded previously but is now due to resume then execution takes place during this part of the update.

Update
yield null
yield WaitForSeconds
yield WWW
yield StartCoroutine

Figure 7.3: Game logic of the execution order

That's awesome, isn't it? How does it know to resume, you ask? Good question, reader. It knows that it should resume because of the logic in the code. There is a fantastic example from the Unity Docs going over a basic fade from opaque to transparent using a coroutine. Let's go through it quickly:

```
void Update()
{
    if (Input.GetKeyDown("f"))
    {
        StartCoroutine(Fade());
    }
}

IEnumerator Fade()
{
    Color c = renderer.material.color;
    for (float alpha = 1f; alpha >= 0; alpha -= 0.1f)
    {
        c.a = alpha;
```

```
            renderer.material.color = c;
            yield return null;
        }
    }
```

I put in bold the three things that may be new to you. `StartCoroutine(Fade())` is asking the application to start a coroutine with the `Fade` method. You will start the coroutine during the start of the game logic at the bottom of the `yield` statements; refer to *Figure 7.3* again for this.

`IEnumerator` is stating that this method is iterable. Remember back to the last time you made a method. The keyword before the name is the type. We use `void` if it returns nothing, but since this will be iterated on, it needs to know. We let the computer know this by adding `IEnumerable` as the return type.

The last part is `yield return null`. This is tricky the first time looking over the `for` loop. In most cases, a `return` will take you out of a loop, but since we have a `yield` there, Unity asks if we've finished with everything in the method. It pauses after subtracting 0.1f from the current alpha and waits for the game logic portion to start again to do it again until it satisfies the `for` loop logic. Once that is completed, it no longer yields.

Summarizing this code, pressing *F* will fade the GameObject this script is on out from the scene. We think you have a good enough grasp of these concepts. Let's get back to the code in our project to finish up our implementation.

Back to the code

OK...we took a little aside to explain some key concepts, but we're back now. Let's open `PhysicsPuzzleTrigger.cs` back up. The concept here is that you have telekinesis and when you move an item close to its trigger volume, it will then, on its own, move into place over a transitional period we define. We've seen `OnTriggerEnter` previously, so that isn't surprising with a volume trigger. We do want it to move on its own, so we need to disable a bunch of fields of the Rigidbody and disable the collider. This is done on lines 28-33 in `PhysicsPuzzleTrigger.cs`.

Now, this is where we get to see new code. We need to set up the references to where the items need to transition from and to as this script is on several GameObjects, so we need to reference their relative positions.

Then we start the coroutine on line 40.

```
StartCoroutine(TransitionTween());
```

Chapter 7 163

We have some code for changing the color of the trigger; this is temporary for debugging.

Then we have a tween loop, which is an animation term for "between" which means the change in movement in our case. We have our while loop running for as long as tweenDuration is set to, normalized from how long it has been from the start. This is defined as delta. We then Lerp the position and Slerp the rotation to the transform we want it to end with:

```
while (Time.time - tweenStart < tweenDuration)
    {
        float delta = (Time.time - tweenStart) / tweenDuration;
        tweenPiece.position = Vector3.Lerp(tweenStartPos, transform.position, delta);
        tweenPiece.eulerAngles = Vector3.Slerp(tweenStartRot, transform.eulerAngles, delta);
        yield return null;
    }
```

Finally, we see the yield return null!

We're now paused until the next game logic loop unless tweenDuration is complete and we don't enter the while loop, which means we have completed the tween. We set the position and angles on line 61 for the moving piece to ensure the transform is ready to be referenced in our UnityAction.

```
tweenPiece.position = transform.position;
tweenPiece.eulerAngles = transform.eulerAngles;
OnPieceSlotted?.Invoke(this,tweenPiece.
GetComponent<PhysicsPuzzlePiece>());
```

Now, we move into our UnityAction:

```
OnPieceSlotted?.Invoke(this, tweenPiece.
GetComponent<PhysicsPuzzlePiece>());
```

This looks interesting. Why is there a question mark there? There is a conditional operator called a "null condition operator", which asks if OnPieceSlotted is null or not before performing the following method. This is another syntactical sugar. You could get the same result by making an if statement checking if OnPieceSlotted is null.

In the case of UnityAction, this is saying something very specific. It's asking if anything has been attached to this action.

If there is a method assigned to this `UnityAction`, then please call whatever function is assigned with the following arguments; the `this` GameObject and the `tweenPiece` as the `PhysicsPuzzlePiece` type.

This is where some magic happens. Remember that we assigned `OnPieceSlotted` to be a static member of the `PhysicsPuzzleTrigger` class? Well, open up `FinalPuzzle.cs` and let's show the power of static members.

On Start, we add a local function named `OnPieceSlotted` to the static `UnityAction` from `PhysicsPuzzleTrigger.OnPieceSlotted`. We know that when our player puts an object into the right position, by the end of the coroutine it needs to update which object it was. Was it the final puzzle or the intro puzzle? We defined that through our enum on `PuzzlePieceType`:

```
void OnPieceSlotted(PhysicsPuzzleTrigger trigger, PhysicsPuzzlePiece piece)
    {
        if (piece.pieceType == PhysicsPuzzlePieceType.Intro)
        {
            Debug.Log("FINAL PUZZLE INTRO SOLVED. Trigger environment transition here");
            tempBridge.SetActive(true);
        }
        else
        {
            numPiecesSlotted += 1;
            if (numPiecesSlotted >= 3)
            {
                Debug.Log("FINAL PUZZLE SOLVED! Trigger portal event");
            }
        }
    }
```

This local method being run from `UnityAction` gives us the trigger and `piece` tells us if we have finished the intro puzzle or if we have worked on the final puzzle. We can use any script later on in the game for this specific mechanic as it's static and available to us. Static is not only fun with socks on the carpet shocking your siblings. It's also magic in programming!

We just did some intermediate-level Unity programming. These tools are usable in so many situations, but they aren't always easy to think about as the first option to the answer of your problem. Take your time and work through each section. Make some coroutines with GameObjects. See if you can make your own `UnityAction` within one script, as we showed above. Test static methods and see how they work, and in time these tools will become natural to you when developing your games.

Summary

What a jam-packed chapter! We went over a lot, so I think we need a small summary here. The concept of physics is already a tough subject to tackle. We're using it for simulation in games on a small scale. We went over the Rigidbody component in its entirety and then dove deep into some brand-new C# work. For C#, we went over:

- Execution order
- Static methods
- `UnityAction` (delegate)
- Coroutines

All these new concepts are tools to use on your next project. Take as much time as needed to digest these concepts. You will see them used in almost every project that you work with.

In the next chapter, we need to add menu systems and a user interface so that the user can have more context for the gameplay.

8
User Interface and Menus

The collection of visual information and components laid out across the screen of a video game is known as the **User Interface** (**UI**). An intuitive UI and menu system creates an opportunity for your players to have quality experiences. This interactivity and direct influence of a game's playable outcome is called **player agency**. Designing for this agency is crucial to creating an intuitive and successful interactive experience within your game world. This agency allows players to interact with the game's narrative and engage within that game space accurately.

User interfaces and menu systems throughout your game also provide player affordances. Player affordances are the communication with your player about how to use an object within the game, conveying controls, and navigating your game world from start to finish.

Game menu systems specifically give the player agency over the various modes of gameplay. These gameplay modes signal to a player when to start and the options and actions available before, during, and after gameplay. Getting the player into the game is important, but during the game, your interface may be more important to the experience.

There are four forms of user interface: **Diegetic**, **Non-diegetic**, **Spatial**, and **Meta**. Spending some time breaking down these UI definitions will give a better understanding of how we will be using them in our project. Then we will look into scripting each of them to give an idea of the proper way to implement them.

This chapter will cover the following topics.

- Defining UI
- UI elements
- UI in our project

- Unity Canvas system
- Unity UI objects

Let's begin by explaining the user interface.

User interface

The need for a user interface is a double-edged sword. You will need to put user interface features in place for the experience to move forward, but this can also easily distract the player from that experience when not done correctly. There isn't always a mechanic that can be made to teach players how to interact with the world they are playing in. This can break immersion, which isn't always bad, but there needs to be an understanding of how one can break this immersion without ruining the experience.

We're going to talk about the four forms of UI, which are broken down across two defined spaces, **Narrative** and **Internal**. **Narrative** lends itself to UI-driven storytelling, whereas **Internal** is functional UI within the game world itself.

> When reading through the various forms of the user interface, realize that these are not exhaustive explanations and will need to be understood more as a tool to help design the right UI for the experience you wish to provide.

While we are going through **Diegetic**, **Non-diegetic**, **Spatial**, and **Meta** UI forms, we will be explaining how the UI fits into a simple 2x2 diagram of Internal and Narrative functions. The 2x2 grid below, in *Figure 8.1*, is a visual representation of how to integrate a holistic view of the UI and incorporate it throughout the overall gameplay experience. In the following paragraphs, each section header of the UI forms will also be supplemented with an "if this, then that" double-answer response.

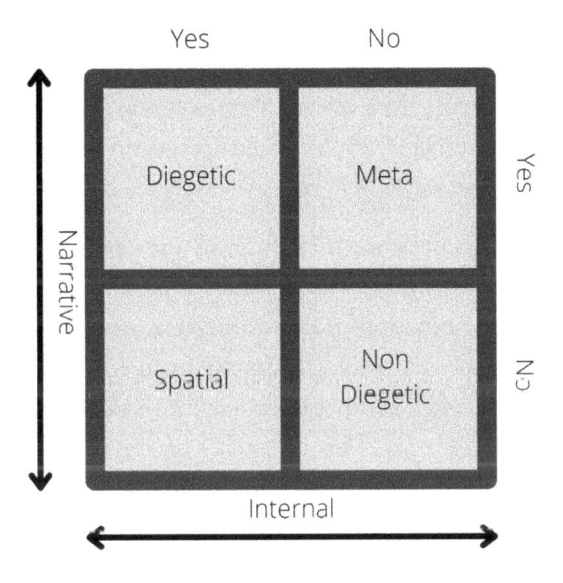

Figure 8.1: 2x2 user interface design

Answering with **Yes** or **No** on both Narrative and Internal on the 2x2 grid above helps us to understand what UI form is needed. Follow along as we describe each of these four forms in detail.

Diegetic — Narrative Yes, Internal Yes

A user interface that blends internal and external spaces is called **Diegetic**. This type of interface commits to not breaking the immersion while providing the information to the player that they need to understand the internal game space.

You may want to convey the location the player needs to go, but you want to give a sense of difficulty. You may, during the story, give the player a direction and provide a compass. When you press a button to pull up the compass, this is giving the player the information without breaking out of the internal space. We will consider this compass when discussing the rest of the four types to see if we can convert it into a different type.

Now that we have explained the Diegetic UI form type, let us take a look at a great example that is within a published game. When explaining Diegetic UI, there is an eerie game that comes to mind, called *Dead Space*. Electronic Arts (EA)'s Visceral Games studio (dissolved and merged into EA Vancouver and EA Montreal; October 17, 2017) created a gritty, survival cosmic horror video game that drew inspiration from other works of horror such as *Resident Evil 4* and the *Silent Hill* series.

The game designers of Visceral Games needed to think of ways the player could look dead center on the screen and focus their attention there as much as possible. That way the player could simultaneously witness the abominations, jump scares, gore, and horrors of *Dead Space's* world, and navigate the narrative of Isaac Clarke. Isaac is the main character of *Dead Space* and the unfortunate spaceship systems engineer that is thrown into a variety of unfortunate situations over a span of years.

How can you do that in a role-playing game where you have a lot of information that your player needs to know? You put that important player information on the character itself. When done this way, the information becomes 3rd person on the screen, allowing the player to still retain a view of the screen and its environment. Isaac's health indicators are on a health bar that is integrated into the lit-up nodes on his spine, seen in *Figure 8.2*, and the stasis meter is incorporated on his right shoulder blade as a partial glowing circular ring. Now the player doesn't need to look away from the main character to know his health and character statistics.

Figure 8.2: Dead Space health visualization

Non-diegetic – Narrative No, Internal No

Looking at the grid, you may think, how can you have any UI that isn't in the narrative or the game space? This is a great question and it's more common than you think! Virtually every menu system and, unintegrated **heads-up display** (HUD) is non-diegetic, as seen in *Figure 8.3*. Pressing play in a game isn't part of the game narrative, but it's part of the game and an important part too.

Figure 8.3: Forza non-diegetic HUD

Let's think about the compass and see if we can convert it into a non-diegetic UI element. Its purpose is to help the player know the direction of where to go. Can we do this without the game characters being aware of it? You could make a minimap that shows the direction the player needs to go and shape it like a compass on the screen. With this being defined, we've decided that yes, you can convert the compass into a non-diegetic form. There are so many examples of a non-diegetic UI element in production, but one of our favorites is in a racing game UI. *Forza* has a clean UI that shows the gear you're in, the speed, and the location in the world to help you along your path on the minimap.

Spatial – Narrative No, Internal Yes

Here is a fun case for user interface design. Spatial UIs exist in the game world, but the characters inside the game are not aware of their existence.

Taking another look at the compass, maybe we want it to be spatial. How can we convey the direction we need to go without the character being aware of it?

There could be a projected compass on the ground that shows the direction of the next waypoint or goal. It only shows up when you look topdown from your character so it doesn't always disturb the gameplay in general. One of the best spatial UI elements in a game is in *Path of Exile*. The items that are on the ground have a colored spire to denote certain item types and the names of the items give a description of what the item may be, as seen in *Figure 8.4* below.

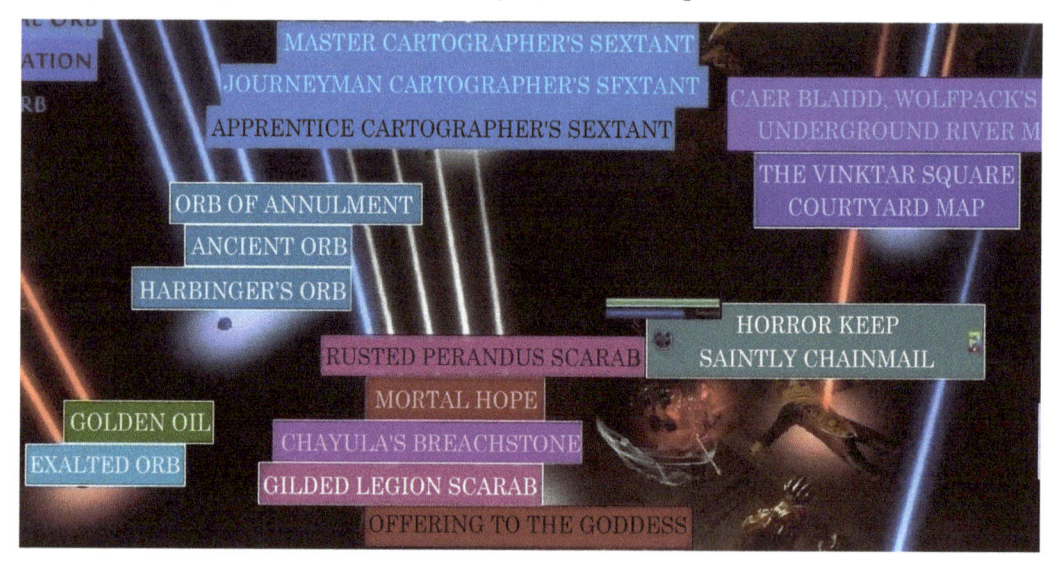

Figure 8.4: Path of Exile spatial item names

The character in the game doesn't know about this screen but it is in the game's space as you need to move your mouse over it to view it.

Meta – Narrative Yes, Internal No

Meta is interesting for a user interface as we can't have the interface in the game world, but the character needs to have knowledge of it. If we look at our compass example and try to transform it into the meta space, we will need to think a bit harder. Breaking the fourth wall by interacting directly with the user while the character is aware of the scenario is rather unique. Let's give it a try.

The outer area of the screen houses the compass degrees and follows the character's rotations. The character looks at their compass and you can see that the direction is or isn't close to the correct location due to the screen UI. This is cumbersome and doesn't feel intuitive.

Chapter 8   173

A much better example of meta is in first-person shooter games. Have you ever played an FPS game and were hit? There is a splatter of blood and a red vignette around the screen. The character knows they were hit and generally makes a sound; the meta UI lets the player know the possibility of death if they keep getting hit. The camera showing the player isn't the player's vision, and we know this, but our rendering with a bloody vignette that darkens and intensifies gives the sense of dramatic life-ending anxiety.

Figure 8.5: Call of Duty Meta screen UI

What we have just discussed are the design methodologies to understand what your UI elements are displaying for the user. As shown, there are several ways to break down a UI element. We will now go over some common terminology in the UI development for games.

UI elements

There are common UI elements that are used during any game. Whether it's the main menu, inventory system, health representation, or a spatial item interaction system, they all serve a single purpose: give the player as much information as possible without directly affecting their immersion too much that it pulls them away from the experience.

In the next few sections, we will cover the topics previously mentioned. These are generalized terms for the user interface and are not supposed to be set in concrete. These are design thoughts following common topics that currently exist for the UI portion of game development.

Use these sections as references for design when thinking about your game projects in the future. We will begin with the **main menu**; coincidentally, this is the menu that will appear first for your players.

Main menu

When a game menu pops up for the first time after loading the game up, this is the first time the developers get to create an emotional response. Is your game a horror game? The font and imagery should reflect this. There are many ways to set up a menu. Do you need a news screen to pop up before you pick your characters when logging in? Does the main menu jump right into gameplay when you press play? Are there several layers of menus that need to be there as the game is focused on menu systems? All of these are legitimate questions.

The simplest way to go about building a menu system is to ensure that it isn't difficult to play the game with its intended difficulty, or connection if it's a multiplayer game. We tend to call this "**low barrier of entry.**" If a player wants to come in and press play without looking into the settings, they should be able to do so. This includes looking at the recommended specs and building the system to allow for that.

The player's experience shouldn't rely on them understanding what their system can handle. A good way to think about this is the game experience from arcade machines or consoles. PlayStation and Xbox require game developers to ensure framerates are high, so the experience is of a good standard. This should also be the case for PC as well as mobile.

Inventory systems

There are other forms of menu systems that are similar in nature but not part of the initial player experience. **Role-playing games (RPGs)** often use an inventory system that shows what you have stored on your character in the form of armor or equipment. This can be used as a bottlenecking system to force players back to the city to sell or upgrade their equipment. It can also be used to help define the experience as the character couldn't possibly hold 30 sets of armor and 200 weapons on them at once while roaming the world. This is an attempt to straddle the line between breaking immersion and keeping realism in check.

Some interesting forms of inventory systems are quest logs and achievements. A quest log is just an inventory of quests that can be completed or removed by finishing the required quest. Achievements are the opposite in that you gain them by performing certain tasks.

Health representation

Health can be represented by "lives left," as in Super Mario Bros. It can also be represented by how many more times you can be hit, such as in the Dead Space reference above. It may not even be represented by a specific value, but an amount of blood on the screen, as seen in Call of Duty. Even more abstract is not health, but a timer left on the screen of how much time you have left to complete a quest or level. All of these can be considered health representations and can look different on the screen using any of the forms we previously spoke about.

Item interaction system

There may be items in your game with which your player needs some help to know that they are interactable. There are two main ways to work through this and both of them can be spatial. Sometimes this will be non-diegetic, which we will go over next.

One way is to make a tooltip on the screen that is only available when your mouse or crosshair is covering the item. This is usually when you want something to be contextual to that specific item. This can be done when the tooltip is in the screen space — this means it's always the same size and is more akin to a floating window. This is the same concept that was shown in the Path of Exile image above. You may also see instead a floating icon around or above the item under the context. This could be for the player to know that they can interact with something. These are similar in nature, but screen space denotes that it's not part of the world and the character isn't aware of it either. This makes it non-diegetic. The second example of the icon floating above the item is spatial as it shows itself in the world, but the character doesn't know about it.

UI in our project

Our project is not user interface-heavy. We purposefully wanted to keep it as light as possible to create a tight immersion within the environment. To keep it as light as possible, we have three major portions to talk about.

- Main menu
- Escape menu
- Spatial UI

To begin, we will talk about the main menu and how that starts our immersion into the game right from the beginning.

Main menu

Our menu is going to be primarily a non-diegetic menu system. From the start of the application, Myvari will be in the woods looking at her book. The menu will be off to the left with the **Title**, **Play**, and **Quit** options available to select. When the **Play** button is pressed, there will be a camera movement with a small cinematic animation that triggers the beginning of the game. Possession of our character happens right after Myvari starts her idle animation after the cinematic animation finishes from the **Play** button press. This system gives a feel that it is within the world as the camera is not fading to black for a scene transition, but it is not part of the world or part of the narrative. Myvari doesn't know the menu system exists and it's not affecting the game world in any way, therefore it is non-diegetic. The screenshot we are showing below in *Figure 8.6* is a mock-up to illustrate the logic without the need for all the art. This is a common tactic when working within game development. In further sections we will go over the implementation of the actual UI.

Figure 8.6: Main menu mock-up

We like the concept of a UI that allows the player to feel like the game they are playing is immediately immersive. When you hit **Play**, the menu should go away and the camera should move into a position where you then take control of the main character. The goal is to not have a loading screen. Keep the players involved as much as possible.

Escape menu

To give as much immersion as possible, we wanted to utilize one of the core features of our character's personality: exploration. To us, this means that we needed the book on her right hip to be a feature of her passage through the game experience. We also knew that we would need to have in-game settings somewhere, which we could also place in the book. This is spatial in that it breaks the immersion of the game as the settings aren't part of the narrative. When Myvari flips to the **Options** portion of the journal, this will feel disjointed enough but will be familiar to someone who is used to playing games. This portion will be spatial as it is part of the world but Myvari doesn't know that it's a menu to close the game. When she is on the left pane, this is all story-driven elements that are part of the world and both Myvari and the player are using it as hints to move forward in the game. In this case, we will call this portion of the menu diegetic as we will be selecting the art to fit as though someone from Myvari's race made this book.

How we will do this is through a small cinematic animation of Myvari pulling the book out and it opening to the journal, which will have small updates depending on where you have been in the game. The book has art to look as though she didn't write in it, but another person of her race did. The book is old and has led her to this cave. There will be markers with small notes to help guide the player if need be. This is a linear progression game, so we will update this at every milestone or sub-milestone. If she is standing still, we will also have her get the book out and read from it, which will bring the immersion of the book being her journal into a closer convergence to keep the experience as congruent as possible.

Figure 8.7: Journal UI mock-up

The journal is an interesting menu system for us. It's acting as an escape menu as well as giving the players more clues about the engagement that Myvari is working through. *Figure 8.7* above shows our mock-up, which we use to visualize what it may look like. This helps us understand where to put the camera, as well as helping the animator know how to animate her grabbing her book out of its holster.

Spatial tooltip

When designing feedback to the player, there are quite a few options as we saw with the compass problem. In our case, we thought about how we could best show the ability to interact with the environment. We settled on a spatial system. This system will be in the form of what is called a tooltip. This tooltip is a small icon that is in the world space above the GameObject that is interactable by the player. We chose to use a spatial system to keep the item within the world for spatial context to the UI element; however, we did not want it to be part of the narrative. This allows us to use a slight bit of immersion breaking to be in stark contrast to the rest of the game. When the player sees the tooltip pop up, it will be interesting. We can use this system throughout the entire vertical slice! We are creating a simple key item example, which will be an icon that floats in the game world, but Myvari will not be privy to its existence. This allows us to make a robust system; if we choose to use a different button for a different type of interaction, we can just change out the icon for the correct button to press.

Figure 8.8: Spatial UI mock-up

This very pink circle is just an item placeholder to be our indicator later on. With it being bright pink, there is no mistaking it for a "completed" item later on!

We have gone over the definition of the user interface and explained our project's use of UI. Now we need to take some time to go over how we actually made the UI work.

Unity UI

Before we dive fully into our implementation of UI in our project, we will go over the basics of Unity's UI system. This will give you an understanding of what items we are using in our systems as well as a couple that we aren't using that you could use in your projects later. There are two main parts to make this work:

- Unity Canvas system
- Unity UI components

We need to go over the Unity Canvas system in a bit of detail first before we start implementing the UI with code so you have a good foundation of its inner workings before trying to add art to it.

Unity canvas system

Unity places its UI inside a canvas system. This is a GameObject that has several components on it by default. To make a canvas, right-click in the **Hierarchy** window and choose **UI**, then **Canvas**. This can be seen in *Figure 8.9* below.

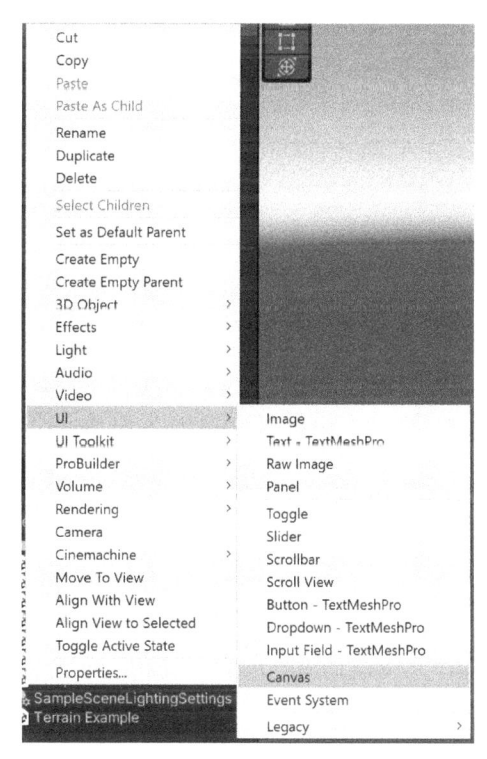

Figure 8.9: Menu to create a canvas

When this gets created, you will have a Canvas GameObject and an Event System GameObject. If there is already an Event System on that level where it was created, only the Canvas would be created.

The Canvas has a Rect transform, and it also has a Canvas component, a Canvas Scalar component, and a Graphic Raycaster component. We will look into each of these in light detail to explain their purpose.

There is also an Event System that could've been created if there wasn't another in the scene hierarchy already. This will house the messaging for input to the UI.

> If you are using the new input system, please make sure to click on this and replace the StandaloneInputModule with the InputSystemUIInputModule. This allows the event system to know which input systems are working in the project.

Why don't we take a look at the components individually, starting with the Rect transform, Canvas, Canvas Scalar, and then the Graphic Raycaster in more detail?

Rect transform

The canvas itself has a Rect transform, but it's meant to be a parent of the other UI, so its Rect transform needs to be read-only. Right-click on the canvas and choose **UI > Button** to make a child button inside the canvas so we can look at the Rect transform clearly.

Below in *Figure 8.10*, you can see the button's Rect transform component in the inspector where you may be expecting the regular Transform component. We still have the position, rotation, and scale options in our Rect transform, but we also have the width, height, pivot, and anchors.

When working with UI, it's best to leave the scale as *1, 1, 1*. This allows the canvas to set the scaling if needed. The safest way to make size changes is through the width and height values.

Rotation will rotate from the pivot location, which is a small blue circle and can be changed from the values of the **Pivot** fields.

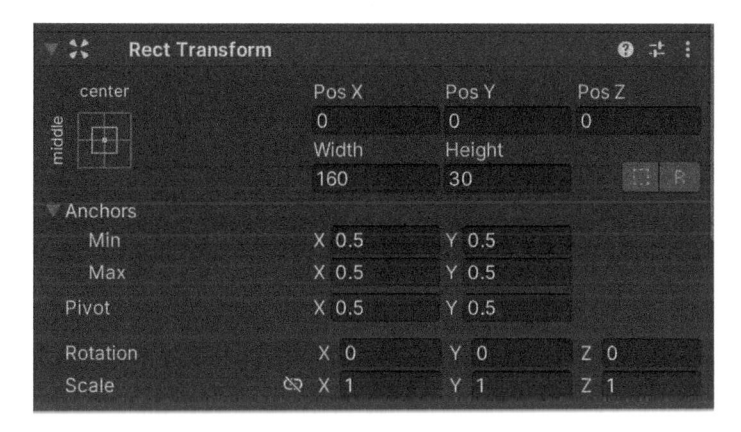

Figure 8.10: Rect Transform component

The position fields will set the local location of the GameObject. When you need to make changes to the size of the UI element, it's best to use the Rect tool instead of scaling. Inside the scene view, there is a Rect tool button, shown in *Figure 8.11* below, which will allow you to change the size of the UI, which will update the position, width, and height.

Figure 8.11: Rect tool used on the selected button

The pivot of the UI element is an *x* or *y* value that is a normalized value to the width and height of the element. This means that a value of 0.5 in both will place the pivot at 50% of the width and height, or local center, of the item.

The last unique item is the anchors. The anchors are designed to allow the UI elements to remain in place, even if the canvas scales. This could happen if you have multiple devices or resolution changes. There are **Anchors** options of **Min/Max**, which will set each anchor to its corresponding normalized value similar to the pivot location. Doing this by hand sometimes takes a little while, so we have a handy tool to make it easier. If you click on the top left of the **Rect Transform** it opens up a useful tool that allows you to select from common anchor options.

This looks like *Figure 8.12* below.

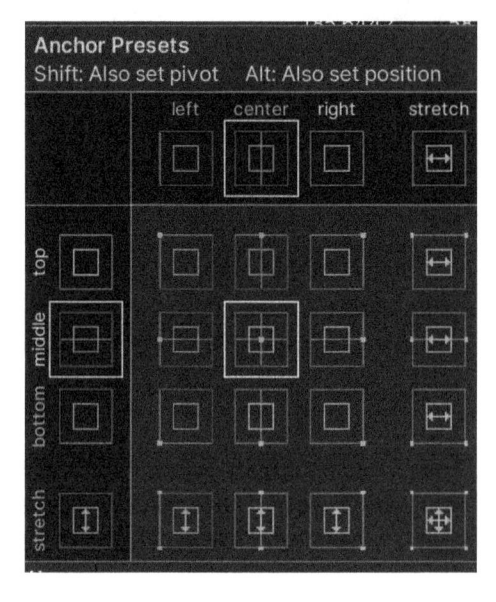

Figure 8.12: Anchor common options

What this tool allows you to do is select the most common anchor positions for the GameObject you are working on. There are two primary types of anchoring: **Positional** and **Stretched**. The 3x3 grid in the middle of this tool will make it so the UI in question will be anchored and not stretch or change when the screen resolution is different from what you have built for. This is a good option only if the resolution will not change drastically. The second type is stretching, which is located around the right and bottom edges. If your game is built with 1920x1080 resolution and the player chooses to play on an ultra-wide monitor, you may want to allow for some scaling on certain UI elements. If it is a 4k monitor with a 16:9 aspect ratio, then you will need to think about stretching all your elements; otherwise, the UI will appear very small.

Anchoring is a bit of an art form. The tricks above that were outlined will treat you well. The best way to go about properly anchoring is by playing the game in the editor and resizing it. It may not give you every scenario, but it will give you a good perspective on how the UI elements are reacting to a resolution change.

Canvas component

The canvas component only houses a few options, but they are crucial! In *Figure 8.13* below you can see the sections that we will go through.

Figure 8.13: Canvas component

We have **Render Mode** with a few options below it: **Pixel Perfect**, **Sort Order**, and **Target Display**. After that, we have **Additional Shader Channels**. Let's look at these options one by one.

Render Mode

There are three render modes that can be chosen: **Screen Space - Overlay**, **Screen Space - Camera**, and **World Space**. They each have a certain type of use and games can have multiple canvases in their world that fit their needs. As we go through them, think about how we might use them in our current project. After we describe all the features of the Unity UI we will get into the implementation.

Screen Space - Overlay

This is a common canvas rendering mode. What is nice about this mode is that it can be used within its own scene and loaded additively to your game for runtime. This allows you to make mobile menus that are separate from the PC monitor menu systems with ease. This works very well; however, it should only be used with simple UI. If you are going to be dragging around UI elements or animating them from a mouse context, such as rollover, then it's best to use the **Camera** option.

A good example of this type of canvas is the main menu or a HUD, which isn't very interactive.

Screen Space - Camera

As with the overlay option, this is a great mode if you are going to be making functions that utilize the `EventTrigger` class. You also cannot instantiate this like overlay mode. It must already be in the scene and have a camera that it will be referencing for bounds. It will attach itself to the camera, so if you make this change and it disappears on you, double-click your camera and it will be right there!

A great example of this mode is something similar to an ARPG where you need to drag and drop equipment to equip the items.

World Space

This rendering mode for the canvas is used when you need a menu that is in the world space. The best way to explain this is through best use cases. You would use this when you want chat bubbles over your character's head in space. You could want landmarks in UI that are selectable, which could potentially use a **World Space** canvas. It would be best if that landmark had text or another form of UI attached to it as well.

Render Mode options

Underneath the **Render Mode** are three options:

- **Pixel Perfect** – This is only used if you are working within 2D space where the UI needs to be exact to every pixel. It helps develop the UI to the constraints of the pixels in creation.
- **Sort Order** – By default the sort order is set to work through the hierarchy under the **Canvas**. The higher up an item is on the hierarchy, the sooner it will be rendered. You can overwrite this by typing in a value. Lower values will render first. Higher values are sent lower down the list. This is helpful if you want a single item to always be at the back. Just put 999 in for the value and it will always be rendered after the others regardless of the hierarchy order.
- **Target Display** – Should be used if you need another UI for a second display. You can set this up to display only on the second display. This can be used for up to eight displays. The use case for this would be for games similar to racing games, which commonly use three curved monitors.

Additional Shader Channels

When in overlay, the UI generally will not include normals, tangents, and so on. Use dropdown shown in *Figure 8.14* to select them.

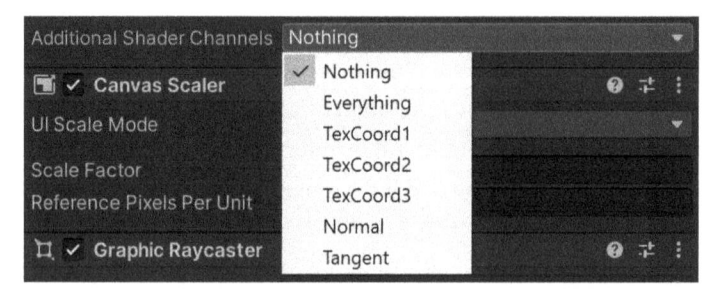

Figure 8.14: Additional Shader Channel options

Chapter 8 185

These would need to be selected if you specifically need them in your UI elements. Otherwise, leave it on **Nothing**.

Canvas Scaler

This component is in charge of making sure the scaling is correct for all the child UI objects under the GameObject with this component attached. It is not only in charge of scaling the UI itself, but also the font sizes and any image borders attached to images.

There are several unique parameters with the Canvas Scaler component. They are placed in the window depending on which of the UI scale modes are chosen. There are three UI scale modes.

Constant Pixel Size

This is used when you need to keep the pixel size the same regardless of the screen changing. The use case for this is if you know that you will be playing this game with a single resolution. If your game can be scaled at all, then you must work through dynamically setting the scale factor and ensuring your pixels per unit are the same as well. These parameters are seen in *Figure 8.15* below.

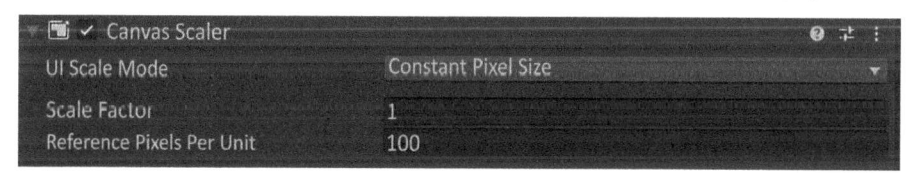

Figure 8.15: Canvas Scaler component Constant Pixel Size UI Scale Mode

If you think that your game will be adjusted at any point then consider working with the **Scale With Screen Size** option.

Scale With Screen Size

When you choose **Scale With Screen Size**, there are different parameters that pop up than with the **Constant Pixel Size** option. As seen below in *Figure 8.16*, we have **Reference Resolution**, **Screen Match Mode**, the **Match** slider, and **Reference Pixels Per Unit**.

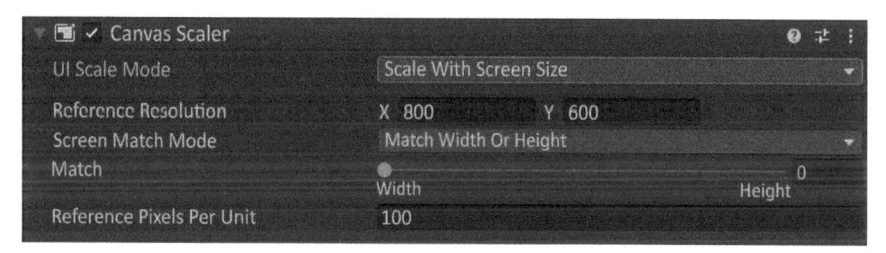

Figure 8.16: Canvas Scaler component Scale With Screen Size mode

- **Reference Resolution** – The resolution you'd expect the most-used screen resolution to be. From there it will scale down or up from the different resolutions the players may be playing from.
- **Screen Match Mode** – Contains three options:
    - **Match Width Or Height** – This will allow the application to match a blend of width to height when it's changed. This works pretty well overall until you hit ultra-wide monitors. This is also the only option where the **Match** slider is available to change. With the next two options, this slider will not be visible.
    - **Expand** – This means that the canvas will scale up but will be no smaller than the reference resolution. This is excellent as it expands width or height needs. This option is by far my favorite to work with.
    - **Shrink** – This option is just like the **Expand** option but it will scale down and not get larger than the **Reference Resolution**. This works well, but you have to work from a large resolution from the start.
- **Reference Pixels Per Unit** – This option refers to how many pixels are in a centimeter (which is a Unity unit). This is very important to pay attention to when you are making a 2D game with sprite options. If you have your sprite set to 100 pixels per unit and this **Reference pixels per unit** is set to 50, your sprite will be twice as big as expected.

Constant Physical Size

This is similar to the **Constant Pixel Size** mode; however, this works with physical units, as seen below in *Figure 8.17*. You may be comfortable with sizing in these units rather than pixels.

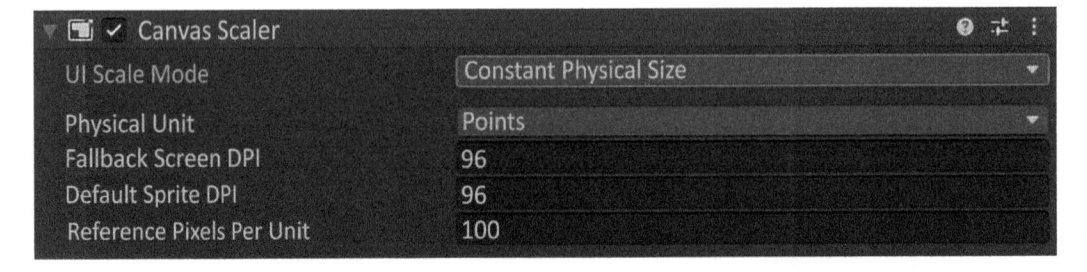

Figure 8.17: Canvas Scaler component Constant Physical Size

If it is the case that these units are better for you to use, then make sure you change the scale of all your fonts to these scales. The list of the physical options is shown below in *Figure 8.18*.

Centimeters
Millimeters
Inches
✓ Points
Picas

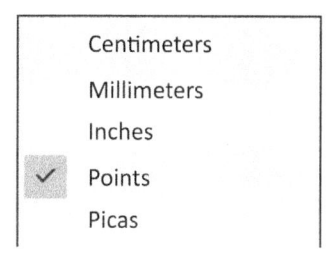

Figure 8.18: Physical unit options

Working with any of these options will force you to change all of your UI items to fit within the scale units of the same type. For example, it is common for sizing in pixels to be 300 wide, whereas 300 centimeters is massive! The scale should probably be 0.1. For this reason we would recommend that you work through your systems and know which one you will be using if you want to use this scaling mode from the beginning.

The last component is the **Graphic Raycaster**. This is the second-to-last default item that comes with the canvas. Let's explain how the **Graphic Raycaster** works with the canvas.

Graphic Raycaster Component

This component is created on the canvas. The purpose for this is to be the function of what your mouse is clicking on. Below are the available parameters for the **Graphic Raycaster**, in *Figure 8.19*:

Graphic Raycaster	
Script	GraphicRaycaster
Ignore Reversed Graphics	✓
Blocking Objects	None
Blocking Mask	Everything

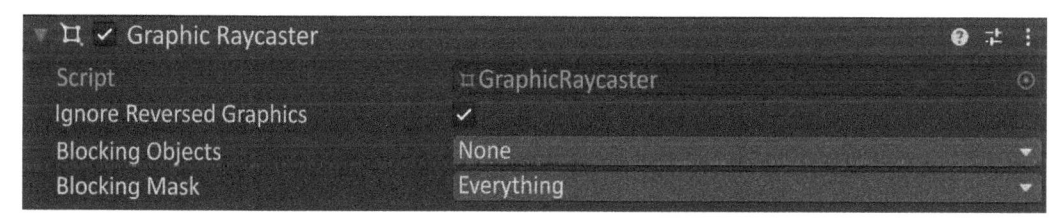

Figure 8.19: GraphicRaycaster Component

There are three parameters to quickly go over here.

- **Ignore Reversed Graphics** – This parameter ensures that you cannot click on objects that are turned around. Remember that backfaces are culled in the camera. You can flip elements of the UI off by flipping them around, but they would still be clickable without this being checked.

- **Blocking Objects** – This allows for items that are 2D or 3D in front of the UI to block clicking the UI. This defaults to none.

- **Blocking Mask** – This parameter allows you to place layers to block the UI. Since UIs are sprites, they are generally a rectangle and can overlap fairly easily. To get around this you can make a UI block layer, which will allow you to place objects in front to block clicking even if it's invisible, with alpha being 0.

We took the time to go over these default items as they are the primary items you will see when you start working with Unity's UI. There are quite a few more options to learn in time as you create more UI, but this foundation will help you get started. Next, we will look into some UI objects to add to your canvas.

Unity UI objects

We now have a canvas! This is great because we've learned how it works with dynamic resolutions and how to set it up for your game's needs. Now we need to add some objects for it to be useful. Unity UI objects are broken up into two types: **Visual** and **Interactive**.

Visual elements are what you expect. They are items that are meant to be visual elements only, but they can be attached to interactive items. The following are examples of these objects, including a description and a visual example:

- **Image** – There are two types of images: **Raw Image** and **Image**. **Raw Image** is only used where you want no border; however, it's generally best to just use the **Image** object. **Images** take sprites and a border can be added to them. You can also tint the sprite within the **Image** component in the inspector. There is also another UI option named **Panel**. This is another UI object with an image component attached designed to be a panel of UI. The only difference between **Image** and **Panel** is that **Panel** will be set to stretch and fill in the entire canvas by default.

Figure 8.20: Default Image and Image UI component

- **Mask** – A **Mask** component will cut out the GameObjects underneath it. This is great for masking out extra items underneath it that may not want to be seen. Below, we added a mask to the image and added another image below it. The outline is the mask; the image that should be a square is cropped on the top and bottom due to the mask hiding it.

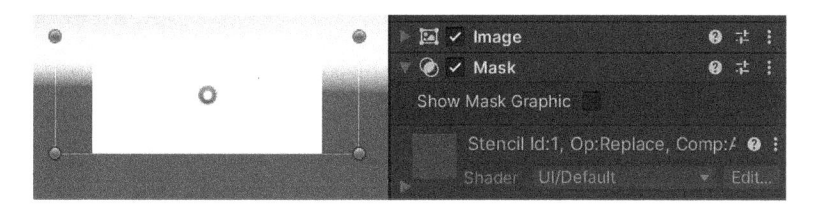

Figure 8.21: Masked default image from Figure 8.20

- **Text** – This is text! Sometimes this is also known as a **Label**. You are able to add a specific font to your UI if you need it. When you create it, you will see **TextMeshPro** after the text option. This is due to **TextMeshPro (TMP)** being so popular that it's been integrated into the core Unity features.

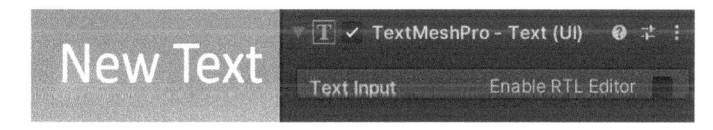

Figure 8.22: TextMeshPro UI component

Interactive items can house visual elements, but they come with interactive `UnityEvents`. The following are examples of these, including a description and a visual example:

- **Button** – This interactive object comes with a label by default in its hierarchy. It also comes with a `UnityEvent` for when it's clicked. It has the ability to be tinted if it's highlighted, pressed, or disabled. This is a primary function of UI with interaction.

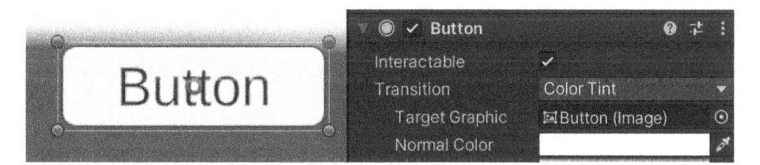

Figure 8.23: Button UI component

- **Dropdown** – A **Dropdown** is a user-selectable field of a predefined group of options. When the user makes a change to this value, it will invoke the `OnValueChanged` `UnityEvent`.

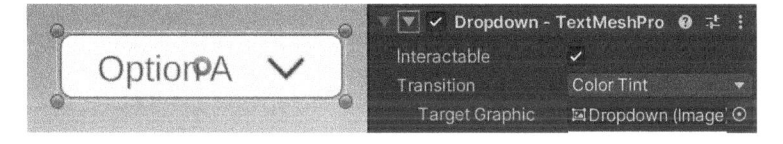

Figure 8.24: Dropdown UI component

- **Input Field** – This is a standard input field where the user clicked into it or "focused" on it. There is an interesting property we'd like to mention called **Content Type**. This allows the developer to error check without needing to write code. Setting this to **Integer Number**, for example, will only allow the user to input numbers. This interactable object has two `UnityEvents`:
    - `OnValueChanged` – This will return the string of what value is currently in the input value every time a change has happened
    - `EndEdit` – This will return the string once the user clicks somewhere else or otherwise loses focus on that input field

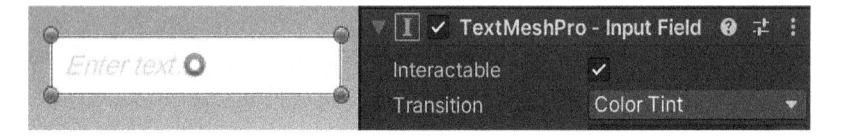

    Figure 8.25: Input Field UI component

- **Scrollbar** – The **Scrollbar** is used generally in conjunction with a **Scroll** Rect. Its purpose is to be a scrollbar for a field if you need something that might be large. The value is from 0 to 1 regardless of how large the scrollbar is, and it can be vertical or horizontal. It also has a `UnityEvent` that can be used to know the `OnValueChanged`, so that you can return the value when you move the scrollbar.

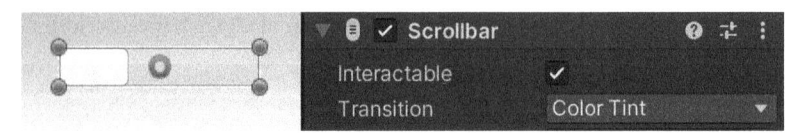

    Figure 8.26: Scrollbar UI component

- **Scroll Rect** – This can also be called a scroll view. This can be put in conjunction with two scroll bars to set up vertical and horizontal scrolling if needed. This is also set up with a mask to hide information outside the mask itself. It also has an `OnValueChanged` `UnityEvent` on the scrolling of the **Scroll** Rect.

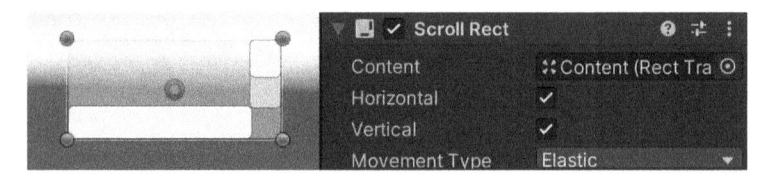

    Figure 8.27: Scroll Rect UI component

- **Slider** – This is a slider that has a draggable object, which will set the value of the slider from a minimum value and a maximum value that you set. It also has a UnityEvent, which returns a value from that min and max value OnValueChanged.

Figure 8.28: Slider UI component

- **Toggle** – This is a checkbox that has a label assigned to it. When clicked, you can use the OnValueChanged UnityEvent to evaluate if it's on or off.

Figure 8.29: Toggle UI component

- **Toggle Group** – If you add toggles to a group, you can set this group to allow only one within the group to be selectable. If you select another one in the assigned grouping, it will switch off the previously on toggle and switch on the selected toggle. There is an **Allow Switch Off** option, which lets you select the currently selected toggle to make none of the groups selected. There is no unique UnityEvent connected to the group itself; however, each toggle still has its own OnValueChanged event that will trigger. One small note, if you are going to make a toggle group, make sure that each toggle has that **Group** assigned in their **Toggle** component.

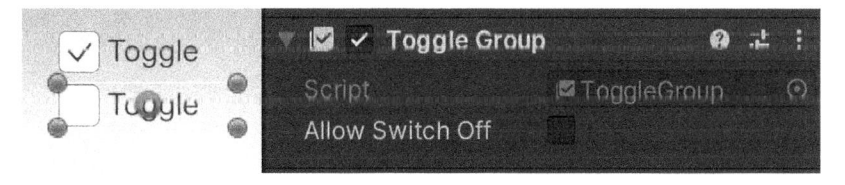

Figure 8.30: Toggle Group UI component

These are all good examples of UI items available for the Unity UI. From here, we need to go through the implementations of the Unity UI to fit our game. We previously went over the design; now we need to look into the code to see how it works when players need to interact with it.

Implementation

We need to now look at our implementation. Knowing what all of the UI objects look like and their purpose is helpful, but we now need to see what it looks like to have them in practice. We will start off with the **Main Menu** before the game starts for the player. After that, we will break into the journal or escape menu. Then we will finish up with the spatial UI for interaction with the game's mechanics.

When reading this part, remember that we will not be going over all of the lines of the script as at this point we assume that you've gotten comfortable with looking at the code that we have on GitHub.

If at any time you feel confused about how the book is laid out for explaining the code, ensure that you pull up the scripts that are being referenced and get yourself realigned. The primary goal of us explaining code in this manner is to be as concise as possible about what we are doing and why. Seeing every line of code doesn't help with that!

That being said, let's get into the main menu implementation.

Main menu implementation

As we wanted this menu to be non-diegetic, but sitting in the world space to give an illusion of space, we chose to go with a **World Space** canvas. Below in *Figure 8.31* is the hierarchy and the inspector with collapsed components that have no changes from the default.

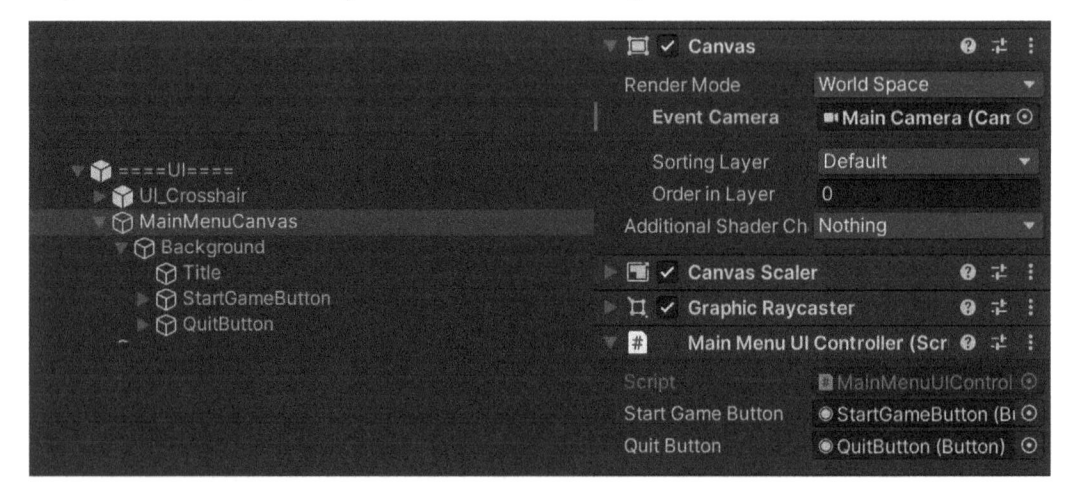

Figure 8.31: Left, hierarchy for MainMenuCanvas; Right, Inspector for Canvas

The `MainMenuUIControl.cs` script is how we will control our main menu. When working with the UI, you need to make sure that you import the UI library:

```
using UnityEngine.UI;
```

When you use the UI library you will be able to access all the UI objects and their methods. Though the next line I'd like to place here isn't specifically part of the UI, I'd like to show you something we haven't talked about yet. This method is called `FindObjectOfType`. We know that there will only be one `MyvariThirdPersonMovement` class in the scene ever, so we are using this method to get it and then ask for its parent so we know the player root.

```
playerRoot = FindObjectOfType<MyvariThirdPersonMovement>().transform.parent;
```

We also need to disable the character and set up listeners for the event system so it knows what to do when we click on the buttons in the canvas.

To disable the character, we have a method we call on awake to turn off what we need to. When using Cinemachine, you want to disable all the cameras that are available or Cinemachine will go to one of the cameras. Then we disable the player's control script only. This allows the characters' animations to keep playing in place, but we just can't control her.

On awake:

```
SetPlayerEnabled(false);
```

Separate private implementation on line 50:

```
void SetPlayerEnabled(bool enable)
    {
        CinemachineVirtualCamera[] cams = playerRoot.GetComponentsInChildren<CinemachineVirtualCamera>(true);
        foreach (CinemachineVirtualCamera cam in cams)
        {
            cam.gameObject.SetActive(enable);
        }
        playerRoot.GetComponentInChildren<MyvariThirdPersonMovement>().enabled = enable;
    }
```

We've set up listeners several times before, but let's take a look at them as well:

```
startGameButton.onClick.AddListener(OnStartGameButtonPressed);
quitButton.onClick.AddListener(OnQuitButtonPressed);
```

What is happening here is that the respective buttons that are in place for startGameButton and quitButton will activate the methods in their listeners when they are clicked.

The OnStartGameButtonPressed method looks like this:

```
void OnStartGameButtonPressed()
    {
        SetPlayerEnabled(true);
        Cursor.lockState = CursorLockMode.Locked;
        Cursor.visible = false;
        this.gameObject.SetActive(false);
    }
```

When it's pressed it sets the character to enabled so we can use the input to move her around, lock and hide the mouse cursor, and disable the main menu so you can't see it anymore. If you hit the quit button, you will close the application. Unity has an easy way to quit the application:

```
Application.Quit();
```

This is the entire main menu! The trickiest part of what we needed to do was to lock the player down. Otherwise, they would've been moveable while the main menu is up, which is not what we wanted in this case. Next, we need to work on the journal.

Journal implementation

In most games, there is a common concept of an escape menu. This is to say, when you press the *Escape* key, you will encounter a menu that generally pauses the gameplay. In our case, we wanted it so when you pressed *Escape*, our character would open up her book and look at it. This would be good as, it allows the game to pause a bit as the camera moves in to see the book and we can house the normal escape menu options, such as resume and quit the game. There will be some similar concepts from the main menu here in this, such as locking and unlocking the cursor. There is also a player enabling method, which is the same as in the main menu as well.

Below, in *Figure 8.32*, is another representation of the hierarchy and script in the inspector for the Journal UI. One of the unique items in the public fields is that we are using an input system as opposed to only relying on the mouse inputs.

Chapter 8

For us to load up the journal, we can press the letter *B* or the *Escape* key.

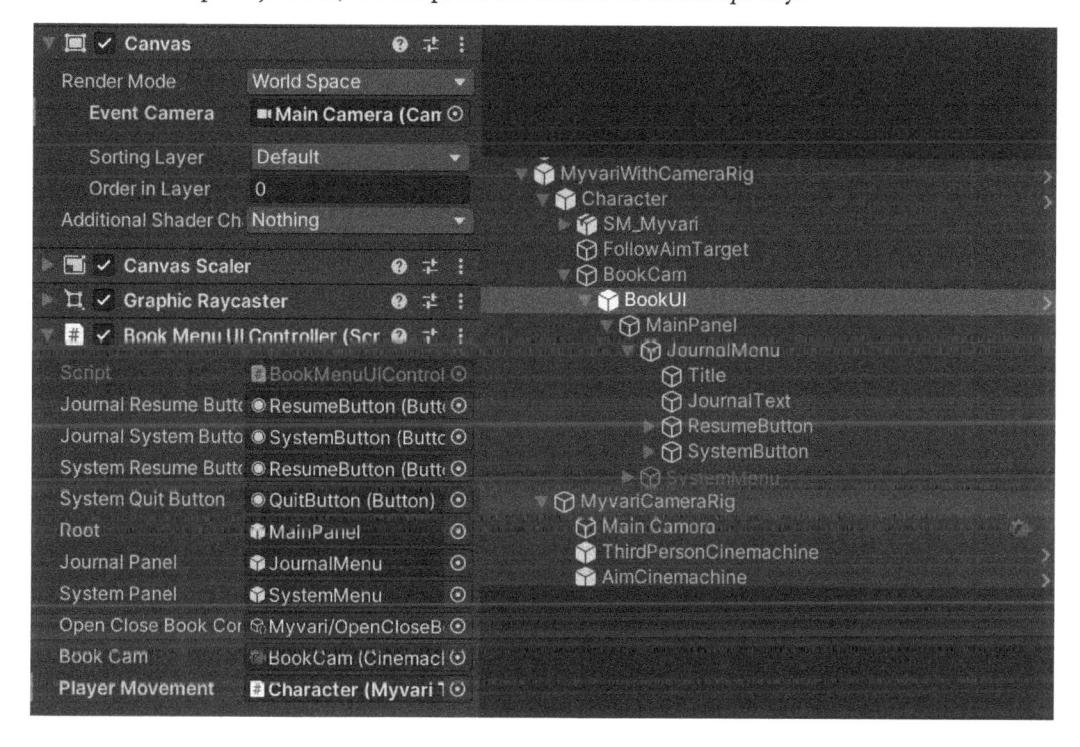

Figure 8.32: Left, Journal hierarchy; Right, Book inspector panel

This is an interesting turning point in the book for us. All of the coding involved with this script has been done previously. I recommend opening the script and looking at it to help remember the prior coding lessons.

The last piece of UI is the spatial UI that helps players know that the item they are looking at is interactable. Let's break this implementation down.

Interaction UI implementation

This is unique to set up as there is no canvas for this item. We will have a single GameObject that is in the scene and we will move it to the location that is needed and turn it off or on depending on what we are looking at if it's intractable. We have a simple GameObject, which is a sphere without a material on it so it's bright pink.

In the script `InteractiveHighlight.cs`, on `awake` we find this GameObject and grab its renderer. If it's not found, then we have an error that lets us know we can't find it.

We grab the mesh renderer so that we can disable it when we don't need to see it.

```
void Awake()
    {
        highlightIndicator = GameObject.
FindGameObjectWithTag("InteractionHighlight");
        if (highlightIndicator == null)
        {
            Debug.LogError("Highlight indicator not found in scene");
        }
        highlightIndicatorRenderer = highlightIndicator.
GetComponent<MeshRenderer>();
    }
```

Now that we have the highlight indicator, we should perform the hiding and movement of the indicator itself. We are using a raycast to know if we are hitting an interactable item or a piece of the game's puzzle pieces. This is a physics method, so we will put this on the fixed update. This will ensure that the code is run in accordance with the physics update timing that we talked about in *Chapter 7, Rigid Bodies and Physics Interaction*.

```
void FixedUpdate()
    {
        Ray ray = new Ray(transform.position, transform.forward);
        if (Physics.Raycast(ray, out RaycastHit hit, maxDistance, rayMask,
QueryTriggerInteraction.Collide))
        {
            highlightIndicator.transform.position = hit.transform.position
+ new Vector3(0f, height, 0f);
            if (!highlightIndicatorRenderer.enable
```

```
    d)
            {
                highlightIndicatorRenderer.enabled = true;
            }
        }
        else
        {
            if (highlightIndicatorRenderer.enabled)
            {
                highlightIndicatorRenderer.enabled = false;
            }
        }
    }
```

As stated previously, the fixed update here runs on physics timing and is checking to see if what is raycast from the center of the screen is hitting items on the two masks. If it is hit and it's within the max distance, then move the highlighted piece and turn on its renderer. If not, then turn it off!

Summary

This chapter was quite meaty with information. Even though we only had three pieces of UI to go over, we needed to break it into all of these pieces to help you with your future projects. You will now also have a strong sense of how other game developers design their UI for their games. During *Chapter 12, Final Touches*, we will be going over the clean-up of it and how polishing the UI makes a difference to the player's experience. In the next chapter, we will go over visual effects and some particle systems.

9
Visual Effects

The game does not currently have all of its features. We've gone from concept to blockout, then developed the game into a state where it is playable. This doesn't mean we are finished quite yet! We need to look at how we can bring more emotional immersion to the player. Luckily for us, Unity provides fantastic assets and tools for us to take the current state of our game and visually turn it up another notch. This is done through various vehicles, such as shaders, particles, and other polishing tools that we will cover in *Chapter 12*, *Final Touches*.

These topics are very complex. For now, we will go over the main focus of visual effects by looking at shaders and particles at a high level. Then, we will progress to an overview of their advanced forms. Because we are using the **Universal Render Pipeline** (**URP**) for this project, we will go over important tools such as Shader Graph, VFX Graph, and Shuriken. Shader Graph visually displays shader detailing and coding. VFX Graph was created to help you understand the various properties of GPU particles. Shuriken, a CPU-focused particle authoring tool, is available in all render pipelines. We will cover that as well.

In this chapter, the following topics will be covered:

- Visual effects overview
- Shader Graph
- Particle Systems:
    - Shuriken
    - VFX Graph

Visual effects overview

Getting started with visual effects may feel daunting at the onset. We currently have a simple scene. The world won't feel alive and immersive without time spent making deliberate answers to questions needing to be solved to progress the narrative and design of the game.

Throughout this book, you've worked through many general game design questions. You've been able to answer them yourself and may use them for any project you may want to work on. Then, you were given the answers we discovered ourselves while creating this project and how it would move forward. We had a pretty good idea of what the feel would be for the player: fantasy exploration in the simplest of terms. We now need to be able to go through our scene and find areas in which we need a touch more fantasy. Exploration is done through the mechanics and narrative design.

Fantasy is a broad term. We could have gone with any theme really. We decided to push through this vague starting point and found a theme of light science fiction focused on an ancient race. These beings hold onto the power of the celestial bodies of the natural space surrounding them. Working with nature, they at some point constructed a cave the player will explore. We need to come up with a way to embody this storytelling through visual gameplay, and the player accepting themselves as the main character of this world is what we are aiming for.

To carry out this visual storytelling, we need to incorporate the multiple visual effects tools available in Unity. Shader Graph allows us to build shaders that can have interesting properties that play with lights and twinkling effects in various ways. Shuriken provides us with particle systems to add ambient dust, glowing particles around bioluminescent plants, and simple details of other fantasy elements. VFX Graph allows us to push simple particles to the limit and bring GPU systems into play. By pushing GPU systems into play, VFX Graph will give us the ability to use many particles. Though this isn't practical, you could spawn tens of millions of particles. Finally, we will use the lighting in Unity to provide hints to the player for where to look and set the mood and tone of the current action, system, or place.

To start this chapter, we will be laying the foundation of terms and going over the individual visual effects tools in detail. After these explanations, we can then expand upon how we incorporate the tools that Unity has to offer into our workspace to create a visually immersive environment. Moving forward, this section may become a useful reference point to come back to re-familiarize yourself with the tools and their purpose.

Shader Graph

Shader Graph is a visual scripting tool designed to allow artist-driven shader creation. Shaders are scripts that inform the graphics pipeline how to render materials. A material is an instance of a shader with parameters set for a certain mesh inside of a GameObject. A simple example of this could be leather. If you think of leather, you could probably think about many different types of leather. What color is it? Is it shiny? Does it have a unique texture? All of these options are parameters in the shader that can be set in the material to render the object properly.

In Unity, a shader is written in **High-Level Shader Language** (**HLSL**). Knowing how to properly write this code requires a detailed understanding of the graphics pipeline in your computer and can be a bit daunting to get going. The graphics pipeline is a complex conceptual model. Simplified, the computer goes through layers and stages to understand what 3D visual graphics are in a scene, then takes that information and renders those visuals to a 2D screen.

In fact, just reading the paragraph above might've seemed a bit confusing. This is natural. There are many moving parts here and we will break this down within this portion of the chapter. In an effort to not dive in too deep with HLSL, we will be focusing purely on Shader Graph. If after spending time in Shader Graph you want to move into a more technical position, we recommend learning HLSL and handwriting shaders. Once you have learned HLSL and handwriting shaders you will have a solid foundation of general shader creation.

Let's go through the setup of Shader Graph first, then how to create a shader. We should then take some time to talk about basic and commonly used nodes that are used to create shaders. Nodes are a visual representation of a block or chunk of code. These nodes can be linked together to create larger functions of visually layered effects.

Setup

We have been talking about using the **URP** project, which should automatically have Shader Graph installed on it. If it isn't installed, you can easily install it by heading to the **Package Manager** and installing it from the Unity Registry packages.

Figure 9.1 below shows what's needed to install Shader Graph properly.

If you have a green checkmark like in the figure below, then it is installed already!

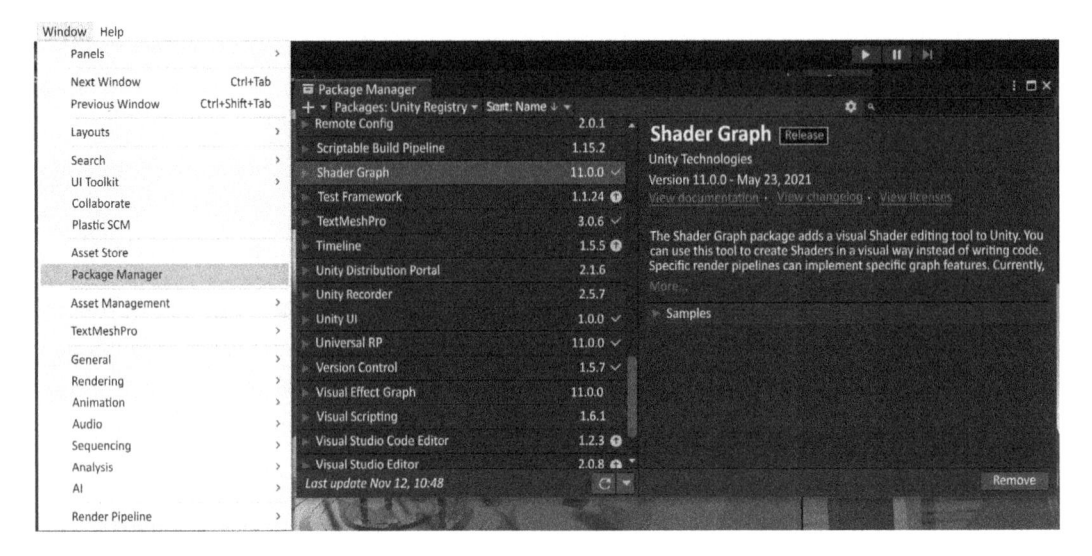

Figure 9.1: Checking if Shader Graph is installed

Now that we have either installed Shader Graph or verified it's installed, let's move on to creating your first shader.

Creation

Right-clicking in an open area of your project window gives you the marking menu for that space. We want to make a new shader, so we mouse over **Create** > **Shader** > **Universal Render Pipeline** and then get four options. These four options are the basics from URP that automatically set up the shader settings for you. Refer to *Figure 9.2* for the path to follow to create your shader.

Chapter 9   203

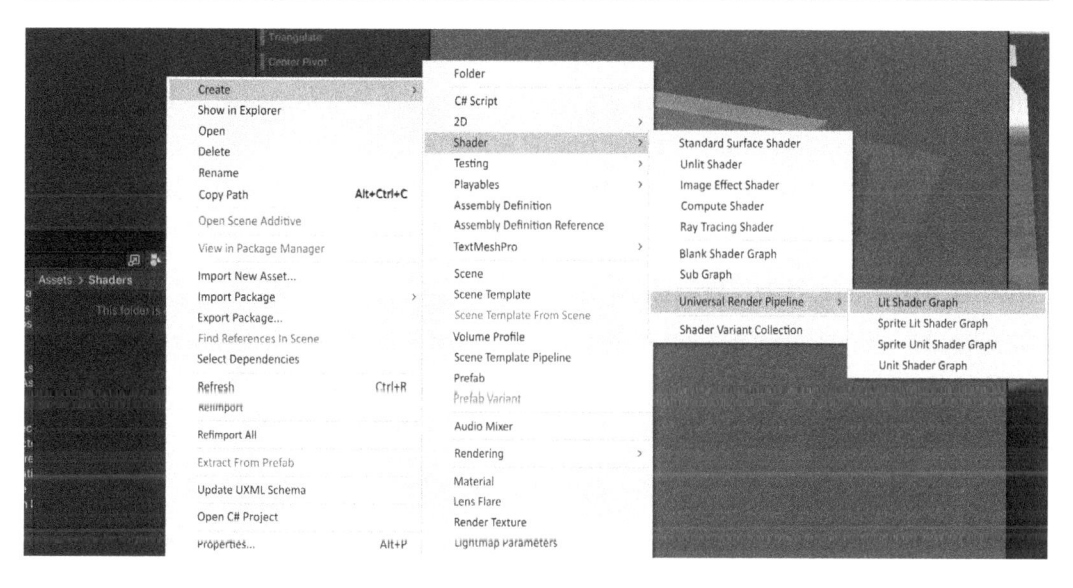

Figure 9.2: Path to create a shader in Unity Editor

You may be wondering, "Which one should I choose?" If so, that is a great question. Let's go over all four of these types just in case you want to mess around with any of the other types after we move along with our choice. From top to bottom we have **Lit**, **Sprite Lit**, **Sprite Unlit**, and **Unlit** Shader Graphs to work with. Let's go through each of these types in that order.

Lit Shader Graph

The Lit Shader Graph lets you render 3D objects with real-world lighting information. The shaders that use this will be using a **Physically Based Rendering** (**PBR**) lighting model. A PBR model allows 3D surfaces to have a photo-realistic quality of materials like stone, wood, glass, plastic, and metals across various lighting conditions. With the Lit Shader's assistance, lighting and reflections across these objects can adhere to dynamic shifts, such as bright light to a dark cave environment, accurately.

Sprite Lit Shader Graph

URP comes with a 2D rendering and lighting system. This system would be used in this graph type as the items that this shader would be rendered on would be sprites. A sprite is a two-dimensional bitmap (an array of binary data that represents the color of each pixel) that is integrated into a larger scene. This will allow the sprites to take in the needed lighting information.

Sprite Unlit Shader Graph

This is similar to the Shader Lit Shader Graph above, but the difference with the Sprite Unlit Shader Graph is that it is considered always fully lit and will take in no lighting information. This graph also only uses the 2D rendering and lighting system in the URP.

Unlit Shader Graph

The unlit type of graph for URP uses the 3D PBR lighting model like the Lit Shader Graph type. The major difference is that it won't take in lighting information. This is the most performant shader in URP.

Shader Graph interface

Choose the Lit Shader Graph type for our Shader Graph. When you right-click in the project window, a new shader file will be created. Double-clicking this file will open the **Shader Graph** window.

There are some pieces we should go over so you can understand what is covered in the following subsections. We need to go over the **Master Stack**, **Blackboard**, **Graph Inspector**, **Main Preview**, and then **Nodes**. In *Figure 9.3* below, four out of five of these sections are displayed. We will be going over them in detail in this chapter.

Chapter 9   205

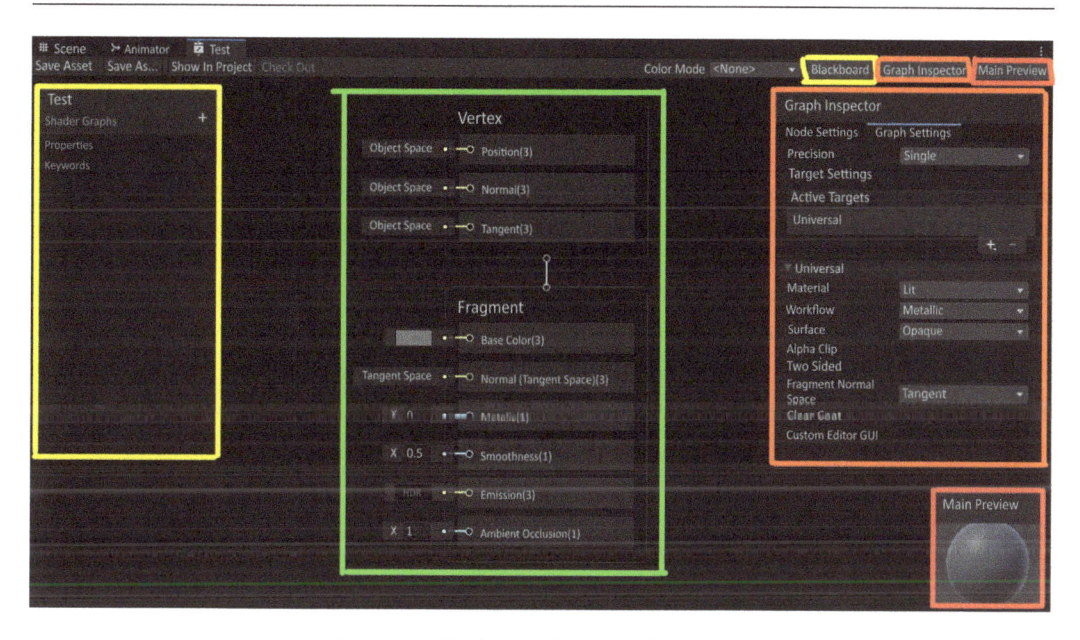

Figure 9.3: Shader Graph window breakdown

Master Stack

The green-outlined item in *Figure 9.3* is the Master Stack. There are two sections to the Master Stack, **Vertex** and **Fragment**. The **Vertex** block of the Master Stack contains instructions to the actual vertexes of the 3D object that the material with this assigned shader will be manipulated. Within this block, you can affect the vertex's **Position**, **Normal**, or **Tangent** attribute. These three attributes occur everywhere in a 2D and 3D environment. **Position** represents a vertex's location in object space. **Normal** is used to calculate which direction light reflects off or is emitted out from the surface. **Tangent** alters the appearance of vertexes on your surface to define the object's horizontal (U) texture direction.

In our case, we do not need to change any of the vertex attributes, so we will move on to the fragment shader portion and leave the object space alone.

Fragment instructions can be thought of as possible pixels on your screen. We can affect the pixels depending on the changes made to the inputs to the stack. The attributes that are listed in the fragment shader depend on the shader type we choose when making the shader.

The blocks inside of the **Fragment** stack are called Fragment Nodes. If you do not need a particular Fragment Node, you can remove it by right-clicking on the **Fragment Node** individually and selecting **Delete**. You can also add other Fragment Nodes to the stack by right-clicking the bottom of the **Fragment** frame and selecting **Add Node**.

In *Figure 9.4*, you can see a selection of all the node choices to add to the stack. If your shader isn't set up to accept those new Fragment Nodes, they will be gray and not usable. For now, let's go through the Lit Shader Fragment options.

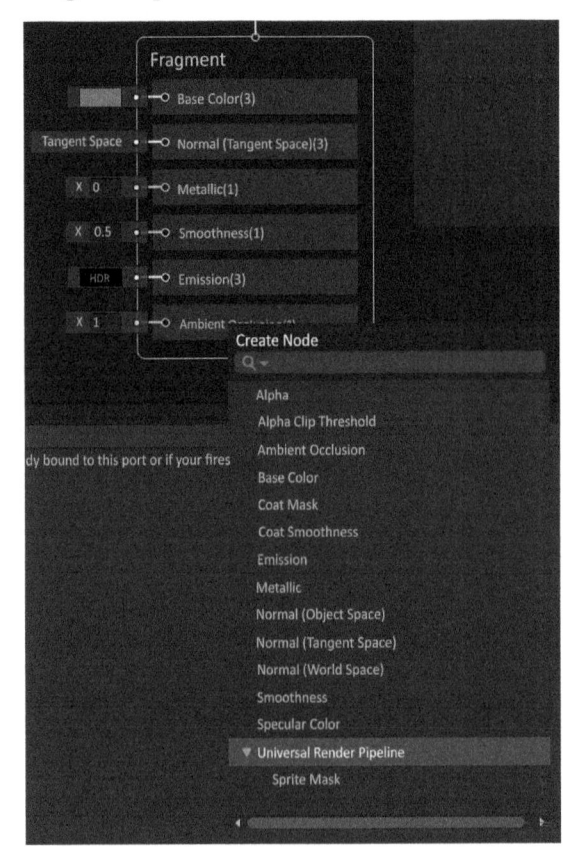

Figure 9.4: Fragment Node options

Chapter 9   207

The Fragment Nodes in the Fragment stack represent the pixels that will potentially be displayed in clip space or on your screen. 3D objects also have a 2D representation of their faces in the form of UVs. UVs are a two-dimensional texture representation of a 3D object. UVs have a flat, 2D axis, 0 (U) to 1 (V) graph. This particular UV graph is a representation of each vertex on this UV plane stretched over a 3D object. The UV graph is also called a UV texture space.

Looking at *Figure 9.5* below, you can see that the geometry has been unwrapped to make it flat. This is like papercraft or origami. Knowing how this works sets up the concept of how shaders can manipulate not only the vertex of a mesh but also the color of the faces.

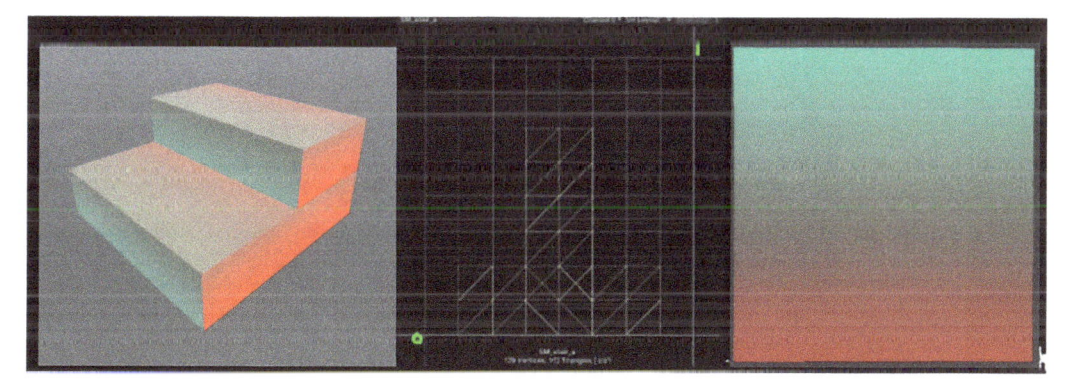

Figure 9.5: Basic mesh, UV layout, gradient on base color

We wanted to show you how we achieved the gradient within Shader Graph for *Figure 9.5*. Though this isn't the simplest graph we could've started with, it does a good job of breaking down some key concepts early.

If you look at *Figure 9.6* below, you will see our graph to build a gradient that we placed in the **Base Color**. The gradient is then applied to the 0-1 space of the 3D object we assigned this material with this shader. It is not a complex shader as it has hardcoded gradients coming from the UV node.

We will add more complexity to the parameters we make in the **Blackboard** in the next section.

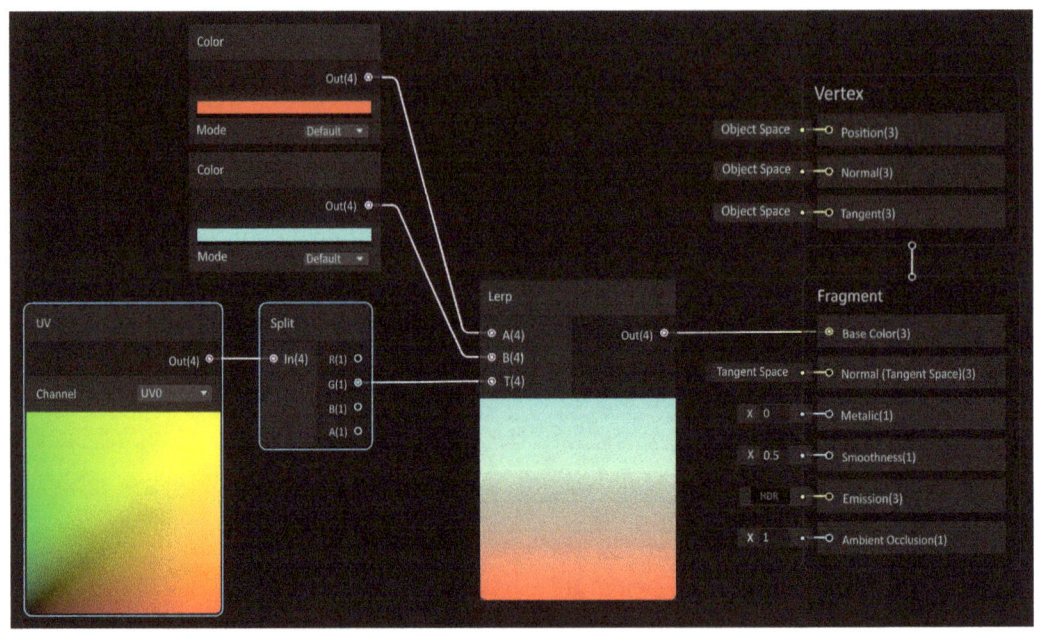

Figure 9.6: Test gradient shader

We will be breaking down commonly used nodes in the next part of this chapter. For now, a quick explanation of what we are doing will help break this down.

Base color

We are taking the UV's 0-1 space, represented here with two gradients, *x* and *y* in the Red and Green channels. Red and Green channels are a part of color space; there are **Red (R)**, **Green (G)**, **Blue (B)**, and **Alpha (A)** channels. RGB represents the color values. The Alpha channel indicates the opacity of each pixel, from 0 (fully transparent) through to 1 (opaque).

We've seen that the 0-1 space starts from the bottom left and ends linearly in the top right in Unity. This means that the Green channel will be a linear gradient from bottom to top. Splitting off that channel allows us to manipulate the 0-1 in a Lerp node, with red replacing black and teal replacing white. There is a lot going on throughout the next few sections, but stick with it! As we break down the nodes, it will be much easier to follow per node.

Normal

Normals tell each fragment how they are supposed to react to light that hits the face.

This is extremely useful to add detail to a face without changing the silhouette, reducing the number of polygons needed for higher detail. Looking at *Figure 9.7* below, you can see that it looks as though there are bumps pulled out of the cube. This isn't a color change; this is light reacting to the surface of the faces. If you look closely, there are no protrusions on the edges. This is because the shape of the cube didn't change. This is just a cube that acts as it does because of the normal maps.

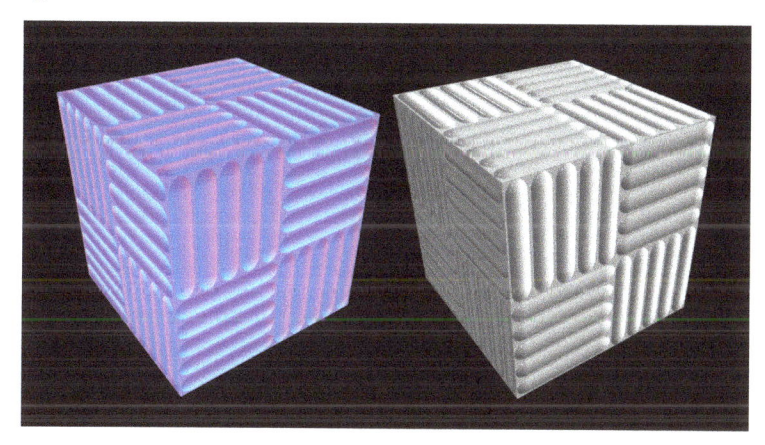

Figure 9.7: Normals on a cube

On the left side of *Figure 9.7*, the left cube is blue due to the normal map using its color scheme from the RGB channels in the tangent space. This means that a flat normal map would represent 0, 0, 1. Red and Green channels are used to represent the shifts in how the light should act on either the *x* tangent or the *y* tangent. When we work with materials in *Chapter 12, Final Touches*, we will go further into detail about the functions of a normal map.

Metallic

Metallic is exactly what it sounds like. This is how metallic the material is! That isn't a great definition though, so let's try to break it down a little.

The metallic field is a scaler float from 0 to 1, with 0 being not metallic and 1 being bare metal. Metallic materials take in their surrounding environment's color. In *Figure 9.8* we have four spheres with four different settings for their material properties. We're only using the URP/Lit shader that comes with URP out of the box to test these out. For this section we will only look at the left two spheres. The far-left sphere is white and the metal setting is set to 0. This material is not taking in any of the environment's color. It's only taking in lighting information and its base color of white.

The second sphere, though it still has white for a base color, has the metallic setting set to 1. The smoothness is set to 0.5 to be neutral, which you will hear more about shortly. If you look closely the second sphere has the Unity default skybox in the color. Now we need to throw in smoothness to this material.

Figure 9.8: From left to right: No metal, all metal, all metal not smooth, all metal all smooth

Smoothness

Continuing with *Figure 9.8*, we will move on to the right two spheres. The third sphere from the left is very interesting. This one has a base color of white, the metal setting set to 1, and smoothness set to 0. This means that the entire sphere is fully diffused! Diffused in this instance means that all the colors of the environment are blended across the whole sphere, leading to an almost perfect true neutral gray. The fourth sphere is the same, but smoothness is set to 1. This means that the entire sphere is reflecting the direct environment.

Emissive

For an object to emit or radiate light you look toward an **emissive map**. The purpose of an emissive map is to be able to push colors to have brighter values than 1. Pushing past the value of 1 allows that part of your object to glow brightly. This is useful for lava, sci-fi lights, or anything you want to emit brightness. Otherwise, the Fragment Node defaults to black and no emission is created.

Figure 9.9: Left is no emission, right has emission with 2.4 intensity, no bloom

This doesn't look like an emissive glowing mushroom! This is due to emission needing a post-processing volume. To do this, create an empty GameObject and name it _PostProcess. We're naming it this to give it a distinctly different name. Using the underscore as a prefix, we're letting our developers know that this object houses logic only. There aren't GameObjects for use in the game itself. Then add a **Volume** component, seen below in *Figure 9.10*.

Figure 9.10: Volume added to post-process GameObject

We're not done yet! We need to add a profile and an override to get our bloom set up. Pressing the **New** button on the right-hand side of the **Volume** component will create a profile for your settings to be added to. This allows you to store those settings for other scenes if you need to. When you add a profile, you will then be able to add an override.

We want to click on **Add Override**, then **Post Process**, and finally **Bloom**. Then select the Intensity Boolean checkbox to allow for intensity to be changed. Change it to 1. The settings are shown below in *Figure 9.11*.

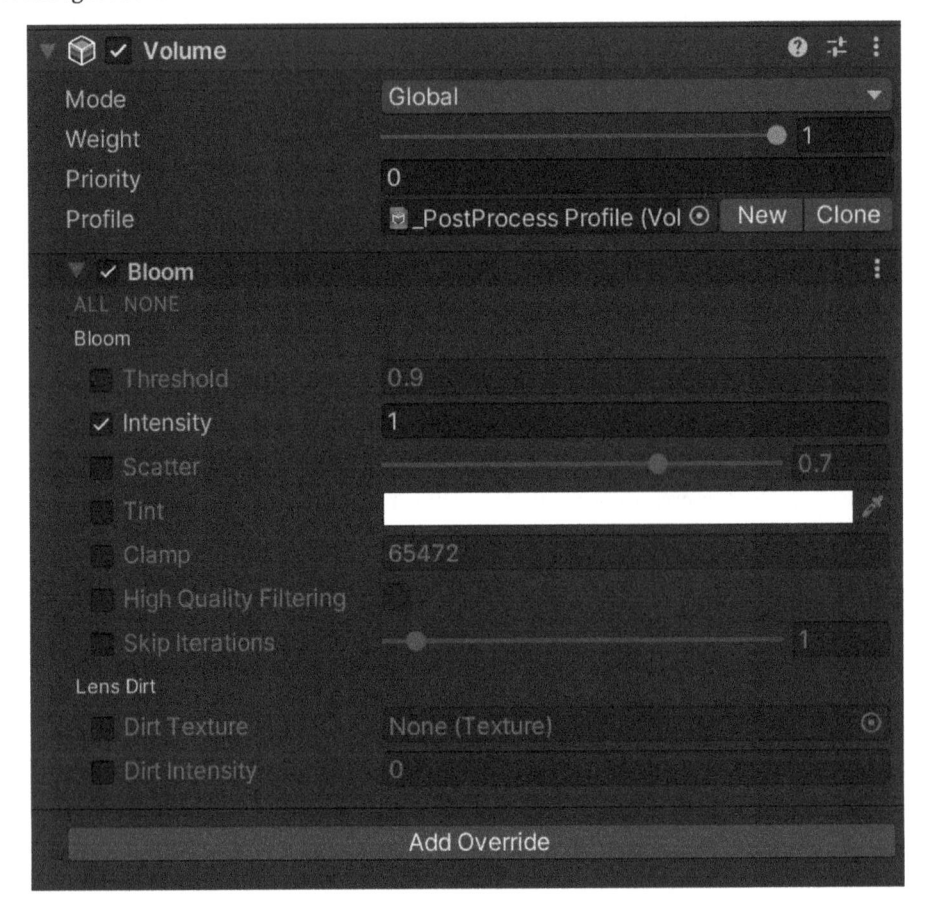

Figure 9.11: Bloom override for post-processing volume

Now we see it emitting light around the mushroom on the screen. This isn't adding light into the scene; it is only adding a brightness value outside of the mesh to the render on the screen.

Chapter 9 213

Figure 9.12: Left: no emissive, Right: emissive and bloom set up

We have a shiny, glowing mushroom! Go forth and add emission to things! We will now look into **Ambient Occlusion**.

Ambient Occlusion

The point of **Ambient Occlusion (AO)** is to add dark spots to sections to show creases. This adds a nice, clean effect of shadows even if there aren't any specific lights making shadows. AO is designed for light at all angles. This attribute expects values from 0 to 1. If you do not have an AO map for your model, it's best to leave it at 1. In *Chapter 12, Finishing Touches*, we will be working with Myvari's material, which will have an AO map to go over.

This was the master stack in summary. Each of the attributes on the stack can be used to provide unique shaders. Something that helps with even more customization is the **Blackboard** part of Shader Graph.

Blackboard

The **Blackboard** allows the user to create properties and keywords to use in shaders that can be dynamically changed in various ways. Properties can be used within the shader or be exposed to the material in the Inspector using the **Exposed** checkbox.

You can locate the **Blackboard** button on the top right of the **Shader Graph** window. Once you click this button, **Blackboard** will open its own separate UI.

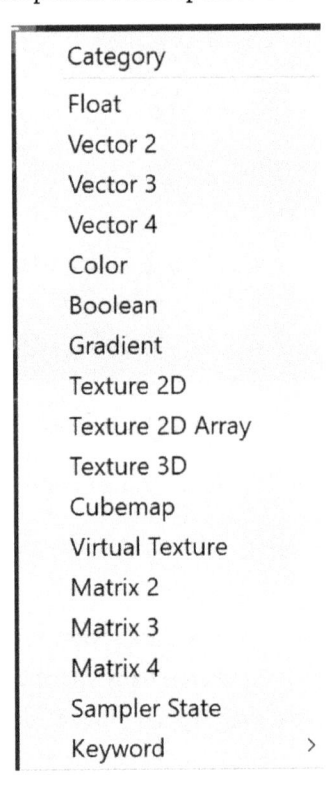

```
Category
Float
Vector 2
Vector 3
Vector 4
Color
Boolean
Gradient
Texture 2D
Texture 2D Array
Texture 3D
Cubemap
Virtual Texture
Matrix 2
Matrix 3
Matrix 4
Sampler State
Keyword                >
```

Figure 9.13: Variable types available in the Blackboard

There are 16 available data types that can be created. These data types can be changed through scripting during runtime as well. Keywords are designed to be changed per material instance during runtime. There are only a few options for this as the compiler needs to account for all the variations. This is handy for things like mobile specifications. You may make an enum (user-defined set of constraints) or list for different systems to change the fidelity (perceptual quality) of the shader to adapt to platform limitations.

Graph Inspector

The **Graph Inspector** gives you the options for the shader type itself. We chose to start with a URP/Lit shader as our base, which sets specific settings in the **Graph Inspector** for us. *Figure 9.14* below shows the **Graph Inspector**. These are the settings that are set by default with the URP/Lit.

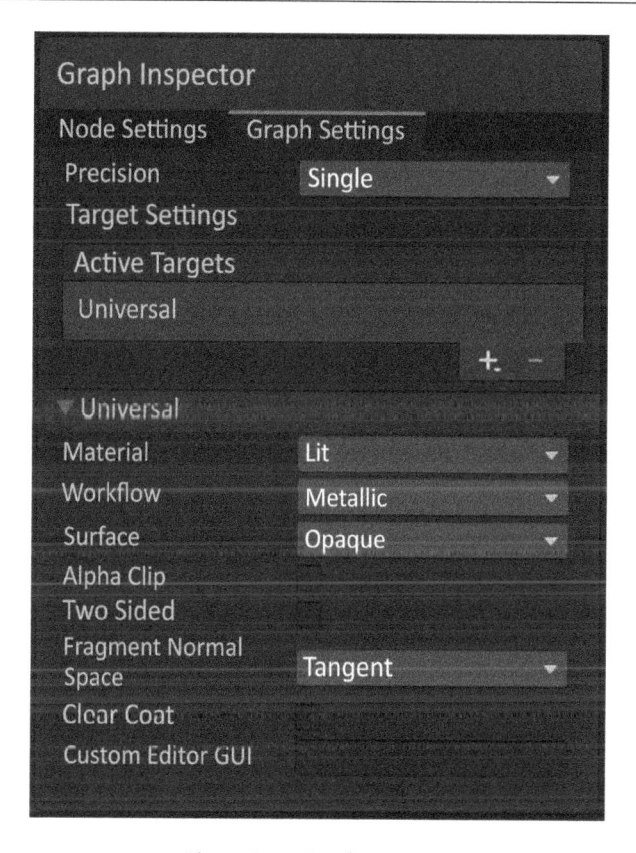

Figure 9.14: Graph Inspector

Each of these properties available to the shader we are building has great use in certain situations. When we go over using them in, *Finishing Touches,* we will explain why we are making the changes to the graph settings. For now, understand that the material we chose was the **Lit** option and it defaults to a metallic opaque workflow. This means that you do not see the color from items behind it as it isn't transparent.

Main Preview

The **Main Preview** is an overall glance at what the shader would look like in the game. The default is a sphere.

You can right-click in the window to access multiple options, such as to include a custom mesh, as noted in *Figure 9.15* below.

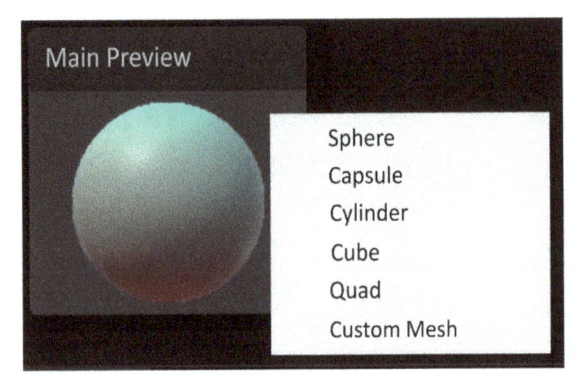

Figure 9.15: Screenshot of the main preview in Shader Graph and its options

Until you plug in some nodes to the Master Stack, this preview will default as a gray sphere. Let's talk about nodes next!

Nodes

A node is a piece of code that will have at least an output but could also have an input depending on the needs of the node. The purpose is to have a change in data to provide manipulation to the input in the attributes on the master stack. If you can recall back in *Figure 9.6*, we showed a few nodes: **Color**, **Lerp**, **Split**, and **UV**. We used them in combination to make the base color be manipulated to show the gradient we made. *Figure 9.16* shows a snippet of the screen when we pressed the spacebar down while our mouse was in the empty gray area of the Shader Graph. There are many nodes that can be used together to make many different effects. You can take the time now to search through the node menu and find the nodes we made in *Figure 9.6* to play with the gradient yourself.

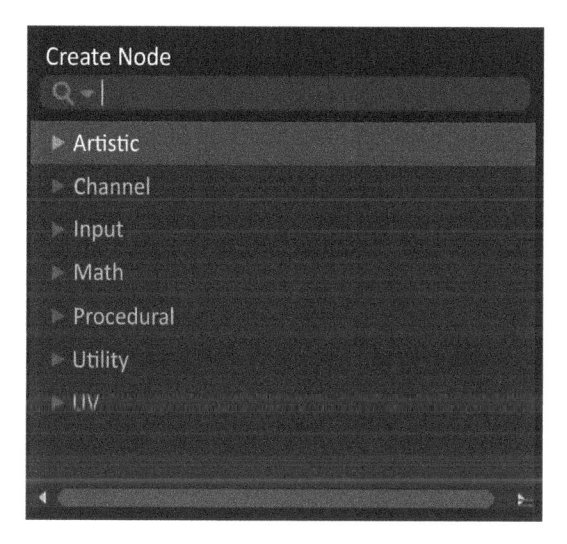

Figure 9.16: Node creation menu

If you took some time to build this out, you may have also opened some of the node groupings and realized that there is a very large number of nodes to choose from. This may cause a little bit of anxiety. Fortunately, we will go over some common nodes that are used in many shaders in the next section.

Commonly used nodes

Below is a simple list of commonly used nodes to make shaders. We want to stress that this isn't the full list of nodes. In fact, there are over 200 nodes now in Shader Graph 10+. Going over all of them could literally be a book or two. The interesting thing about these sets of nodes is that they can be built up to make some incredible shaders. Something to keep in mind when reading about these is that there may be information in the previous node that helps describe the current node you are reading. Read through them all even if you're reasonably comfortable with, say, knowing how to add, for example.

Add

To be able to explain **Add**, we need to make sure you remember that 0 means absence, or the color black in this case. This means that a value of 1 is white. We normalize our values on a 0-1 scale across many applications. You may remember that UV coordinates are also between 0 and 1. This is no mistake! So, if I had two scalars, or Vector1s, and added them, the value would be greater.

Let's show a quick example: 0.4 + 0.4 = 0.8.

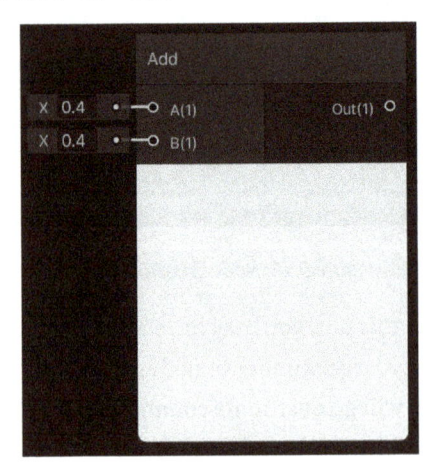

Figure 9.17: Add node

0.4 is a darker-than-medium-gray value. If we add two of them together, we almost get white! 0.8 is 80% to pure white in value, seen in *Figure 9.17*.

Color

This node is a Vector4 with nice visual sugar on top. Vector4 (*0, 0, 0, 0*) represents Red, Green, Blue, and Alpha in shader values. **Color** has an interface for you to select the color you want, and it will set up the RGB values for you with an Alpha slider for that value while outputting a Vector4.

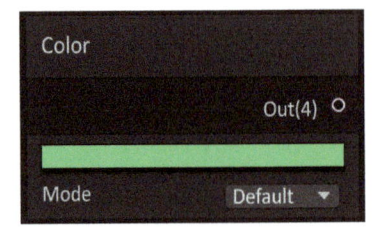

Figure 9.18: Color node

This would be difficult with the Vector4 node as there is no color visual to know what your values need to be.

Lerp

Lerp stands for **Linear Interpolation**. The Lerp node can be used in many applications. One instance is how we set up a gradient to be used for the base color in *Figure 9.6*. There are three inputs: A, B, and T. You can think of it as A is 0, B is 1, and T is the driver. The driver (T) is a value of 0-1. However, the value will map to the value of A, B, and the values in between. If T is at 0, it will display an 100% value of what is in A. If T has a value of 1, it will display an 100% value of B. Now, if T is at 0.4, then that will be in between the values of A and B: 40% A and 60% B.

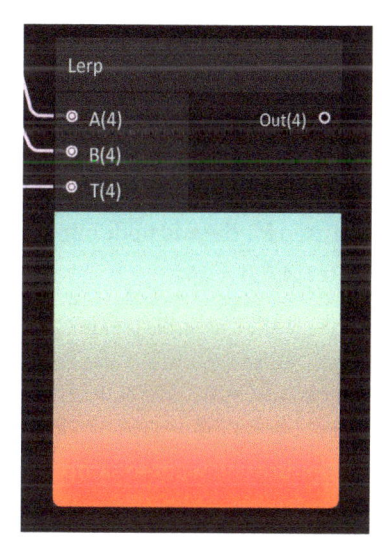

Figure 9.19: Lerp node

This is difficult to visualize with just numbers alone. Luckily, in *Figure 9.19* we used the UV to input T as a gradient. This allows us to see the 0-1 going from bottom to top. You are seeing a gradient from A to B from bottom to top.

Multiply

We've seen the **Add** and **Lerp** nodes; now we need to work through another operation, **Multiply**. By the nature of basic arithmetic, **Multiply** will make the value lower.

This is happening because we are in the range of 0-1. Let's put together an example in *Figure 9.20*.

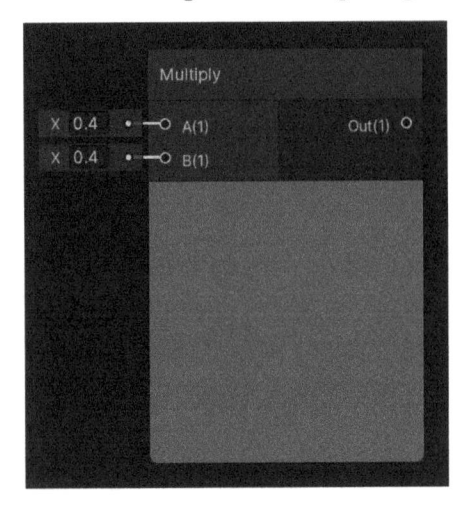

Figure 9.20: Multiply node

We have used the same example we used for the add node but we are using multiplication instead of using addition. Simple math states .4 * .4 = .16.

Sample Texture 2D

This node allows you to take textures you have authored in other **Digital Content Creation (DCC)** software such as Photoshop and use the color information to manipulate the attributes of the master stack. There are two inputs, the texture you want to sample and the UVs, as seen in *Figure 9.21*.

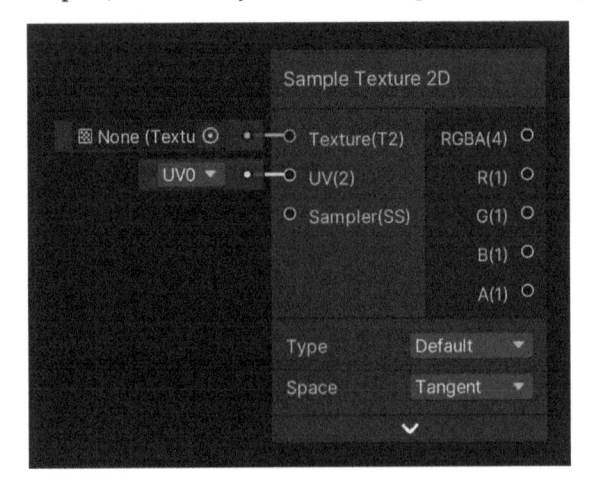

Figure 9.21: Sample Texture 2D

The UV node allows you to manipulate the UV coordinates of your mesh. A nice feature of this node is that it outputs the Vector4 as well as each float individually from the node itself.

Saturate

There may be a time when your values go above 1. This may happen because you are working with multiple nodes that push your values outside the 0-1 range.

Figure 9.22: Saturate node

If this happens, you can input the data into a saturate node and it will return all of your values within the 0-1 range. Place the float value in the **In** portion, and the **Out** value will be normalized to the 0-1 range.

Split

As we saw in the **Sample Texture 2D node**, the Vector4 was split into individual outputs. This isn't always the case. The **Color** node only outputs a Vector4. If you only want to use the Red channel value from **Color**, how could you get it? You guessed it, a split node. Input a Vector2, 3, or 4 and use whichever channel you desire as a float.

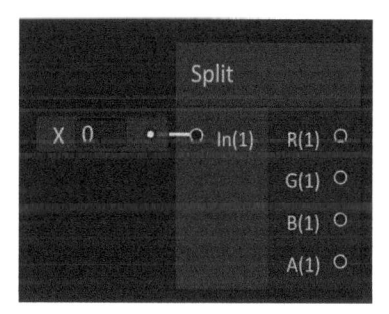

Figure 9.23: Split node

This is very helpful to be able to break out an image that you put four grayscale images onto. We call that **channel packing** so you can have three images on one texture lookup.

UV

There may be a time when you need to manipulate the UVs of the object you want to render. A reason for this may be that you want to tile the UVs because the scale of the item was larger or smaller than what was intended. Another reason to use the UV node is that it automatically creates horizontal and vertical gradients.

Figure 9.24: UV node

If split, the R channel is the horizontal gradient and the G channel is the vertical gradient.

Vectors

These guys are used everywhere. You'll notice that a Vector1 is named a **Float**. Another name for Vector1 is Scalar. Something else you may have noticed is that the outputs are all different colors. Float is cyan, Vector2 is green, Vector3 is yellow, and Vector4 is pink. This is incredibly useful to know the colors as they are shown on the connection lines between the nodes. These nodes are used in infinite use cases. Do you need three points of data? Vector3!

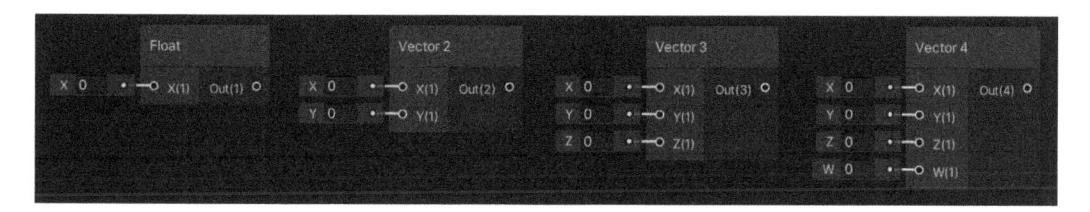

Figure 9.25: Vector nodes

With all of these basic nodes, you can make some powerful shaders to make beautiful materials with. In *Chapter 12, Finishing Touches*, we will be covering shaders for multiple purposes and showing how we use these nodes to create some nice visual candy. Now let's move away from Shader Graph and work with Particle Systems so we can add nice visual effects to our experiences.

Particle Systems

When you think of visual effects in a video game, the first thing that pops into your head most likely is the trails of legendary weapons in ARPGs or the amazing explosions from intense first-person-shooter campaigns. Whatever popped into your head, there are systems that allow for these effects to happen. Particle Systems allow for the spawning of meshes with certain rules to create these effects. Two of them in Unity are Shuriken and VFX Graph.

Shuriken

This system is full of features to help spawn 3D meshes (structural collection of vertices, edges, and faces that define a 3D object). You can create fire embers, trails, explosions, smoke, and everything else to help sell the experience that has been defined. As you can see in *Figure 9.26* there are a lot of options to go over. We will leave the explanation of this to the examples covered in *Chapter 12, Finishing Touches* when we create Shuriken-based effects.

Some high-level knowledge of Shuriken to know is that it is a Particle System that uses the CPU to direct the particles.

This limits the amount of particles that can spawn directly on that hardware.

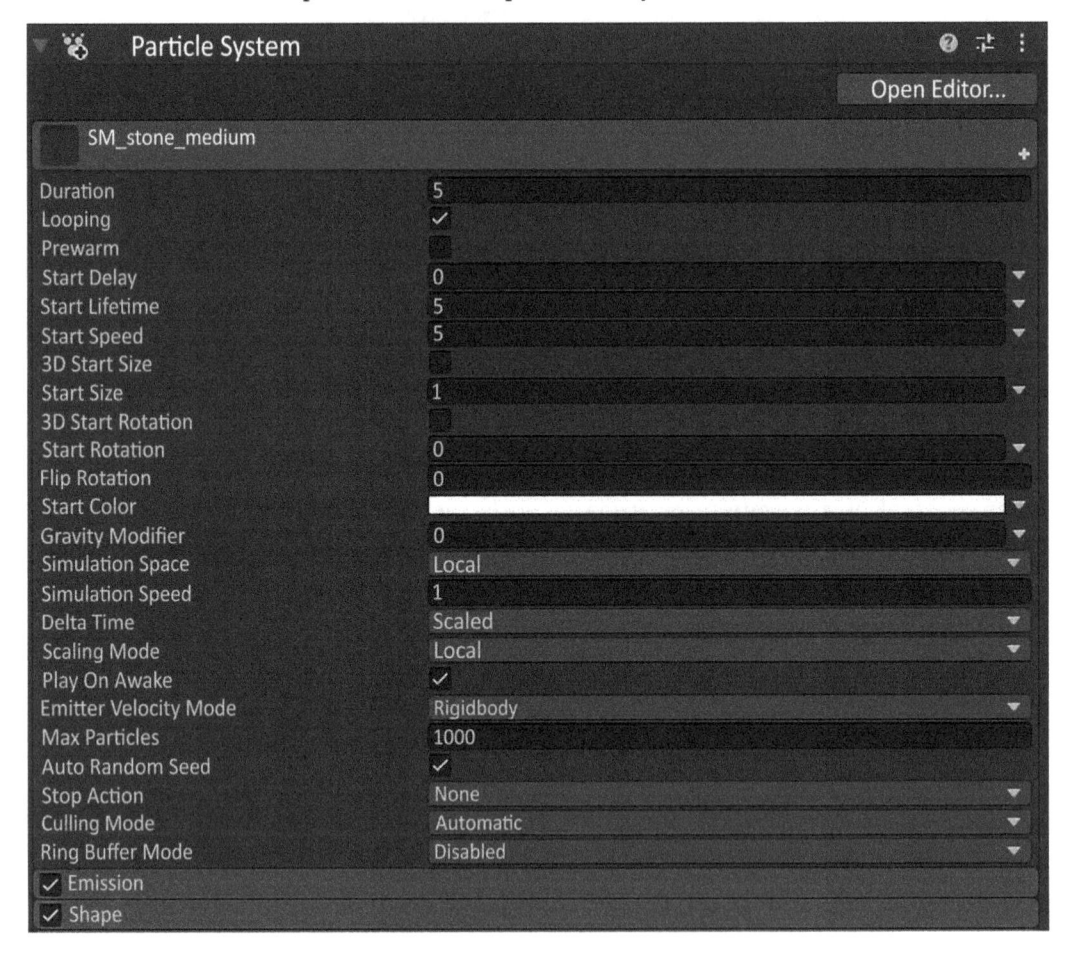

Figure 9.26: Shuriken Particle System

Shuriken is fantastic for particle systems on the CPU, but if you want to have large amounts of particles moving around, VFX Graph is the way to go. This makes GPU-driven particles and can handle many thousands of particles at once.

VFX Graph

Firstly, you will most likely need to install VFX Graph. Open the **Package Manager** as you have done before and find **Visual Effects Graph** from within **Unity Registry** and install it! After you've finished this, you will need to create a VFX Graph system. In your project window, right-click and then select **Create > Visual Effects > Visual Effects Graph**.

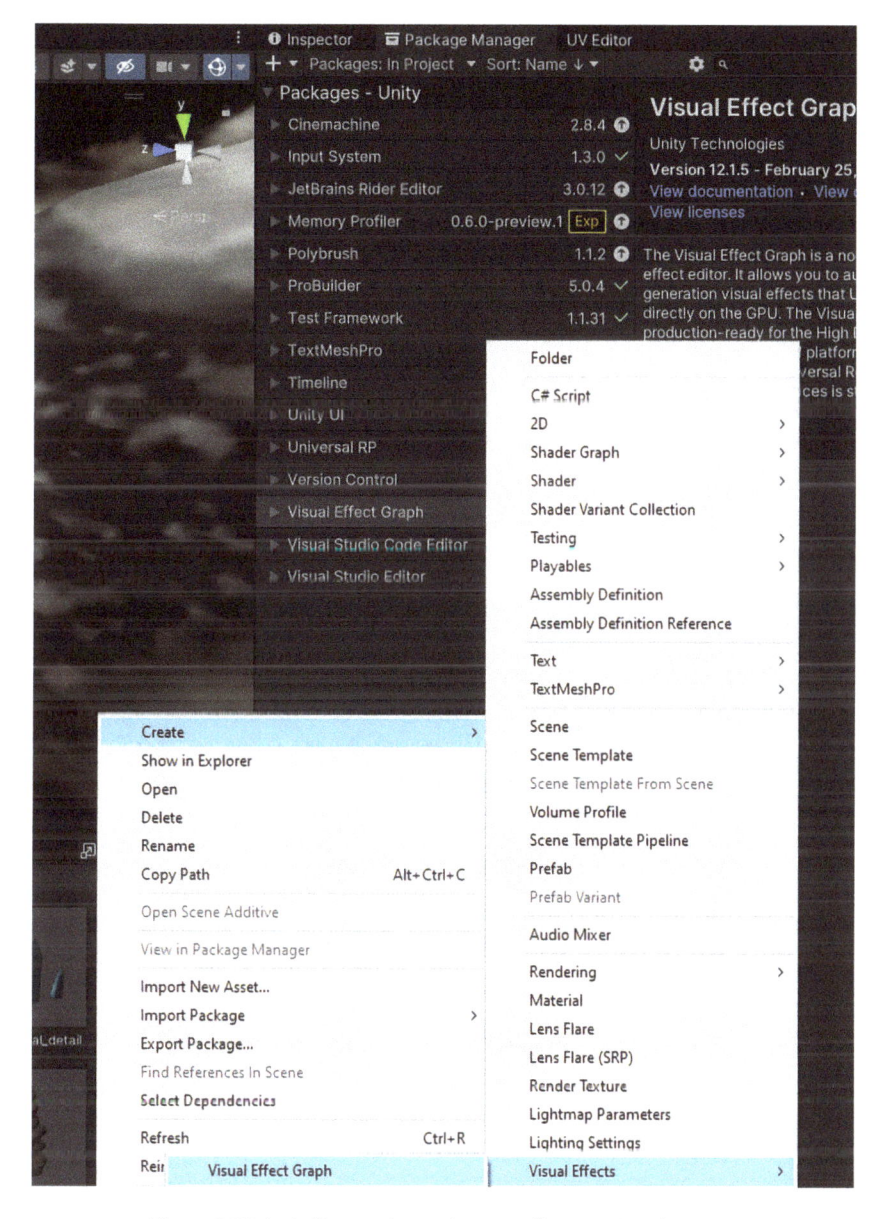

Figure 9.27: Installing and creating your first VFX Graph system

Opening VFX Graph will present you with a new window. This window is like the **Shader Graph**. You'll notice there is a **Blackboard**, which we can use to create parameters that can be changed at runtime and is exposed in the inspector.

There is a UI that is unique to the VFX Graph and a few specific terms: **Contexts**, **Blocks**, **Nodes**, and **Variables**. **Contexts** are portions of the system broken down, such as **Spawning**, **Initialization**, **Update**, and **Output**.

Each of these **contexts** has **blocks** inside of them and can be added to the **contexts** by right-clicking. The **Spawning context** controls how many instances of the system feeds into an **Initialize context**. **Initialize context** processes the **Spawn Event** and engages a new particle simulation. **Update context** takes in the **Initialized** particles and executes explicit behaviors upon certain conditions. **Output contexts** account for the simulation data and render every living particle according to the **Output context** configuration. However, **Output context** does not modify simulated data.

The first context is spawning. This context will allow you to add blocks to affect the spawning logic of each system. There are some questions that should be considered here: How many particles should spawn from this system? How quickly should those particles spawn? When are they spawned?

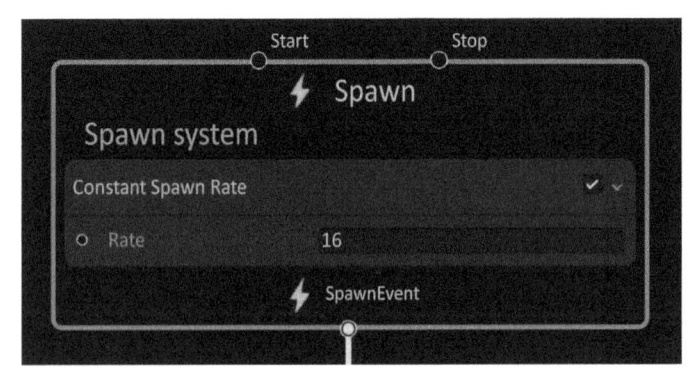

Figure 9.28: Spawn context

After the spawning is completed, you need to have parameters to initialize them with. These blocks answer these types of questions: Where do the particles spawn? Are they spawned moving or do they have velocity? How long does each particle live for?

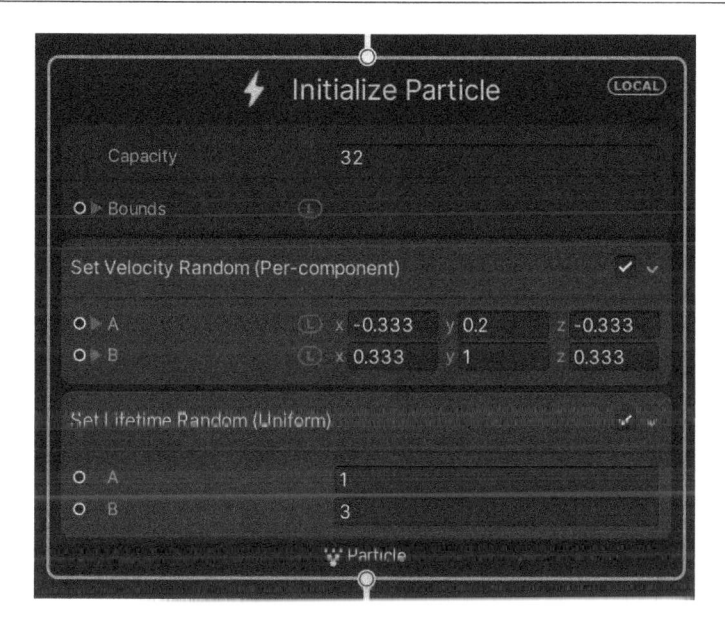

Figure 9.29: Initialize context

Now that you have them spawning, it may be a good idea to add some unique behavior to them as they update, or they will be floating sphere gradients. You can expect this to answer the ultimate question: How will the particles change over time?

Figure 9.30: Update context

Then finally, as you have an understanding of how many particles there are, where the particles are, and what the particles are doing, you can now decide what they will look like.

The questions are: Which way are the particles facing? What shader is being used?

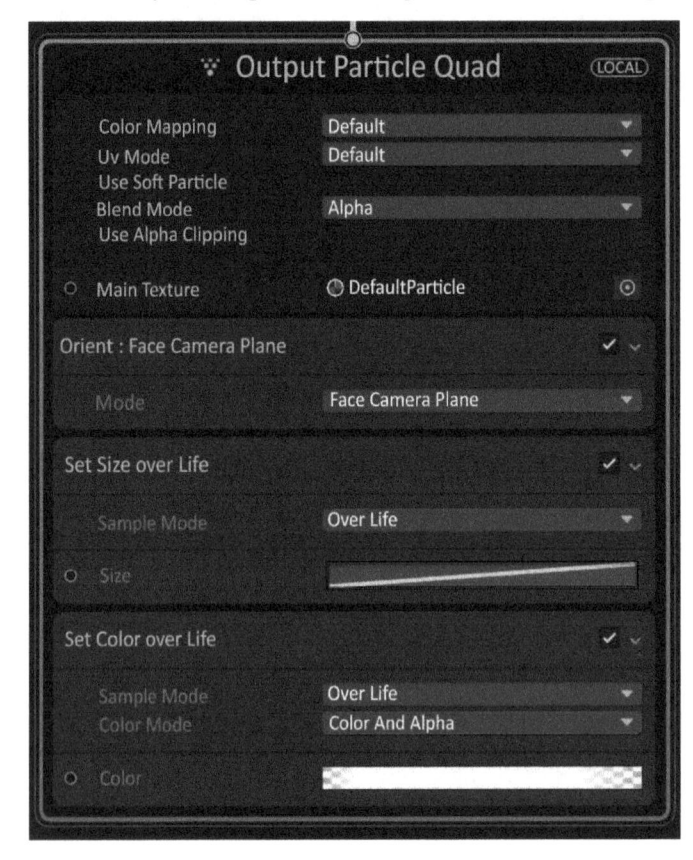

Figure 9.31: Output context

You may have noticed the left side of the blocks sometimes have circle inputs like the Shader Graph. If you thought that you could put some input to this, maybe from nodes, then you're correct! There are nodes that you can work through to get the right data flowing to the blocks that are in each context.

Nodes

As this was in Shader Graph, the nodes are meant to take data values and manipulate them in a way to get the desired outcome. In VFX Graph's case the values are meant to be read into one of the blocks as opposed to one of the attributes from the **Master Stack**. For the most part you will utilize the **Operator** nodes and variables that are created in the **Blackboard** to complete the complex maths.

Summary

We learned that visual effects have heavy technical implications through two major sources in Unity: shaders and particles. Taking our time through shaders, we built an example of a material on a 3D object to get the concept down so when we have multiple different scenarios, we can follow how the shader was created. This was done through Shader Graph. After that, we dove into the concept of particles. Shuriken was shown to get a simple understanding of CPU particles and will be used in later chapters to explain the finishing touches. GPU particles are created through VFX Graph; we went over the interface and some vocabulary of VFX Graph so when we use it later, there is an understanding to work off.

Visual effects are a very large topic to master. Mastering these tools takes a long time. Take your time when working through this and fail fast. This will guide you through understanding visual effects.

The next chapter covers the implementation of sound in the game. Sounds are generally overlooked until nearly the end of games, but they are integral to ensuring the product has captivating emotional tie-ins with the environment and the character. We will go over implementations, some sound design, and other sound-focused knowledge points in the next chapter.

10
Sound Effects

Sound effects! Sound is the only part of a video game that comes from the real world and makes it into the game. Using microphones, sound designers will record common video game sounds such as voiceovers, music, UI sounds, weapons, and ambient sounds to help bring a game to life! Sound tends to have a very subtle effect on how players perceive a video game's quality. A good-looking animation in a game can only be as good as its sound.

In this chapter, we will be going over the five elements of selecting or designing sounds. These are **Source, Envelope, Pitch, Frequency,** and **Layering**. Understanding these five elements will give you a strong foundation to ensure your sounds fit the overall design of the narrative, character, environment, and mechanics we've worked through so far. Then we will go into how to scale these elements in the game engine with our code and mixing! Sounds tell a story on an individual sound effect basis as well as working together to tell a greater, more in-depth story. Finally, we will go through specific examples of our sound design in our project as well as their implementation in Unity. These examples include magical sounds, footstep sounds, and ambient sounds. Here's a quick summary of this chapter:

- The five elements of sound design
- Designing for scale
- Our project's sound design and implementation
- Triggering sound through player interaction

Sound... design?

Sound design! The forgotten stepchild of video games, but also the soul and emotion behind them.

A straightforward explanation of sound design is that a sound is recorded, processed, and then coded directly into a game. Therefore, this makes sound the only part of a video game that comes directly from the real world.

Any sound that we reference in this chapter can be found in /Assets/Sounds/[Name].

The five elements of sound design

The elements of sound design we'll be discussing are source, envelope, pitch, frequency, and layering. These apply to the process of making an individual sound effect, as well as a broader scope of how sounds work together in a game.

Source

A source can be a person, place, or thing from which your inspiration comes or is obtained. Your source is what helps your listener understand the real-world characteristics of your sound. If you record the sound of a footstep hitting a grassy surface versus a concrete surface, the minute qualities and differences between these two sounds help us distinguish them. And thus, we can utilize the source as a creative limitation in creating our sounds authentically.

Limitations are what artists use to cut out all of the clutter in our brains to help create their visions. So, in our recording process, if we needed a magical water sound in a video game, we would record some water as a base layer. Or, if we wanted to record the sound for an animation of a dog rolling in dirt, the first and best thing to record would be the sound of a dog rolling in dirt. What we are creating sounds for helps us select what to record!

Recording sounds can be a difficult process and has an entire art form behind it; while it will help with your growth as a sound designer, I highly recommend using existing sound libraries. Almost any sound that you can think of has already been recorded, so it makes more sense to just buy or download sounds online! This will help speed up your workflow drastically. If you don't want to use sound libraries, then you can use a microphone! Using a microphone is a very in-depth process that we won't be covering in this book because you could literally write entire books on this art.

Here are some popular free websites and sound libraries:

- Blipsounds: https://blipsounds.com/community-library/
- Andrew V Scott: https://www.andrewvscott.com/Building-A-Large-SFX-Library-for-Free
- SKYES Audio: https://www.skyesaudio.com/blog/2019/4/1/the-ultimate-free-sound-effects-list-free-to-download
- Freesound: https://freesound.org/

There are many more that can be found with some internet searching. Don't be afraid to look around to find what fits your needs.

In video games, the source of a sound effect is usually determined by what you see visually. For an ice mage that casts an icy wind spell, you'd limit yourself to using wind and ice sounds to get started. If you have a gun made of jello that shoots tiny horses with the power of radioactive farts, you'll likely utilize jello, horses, farting, and gun sounds.

So, if we take a magic sword that has metal textures, and purple magic VFX that runs along the blade, what kind of sounds are we going to look for? You've probably put together that we'll use sounds from a magic sound library and some metallic ringing sounds.

Another way to determine your source is via story context. The same magic sword may look like it's magic, but maybe the writers of the game determined the blade uses futuristic magic so you need to use sci-fi sound elements.

It should be mentioned that there are many games that have limitations where the sound must fill in the gaps. A game that emulates graphics from an Atari 2600 with realistic sound design might require some imagination. A green area that your player walks on could be grass or a toxic waste dump depending on the context of the game's world.

Envelopes

An envelope is a way for sound designers to explain the volume of a sound over time (volume as in decibels, not 3D models). The two parts of an envelope you'll use are the "attack" and "release."

The attack, shown below in *Figure 10.1*, is the start of the sound, and the release is the end of the sound. We describe the attack and release of a sound by speed (i.e., fast and slow).

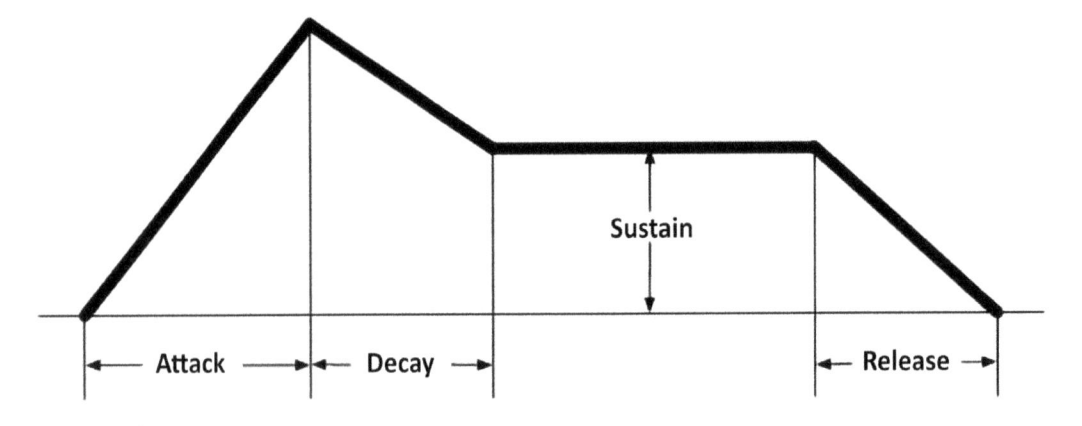

Figure 10.1: Envelope explanation

Attack

An example of a sound with a slow attack would be something like a "sword whoosh" sound effect when a sword is slashed through the air. The sound starts off being almost inaudible and raises in volume over the course of half of a second. We can make the attack even slower by making the volume raise over the course of a few seconds. You can see a direct visual in *Figure 10.2* of how the envelope would look in its waveform. Sounds with a slower attack tend to appear more subtle and gentle to the player. Some other examples of sounds with a slow attack would be a car passing by or a kettle getting ready to whistle.

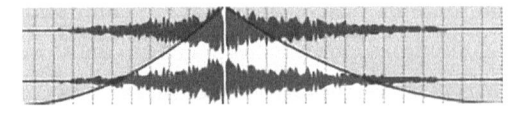

Figure 10.2: Fast attack sound

An example of a sound with a fast attack as in *Figure 10.2* would be a punching sound effect. As soon as the sound starts, it will be almost at max volume, creating a transient sound. A transient sound is a sound with a faster attack, seeming more aggressive to the player, usually to create an impact of sorts to convey power or shock the player. Some other examples of a sound with a fast attack would be a gun firing, a cymbal crash as seen in *Figure 10.3*, or a hammer hitting an anvil.

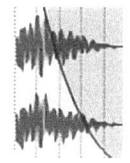

Figure 10.3: Cymbal crash example of fast attack

Release

Then we have the release of a sound. As you can probably guess, we'll be using speed to determine the nature of the release. An example of a sound with a slower release would be a car engine turning off or an explosion. Most sound effects will have a slower release as it sounds more appealing.

There aren't many examples that you will hear in video games that will have a short release. A hard cutoff in a sound effect is unnatural and unpleasant to hear in most cases, barring some advanced stylized techniques. A sound with a slow release could be a big gong ringing out, or the sound of a car driving into the distance while you hear the sound's volume dissipate. For the sake of example, here is what a slow release looks like:

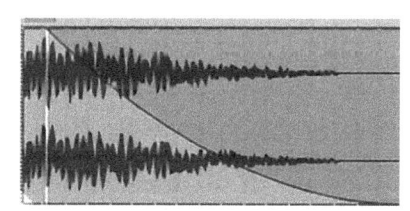

Figure 10.4: Slow release sound

And here is what a fast release looks like:

Figure 10.5: Fast release sound

Another element of sound is pitch.

Pitch

Pitch is an element of sound that determines its "highness" or "lowness."

This is probably one of the easiest concepts to grasp as we hear it in movies, video games, and even day-to-day life. A big, buff character in an animated movie will commonly have a low-pitched voice, while a smaller, cuter character might have a high-pitched voice.

The example given above is one of the most common reasons to control the pitch of a sound effect – size. The other one is speed. Think of a car that is going slowly versus one that is going quickly. The one that is going faster has an engine revving at a higher pitch while an idle or slow-moving car will resonate low-frequency bellows.

To fully understand pitch, it will help to understand frequency, which is directly tied to it.

Frequency

Frequency is the most complicated element to explain, but it's one of the most important to understand. You have probably listened to music in a car or on a stereo and have seen the option to control "bass" or "treble." Treble refers to "higher frequencies" while bass refers to "lower frequencies." The human hearing range is from 20 Hz to 20,000 Hz (Hertz), and many sounds, no matter if they sound high-pitched or low-pitched, hit every single frequency. When you play a sound in your car and turn down the "bass," you're turning down the lower frequencies.

The best example is white noise. White noise is simply a sound that plays every single frequency at the same volume. If you've never heard it, it sounds like TV static. You can listen to the sound in /Assets/Sounds/WhiteNoise.wav. You can find it in the project on GitHub, which you can find a link for in this book's *Preface*.

The weird part about this sound is that, just by listening, it feels like the sound consists mostly of higher frequencies. But we can use a tool called an equalizer (or EQ for short) to visualize the frequencies that are playing, as well as controlling the volume of individual frequencies.

Generally, higher frequencies are perceived as louder, which is an important fact to consider when making sounds for your game. If you want to make a sound stand out, including higher frequencies will help quite a bit, while cutting them out might help blend sounds into the background. But if you want every sound to stand out, but also want them to have weight and power, we will have to utilize our lower frequencies. So, a balance must be struck.

The yellow lines on this graph indicate where the frequencies are hitting, and you can see that it's practically at the same volume across the whole spectrum. This means that every single frequency has generally the same frequency volume.

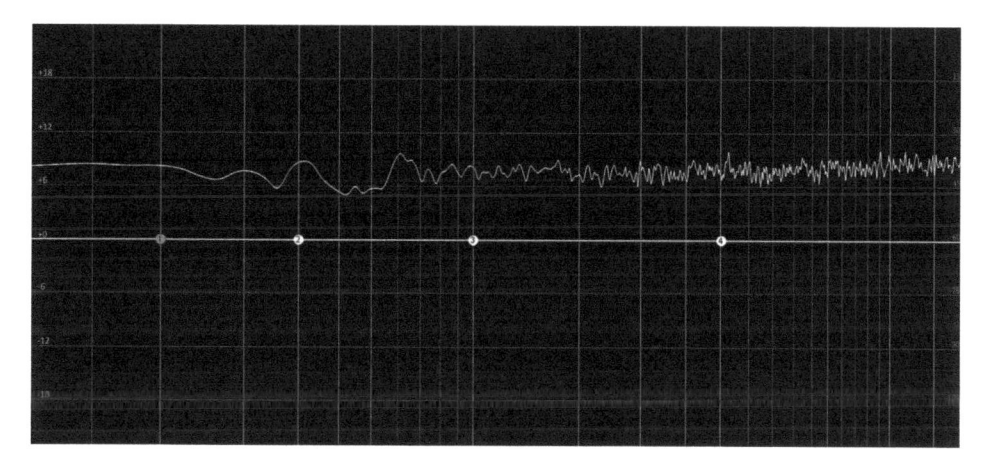

Figure 10.6: Example of similar-frequency volume

I've provided a few sounds below so you can all hear the differences when we remove the lower and higher frequencies, along with a graph showing which frequencies we removed. As you listen, you'll hear and see that every sound seems to cover higher and lower frequencies to a certain degree, and we can control these frequencies to elicit unique feelings with each sound.

Listen to `Assets/Sounds/Explosion.wav` then `Assets/Sounds/ExplosionLP.wav` to hear what it's like to have the higher frequencies cut. And then listen to `ExplosionHP.wav` to hear what it's like to have the lower frequencies cut out.

Listen to `Assets/Sounds/BeamSword.wav` then `Assets/Sounds/BeamSwordLP.wav` to hear what it's like to have the higher frequencies cut. And then listen to `BeamSwordHP.wav` to hear what it's like to have the lower frequencies cut out.

Listen to `Assets/Sounds/MagicIceSpell.wav` then `Assets/Sounds/MagicIceSpellLP.wav` to hear what it's like to have the higher frequencies cut. And then listen to `MagicIceSpellHP.wav` to hear what it's like to have the lower frequencies cut out.

Listen to `Assets/Sounds/Footstep.wav` then `Assets/Sounds/FootstepLP.wav` to hear what it's like to have the higher frequencies cut. And then listen to `Assets/Sounds/FootstepHP.wav` to hear what it's like to have the lower frequencies cut out.

The reason frequency is one of the toughest concepts to grasp is because your ears aren't trained to listen for it. We just hear a sound and know whether it sounds good or not.

Layering

Layering is the simplest concept to grasp of the five elements. While visual mediums are almost all multiplicative, sound mediums are additive. Layering is simply the process of playing multiple sounds at the same time in a unique sequence.

Next, we have four unique sound effects that stand alone. We have the "impact," the "bloom," the "tail," and the "bass." If you listen to each on their own, they feel empty, but as soon as we add them all together, we have a beautiful explosion sound.

This is a useful process because we can take a source like "Sci-fi Energy" and "Metal Sword" and combine these together to make a "Sci-Fi Energy Sword." Or, we can take our horse fart gun and choose our layers based on the description and functionality of the gun. Listen to `Assets/Sounds/ScifiEnergySword01.wav`, then `Assets/Sounds/ScifiEnergySword02.wav`, then `Assets/Sounds/ScifiEnergySword03.wav`.

Layering also allows us to break down our frequencies to more isolated parts. We can take a sound that is primarily lower frequencies and add it to a regular sound to give it more weight and power. Listen to `Assets/Sounds/Splash01.wav`, then listen to the lower frequencies added to `Assets/Sounds/Splash02.wav` to hear how it becomes more powerful.

We can also layer together two sounds with different envelopes, one with a long attack, and one with a fast attack to create a cool buildup effect to add impact. Listen to `Assets/Sounds/EarthSpell01.wav` to hear the sound before we add a buildup, and then listen to `Assets/Sounds/EarthSpell02.wav` to hear what happens when we add a buildup to hear how we can change the story of our sound!

Now that we've gone over what makes up a sound and how it applies to a single sound effect being created, we'll go over the applications of these five elements on a broader scale of a game.

Designing for scale

Unlike art, which is multiplicative, making sound effects is a completely additive process. As an example, if we have 100 sounds without paying attention to the volume or frequency range of them, this can end up creating a lot of clutter. In the space of a video game, we must be prepared for any sounds, whether it's a sword swipe, ambient sound, an orchestral score, or a voiceover reading, to be played at the same time. We have tools to control these sounds individually, but we must make sure that we have what's called a balanced mix.

How to approach making sounds for a game

So where do sounds go in your game? Sounds can often go overlooked since they are technically not necessary to make what is defined as a "game." And because of this, it's tough to think immediately about what needs sound and what doesn't.

Put quite simply, I like to look for anything that moves in a game. Even down to the smallest subtleties. Adding sounds for an NPC can include breathing, the sound of their feet hitting a surface, the sound of their clothes rustling... All of these are viable sounds to put into a game. We'll talk about some reasons later in *Chapter 11* as to why this much attention to detail might be difficult to achieve.

Sometimes the art in a game is minimal. What you see isn't quite enough information, so use your imagination as to what sounds could be included! The more you add to the sound, the better. Sometimes a game can be nothing but pixel-art, and you might be incentivized to add fewer sounds, but you should always think about what attention to detail you can hear that isn't being seen! If a player falls into a pit where you can't see what's happening, creating an audible experience can tell a more detailed story than visuals can allow! Maybe there are spikes, a bottomless pit, or lava! We would want the player to hear the bubbles of the lava, the impact of the spikes impaling the player, or the whistle of a player falling off a steep cliff!

Our project's sound design and implementation

We find that the best way to learn is to jump in headfirst and start understanding how things work. This process is relatively simple now that we've gone over the Unity engine.

Getting our first sound to play

To start off, let's get some audio files into our project. We'll start by creating a folder called Audio in Unity, and then dragging our Assets/Sounds/TestTone.wav file into it.

Now that we have our audio in the folder, let's create an empty GameObject in the scene right by our player. We're going to begin by placing an object in the scene next to our character. For now, let's call this GameObject Sound Emitter.

As it stands, this GameObject won't do anything. So, let's click and drag our audio from its Unity folder directly into our Sound Emitter GameObject's inspector.

This will automatically create an **Audio Source** component on the GameObject. This is what allows our sound effects to play in Unity! Let's go ahead and hit play to see what happens!

If you followed properly, you likely already heard your first sound! Congrats! This is of course just a placeholder sound, so we'll focus more on adding other sounds that we'll use in the game. In this process, we'll go over the parameters we can change on the **Audio Source** component.

Organization

To better organize this project, let's go ahead and add a new prefab called ====SFX====. We will put all our sound effects that exist in our scene into here.

In addition to this, we'll create two new folders in /Assets/Sounds/ in our GitHub project. We'll have a sources folder and a prefabs folder.

Music

Music is a massive part of video games. Sound effects help bring a game to life through detailed ambient sounds, player sounds, and expressive voiceovers, but music is what helps drive moment-to-moment emotions for the player.

You might have some questions about the difference between sounds and music. Technically they are the same, but to make it easier to communicate about them, most professional sound designers will consider music to be the score, or pitched instruments like piano, violins, guitars, and drums working together to make a cohesive song or musical track to listen to as background music. Meanwhile, sound effects are usually real-life instances like footsteps, swords, UI sounds, etc.

Let's add music to our game! To add music to our game, all we must do is take our SFX GameObject that's in our scene and rename it to Music.

Let's give our Assets/Sounds/Music_01.wav a listen. First, select the audio file in your folder and click the looping button at the bottom of the inspector. It's the button right above the waveform to the far right, seen in *Figure 10.7* below.

Figure 10.7: Wave play UI in inspector

Now, hit the **Play** button, which is the sideways triangle to the right in the inspector, but to the left of the looping button.

If you listen to the music all the way through until the end, you'll recognize that the music is a seamless loop! To hear this in action in the game, let's take our Sound Emitter GameObject in the scene, and rename it to Music.

Next, let's click and drag our music into our new `Music` GameObject. We'll be putting it into the **AudioClip** space of our **Audio Source** component seen in *Figure 10.8*.

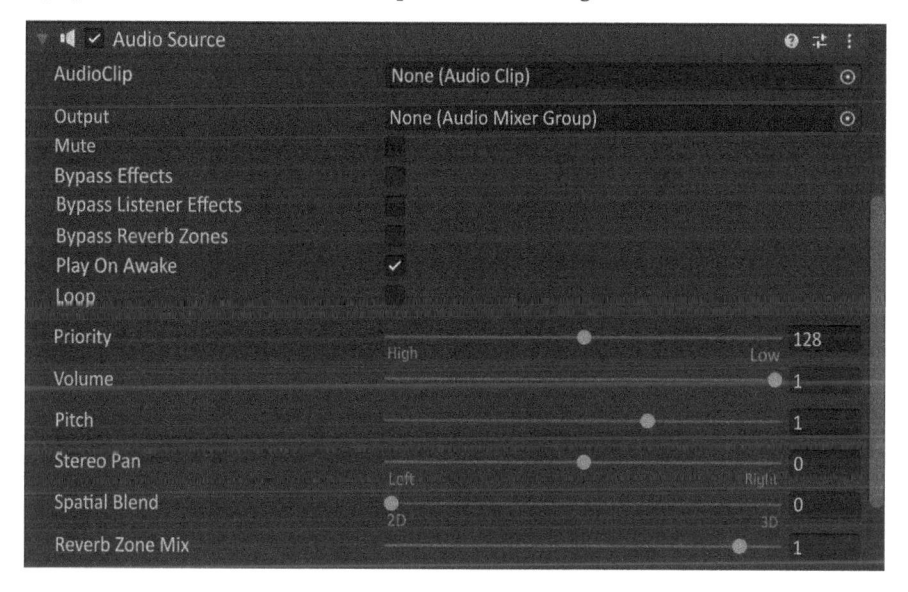

Figure 10.8: Audio Source component

If we were to test playing the game right now, we would be able to hear sound but it would stop eventually. But we pressed the looping button in the inspector for the .wav file, right? So why isn't it working?

Well, that looping button was strictly for playback in that one instance. If we want to loop the sound on the **Audio Source** component, we must check **Loop** as on, seen under **Play On Awake** in *Figure 10.8*. Now if we play the game, our music will loop! How exciting!

Later on in this chapter, we will adjust the volumes of all of the sounds in the game, otherwise called "the mix," or "mixing the game." We aren't going to mix the game immediately because the volume of every sound in a game is entirely dependent on how it sounds relative to other sound effects!

2D sounds

Up until now, we've only heard 2D sound effects. 2D sound effects are sounds that have no in-game location and will play anywhere for the player. No matter where you move on the map, a 2D sound will play as a consistent trigger.

The following is a list of 2D sounds that you've likely heard while playing video games:

- **Music**: Intro music that plays during the opening menu before you press play
- **UI**: Pressing a button, hearing the "click" of the button
- **Voiceover**: The narrator speaking over gameplay
- **Ambient sound**: General sound being played when in an area, such as wind

All the categories above can be triggered by player action, by a game event, by just starting the game, or by entering a new area of a game. But not all of them will exist in a 3D space in the game. This makes them 2D sound effects.

So now that we've gone over what 2D sounds are, let's talk about 3D sounds.

3D sounds

Unlike 2D sounds, 3D sounds exist in the world of the game. When you play a game, you can usually tell what sounds are 3D by moving around in the world and hearing what sounds occur in which ear. This is called panning.

Panning is the stereo quality of a sound. Have you ever listened to a song with headphones on and taken them off one of your ears only to hear some of the instruments playing instead of the full song? This is what panning is! The music producers who made that song purposefully put those instruments in one ear to create better "stereo imaging" (we won't be going much deeper than this, I promise).

So in the real world, if someone is speaking on your left, you will hear them in your left ear while you won't hear them as much in your right ear. We want to recreate this feeling in video games. So, we define positional sound as 3D sounds.

Using 3D sounds

Let's do a little experiment. Let's take our `Music` GameObject and move the `Spatial Blend` option from `0` to `1`.

We now have spatial audio! This means that our sounds will be in 3D!

As it stands, it might be difficult to pinpoint exactly where the music is playing from because there's no visual indicator for it. So, to fix this, I like to create a sphere GameObject as a child of our audio source to visualize exactly where it lies!

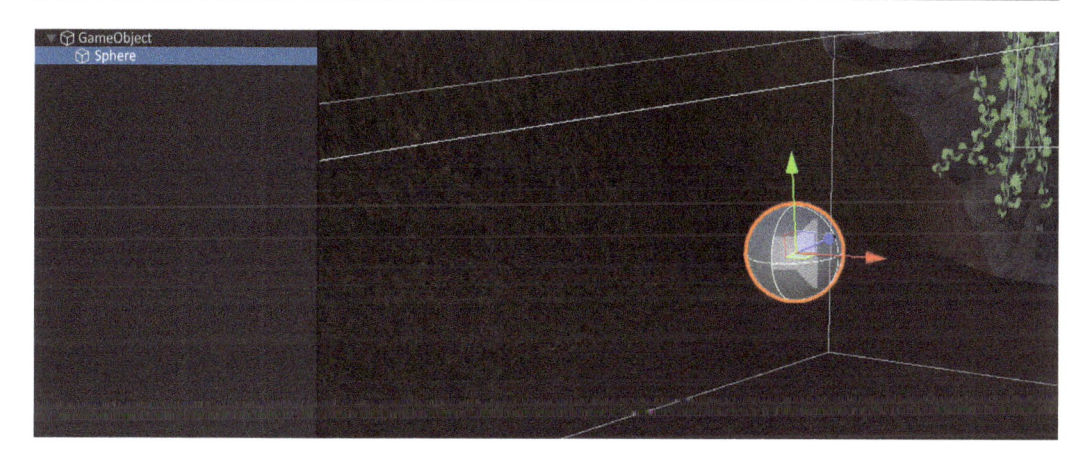

Figure 10.9: Sphere GameObject being set to a child object

Now when we hit **play**, we can see exactly where the audio source is playing from! Next, we will talk about how to control the parameters of our 3D sound effects.

Audio listener part I

How are we able to hear sounds in a game? We hear them through our audio listener. It's a component that we can place on any GameObject that acts as a virtual pair of ears. Placing this listener in most cases is very simple, but sometimes we require more complex integration.

In a game that uses a first-person camera, it's simple: we just add the listener to the camera GameObject and we call it a day.

We use an audio listener on the camera because it acts as the ears of the player. But sometimes the camera can be in an isometric view, and the camera is too far from the player to properly pan and hear sounds as they move around in the world, so we offset the audio listener on a new GameObject to be offset from the camera.

We'll get back to this in the *Audio listener part II* section. For now, let's set up some 3D sound settings. We won't be able to utilize the audio listener in a practical sense until we get our 3D sounds set up.

3D sound settings

When you hear a sound in real life, you can usually get close to it and it will become louder, while when you get further away from it, it gets quieter, and eventually becomes silent. We can control this effect using the 3D sound settings on our **Audio Source** component.

We'll be focusing on **Min Distance** and **Max Distance** for our 3D sound settings.

Go ahead and change **Max Distance** to 10 in the **Audio Source** component and hit **Play**. Assuming you still have the sphere on your GameObject, get closer and further away from it in-game. To help visualize this further, let's undock our scene tab in Unity and put it side by side with our **Game** tab.

Now that we've done this, we can visualize the min and **max distance** with a wireframe gizmo sphere in-game! And we can see that when we move our player outside of the range of the sphere, we will no longer hear the sound.

With our **max distance** slider, we can control the distance from where we can hear the sound. And with **Min Distance**, we can control at what point the sound will be the loudest. Let's go ahead and change the min distance to 3. You'll notice that the smaller sphere inside of the larger sphere changes, as shown later in the chapter in *Figure 10.17*.

When we move our player inside of this sphere, you will notice that there is no panning. This is because the sound has reached its maximum volume, and inside of the smaller sphere, the sound will turn into a 2D sound!

Lastly, we just want to take **Volume Rolloff** and set it to **Linear Rolloff** instead of **Logarithmic**. The reason we do this is when you change the max distance to a number less than 500 in **Logarithmic** mode, the sound doesn't actually get cut off at that distance. So if we were to set the max distance to 10, then we would continue to hear it even if we're 400 units across the map, even though we set the max distance to much less than this.

For reference's sake, here is **Logarithmic**:

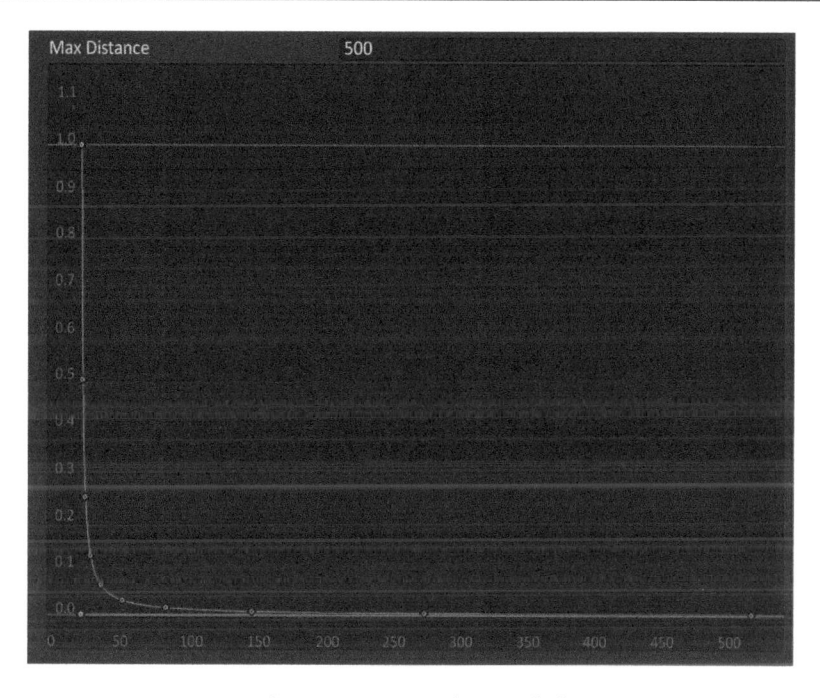

Figure 10.10: Logarithmic Rolloff

And here is **Linear**:

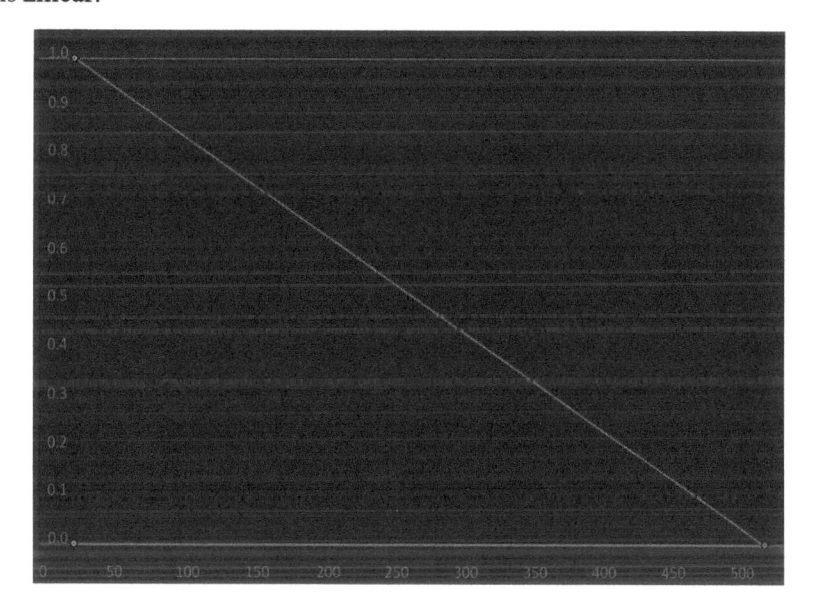

Figure 10.11: Linear Rolloff

Audio listener part II

You may have noticed that the audio feels a tiny bit off while your player is inside of the sphere. Usually, when our player passes the sphere, it isn't at its loudest; it only reaches its loudest when the camera is next to the sphere. This is because the audio listener for Unity defaults to being set on the camera.

In a third-person game, like the one we're making, we'll want to add it to the player, but there's a catch. We want it on the player without rotating with the player. We want to rotate it with the camera, showing the selection in *Figure 10.12* below.

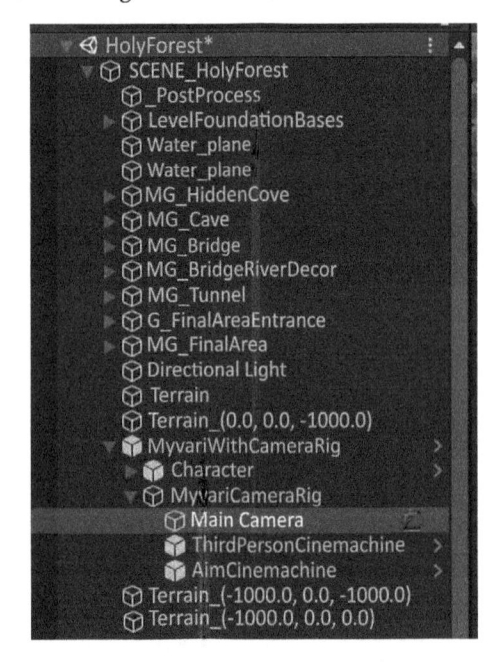

Figure 10.12: Selecting the camera in the Hierarchy

If we open our scene, we can see that `MyvariWithCameraRig` has `Main Camera` attached. And inside the inspector, we'll find a component called **Audio Listener**, shown below in *Figure 10.13*.

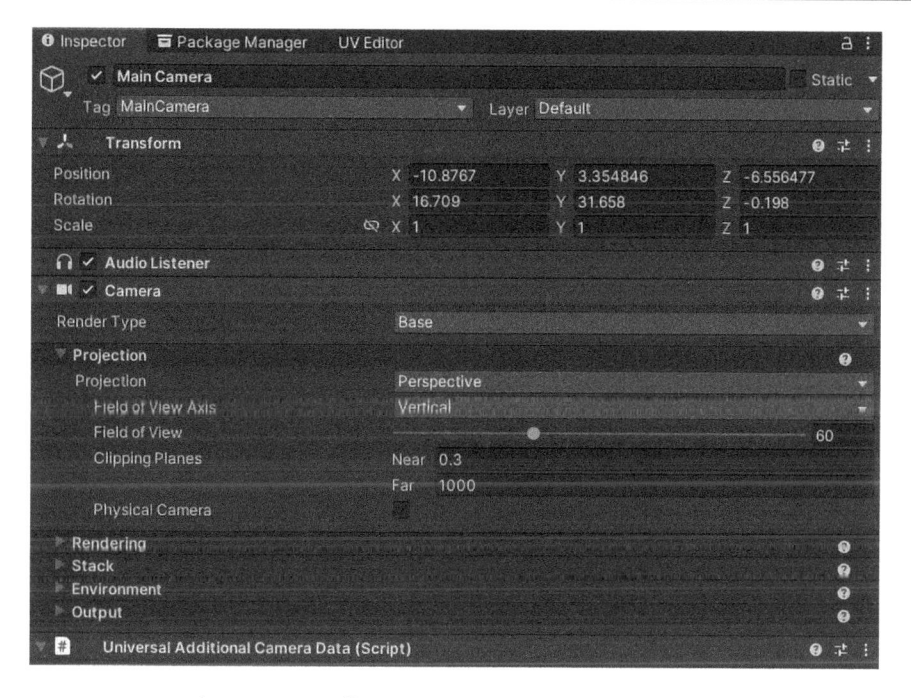

Figure 10.13: Audio Listener on Main Camera in Inspector

Now as an experiment, let's remove the **Audio Listener** here, and move it directly onto our main character. Just placing it on the `Character` GameObject will work just fine.

Now play the game, and move about and away from our sphere object, and rotate around it. You'll notice that the panning is all over the place! From our perspective watching the character, it's hard to tell where information is coming from because we're not in the shoes of our character; we have a third-person perspective.

In a game like this, we could probably get away with just placing our **Audio Listener** on the camera, but it would help quite a bit to have it on our character model. But we can't do that because the player isn't locked by its rotation.

But there's a solution to this! In most games, we would have to add it as a child GameObject to `Main Camera` inside of the `MyvariWithCameraRig` GameObject. But here, we've already done most of the work, because the root `MyvariWithCameraRig` transform is already lined up with the character model!

All we must do is create a new GameObject inside of the root `MyvariWithCameraRig`, rename it `Listener`, as seen in *Figure 10.14*, and we can add our **Audio Listener** component to it.

Figure 10.14: New GameObject to place our Audio Listener onto

Next, we can take this `Listener` GameObject and move it up on the *y* axis so it lines up right next to the ears of our character, seen by the transform gizmo below in *Figure 10.15*.

Figure 10.15: Audio Listener GameObject lined up to head height on Myvari

I moved it up by 1.5 units on the *y* axis. Now when we move around, the `transform` of the `Listener` GameObject will move alongside the camera. Our 3D sounds will now play relative to the character's position instead of the camera!

Adding 3D ambient sounds to the game

How often in your life do you experience absolute silence? You might think that enjoying a quiet evening in your living room has absolute silence, but you still can hear your air conditioning, the refrigerator running, sounds outside your window, etc.

These sounds mentioned of course are very quiet, but the point is that we never truly experience absolute silence!

So even in our video games, if our player is idle, not moving, and staying completely still, it helps a lot to always have some sort of sound. This is where ambient sounds come in.

Ambient sounds can be generally defined as "sounds that exist in a 3D space but don't move." In our Holy Forest project, we can add sound for trees rustling, the interior of the cave, the portal humming, magical energies emitting from an object, rivers, and more!

To add an ambient sound is quite simple. We've technically already done this! The sound we listened to in the *3D sound settings* section can technically be seen as ambient sound.

Let's start with a very simple ambient sound of trees rustling in our scene.

Let's take our `Assets/Sounds/AMB_Trees3D.wav` file and drop it into an **audio source** component on a GameObject. Let's set **Volume Rolloff** to **Linear Rolloff** and set **Spatial Blend** to 1. Next, let's keep our min distance to 1 and our max distance to 5.

Once we've done this, we can place our GameObject's transform values as in the following image. The transform in the image reflects the ambient sound GameObject seen in *Figure 10.16*, and is physically available in the scene under **Sound**, in the hierarchy for the first AMB_Trees3D GameObject.

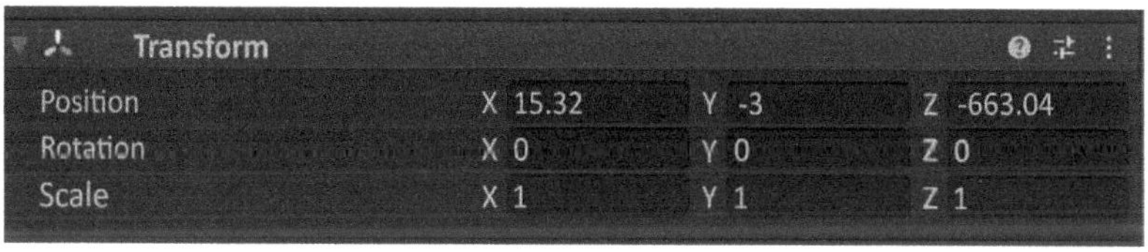

Transform			
Position	X 15.32	Y -3	Z -663.04
Rotation	X 0	Y 0	Z 0
Scale	X 1	Y 1	Z 1

Figure 10.16: Ambient Tree 3D sound transform

We're going to put it on the bigger tree to the left of where our player spawns. In the following image, you can see our sound gizmo placed in the scene.

You can see this in *Figure 10.17* below as well as in the scene. Double-clicking on the `AMB_Trees3D` GameObject in the hierarchy will bring you physically to that location in the scene.

Figure 10.17: Gizmo for the ambient audio source

Lastly, we just want to make sure that **Play On Awake** is checked on so the sound plays immediately when the scene starts, as shown below in *Figure 10.18*.

Figure 10.18: Ensuring Play On Awake is set to True

Now let's press **Play**. And here we will see that the sound plays properly in the game! It will work exactly as our previous sound did, where we can hear it directionally, and the sound will eventually cut out when we leave the radius of the tree!

Filling out our ambient sounds

For the remainder of the ambient sounds, it will be a rinse and repeat of what we've just done. We'll include the min/max ranges and the positions of our ambient sounds as well as the audio files that we feel work for each ambient item. In the scene we have the ambient sounds set up under ====AMB====, as seen in *Figure 10.19* below. I strongly encourage you to listen to the ambient sounds and see how they sound to you!

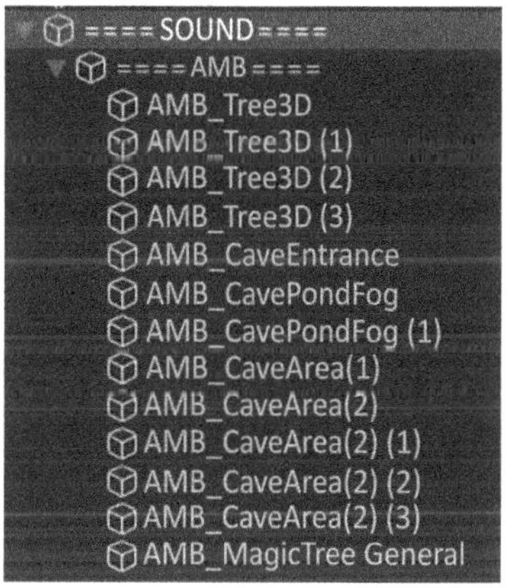

Figure 10.19: List of ambient sounds in the hierarchy

2D ambience

If you walk around our newly filled-out scene, you'll notice that it feels much more alive now! However, you'll notice that in certain spots, you'll hear silence, and as we've learned, hearing absolute silence is not something we ever want our players to experience in the game!

Let's add an audio source to our ====SOUND==== parent GameObject and throw in our General2D_Amb.wav.

Triggering sound through player interaction

All the sounds we've created so far are sounds that will play as soon as you enter a scene. This happens because we have **Play On Awake** checked in the **Audio Source** component.

If we don't have this checked, sounds will never play. But what's cool is we get to trigger sounds in other ways!

Triggering sound through Unity events

Let's get a sound for our first stairs puzzle. This one will be quite easy. The easiest way for us to add our sound will be to add an **Audio Source** component directly to the trigger region GameObject. Let's find `LeftStairsTrigger` and scroll down in the **Inspector** until we find the **Interactio Trigger** script, as shown in *Figure 10.20*.

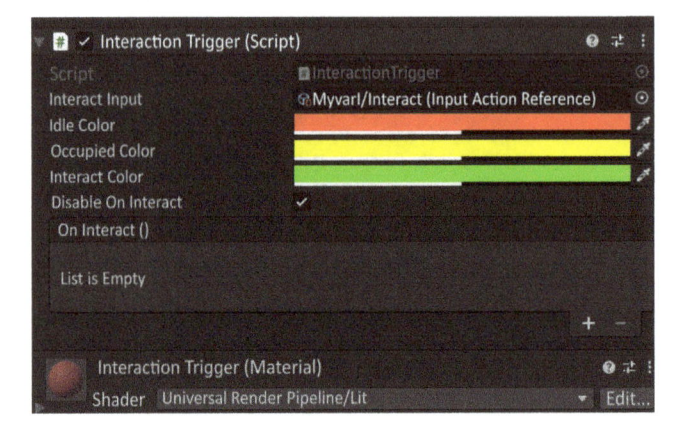

Figure 10.20: Interaction Trigger script on the LeftStairsTrigger GameObject

If you recall, we made a `UnityEvent` called `OnInteract`, which we can utilize with our **Audio Source** component! Go ahead and click **Add Component** at the bottom of the inspector and select **Audio Source**.

Next, drag and drop the `StairsPuzzleSuccess.wav` file into the **Audio Source** component. We will leave the **Audio Source** as 2D since the sound that we're playing is a reward jingle.

Now, click the + in the `OnInteract UnityEvent`, and in the field that says `None (Object)`, drag and drop your **Audio Source** component, as shown in *Figure 10.21*.

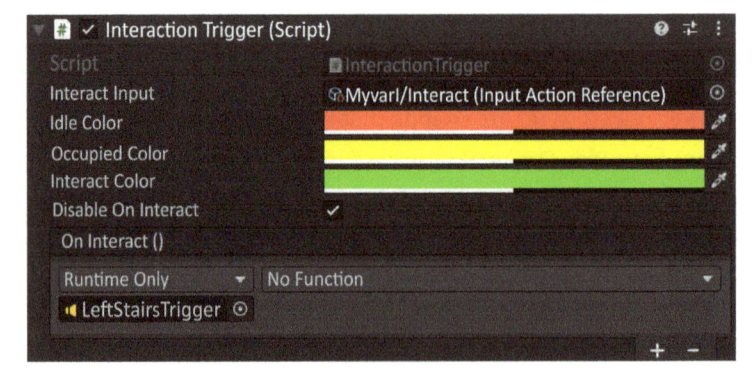

Figure 10.21: Sound added to Interaction Trigger

Next, you'll see the dropdown that currently is labeled as No Function. Let's click this and go down to **AudioSource** and then to **Play ()**, as in *Figure 10.22* below.

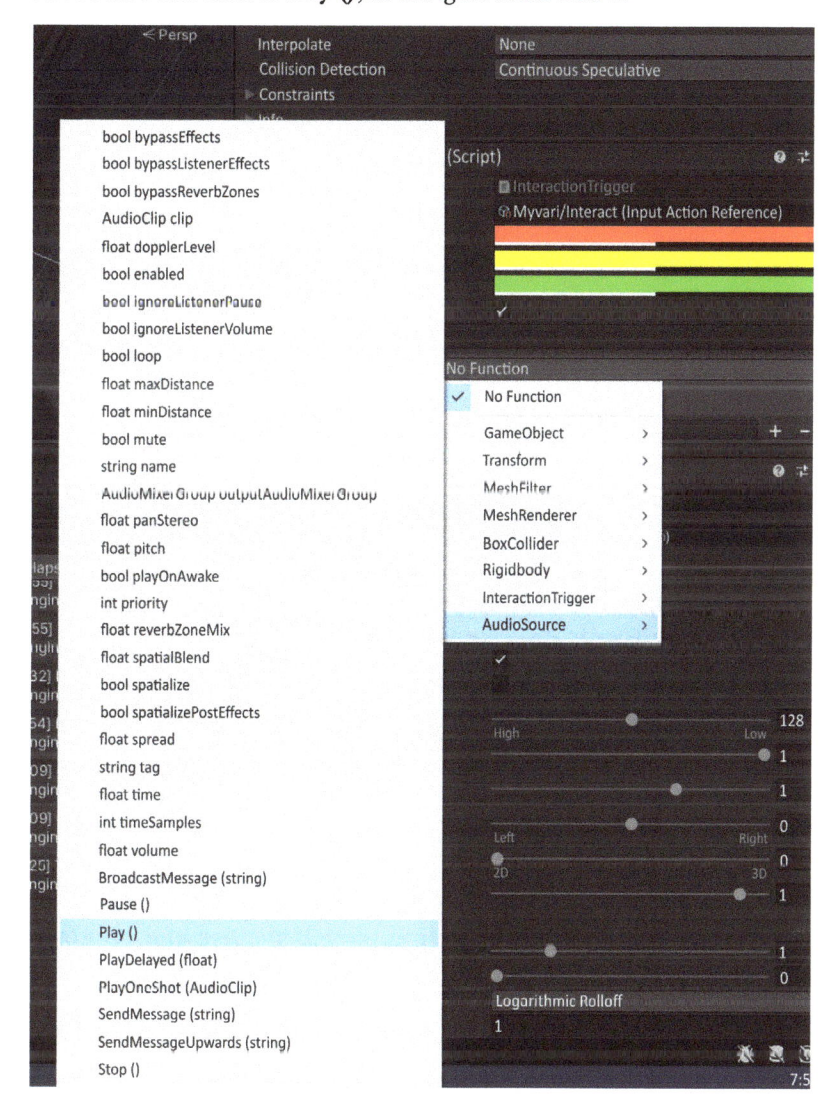

Figure 10.22: Adding the Play method to the sound object on interact

This will ensure that we play our audio file when we activate `LeftStairsTrigger`. Go ahead and hit play and navigate to `LeftStairsTrigger`. Once you do this, you'll hear our sound! Let's go ahead and repeat the same exact process for `RightStairsTrigger`.

Rotating puzzle sounds

For the first time, we'll be triggering sound directly in code. This will be a fairly simple process of making our **Audio Source** variable publicly available through code. Then we just trigger it.

We'll be adding the following sounds:

- A sound that plays when the puzzle is complete
- A sound for when the spire starts moving

Let's start with the simplest one, our "puzzle complete" sound. This will play when all the spires are aligned, and the door opens. Go into our `First Puzzle` prefab in our scene and open up the `FirstPuzzle.cs` script. This script is where we will add our code, as in *Figure 10.23*. On line 173, go ahead and type in:

```
public AudioSource puzzleCompleteSFX;
```

```
168       /// <summary>
169       /// TEMP: Reference to door, hidden when puzzle is solved
170       /// </summary>
171       GameObject tempDoor;
172
173       public AudioSource puzzleCompleteSFX;
174
175       /// <summary>
176       /// Initialization
177       /// </summary>
178       void Start()
179       {
```

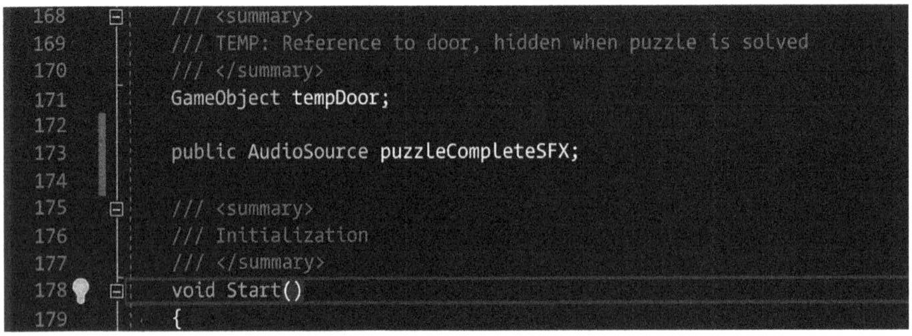

Figure 10.23: Public Audio Source added to the first puzzle script

Now go back to the `First Puzzle` prefab in our scene, open up the inspector, and add an **Audio Source** component. On this **Audio Source**, we will uncheck **Play on Awake** and drag `FirstPuzzleJingle.wav` into it.

Next, in the same way we dragged and dropped our audio component into the `UnityEvent`, we will drag and drop the Audio Source into the new serialized field labeled `Puzzle Complete SFX` on our `FirstPuzzle` script component, seen in *Figure 10.24*.

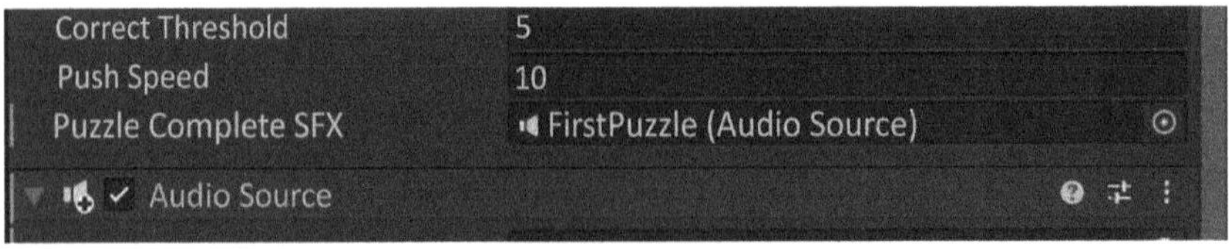

Correct Threshold	5
Push Speed	10
Puzzle Complete SFX	FirstPuzzle (Audio Source)
Audio Source	

Figure 10.24: Dragging and dropping an audio file into the Audio Source component

Chapter 10

Now our last step is to go to the `CheckForVictory()` function inside the `FirstPuzzle.cs` script and go into the `if` statement on line 241. Right before `return true` on line 245, in *Figure 10.25*, we are going to add the following:

```
// Everything is aligned so display the victory
if (outerAligned && middleAligned && innerAligned)
{
    puzzleCompleteSFX.Play();

    return true;
}
return false;
```

Figure 10.25: Adding Play to the Audio Source

Now let's go into our game and see if it works. When we enter the game, we should be able to activate our puzzle and hear sound when we successfully rotate the spires!

Tree puzzle

Using the same method as before, let's add a sound that plays when we put the ball on the bridge, when we solve part of the puzzle, and when we complete the final puzzle. We'll open `FinalPuzzle.cs` and add:

- `IntroPuzzleSolved.wav` on line 31
- `FinalPuzzlePartial.wav` on line 38
- `FinalPuzzleSolved.wav` on line 41

Summary

Congrats! We've just taken our first steps to understanding audio in video games. We've gone over what makes up a sound effect, broken down the five parts of sound design, learned about audio listeners and the differences between music and sound, learned how to use 3D sound, and learned how to trigger Audio Source components through code! This is a great start to breathing life into our game through sound. In *Chapter 12*, *Final Touches*, while polishing audio, we will go over some extra tips to make your audio go that one step further.

In the next chapter, we'll move on to building our project so you can share it with others.

11
Build and Test

At this point in the development journey, we've gone through a great amount of work together. We should now have a vertical slice of a game that, so far, we've been able to play in the Unity Editor and it's working. This is wonderful, but are you going to expect your players to download Unity and open the package up, then play it in the editor? I think not! This is where we want to build the game project out into an executable. In this chapter, we will go over how to build your game out so it can be published and tested and ultimately get into the hands of players.

You will learn about:

- Building from Unity
- Testing—functional, performance, playtesting, soak, and localization testing
- User Experience (UX)

Building with Unity

We've worked very hard to put together an experience. We now need to be able to get it out to people. To do this, we need to tell Unity a couple of things. It needs to know what you are building for, such as which scenes should be built within the application, which platform, and additional options that affect the build output executable.

Where we are now in the vertical slice is a good place to build at. This may not always be the case in every project. In most cases, the best way to work with the build is this: build early, build often. In our case, we needed to wait until we had some mechanics and a standard playthrough from our two major puzzles before we decided to build.

In *Figure 11.1* you can see the **Build Settings** menu, which is found under **File > Build Settings**. Below the image, we will break down each of these settings.

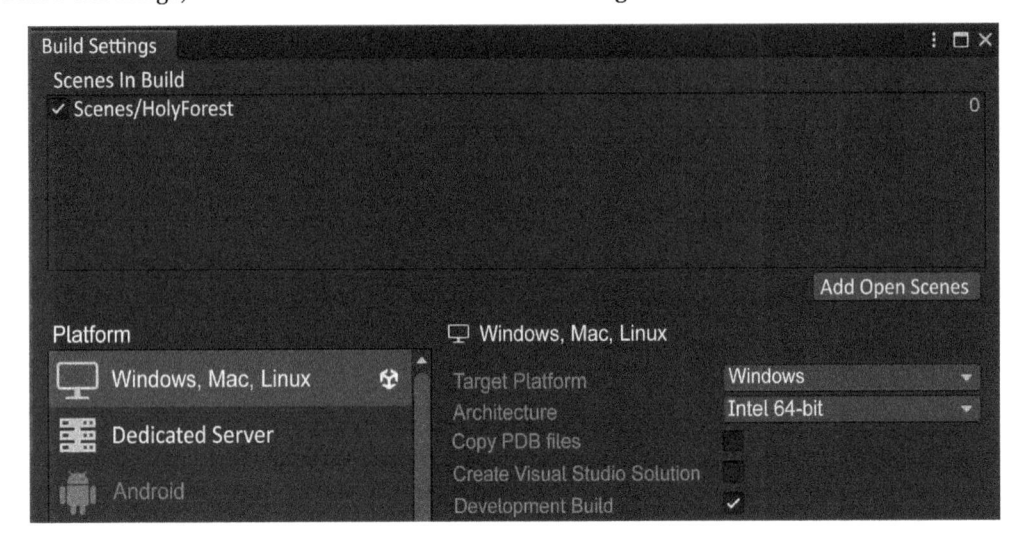

Figure 11.1: Build settings

The first block we see is **Scenes In Build**. As it is at the top, we should have a feeling that it's important. This automatically places the default scene into the box, but there may be other scenes that you want. You may have another scene for menu systems or another map that might be a tutorial level. The key factor here is to have the scenes that you want in the game in this box; you can just drag the scenes from the project window into the **Scenes In Build** box.

> The top scene in this list will always be the first scene that is loaded.

Below the **Scenes In Build** block, the GUI is split into two sections, **Platform** and then settings for that platform. On the left, we choose which platform we want to build for. After that, the settings for that platform will be on the right side. We will go over just the **PC, Mac & Linux Standalone** options.

If you are building for any other platform, the Unity documentation will help guide you through the building process. We will be describing most of the parameters that are available below. Console and mobile choices will have a few different available parameters specific to their target platform's needs.

Target platform

This option is simple enough: which platform would you like to target with this build? The choices here are Windows, macOS, and Linux. We are building for Windows with this vertical slice.

Architecture

We need to know what CPU architecture we should be planning on. A 32-bit OS will require your game to use less than 4 GB of RAM. You can do this, but you can use 64-bit for smaller games as well; it will not hurt your game. In general, 64-bit should be the way to go.

Server Build

Unity can create a server for your game if you are working on a multiplayer game. This will build the player settings with no visual elements. It will also build managed scripts that are defined for multiplayer. We will not be working with this, but know the option is there. We also will not be going over multiplayer development with Unity as that would be a much different project from the beginning.

Copy PDB files

This is a Windows-platform-only setting. It will allow you to build in the Microsoft program database for debugging. We will not be using this either in our build.

Create Visual Studio Solution

This is also a Windows platform-only setting. Enabling this will allow you to build from Visual Studio instead of only from **Build Settings** menu. If you are targeting macOS, there would instead be a **Create Xcode Project** checkbox.

Development Build

Enabling this will allow debugging, including the Profiler. The Profiler is an analyzer to know what is being performed during runtime.

We will be going over this thoroughly in the *Testing* section of this chapter. There are also defined settings that will be included. This is very good for when you need to test your application and are worried about performance. You especially need to keep it in mind if you have a tight visual budget. There is a term that is used called "benchmarking." This term refers to testing your build on a target machine. If you choose a lower-end computer to test on, note its specs and build the game in development mode so that you can run the Profiler while it's running. Once you have the benchmark, you can make some educated guesses on how it will run on higher-end and lower-end machines.

Autoconnect Profiler

If you have **Development Build** turned on, then you can enable this setting. It will automatically connect the Profiler that we talked about above in the *Development Build* section.

Deep Profiling Support

This also requires the development build to be enabled. This enables the Unity Profiler to record more detailed data. This will not be the best option for checking performance as there could be some slowing down of executing scripts. The primary purpose of a deep profiling build is to get a specific cause of managed applications by recording all function calls.

Since every method will be recorded individually, deep profiling provides a very clear view of what is being called and when. Some bugs during gameplay can be lured out and caught more easily with a deep profile.

Script Debugging

Enabling this also needs **Development Build** enabled and it adds debugging symbols to the script code. This will allow the **IDE (Integrated Development Editor**, such as Visual Studio) to be attached to the game when it runs to debug it through your breakpoints and debugging systems. When you select this, another option will pop up as shown below in *Figure 11.2*:

Figure 11.2: Wait For Managed Debugger build setting option

The **Wait For Managed Debugger** option, if enabled, will wait until the IDE is looking for the build to ask for the connection. No scripts will be executed until there is a connection with the debugger.

Scripts Only Build

There may come a time when you find some bugs and need to be able to make some changes, but you don't want to build everything. Data files can get to be very large. We have talked previously in this book about how iteration matters more than almost anything. This can significantly reduce the time between iterations of debugging.

This option will only build the scripts and keep all the data files intact.

Compression Method

There are three options here: **Default, LZ4,** and **LZ4HC. Default** means no compression. No compression will have a runnable file on Windows, Mac, and Linux right away. On Android builds, it will build as a ZIP file.

LZ4 is useful for development builds as the data stored will be compressed and unpacked or decompressed during runtime. Scene and asset loading depend on disk read speeds. This is another option that can be used to help iteration speeds as the build time is faster than the default. An interesting note is that LZ4 decompression on Android is faster than the default ZIP.

LZ4HC is a high-compression version of LZ4, which will take longer to build as it compresses the build further. This is a great option for release builds after spending time debugging.

Starting with **Default** for quick tests in gameplay testing is a good idea. After you get to the point where you need to development build and debug, use LZ4. Then after you're ready to make releases, build on LZ4HC.

Testing

Testing a game is a broad concept. There are large testing portions that are more common and some smaller, more specific ones. The more common testing patterns we see are:

- Functional
- Performance
- Playtesting
- Soak
- Localization

If you research game QA or game testing, you will find several other names for testing, and a studio may have their own specific testing that is their form of best practice.

None of this is wrong. The testing we will explain from the list above is seen in almost every studio. Let's break down the first in the list, functional testing.

Functional testing

Your testing started well before you got to this chapter. Every time you pressed play to check if a script did what it was supposed to do, you tested that script alongside the rest of the game. This is part of the iterative nature of game development and is also called functional testing.

Functional testing has a very direct name! It's testing for the game's functions. A few examples of the scope of the functions being tested are:

- Animation – Looking for animations that don't work together or character rigs that are broken. This is carried out by testing mechanics and movements where the character animation is being transitioned to other animations.
- Audio elements and quality – Listening intently for the purpose of hearing imperfections at specific times. Examples of this might be listening for footstep sounds that sound wrong, ambient noises for objects that aren't there, and anywhere sound is incorrectly placed.
- Cinematics – Playing through the cinematics to find any out-of-place sounds, visuals, animations, or timing of the entire cinematic.
- Instructions or tutorials – There could be instructions on how to play the game. These instructions should be written properly and make sense to the controller scheme the player is using.
- Mechanics interaction – Playing through all the mechanics to feel them out, checking to see if they are working as intended and can be completed if there is completion.
- Sorting – This is a visual check dealing with transparency issues. Layers on the screen need to know their layer on the screen. Some effects and UI will have a hard time knowing what is on top to be sorted properly. This takes testing with multiple scenarios to ensure that the GameObjects with transparency are sorting properly.

- Usability – Usability has its own thread of work that can be tested, but in this case, we are looking for controller schemes that make sense and work. An example is the **A** button being used for a jump; this is so common that if something else is used, it would need to be explained thoroughly as to why.
- UI (menu structure, resolution, aspect ratio, font sizing) – The user interface needs to be checked thoroughly for many parts. How does it look when it's scaled? Do the colors look correct? Can you understand how the menu flows? Every small problem that pops up will be seen by the majority of users. They need to be documented to be fixed.

As you can see, functional testing is thorough and needs to be iterated on to make sure that the game's functions all make sense to the player and work properly. When you're playing the game to test a single mechanic, this is a great practice, but it is only checking out that mechanic in a bubble. The rest of the game could potentially be affected by the changes you are making. Strong functional testing done early and often will make your project that much cleaner and more positive in the end.

While working through functional testing, you may encounter hitches in rendering, making the framerate low. If this happens, take note and add it to the list of performance testing that will be done as well. Since we're on the topic, let's go into how to performance test in Unity.

Performance testing

Inside Unity, we have four sources of analysis:

- Unity Profiler
- Memory Profiler
- Frame debugger
- Physics debugger and Profiler

All four of these analysis tools have their own specific uses to help define what might be causing an issue. We will go through them to a basic degree to get familiar with each one. Starting off, we need to go over the most commonly used one, Unity Profiler.

Unity profiler

To perform profiling, you will need to use Unity's analyzing tool, the Profiler, which looks as in *Figure 11.3* below:

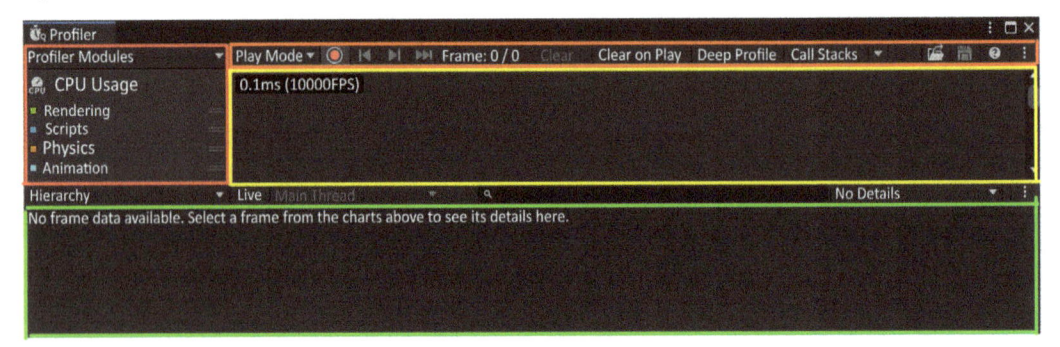

Figure 11.3: Unity's Profiler window example

The profiling tool helps with identifying CPU use, memory usage, and rendering time. When you open the Profiler by going to **Window > Analysis > Profiler,** you will see four sections, as displayed in *Figure 11.3* above. The four sections are:

- (Red) Profiler modules – This section contains what profile modules are in use and has colors to show what is taking place when the recording of the Profiler starts.
- (Orange) Profiler controls – These controls are for setting up what the Profiler is doing. Here you can start recording and change modes or the Profiler tool.
- (Yellow) Frame charts – This shows the individual frames as a stacked chart over time and curves for rendering passes.
- (Green) Module details panels – The module details panels explain every section of the selected frame broken down over a percentage of use on the thread requested. **Default** is the main thread.

As an example, in the profile below in *Figure 11.4*, we have a frame selected while playing our game; I recorded 7800 frames while moving Myvari around. You can see that we're currently running close to 60 frames per second. I wanted to know what was taking the most CPU time from the **PlayerLoop** — in this case, it was the game being played in the editor at ~80%. Scrolling down the **PlayerLoop,** we see that the forward renderer is the heaviest task on the main thread. There is not a lot going on currently in the scene, which is why we're running an average of 60 FPS.

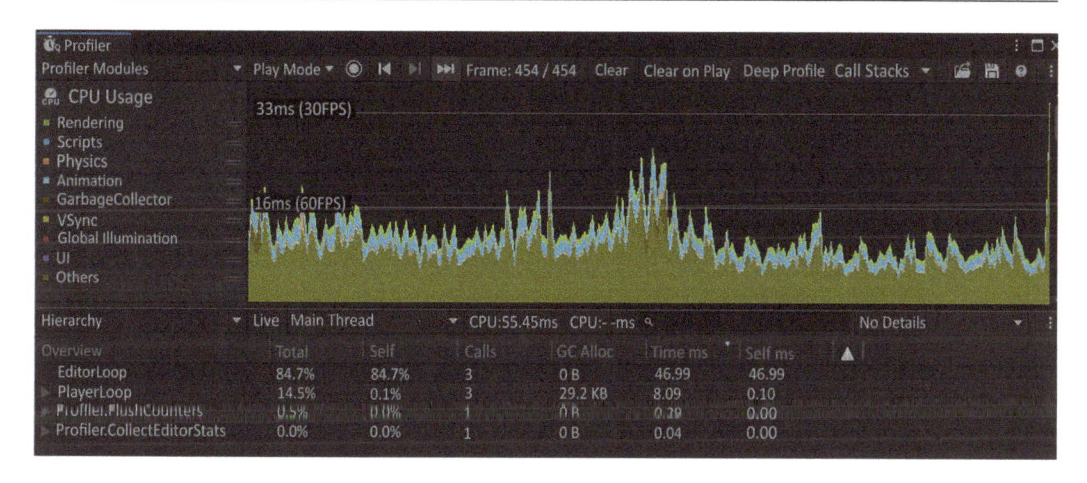

Figure 11.4: Profiler with frame selected

You can see how much information comes along with the Profiler. This is fantastic information when you want to see what might be causing your game to have a lower framerate.

Memory Profiler

This tool, as expected, profiles the memory of the editor. You can also run the memory profiler on a standalone build if **Development Build** is selected in the **Build Settings** menu. The limitation here is that you cannot run the memory Profiler on a release build, just as with the Unity Profiler we saw previously. The Memory Profiler also isn't automatically added to the Unity project. It is a package that can be added. To add it, follow along below.

To add the Memory Profiler, go to your **Package Manager** and add a package by name. This can be done by selecting the options as shown in *Figure 11.5* and then adding com.unity.memoryProfiler to the **Add package by name** field:

Figure 11.5: (Left) Add package by name, (right) Adding the Memory Profiler

When it's installed, you can access the Memory Profiler by going to **Windows > Analysis > Memory Profiler**. When it first loads, you will see a blank middle section with an option to create a snapshot. If you press play and then take a snapshot, you will get a similar screen to what we have here. There is a large amount of info to go over within this Profiler. The primary use of this is if you have a low framerate and you want to check memory usage or if during a soak test you are seeing crashes. You can see, through multiple snapshots in time, what memory is being used.

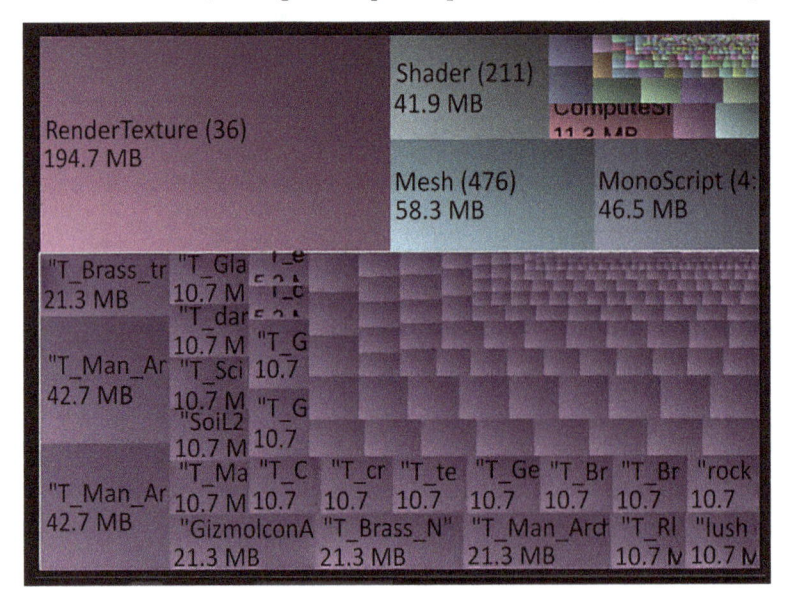

Figure 11.6: Memory Profiler

While looking at a snapshot, the center area breaks down all the memory in that snapshot. In the bottom area, there are blocks of everything used in groups. You can select the groups to break them down even further. We did this to the bottom mauve-colored block, which is used to display Texture2D. We already knew that this would have? a large memory footprint as it's the texturing for all the architecture. It needed to be fairly large.

If the memory looks as you expected, then it may be a good idea to look at the frame debugger to check what could be loading in specific frames that could cause issues. Let's look into that tool next.

Frame debugger

Being able to see an individual frame and how the draw calls were constructed to give you the rendering of that frame can be very helpful for debugging visual artifacts. You may have used this when you were doing functional testing and found sorting issues. You can now load the frame debugger up and see when each item was rendered. From this point, you will have the knowledge to be able to work through why it was rendered in the wrong order.

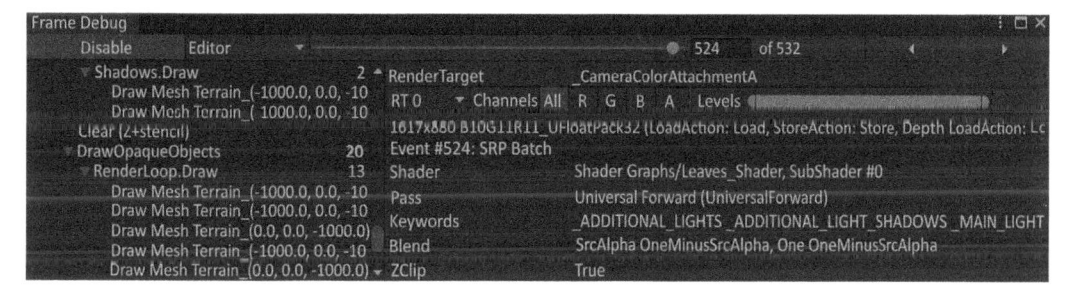

Figure 11.7: Frame debugger

Another strong feature of the frame debugger is that you are able to see what Shader properties were set on the item that was being rendered, as shown in *Figure 11.7* above. This is useful as when you are setting Shader properties procedurally, you may have an expectation of the Shader properties using certain textures of variables. If they aren't as expected, then it would be a great idea to check out the frame and see what it is set to. This could lead to finding out that for one frame it was set to what you expected but then overridden. This could help lead you to the right script that is changing your Shader properties a frame or two after your expected values are being set.

Physics debugger and Profiler module

For physics, we have both a debugger and a Profiler module. The physics debugger is a visualization tool to know what physics collisions are in the scene and what they should or should not be able to collide with. As you saw in *Chapter 7, Rigid Bodies and Physics Interaction*, the Rigidbody is complicated in its optimization settings for physics properties. Being able to visualize what type of collider is on what and where is a great help to knowing what objects are doing when and why. In *Figure 11.8* below, you can see in the scene which objects are physics objects.

Opening the **Colors** section of the physics debugger will allow you to colorize them according to what you might need to debug:

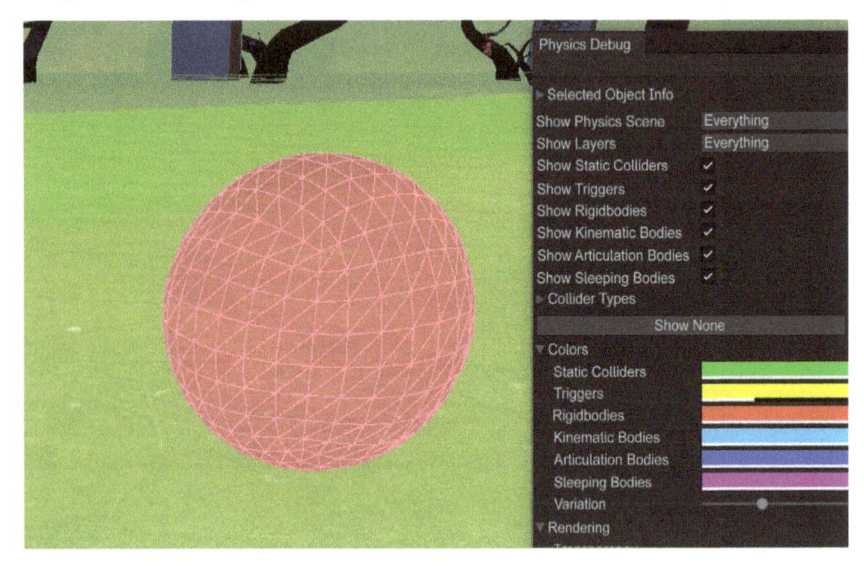

Figure 11.8: Physics Debugger

After you have identified any physics issues from the GameObjects visualized by the physics debugger we have another tool to gather more information. Fortunately for us, we also have the physics Profiler module to be able to help us with any physics issues that are being visualized so we can look up the issue. The physics Profiler module is in the Unity Profiler and will help find answers to the physics discrepancies you may see when the debugger is on.

To see what the physics Profiler module looks like, see *Figure 11.9* below:

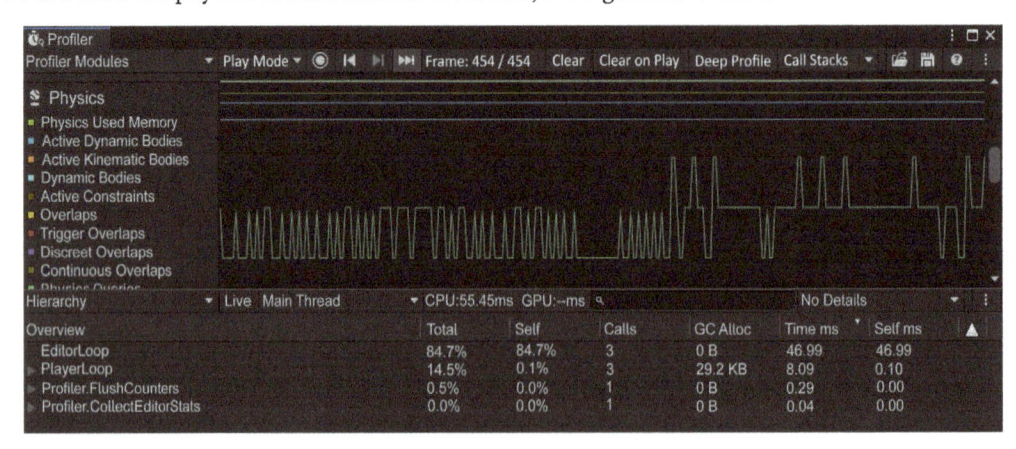

Figure 11.9: Physics Profiler module

The use of this may not be understood at this point as we don't have a case with our physics mechanics to show a direct problem. We don't have fast-moving items that can cause a lot of physics issues. If your game does have fast-moving objects, when you are recording your Profiler and noticing GameObjects clipping through other GameObjects when they shouldn't, this module would be good to see the total memory used. It's possible that the memory being used is not allowing for the physics to update fast enough to get the active body information.

Physics debugging can take time to get to an answer as this needs to happen while the physics work is taking place. Be patient with this debugging and use as many tools as possible to get the answer you need.

Now that we've gone over all of the debugging tools, we need to test the game with others outside of our team. This is called playtesting. Let's get the game into others' hands.

Playtesting

This is a difficult problem to assess. At first, it may be a good idea to test internally with you and your team, friends, and allies. You ask them to play the game and see how they feel about it. This is not meant to build your ego. You need to be there when they are playing and ask them to speak out loud about how they feel about the experience. Do not prompt them on anything. You want them to give you genuine feelings and if they speak to the intended experience, you're on the right track.

Even if the game's art isn't in place and the menu systems are blocky objects with Arial font placeholding for later, none of that detracts from the core game experience. One example is the visceral response when someone enters the first emotional touchpoint you want to evoke. For our project, we want to give a sense of wonder. This is close to confusion, so we need to be deliberate in placement and light usage to encourage adventuring on the player's terms. If they say things such as, "I wonder what's over there," we are leaning into that sense of wonder.

At the same time, they may say that same sentence, but you didn't have anything planned. Let them explore wherever they thought there might be something and take note. It would be a good idea to put something there. Allow that inherent wonderment to take your design further than you have already gone. It almost doesn't matter what would be there if there is a kind of interaction. An example of this is an area that has nothing to do with the narrative that's off to the side just slightly, being available to move into. When testers move into spots on the map that you don't expect them to, take that as an opportunity for engagement. You could build it up as a scenic view. When you walk over there, the camera pans out a bit to take in the view. This isn't an addition to the story, but the sense of wonder was fulfilled. Something happened when you explored.

Exploration may not be a large portion of your game; maybe your title is a socially focused experience. The need for interaction is high for any player that is inside a multiplayer game. In what ways can you interact with your friends when playing together? An extremely good example of this is FromSoftware's multiplayer interaction system. The social interaction in FromSoftware's game — for example *Elden Ring* — allows you to leave short messages with specific words, but you can also use emotes and the message will play your character as a ghost with your small message and the emote. This allows interaction with the emotes that you may have found. This is a very interesting way to allow interaction within a game that is defined by its ability to make you feel alone and weak.

After they are done playing, take all your notes and thank them for their time. You do not need to implement everything you wrote down from their test, but after you have five people test it, there will be trends. Take care of those trends first.

Soak testing

Soak testing isn't an intuitive name. We aren't going to dunk our computers into a bath; we will just let the game run for 24 hours idly. Your character is in the game, live, just sitting by itself while the game plays out. The reason for this is to attempt to bring out any possible memory leaks in the game.

A memory leak is when there is some memory that isn't being taken care of somewhere. Let's say we have a particle that is falling from a tree for some nice ambiance. The particle is set to die, but an accidental couple of extra 0s were added so now instead of lasting for 10 seconds, it's lasting for 1000 seconds. This might not be a problem when you are running around in the game as when you leave, the particles will get culled. But if you let the game idle, all the particle systems making leaves will pile up and several thousand leaves on the ground might cause performance to tank hard. This would need fixing, and wouldn't have been possible without soak testing.

Localization testing

Localization is the act of translating the game to be experienced in another language. This test can take longer than expected and you need to be patient. Every menu item, dialogue line, and description needs to be considered for this testing portion. Translation also isn't just a word-for-word explanation. Some languages require more context for their descriptions, which can lead to very confusing translations if not paid close attention to.

When localizing a game, take care not to rush this process. It can completely throw off another culture's experience, which would be a shame!

User experience, or UX

UX can be defined as the sum of the parts within branding, design, and usability. For our part, we will briefly cover how branding plays its part in the UX role. We will then speak about design only a little bit as we've covered design for the fundamental parts of this project already. After we cover those quickly, we can then move into usability. Let's go for it!

Branding

To cover this broadly, branding through a UX lens is about how the overall experience the user will take through the journey of the game will need to also be reflected in the branding. For an overly contrasted example, think about if a horror game's branding used soft tones and pastels with flowers and happy music as their marketing material. This obviously doesn't fit the branding of the game and will cause dissonance in the user's experience.

The purpose and point of UX as a defined part of development is that deliberate cohesive actions are paid attention to. The time spent on UX should ensure that all the designed parts, including the logo, marketing material, and the game parts, are part of a whole, unified experience.

Design

We've covered a lot of design in this book so far. Interestingly, we've covered all of our design in a bit of a siloed manner. Sometimes this can cause an issue, but luckily for our project we really focused this game on the character design. The rest of the design was built around the past of her race, which provided answers to questions for visual cues.

The pacing of the game is dealt with through the style of gameplay and mechanics being focused on environmental narratives. With those three parts combined, it turned out to be a cohesive project already. This does a good job of validating the time we spent on design within every part. Good job sticking with it!

Usability

After you've hooked a user through your exquisite branding and intelligent and cohesive design, they should be able to use the product. For games, usability is all focused on interactions. This shouldn't be much surprise as we've defined this as a pillar for experience in *Chapter 6, Interactions and Mechanics*. We've worked through overall interaction with the player; however, there is no defined affordance. We need to work through how the player knows they can perform the interactions.

We will go over the major portions of the vertical slice here, starting with the initial problem of getting to the first puzzle, then moving on to the first puzzle itself. After that, we need to bring about how the next mechanic, telekinesis, will be introduced, and then lastly the final puzzle.

Initial problem

Within the starting cave section, we have a blocked stairway where the player needs to interact with two objects to unlock. There are several things we will use to give affordance to the player, so they know how to perform the needed task:

- Light pooling
- Worldspace UI
- Satisfy the action

Light pooling is a small part of environment or level design that allows the player to feel as though they should be heading in that direction. If a tunnel is dark and there is a light at the end, the player will tend to head toward that light. We can use this method to have glowing objects or lights near a button that needs to be pressed.

Now that they are near it, when they mouse near enough, we will pop up a worldspace UI for interaction. This button should be the same as every other interaction of this type. For this game, our interaction is the *E* key on the keyboard.

After you use the interactive button, there needs to be something that satisfies the use of that action. In this case, it's a button in a rock. It will animate to set itself in place, glow from being used, and trigger a sound to fully indicate that the user used their affordance.

First puzzle

When you first come up to the first puzzle, it may not be immediately understood that the player's purpose is to move the stones into a position. We used one primary key usability feature, among others which will seem similar. Let's list them out again:

- Light pooling
- Hero art piece
- Worldspace UI
- Camera positioning (the key factor previously mentioned)
- Satisfy the action

We previously went over light pooling as a concept for positioning. In this case, we will be using light pooling to draw visual attention to a place to move to. The thing to look at is the door as it has the answer to the puzzle laid out in front of you.

The art piece we are light pooling to is the answer to the puzzle. It's directly placed at the next position you are headed and right in front of you when you exit the stairs, and it's lit up. There is no barrier to entry on what you should be looking at when you get to the top of the stairs. That is what we like to do for our players. Let them get a feel for exploration but know they are looking at the right place when they do.

Our worldspace UI is the same as before, but we are using it to let the player know they can interact with the puzzle piece when they get close to the moveable pieces.

The key factor to moving in the next section is the camera movement. When you enter the space of the puzzle, the camera will gently move up to a position that will represent the successful movement of the pillars in coordination with the art piece on the door when you first entered.

After the player moves the pillars into position, there are loud sounds of rocks being put into place and connections of what might sound like a large lock tumbler falling into place. When the final pillar is in place, the entire piece moves into the finalized complete position and the camera moves back to their shoulder while a pillar rises in the middle to allow the player to press the "door open" button.

Introduction to a secondary mechanic

We've been explaining players' affordances and how to get them to do the actions. You can add new mechanics without breaking the experience as long as you take care to introduce them in a deliberate manner. So far, Myvari has only been an explorer. We want her to have slight telekinesis powers from her ancient blood. We could just have them active and put something in her way, but that isn't very fun, and the experience isn't as strong.

To get ourselves a new mechanic and hopefully draw the player into caring about our main character, what we will do is give two actions that at first don't directly involve the player, but they do involve Myvari. The first thing that we will do is, while walking out in a thin area on the side of the mountain, we will have a large rock come tumbling down the mountain. There will be a cinematic that will happen where she will be alarmed, and she will defend herself by putting up her arm, which triggers her telekinesis just slightly, and she will maneuver the rock to the side slightly so that is crashes down the mountain instead of on top of Myvari herself.

Next, after some small exploration, the player will come across an area where they cannot enter the next area, but can see it. There is a pillar that looks like the one that opened the first door from the first puzzle, but it's separated. We will use a new form of worldspace UI and when you hover over the broken piece, it will be outlined and the interact button will pop up. This outline will have a similar color to what was used when the telekinesis happened with the rock and when you interact with it, you will put your hand out and pick it up. It will, when close enough to the pillar, automatically fix itself, which triggers many visual changes to the area you are in.

In conclusion, we are using small examples of telekinesis to introduce this slowly and in a way that befits the character. This is a good use of usability as the player gets to grow with the character. We can now take what we learned here and push it into the final puzzle, which uses this telekinesis as a primary mechanic.

Final puzzle

It's interesting how much effort it takes to make an experience strong! Those lead-up efforts for describing a mechanic are the glue that makes the experience a matter of immersion instead of just another button to press to make the character do something.

We now enter the final puzzle and there are similar means for player affordances that you've seen previously. We will use slightly different means as the items used in the mechanic are different, but the overall concept is driven by the environment. You will see these UX usability functions in the final puzzle area:

- Light pooling
- Connection to the hero art piece
- Worldspace UI
- Satisfy the action

As always, we use lighting to help our players understand the next move subtly. There is a large light coming from behind our hero piece (main focus) tree, meaning it has narrative implications and needed more authored treatment, which shows a glow coming from each of the cables attached to the architecture. If you follow the cables, they flow through large pillars.

Those pillars are connected to the hero art piece, which is the central tree. The thing is that the pillars themselves are missing something. That something is on the ground in multiple locations around the tree's area. Moving your mouse to look at these larger spherical objects shows you can interact with them.

The interaction, in this case, is the worldspace UI. This is the outline that we already saw previously coming across the water bridge when we picked up the piece to complete the pillar. Picking up the object and moving it near the empty location with the same shape lights up the cables, which needs to be done in a certain order to get power to the tree. This is only slowed down by the character's ability to notice some cabling is broken or not connected properly.

Satisfying the action comes from the nice energy flowing from the cables toward the tree with each placement of the object. By the end, the tree will light up in a cinematic and open a section that reveals a tiara. Myvari grabs the tiara and places it on her head to unlock her place as the final princess of her ancient race.

This ends the vertical slice when the portal turns on from the completion of the puzzle and she walks through it, excited for the next step of the adventure.

Summary

You might be thinking, "what's next?" This is a great question. You have a game that is built and has gone through some testing with some bug fixes. It's a playable item in this case and could provide plenty of context to investors to continue the journey of getting a game funded or published.

What we will go over next are polishing techniques to try for beauty and UX to take the front seat. We're calling these finishing touches as we know that the vertical slice is in a good state to add final touches to it only. Take some time in the next chapter to see all the tasks we can do to push our brand and quality into the game.

12

Finishing Touches

Welcome to the *Finishing Touches* chapter! There is a misconception about how long games take to make and the overall difficulty of game development. This chapter will act as a toolbox to guide you in finishing your projects. This isn't a straightforward next step, but rather an open box for you to see what we're using to polish up our vertical slice. An interesting feature of the polishing process is that it covers a good 80% of game development. This might sound unintuitive; however, if you've been paying attention to the screenshots during the development, you will have noticed that we don't have a complete game by any stretch of the imagination at this point from a consumer's point of view. The mechanics work and the game is an experience by now, just not a complete one.

This chapter will go over:

- Overview
- Asset finalization
- Lighting
- Sound polish

Overview

Finishing touches are extremely important to a complete experience. We need to take what we have and tighten up all the stitches. This is done in several ways.

Lighting and sound are very difficult to finalize prior to this point. There can be **research and development (R&D)**, but unless the game's focus is one of those two topics, you won't be getting finalized lighting or sound until there are finalized assets in the game, as seen in the list in the following section. You're correct in wondering why we had a chapter on sound before this. We wanted to go over the basics of sound in general and get you familiar with the concept of sound design and its implementation within Unity.

Lighting could be worked on early to set a mood but will need to be finalized after environments and light pools are well defined and firm in place. Again, if lighting and mood are going to be in the experience, then heavy lighting R&D will need to take place even in the blocking-in stages of development. All the conversations here about lighting will guide you during that stage too if it's needed.

The way this will work is that there will be specific actions that we will cover in all three of the major sections in this chapter. These actions are specific to our project but could help you with your future projects all the same. Think of them as tools instead of a tutorial. Some of them may need programming, and some of them may not.

As most of the mechanics have been programmed to a certain degree, we will focus first on asset finalization. Remember, as we said, it's hard to get lighting and sound if the assets aren't done. Let's start there!

Asset finalization

This section will be awesome. There are so many great art assets and finishing touches that we can go over. Here is a list of tools we used that may help you in your projects in the future:

- Stylized pass on assets
- Detail normals
- Architecture cleanup
- Texture blending
- Environment clutter
- Detail meshes
- Effects
- Cinematics
- Secondary animation

Chapter 12

The way we will go through these sections is that we will have an explanation of why we will be doing this for our project, which may help you decide if you need to perform these polishing touches on your own projects in the future. After that, we will cover the literal steps that we took so that you can see how they are done. Interestingly, the actual steps we are taking may not be the only way to achieve these finishing touches. The best way to take these actions is as a concept or a starting point as the needs will be different for your project. We will begin our finishing touches with a stylized pass on our assets.

Stylized pass on assets

When defining an art style, we begin with broad strokes. Even if you take the time to outline the art direction, once you get to the polishing phase, you will need to make a pass on it to get the finishing touches in place. In our case, we found that our assets didn't have enough of a stylized look to them to fit our art direction. The word stylized is used very often and it has the right to be used often for games as it means to just not look realistic. In our case, we want the stylizing to make everything feel more illustrative in nature. This means we need to push all our contrasting silhouettes and colors into the textures. We also need broader line weights in our textures.

A good example within our project is Myvari's necklace. This art piece needs to stand out as it is the primary focus of Myvari's telekinesis. We also know that we will be seeing it up close during cinematics, so we need to ensure that we put time into designing this piece.

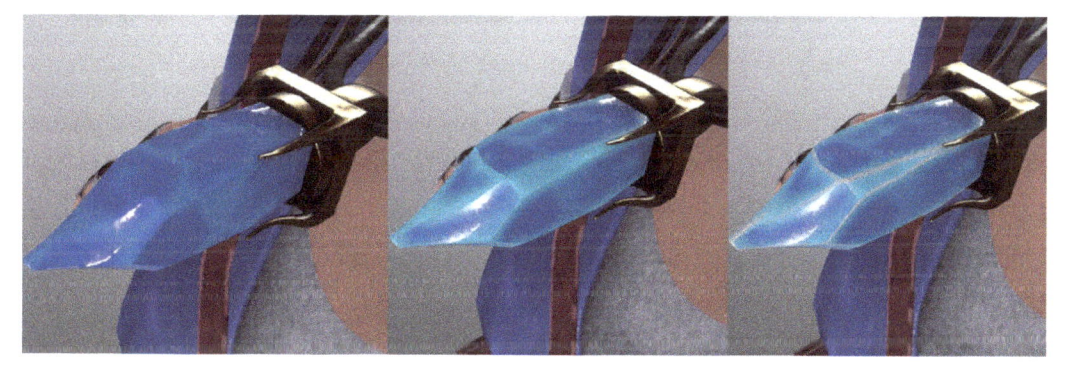

Figure 12.1: Stylized passes for Myvari's necklace

This needs to happen throughout all the art pieces to have as much consistency as possible within the character and the world. Once the stylized pass is completed, some models may need to have small details added. We call them "detail normals." Let's go over them now!

Detail normals

A detail normal can sometimes be considered part of the stylized pass. In our case, we wanted this to be a standout part of the art direction overall, so we pulled it out of the stylized pass. We want to drive home the stylized nature of the silhouettes in the models; however, we want to give the materials themselves a sense of realism. Leather will need to look like leather, and bark should look like bark. Below in *Figure 12.2*, we have a detail normal on the mushroom to give a bit of extra nuance to it. The left image has base normals and texture. The right image has detail normals layered on top.

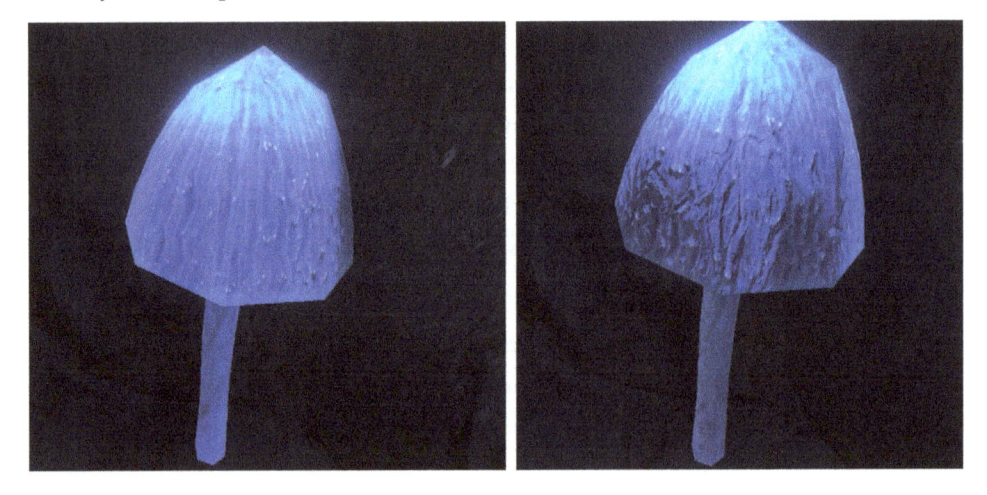

Figure 12.2: Left, no detail normal; Right, detail normal added

Detail textures are also interesting as they are generally smaller details from a tileable texture that won't fit nicely on the texture itself due to the sizing of the model's texture. To gain the small details, we layered them in the shader.

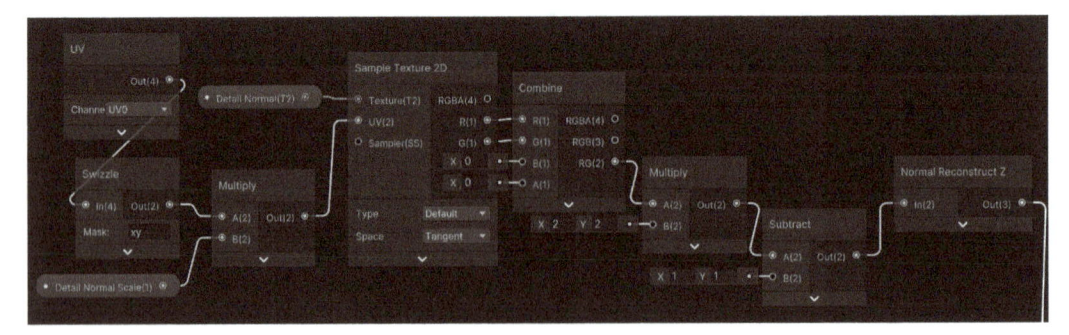

Figure 12.3: Detail normals

Above is the shader we are using for our detail normal in *Figure 12.3*. The way we will break this down is by following the data connection points and explaining the reasoning per node. To start off, we begin with a UV node.

UV node – This node sets the UV space you will be manipulating. The dropdown allows you to choose which UV map to manipulate. Since we are using the main UV channel, we will keep it at UV0. We will take the output of the UV node and input it into a Swizzle node.

Swizzle node – The Swizzle node allows users to take an input and mix the channels to create an output with the data amount that is needed. You'll notice that we have set xy as the output. Our input is a pin line, which refers to a Vector4, which is shown in the input of the Swizzle as well. We only need the red and green channels in this case, so we just request the xy or rg channel and we get a Vector2 output green line. Unity's Shader Graph already culls the rest of the channels, so we do not specifically need this, but it's a good habit to only use the channels that you need to work with. We take this output into a Multiply node.

Multiply node – We use a float parameter here for the customizability of the UVs down the line alongside the Swizzle input. The **Detail Normal Scale** parameter is exposed so we can make a change in the inspector later on, tweaking it to our needs. The output of this will go into the UV channel of a Sample Texture 2D node.

Sample Texture 2D node – Another input to this node is our texture 2D parameter detail normal. We need to make sure that the **Space** option is set to **Tangent** as we will be affecting the tangents to reconstruct the normal later on. We will be taking the output and getting to a Vector2 once again, but with a different method than Swizzle. We will be using a Combine node from the individual channels on the Sample Texture 2D node.

Combine node – Taking in the R and G from the Sample Texture 2D node output, we combine it to make a Vector2 that is sampling the texture we want and following the UVs we're setting. Now we need to take this Vector2 into a scale and bias it into a different range.

Scale and Bias nodes (using multiply and subtract) – The next two nodes are a basic math function to transform the (0 to 1) range to a (-1 to 1) range. We do this by multiplying by 2 and then subtracting 1 on both the X and Y vectors. This is important to us as we may want the normal to appear as concave, or going into the model. After we finish this function, we will take the output into a Normal Reconstruct Z node.

Normal Reconstruct Z node – This node's purpose is to derive the correct Z values for the input of R and G from the normal map we chose in the Sample Texture 2D node.

After this there are three more steps. We will be following individual figures for these next steps. We will take the output of this node and move it into a Normal Strength node.

Normal Strength node – Plugging into the Normal Strength node are the normals we had as an output from the Normal Reconstruct Z node. There is also a float value for which we created a parameter named **Detail Normal Strength**. This can be seen below in *Figure 12.4*. We're using this node so that if the normal map seems like it might have too much detail or is not visually appealing, we can tone it down a little. The parameter we set in the **Strength** input allows us to dynamically set the Detail Normal Strength per material.

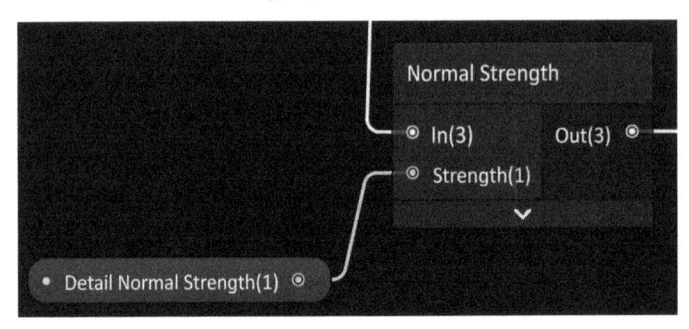

Figure 12.4: Normal Strength node

We take the output of this and put it into a Normal Blend node.

Normal Blend node – We ultimately want these detail normals to be layered with the normal of the mesh itself. This is the node that we will be doing this with.

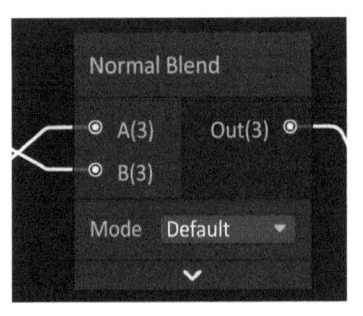

Figure 12.5: Normal Blend node

It will output a normal map with both normals inside the data. We will then place the output into a Boolean keyword parameter, which we named `Detail Normal?`.

Boolean keyword – This Boolean keyword is designed in a way to allow us to either use a detail normal or not. Since this shader is being used across many materials, we need a way to exclude a detail normal from being needed if a mesh may not have one. We've done this by having the input for On be the blended normals of the mesh and the detail normal. If it's set to Off then just the mesh normal will be accepted.

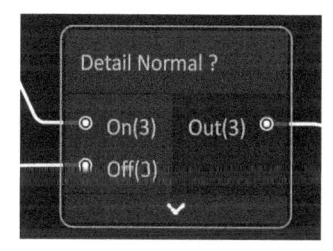

Figure 12.6: Detail normal Boolean keyword

The output of this will then go into the **Master Stack Normal** input. When you create a material, if you want to have a detail normal, all you need to do is select On with the checkbox of the Detail Normal? parameter.

Next, we will work through cleaning up the architecture.

Architecture cleanup

The silhouettes of the current buildings may look good, but does the architecture make sense? This is an interesting design issue with building shapes. We need to ensure that the architecture looks like something that might be built by a living creature. This is a difficult task to get right as the creatures we're looking to emulate don't exist! They are fictional creatures, which means we need to be very clear on the path we take when architecting for them.

We know that they are focused on celestial bodies and time concepts. The shapes of space, planets, and the concept of time need to take part in the silhouettes of the buildings and materials. This may not mean an entire remodel of the pieces but more pushing the shapes so the language stands out enough to fit the culture we're designing for.

We also need to get rid of some geometry that won't ever be seen. This is in order to optimize the game and is important. In games, if you cannot see it, then it doesn't need to render. Therefore, we do something called **backface culling**. This means that if you were to look at the back half of a sphere from the inside it would be invisible.

The backside of an object isn't rendered as it's not seen. If you didn't do that then the sphere would have to render all the inside faces, which would be a waste of precious computer time; we need to render everything else.

Texture blending

When building terrain or larger objects that need to connect, there is always a bit of a line that shows that the objects are 3D meshes. This is a common problem, and it can hurt immersion or break the experience if not worked with closely. There are several ways to make this better. You may add another mesh on top of the split. You could also layer or overlap the meshes to make a break in the model to let the player think that it was meant to be slightly broken. You could also perform something called **texture blending**.

One way that we have done this is through Y-up materials. They may have other names as well, but I call them that due to using the Y-up axis to blend in materials. What we do is ask the shader to blend in positive Y of the world normal values. We use this value at the Lerp value in our shader where the base texture is on the A channel and B is the moss or snow texture. Let's look at *Figures 12.7* through *12.9* below for screenshots of the Shadergraph imagery. In *Figure 12.7*, we're showing some rocks that have a single UV set with a rock texture. These rocks are exactly the same except we've duplicated them and rotated them to show the shader that we put together that places the texture on the world normals.

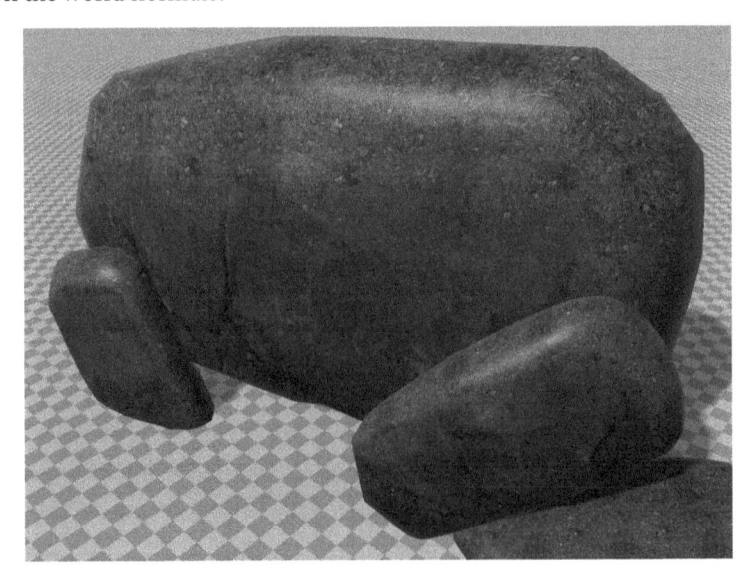

Figure 12.7: Rocks with our Y-up shader applied

Chapter 12

The textures applied to this aren't final moss textures, but they are designed to be contrasted to the rock to show the textures separately. This allows us to work through the differences easily with visuals. You'll notice that the rocks are the same, but scaled and rotated. This is a strong way to provide reuse within your meshes in your scene so you don't have to model so many rocks! Let's look at the Shadergraph on how this works next.

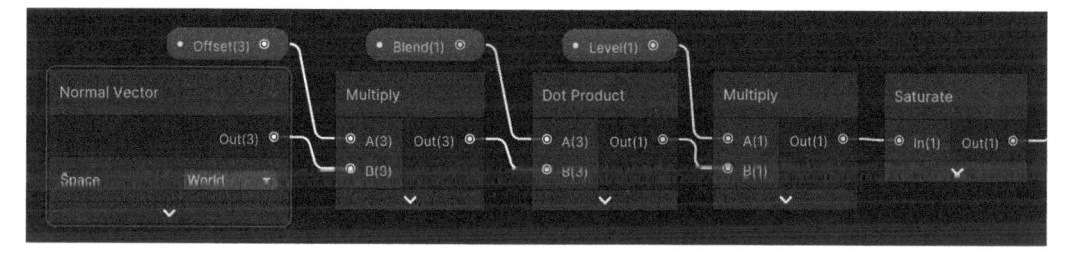

Figure 12.8: World normal Y-up for T value of Lerp

We need to plan out how we will split the rendering of the texture on the mesh. The interesting thing is that we need to make the texture always appear on the top of the mesh regardless of how it's rotated. We decided to take the normal vector of the world space and then multiply it by a Vector3 that we named Offset. We want the positive Y, so the default value of our Offset parameter will be (0, 1, 0). We have two more blending parameters. They are Blend and Level and they are both floats. The **Blend** parameter is a hard value from 0 to 1. With 0 there is no blending and the rock is the only texture, and with 1 there is no blending where the other texture has a hard line. This is complemented with the Level parameter. The Level parameter should be set to **Slider** with the min value set to 0 and the max to 100, and the **Default** set to 1; these can be set in the **Node Settings** in the **Graph Inspector**. We added it in this shader to show that you can add more tools for your artists per material. At the end of this line of data is a saturate.

This ensures that the data sticks to the 0-1 range, which is what we need to be the T value of the Lerp, which we will go over next.

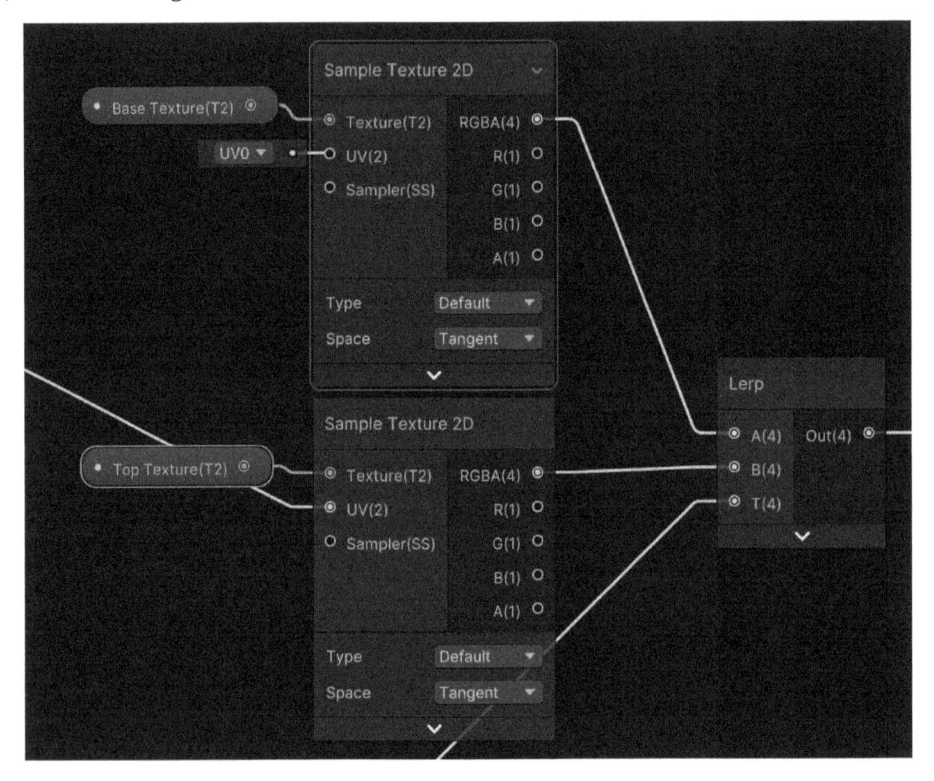

Figure 12.9: Texture lookups and Lerp

Above in *Figure 12.9* is our Lerp. Value is the base texture, and B is the Y-up texture. T is the output of our saturate in *Figure 12.8*. The output of the Lerp is going into our base color. This is only the beginning and you can bolster this by using normal maps and height maps to help mix the channels to make them even more seamless. We currently aren't using extra maps in this shader, but the concept uses the exact same nodes, just with the additional maps as inputs.

Environment clutter

This is a job all on its own. Those who work with environment clutter are known in the industry as clutter artists. Their job is to place items to make the environment feel lived in. Currently, we have an environment that is mechanically designed. We know where Myvari needs to be to trigger cinematics. We know how she will work with the physics puzzles. What we don't know is how the people lived in this space previously.

What were these spaces used for before there were puzzles to open the doors? Should there be broken things around or did it all break down a long time ago? Should there be spiderwebs or plants growing over some pieces?

The clutter artists will have a set of small items to place around to make it feel like there was something going on here at one point in time. This is where we have an opportunity to tell small stories in every section.

Detail meshes

Unity terrain can house detail meshes to place simple meshes, such as grass or small rocks. We explained this in *Chapter 5*, *Environment*, in the *Painting details* section briefly. The primary reason it's in this chapter is to explain that there is more work to be done with the details. This is very similar to the clutter artist's work; however, this isn't specific to how the space was lived in but to develop the nature. In our case, we are using it for grass and rocks. We need to make sure that the grass and rocks are in a spot that makes sense.

This is primarily working through the finer details of cleaning up the scene in regard to the detail meshes.

Effects

Polishing effects are similar to polishing animations. They need to be finessed to ensure that it is stimulating the correct emotions of the viewer. Most of the effects in this vertical slice are meant to be ambient. We will be covering two effects. The first one will be the blocker to the stairs in the first portion of the cave. The second one will be Myvari's telekinesis. We chose these two effects to cover in the book as they are quite unique from each other.

Stair blocker

The stair blocker is there to create an obstacle for the player in going up the stairs. They need to find a way to disable this so they can progress. We decided to go with arcane energy moving upward in front of the stairs. This will be done purely through a shader, which means we will cover some simple techniques in the Shader Graph.

The image shown here, in *Figure 12.10*, of the effect is static, so jump into the project and look at the first puzzle area in front of the stairs.

Figure 12.10: Stair blocking effect

This effect is made by utilizing a channel-packed texture with three unique cloud textures. The cloud textures are a grayscale perlin noise in Adobe Photoshop. We took each layer and placed it in the Red, Green, and Blue channels to have three textures in one image. This allows us to use multiple different clouds to build our own noise pattern when animating its UVs. To make this effect work, we needed a way to animate these UVs in multiple ways. We chose an A set and a B set, which we created in our parameters. Let's go through all of our parameters to make sure we are on the same page. We will explain why we have each parameter as we grow out of this effect as seen in *Figure 12.11* below.

We have **Color**, which will be setting the overall color of the arcane magic. **Cloud Tex** will be the texture you can use for this shader. We then have **Offset** and **Tiling** with both an A and B version. We will cover the two parameters soon. Then we have two edges that are used for a Smoothstep node.

We need to first figure out how to make our texture animate. We will be using **Tiling**, **Offset**, and **Cloud Tex** to perform this initial section of the shader.

Chapter 12

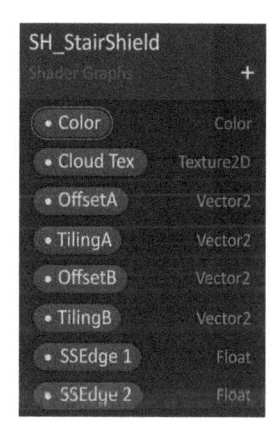

Figure 12.11: StairShield parameters from Blackboard

Looking at *Figure 12.12* below, we've previously seen the Sample Texture 2D and **Multiply** nodes. Let's go over the **Time** node. This node gives you access to the game time, the sin and cos of the game time, the delta time, and a smoothed delta. We will be using game time and multiplying it by a constant value for our speed. The next node that is new is the **Tiling And Offset** node. This node is a utility node to help deal with tiling and offsetting the UVs on a mesh that the material will be applied to. We assign the offset Vector2 to the multiplication of time. This will provide a moving value for our offset. This will animate the UVs in the direction you want them to move.

The last part is to plug the Tiling And Offset node into the UV input of the Sample Texture 2D node. You aren't seeing the Offset and Tiling B set in this image as it's the same nodes with different parameters. The reason we want to have multiple sets is that we want to have independent textures with different speeds and UV tiling scales. This makes a dynamic texture in the output.

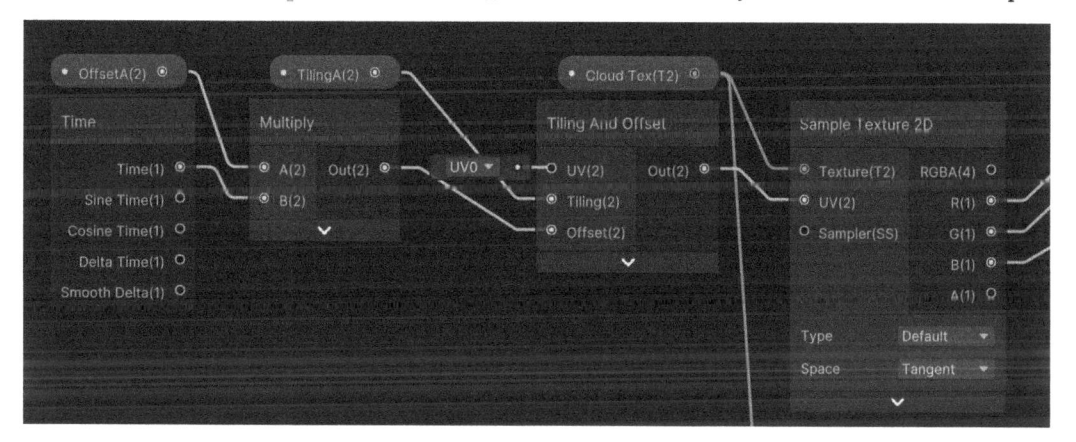

Figure 12.12: Offset and Tiling for our cloud texture

We need to put together a seemingly never-ending tiling pattern. All of these noise patterns are tiling in both horizontal and vertical directions. Sometimes this is called a four-way tiling texture. We had planned to move Offset A up in the Y axis by a faster amount and then Offset B a bit slower. We would also tile the B set somewhere between .5 and .75. This would give us a totally different set of noise to layer on top of the other.

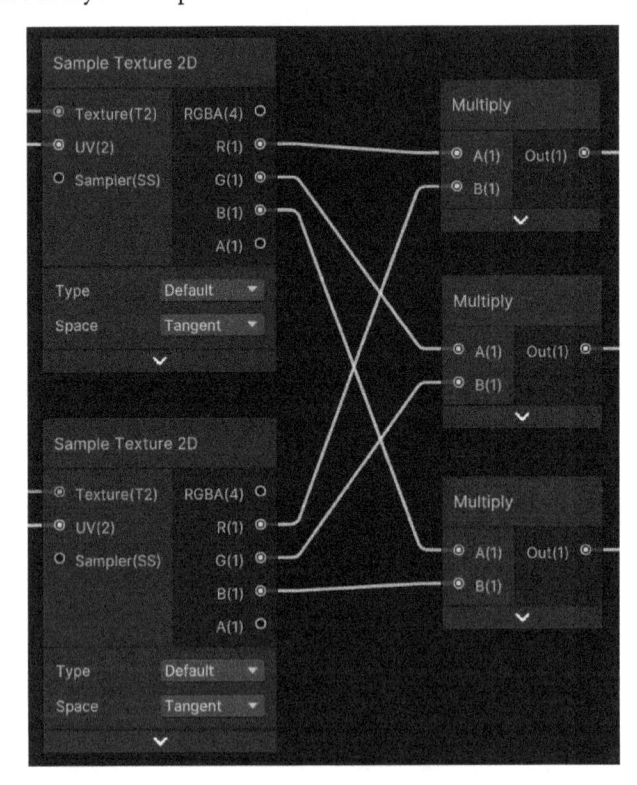

Figure 12.13: Crossing the channels

In *Figure 12.13* above we are making three dynamic images to put together. Both Sample Texture 2D nodes have different tiling settings and different offsets moving in time. Putting them together with a multiply will inevitably create a living cloud structure as they cross paths. We're doing that with all three channels (R, G, B). Next, we will multiply each of these by 5 to force the entire image channels higher than their original. Then we add together the three channels into one output by adding the first two multiplied nodes, then adding the third one to that, as seen below in *Figure 12.14*.

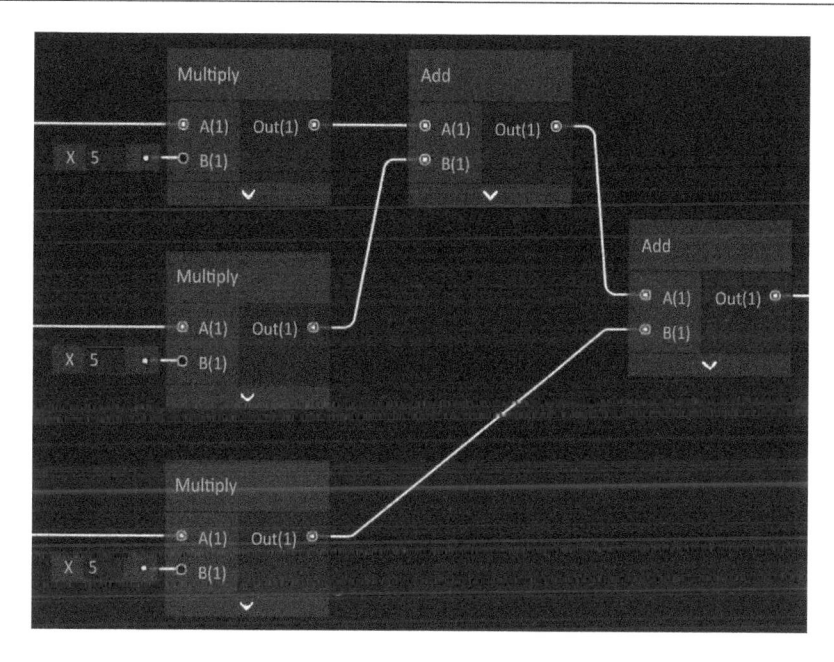

Figure 12.14: Multiply and Add

Now that we have a single data stream with movement, we can push values to make a more interesting effect. We like to smoothstep data to push anything that is close to 0 to 0 and what is close to 1 to 1. This makes the layered data make interesting shapes as seen in *Figure 12.15* below. The problem with this is the overall cloudiness is lost in that process, so we want to add in the previous **Add** and then saturate it to make sure it's within the range 0-1 and then multiply it by a color parameter so we change the color in the inspector.

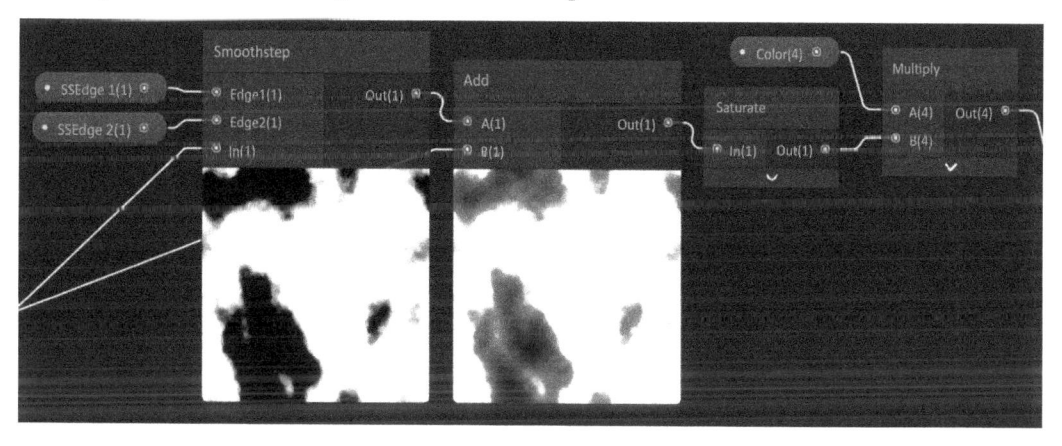

Figure 12.15: Smoothstep and color

The output of the color node will go into the base color. We then make a material that uses the SH_StairShield shader, then apply it to a plane in the scene where we wanted to show there is something blocking the stairs.

Shuriken system – stair blocker particles layer

We like the way the stair block feels, but the effects need layers to feel like well-made art. We also needed to spend a bit of time going over Shuriken itself. This effect will go over some basic portions of Shuriken for producing simple effects to layer into your world. What we will be creating is a stretched sprite moving upward to give more energy to the stair blocker.

To begin, we wanted to make something with a default item to show the power of particle systems. We are using the ParticlesUnlit material, which is a simple radial gradient from the center. We sometimes call these "math dots" as they can be created without a texture. We want to spawn particles that have a lot of energy upward but get slowed down near the end of their life and fade out. We will go through the settings below to make this happen; however, we encourage you to look in the project at the particle system and play with the settings. Make some changes to see if you can make something you feel looks better. Share it on Discord!

The Shuriken system has a large number of parameters inside the modules. We will only be going over the ones we modified and needed to enable for this simple system. We implore you to look through the Unity documentation for an explanation of all the parameters and modules. Let's look at the main module first, below in *Figure 12.16*.

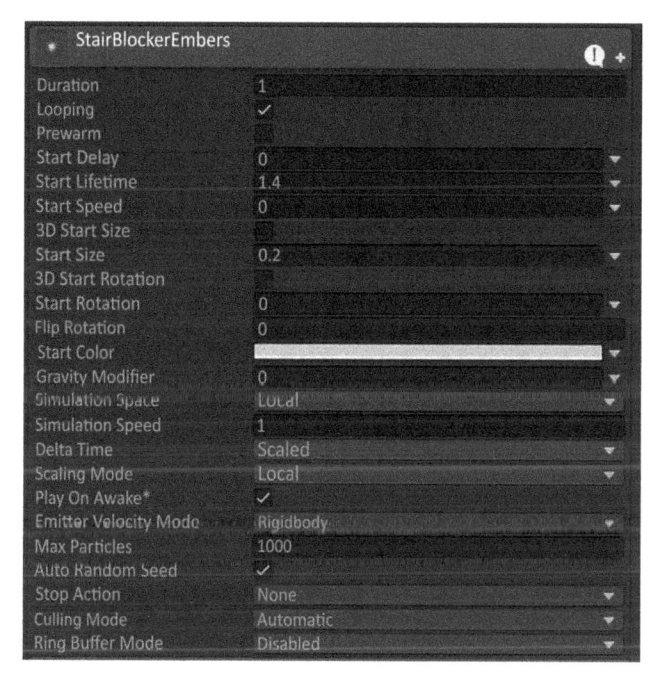

Figure 12.16: Shuriken main module

The only parameters we made changes to here were **Start Lifetime**, changing it to 1.4, and **Start Speed**, setting it to 0. We made the lifetime change after making all of the other changes as we didn't know exactly how long we wanted this particle system to live. The **Start Speed** we put to 0 because we knew we wanted to control the velocity. We also modified the color but we'll override the color in the **Color Over Life** module later on. The next module we will go over is **Emission**.

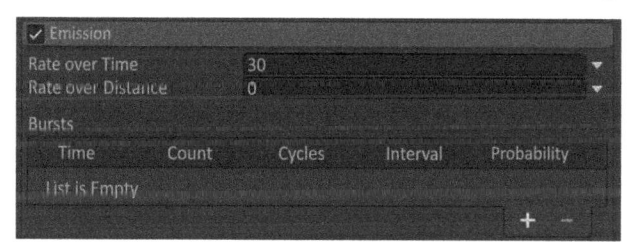

Figure 12.17: Emission module

As seen above in *Figure 12.17*, this is the **Emission** module. We changed **Rate over Time** to 30 to make sure we have plenty of particles spawning. The emission of your particles is highly dependent on what you need to convey. For us, we wanted to have enough to add to the stair barrier shader, but not too much that we overpower it.

We now have a bunch of particles spawning, but we know we want it to be spawning near the bottom of the stair blocker. We will use the **Shape** module to restrict the spawning to a location that makes sense to the purpose of the effect.

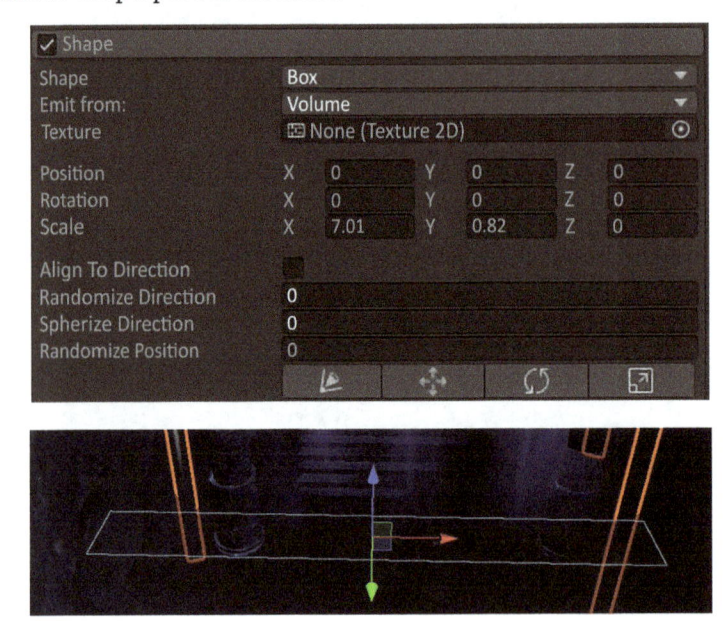

Figure 12.18: Shape module and shape placed in game

We chose the shape to be a box as we wanted the particles to spawn from the bottom of the stair blocker and move up from there to follow the flow of the movement. We then needed to get these particles moving. We know we wanted them moving upward quickly, thus setting 100 in **Linear Z**, shown in *Figure 12.19* below. This blasts them off to space, but we want to add a drag component to our velocity to slow them down near the top. This comes from the limit **Velocity over Lifetime**.

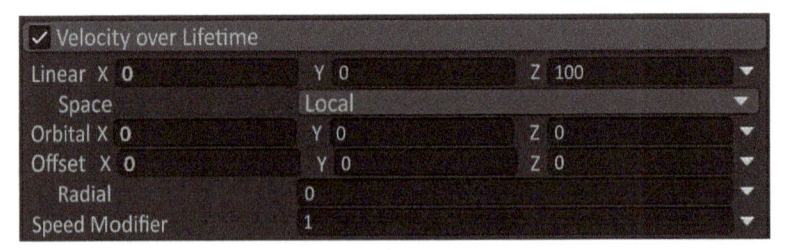

Figure 12.19: Velocity over Lifetime module

Figure 12.20 below shows where we will add drag to our particles. We're keeping the drag at a constant value and setting it to 5. This value gave it a nice drag. This value wasn't known beforehand; we just play around with it until it feels like what we're looking for.

Figure 12.20: Limit Velocity over Lifetime module

Next, we need to colorize these particles as they are just white math dots going upward. Enabling the **Color over Lifetime** module, seen below in *Figure 12.21*, allows you to define a gradient where the left side is the beginning of the particle's life, and the right side is the end of the particle's life, including the alpha of the particle if your material is set up to accept alpha.

Figure 12.21: Color over Lifetime

Clicking on the gradient will pop up a gradient editor, which is seen below in *Figure 12.22*. The top of the gradient is the alpha and the bottom is for the color. Try to change the color on them to see it change the particles!

Figure 12.22: Gradient Editor

Now we set the render mode from the **Renderer** module. Since we knew that we wanted the particles from the beginning to be stretched from the velocity, we changed this setting to **Stretched Billboard** very early. If you decided to follow along with this particle creation, your particles would look like colored dots instead of streaks.

Changing the **Render Mode** to **Stretched Billboard** will fix that, as shown below in *Figure 12.23*. We also set **Speed Scale** to 0.1 as they are moving very fast, which makes them stretch very far if you go much higher than 0.1.

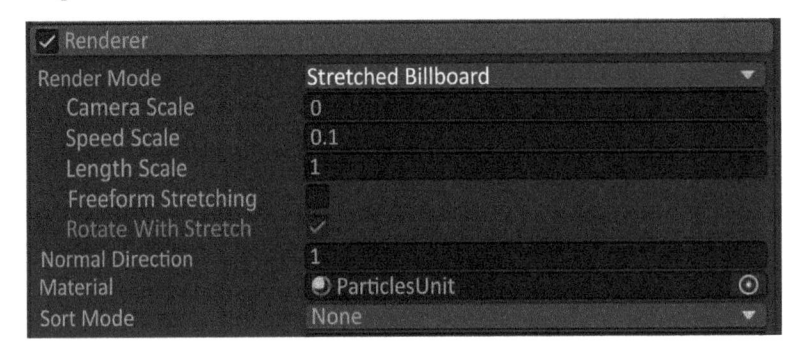

Figure 12.23: Renderer module

By going through these, we have just shown a simple example of a stretched particle to show some of the systems available. The power comes into play when you add shaders to the particles. A well-designed visual effect can trigger the emotion of an action happening. Though this may seem daunting at first, if you break down what you need, it becomes more of a fun time playing with the settings to get the right feel for your need. You will see other Shuriken effects around the level when you get into the project. Feel free to break them apart and put them back together to learn about the differences in the settings and how they play a part in the role of the visual effect.

We will be going over VFX Graph in the next section. This is another particle system creator that allows us to create GPU particles. This is a different way of working as it has its own system design and UI outside of the inspector. Let's get into an example we are using in the project.

VFX Graph – Myvari's telekinesis

Telekinesis can look like anything. We want it to seem as though Myvari is harnessing celestial energy that is flowing from her toward the object she is controlling. For this portion, we will cover how we set up the entire VFX Graph, shader, and a bit of code for implementation.

Chapter 12

We will assume that you have the VFX Graph package installed already and have opened up the FX_BeamSetup **Visual Effect Asset**.

The **Spawn** context starts out by default with a constant spawn rate block in this context. We want to just burst one time with 32 particles that we want to manipulate as long as the strip is up. We deleted the constant spawn and put in place a **Single Burst** block instead, as seen in *Figure 12.24* below.

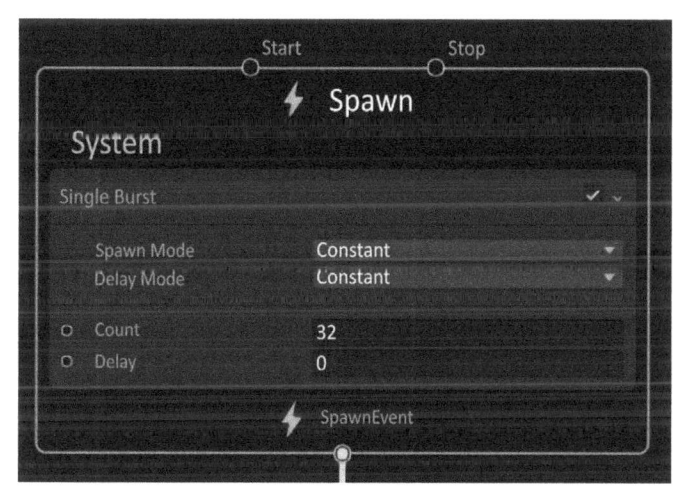

Figure 12.24: Spawn context

The number 32 wasn't a special number from the beginning. We weren't sure how many we would need, but it's easy enough to add more during the process of creating the strip. Below in *Figure 12.25* is our **Initialize** context. We need to set **Particle Per Strip Count** to the same number as the spawn in the burst above. We want a **Set Size** block and a **Set Custom Attribute** block. This attribute block will be a float data type and we called it InterpolatedPosition.

The reason we called it this is that we want to have an index of every particle so we can individually place them where we want them.

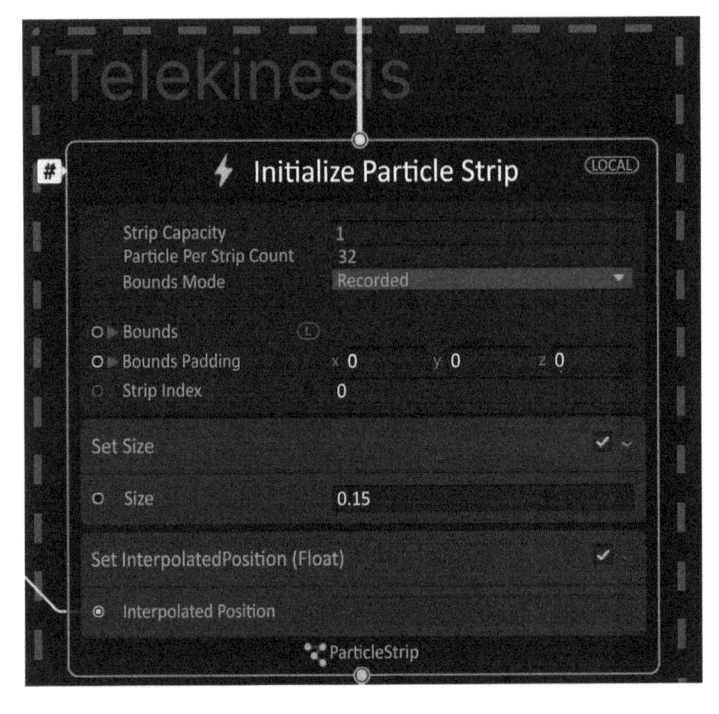

Figure 12.25: Initialize context

We can see in *Figure 12.26* below that we are getting the particle index and then dividing it by one less than the total amount. The index starts at 0, so we need to start from one below the number we spawned. This gives us a value that we can work with and is stored in the float custom attribute we made.

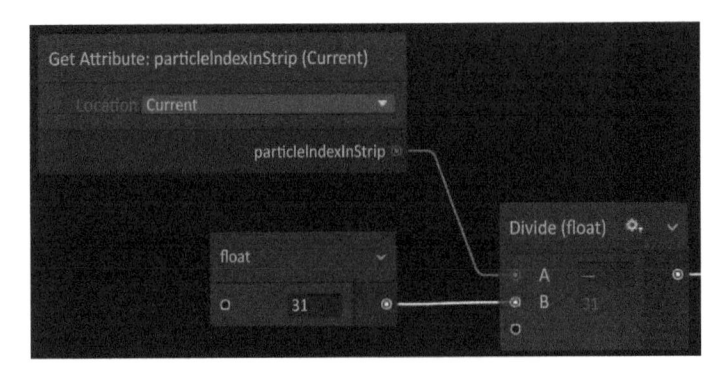

Figure 12.26: Particle Index nodes

Now we have a particle strip that needs to have a position to go to. We will make two transform parameters in the blackboard just like we do in the Shader Graph. We named them BeamStart and BeamEnd. We will Lerp the particles' positions from the beam start to the beam end according to the interpolated position float we initialized with. Looking at *Figure 12.27* below, you can see how we connect them together. The output of the Lerp will go to the **Update Context**.

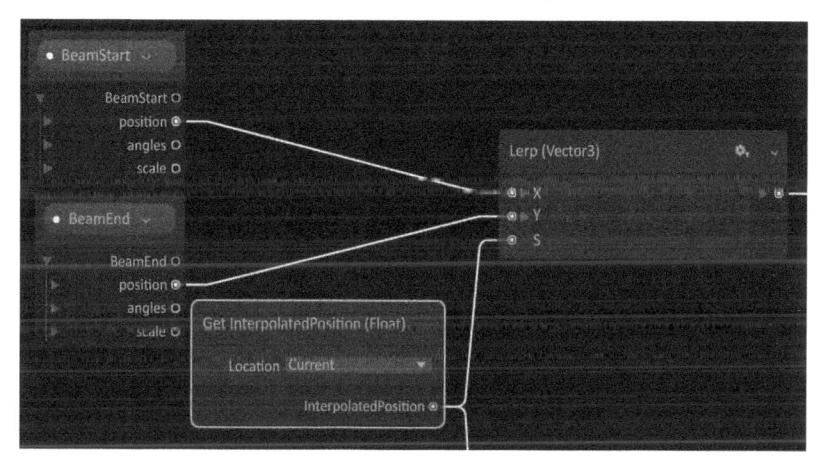

Figure 12.27: Positioning the beam

In the update context we have two blocks as seen below in *Figure 12.28*: **Set Position** and **Add Position**. We will be adding the output of the Lerp for their position into this block. There is one trick that will make some strange movement happen. On the **Set Position** block there is a small *w* in the middle. If it is an *L*, then that means it's moving the local position. This will cause double transforms when moving around the GameObjects. If you click on the *L* it will change to *w*, which stands for world space. It is fine to leave **Add Position** in local space.

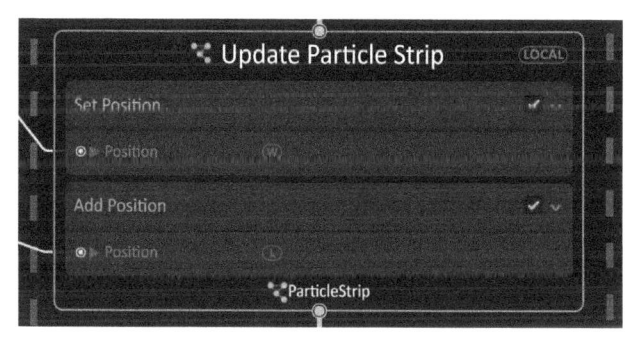

Figure 12.28: Update context

Currently we have a straight beam from start to end. This is fine for testing, but we need something a bit more fun. Let's add some turbulence so it isn't so rigid. We will use the Add Position block and the input for that will be some manipulations of 3D noise. This has a few more nodes to make the right data for nice turbulence, but we will walk through them.

Looking at *Figure 12.29* below, these five nodes are all we need. We want to get our current position, then add that to time. We have a **Multiply** node in between there so we could speed up or slow down the time value. This could be a variable that's tunable as well. After **Add** is a **Perlin Noise 3D**. The values here are purely subjective. Place your coordinates in the **Coordinate** slot and then place the output derivates into the **Add Position** block input in the **Update** context. From there, play around with the values until it gives you the nice turbulence you want. There is a problem with this approach. This will update every particle, including the beam start and beam end. This feels odd as we wanted it to come from our character's hand.

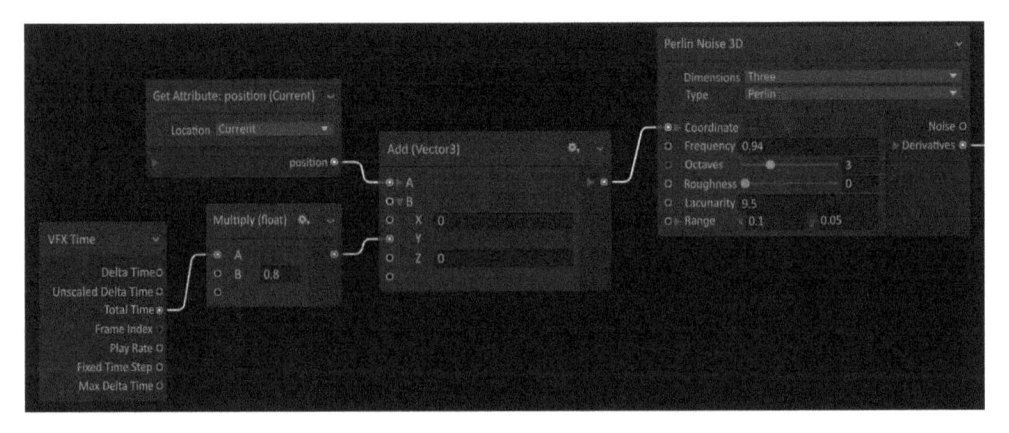

Figure 12.29: 3D Perlin Noise for turbulence

To ensure that the beam start and end are independent of this, we went with a simple gradient to tell the position whether or not it should be using the turbulence. Looking at *Figure 12.30*, we see that we take the interpolated position value and sample it across that interpolation with time. The gradient now acts as a transfer to which particle will be affected. The 0 value at the beginning and end of the strip will make 0 values multiplied with the derivatives from the noise generator. Now we plug this into the **Add Position** block.

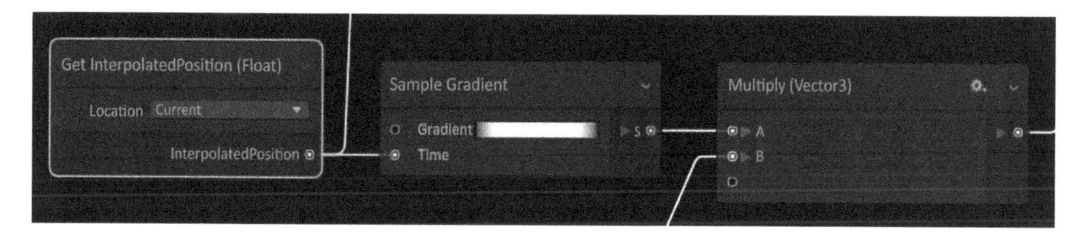

Figure 12.30: Mask for the turbulence

We're in the home stretch for setting up the VFX Graph portion. The **Output** context is shown in *Figure 12.31*. By default this will be an **Output Particle Quad**. This won't do us any good, so delete it if you have it on your VFX Graph and press the spacebar to make a new node. Then type particlestrip. You're looking for the **Output ParticleStrip Quad**. The one below has unlit in the name; this is due to the material being used.

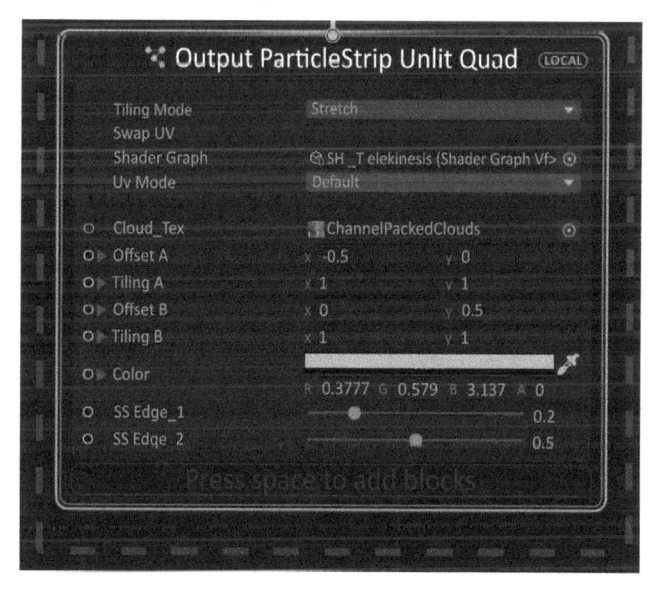

Figure 12.31: Output ParticleStrip Quad context

The shader is a duplicate of SH_StairShield with one change. In the **Graph** inspector, the **Support VFX Graph** Boolean is set to true. This shader has enough versatility to get the job done for now. We may change the texture before its final use, but for now it has what we need to get it going. We then assign it to the Shadergraph attribute in the output context. This will expose the parameters in the shader.

There are two more steps to finalize this effect. We need to create the GameObject's beam start and beam end, and then implement this effect by placing the locations of the GameObjects during gameplay.

To start, let's make our prefab. Below in *Figure 12.32* we made an empty GameObject and named it Telekinesis. Then we placed the beam setup object as a child and set its position at 0, 0, 0. Then we created two more empty GameObjects and named them BeamStart and BeamEnd. We also set these positions at 0, 0, 0.

Figure 12.32: Telekinesis prefab

There is a component you can add to VFX Graph assets called **VFX Property Binder**. Add this component to the FX_BeamSetup GameObject. We then create two bound properties to the transform and name them the same as the properties in the VFX Graph (BeamStart and BeamEnd). Drag the GameObject into the **Target** slot to reference the GameObject's transform. Do the same for BeamEnd. This will look like *Figure 12.33* below.

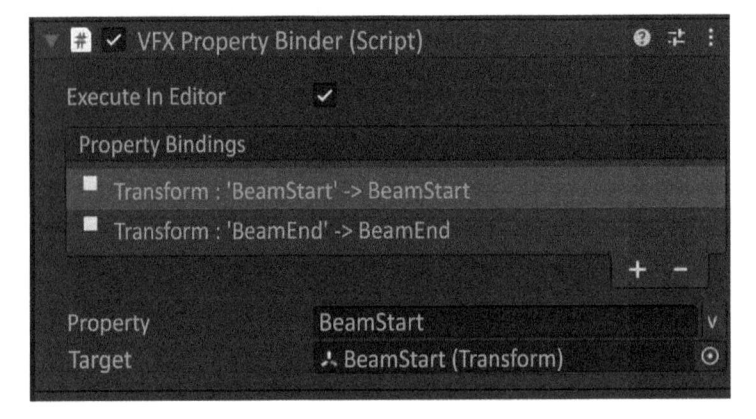

Figure 12.33: VFX Property Binder component

We now need to go over the implementation. The considerations here are that the start of the beam needed to come from our character's left hand. We also know we need the end to be attached to the item we are controlling with physics. We also need to turn on and off the visual effect only when the interact button is interacting with a physics puzzle item. We will be working with DragRigidBody.cs.

This script takes the center of the screen as a point of reference and if you are within range of the physics item that you can interact with, it will give Myvari control of that Rigidbody from the use of the physics puzzle pieces scripts we went over in *Chapter 6, Interactions and Mechanics*.

Fields to add:

```
public VisualEffect telekinesis;
public Transform leftWristLoc;
public Transform beamStart;
public Transform beamEnd;
```

These will be assigned in the editor and should be self-explanatory except possibly the `leftWristLoc`. This transform is from Myvari's joints in her hierarchy. Expand her hierarchy and drag the left wrist onto this slot in the inspector.

In the update, we want to turn off the beam if the interact button is released.

```
if (control.wasReleasedThisFrame)
    {
        //Release selected Rigidbody if there any
        selectedRigidbody = null;

        telekinesis.enabled = false;
    }
```

After this we need to work with the `FixedUpdate`. We are working with physics, so we need to ask the program to check if we have a Rigidbody, and on the `FixedUpdate`, we will turn on the beam if true and set the positions of the `beamStart` and `beamEnd` at every `FixedUpdate` loop with the physics.

```
if (selectedRigidbody)
    {
        telekinesis.enabled = true;
        ...
        beamStart.position = leftWristLoc.position;
        beamEnd.position = selectedRigidbody.gameObject.transform.
position;
    }
```

This is it! Save your files, get back in the editor, and assign the transforms and visual effects to the script. This script is located in Main Camera. *Figure 12.34* below shows the selected object with the script.

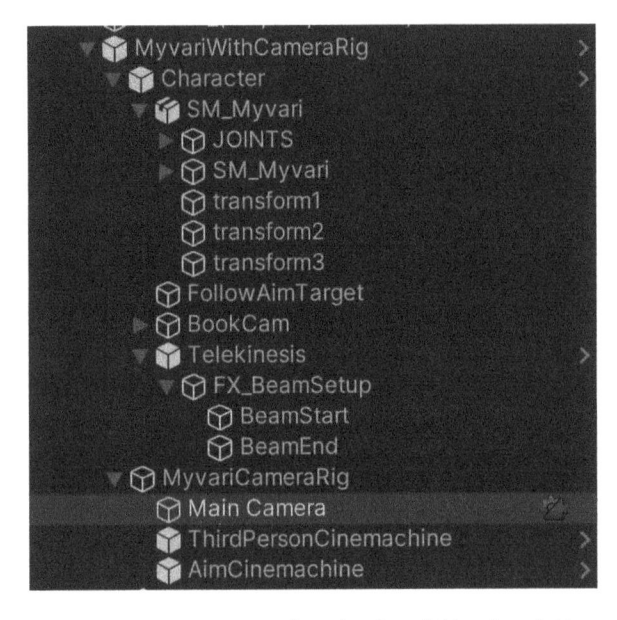

Figure 12.34: Main Camera location for telekinesis scripting

Particle effects and shader work are always interesting problems to be handled with care. Too much of a good thing ends up not feeling good. When working through a level, take a moment to think about the tiny details and see if it makes sense to add small movements to sell the experience.

From the above two effects, there is quite a bit of thought put into each visual effect no matter the size of the effect. Take your time going through each effect in the game to break down the parts.

Cinematics

In our project, we're using cinematics for three purposes. The first one is to explain that the area has been around a long time, so the areas are fragile. The second one is showing the player that Myvari has innate powers by her defending herself against a falling boulder. The third cinematic is the ending scene when she puts on her tiara and goes through the portal after finishing the final puzzle.

The way that we work through cinematics is we export the models while they are in place in the environment. This allows us to make sure that our cinematics match with the environment with as much precision as possible.

Secondary animation

Sometimes there needs to be additional animation that is easier to simulate than it is to rig and hand-key. Hair is a good example of this. The actions that hair takes are a secondary animation after momentum is gained. Hand-keying this is possible but takes a lot of patience and can be done instead with physics. We will be using Unity's Spring Joint component for this. There are also several assets in Unity's Asset Store that have been made to make this process more robust. If you need just simple physics for your secondary animation, it can be done through the Unity physics Rigidbody component, the Spring Joint component, and capsule colliders.

Lighting

We've decided to put lighting in the finishing touches, but this could have had its own book. This is one of those topics that are a massive rabbit hole. We wanted to go over some basics of lighting here and the reason why it's important to pay attention to lighting, as well as highlighting a few polishing tools and how to use lighting in Unity.

First, we need to explain that lighting is an art. The purpose of lighting includes defining 3D form, providing mood, and designing methods for gameplay. After we go through a few design thoughts on lighting, we will take a tour of the Unity mixed lighting, lightmaps, reflection, and light probes.

3D form

Without lighting, a 3D form is flat. In fact, we use unlit shaders for most effects. One reason is that we don't need to add shadowing and lighting for small shiny effects that will only be on screen for a short time. They are flat and don't need lighting to help define them; their texture shape does that work for it.

Providing mood

This goes along with the design of the areas but is focused specifically on the lighting. Is the alleyway getting darker as you walk down it? This could push a sense of danger or nervousness in your player. Do you want unnatural lighting colors around certain areas to give an arcane feeling inside a mage's house? Completely possible! All of these decisions should be thought about when placing lighting. In the same vein as mood, we could want our lights to define the gameplay.

Gameplay design

Gameplay can be defined through light in many ways. In fact, your entire game could be designed around light.

Horror games often use light sources as a way to push away enemies, but it's limited to a small timer as your batteries are inevitably running out! Taking a unique route, an older game named Boktai used a light sensor peripheral for the Game Boy to charge up your weapons, and if you played it in the dark the game was more difficult.

These concepts are a bit on the edge of gameplay elements. We could just use light to give the player an idea of where to go, or where to stay away from. We probably have a good idea now about general concepts of lighting design and how it can influence the player's experience. Let's dig into Unity lighting.

Unity lighting

To get to a polished state we need to go over the basics first. This will be an overview of what you are capable of doing in Unity for lighting, and then we will be going over what settings and uses we have for our project. Built-in renderer, URP, and HDRP lighting are all different from each other. We will be talking about URP lighting specifically. We will also be pushing for a certain feel and explaining features that helped us achieve the desired look that we aimed for in our vertical slice. Each lighting asset can be configured in different ways, which means that these steps will only give as much help as needed to get your feet wet with lighting. After you go through this and play around with what we explain, we highly recommend reading the documentation for other lighting objects for different rendering pipelines depending on the needs of your project. Now that we've gone over the construct of lighting here, we will begin by talking about mixed lighting.

Mixed lighting

We're taking a slight shortcut here by going into mixed lighting from the start. To utilize mixed lighting properly, you need to be using indirect baked lighting and dynamic lighting. We will touch on both right now, then get back to mixed lighting.

Indirect baked lighting

Real-time lights, that are casting light rays onto static GameObjects bouncing off geometry in the world, will be baked onto a lightmap. Those terms are new! Static game objects are defined by selecting the **Static** checkbox in the inspector, as seen in *Figure 12.35* below.

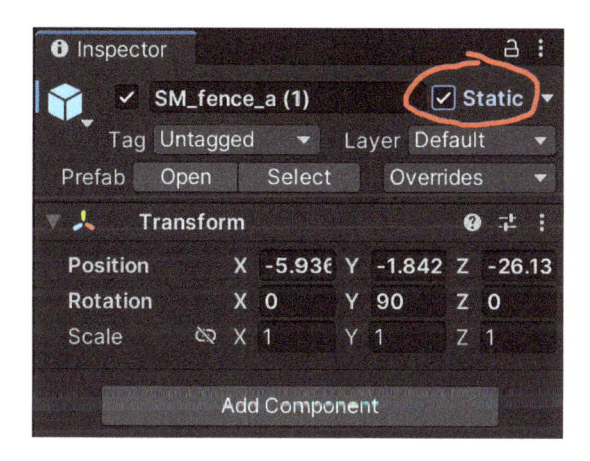

Figure 12.35: Static checkbox

hen this is selected, when the game is baking its lightmaps into the Lightmap UVs, it will know to add this to the items to bake. You would only choose this to be static if you know for certain you will never move the GameObject that you would make static. We are fairly certain this concrete fence will remain solid the entire game, so we selected it as static. The next term is lightmap. This is a secondary set of UVs that are not allowed to overlap with the object that you want to bake the lighting onto. When you import a model, you can let Unity generate the lightmap UVs for you, and it does a decent job at taking care of this. You can do this by selecting the FBX for the 3D model and choosing **Generate Lightmap UVs**, as in *Figure 12.36* below.

When you select the checkbox, Lightmap UV settings will show up. These values are the average per object you have in your scene. These settings will do a decent job of setting up the basics but you may need to look into each attribute to make sure each object receives light the way you would expect it to.

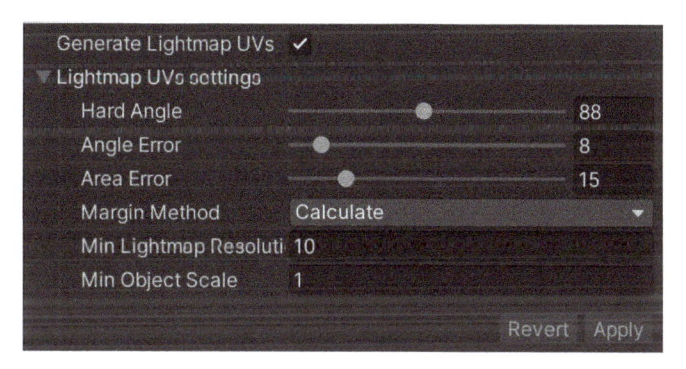

Figure 12.36: Generate Lightmap UVs option

That is for the objects that receive light. As for the lights, you can set any available light to be a baked light. Directional, spot, point, and area light are all available to be added to lightmaps when generating or baking lighting.

Dynamic lighting

This is also referred to as real-time lighting. Real-time lighting has to deal with real-time shadows and many settings involved with this. Real-time lighting is applied to any item that wasn't chosen as static. Skeletal meshes are always real time as they cannot be static. Their nature is to move!

In our URP asset we can see that in the **Shadows** settings, we can set the distance to where the quality of shadows goes down. Below in *Figure 12.37* you can see this range in the **Shadows** section.

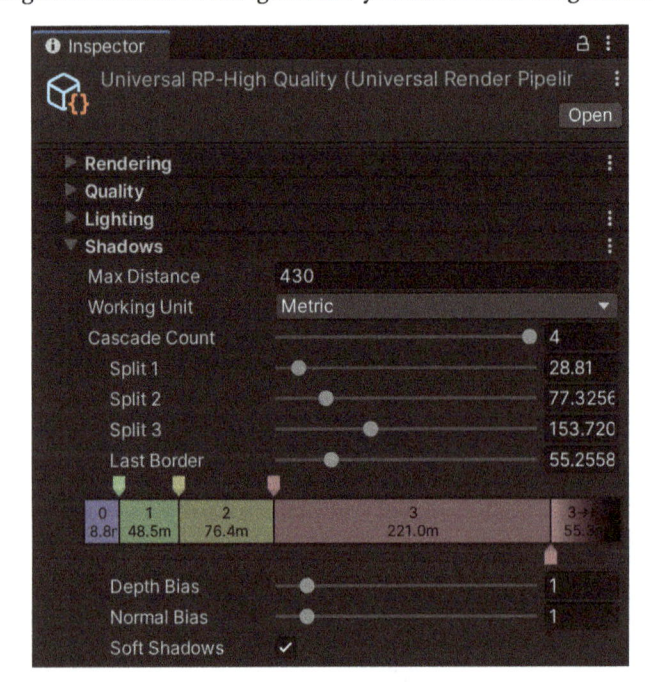

Figure 12.37: URP Shadows settings

Each real-time light will use these settings for the shadows. **Cascades** are how many times the light quality goes down. It's set in meters by default. This can help us design the limits as we know how tall our characters should be in general. 1 Unity unit is by default 1 meter. You could set up a test scene to see what the shadows would look like for the distance of each cascade to help make these decisions.

Something that's unique to real-time lights is the four lights that are available.

The directional, point, and spot lights are available for real-time lighting information. Area lights cannot create real-time shadows.

Now that we've gone over the basics of real-time and indirect lighting, we need to get back into mixed lighting mode. First, we need to let you know how to put lights on the scene. In *Figure 12.38* below you can see the list of lights. You can access this menu just as you create any GameObject, by right-clicking in the hierarchy or going to the GameObject menu and hovering over the **Light** option to get the submenu seen in *Figure 12.38*.

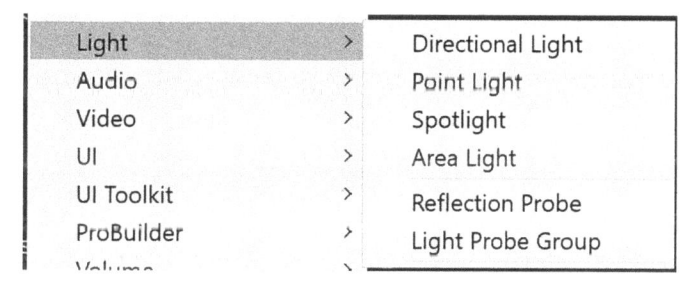

Figure 12.38: Light options

Now we need to get back to mixed lighting. We've talked about both lighting modes. Some games may only use baked lighting while some games might only use real-time lighting. The majority will use both in URP. When you select any light that you make, the inspector has an option to choose real-time, mixed, or baked. Remember, baked means baked indirect light. The best part of mixed is that it allows the light to be baked where it is, but acts as dynamic when introduced to a non-static GameObject. This is useful for the directional light. This light acts like the sun, so we want it to bake for the static items, but be dynamic for the character or anything non-static. You can see this selected within the inspector in *Figure 12.39* below.

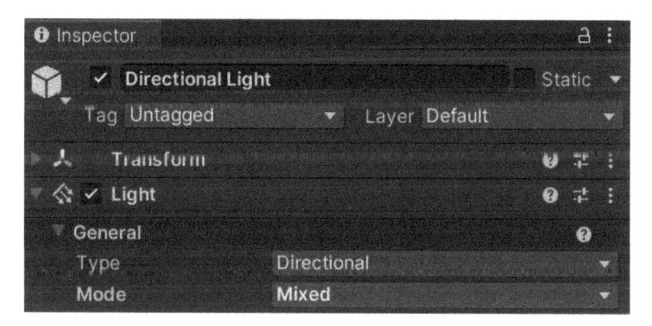

Figure 12.39: Directional light set to mixed

Even after you've set all the meshes to static that you need to, and placed lights and set them to either real-time, baked, or mixed, you still need to set up your lighting settings within the lighting window. To get there, use the screenshot below, in *Figure 12.40*.

Figure 12.40: Path to the lighting window

Within the window that pops up, you will have several tunable settings. These settings are going to be unique for every project. We know that we want some nice shadow fidelity. This means we need more samples and higher resolution for our lightmaps. We're also going to be fairly close to the character in the game and during cinematics, which is still real time. These factors need to be considered when thinking about your settings. You could potentially crank up the settings and have nice shadows with a huge light bake, but then your real-time shadows might not be able to handle it and will be blocky, which will cause the game to have a strange feel to it. It's good to consider the system your game will be played on and thoroughly test the performance again after adding more lights and lightmaps.

There is another tool to use to gain more accurate real-time lighting information inside Unity without needing to have a lot of real-time lights. It is called light probes. Let's take a look at that tool.

Light probes

Creating light probes is as easy as going to your **Light** GameObject group and selecting **Light Probe Group**.

You can see this in the options three figures above in *Figure 12.38*. What this tool does is sample the lighting information at points in 3D which are shown in *Figure 12.42*. That information is then used in real time even if the lighting is baked information only. This is very helpful if you want to use the coloration from an area light (which is only baked) and add it to a character. Think about a light on a wall where you don't need to cast a shadow or for it to be real time. Instead of being resource-intensive, you can just use light probes around that area and it will help pick up on non-static geometry in real time.

To set this up though, you need to place light probes by hand. There are assets on the Asset Store to automatically place them but keep in mind that anything automated in the entertainment industry needs to have an artist's input to achieve what the experience needs.

Light Probe Group when editing the group looks like *Figure 12.41* below in the inspector.

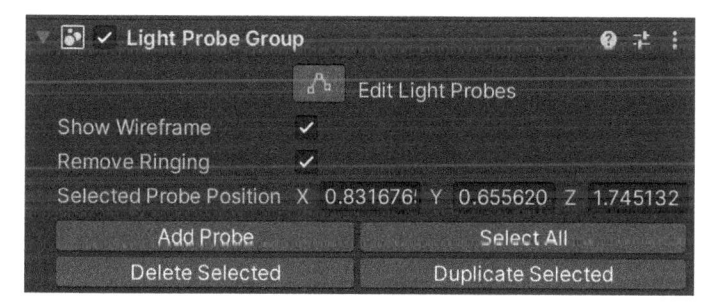

Figure 12.41: Light Probe Group component in inspector

You can add, delete, select all, and duplicate selected. When you're placing Light Probes, just know that they are averages of multiple color locations. These aren't a perfect representation of the light in one area, but more of an approximation to give a bit of extra boost to ensure the mood is kept for the real-time actors in the game. With that being said, add probes until they form a nice lattice. The more you have, the more computational power it will take. For each project, as usual, it will depend on the system to know how many light probes will be allowed for performance.

After you've placed them, you can either press play and walk around, or just drag your non-static GameObjects around the scene to see the lighting shift slightly.

Here is an example of the initial hallway of our vertical slice's light probe lattice in *Figure 12.42*.

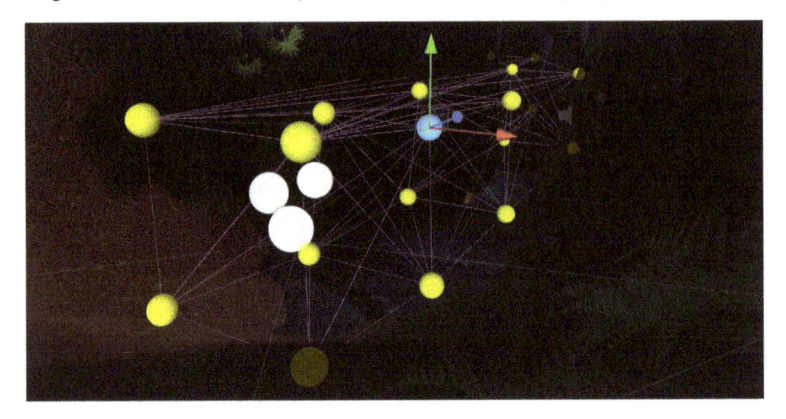

Figure 12.42: Light Probe lattice

This can take some time and will be done after placing your lights. If you change up your lighting configuration, make sure to rethink your light probes as well afterward. There is just one last thing before we get to polishing sound. We want to go over reflections.

Reflection probe

There are materials in the world that reflect the color of the environment. These are metallic and/or glossy materials. The problem is, what do they reflect? I'm happy you asked that because Unity initially will create a reflection map of just the skybox so there is something reflected in those materials. There is another tool you can add to your scene, which is a reflection probe that will allow you to designate a volume that has the reflection data in that area. You can also have overlapping volumes.

This is an interesting issue as it's not a perfect representation as the probe's reflection position is from the center of the position of that probe. If you have a large area, and you need to be very close to the reflections while also needing that reflection to be accurate, you will need multiple reflection probes, with each probe's volumes only as large as you need them. The smaller the volume, the crisper the reflection image. These types of things won't be very clear until you have run around the world and looked for this or worked through the cinematics of your game and seen a strange-looking reflection. There is a small caveat here; you can create real-time reflections, but they are very expensive. These should be used with caution. That is until we all have quantum computers in our houses.

To create a reflection probe, the option is in the same place as all the rest of the lighting, in the GameObject menu under **Lighting**.

When you create the probe and place it in the location you want to reflect around, you will have to then use the inspector to edit the volume, which looks like the below *Figure 12.43*.

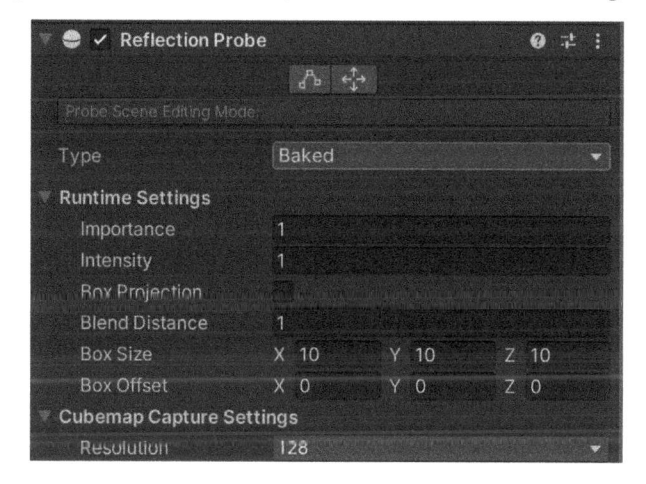

Figure 12.43: Reflection Probe component in the inspector

The top-center two icons are for editing and moving the volume. Selecting the points icon gives you access to the volume's shape to shrink and grow it to your needs. The type can be **Baked**, **Real-time**, or **Custom**. **Baked** will only be baked once and cannot change during runtime. **Real-time** changes as the game is running every frame. **Custom** allows you to place your own custom cubemap instead of sampling the environment. This could be useful if you want to distort the environment in the reflections! The cubemap settings are to tweak the cubemap's scale and parameters to increase the needed fidelity at a performance cost.

One of the most important settings is the **Importance** setting! This setting is an integer that you set to tell the game which reflection probe is being displayed when there are overlapping reflection volumes.

The way this works is that the higher the number, the higher the importance. If you have two overlapping volumes, such as inside the entrance to a cave versus right outside of it, you would then set the hallway to importance level 2. This way when you enter the volume that is of higher importance, the reflection probe will switch to it. This can cause some popping on very close reflection surfaces. Play through your game and pay attention to reflections when they transition.

Adding lighting overall is a fun task. It can greatly improve the graphical quality of your game and there are some great tricks to set that up. Next up is sound polish.

Sound polish

We have a few things we can do to make sounds in our game more believable. Sound polish comes down to tweaking the volume of sounds, changing the minimum and maximum attenuation distances, and even replacing sounds that you feel don't sound good.

These are all things we've adjusted throughout the project already. For example, on one of our first ambiences, we can adjust the volume or pitch to see what feels right. Or we can change the minimum or maximum distances on the attenuation, add sounds that we may have missed, make sure that certain sounds that are more important are louder than others, etc.

Overall, mixing and sound polish is a very iterative process of just manipulating the values and replacing sounds with other sounds to get a feel for what's best. You never know how a sound will fit with the rest of the sounds until you place it in the game.

Triggering sound through animation events

We wanted to show you how to add sound to an animation event. It's quite an easy process as we already know how to add animation events, and how to trigger sounds using `AudioSource` components. We'll be adding footstep sounds to our character walking.

First let's select our character, the `MyvariWithCameraRig`:

Figure 12.44: MyvariWithCameraRig

Then let's drop down into its child objects to find the `SM_Myvari` GameObject. Here you will see the animator component! We only need a few things here.

Chapter 12

First, let's create a new script and call it AnimationSounds, then we'll put this right below our **Animator Component**. After this, we'll add our AudioSource component. It should all look something like *Figure 12.45* below:

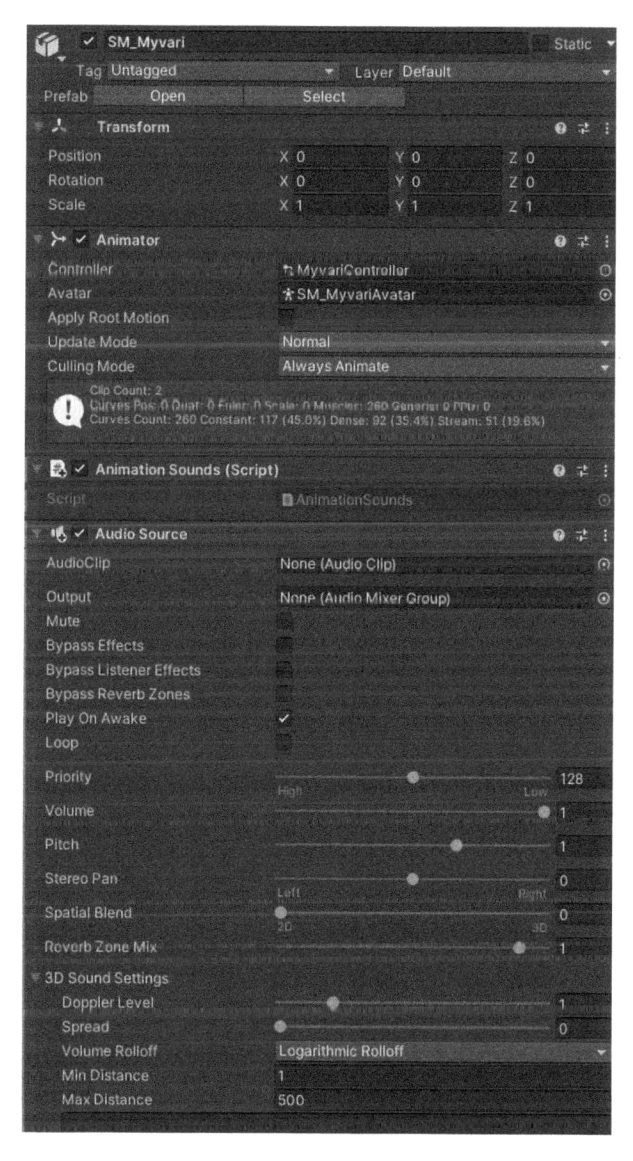

Figure 12.45: SM_Myvari inspector window

Before we continue forward, let's add a function to our AnimationSounds script. Remove the **Start** and **Update** functions and add a new one called PlaySound(). Above this new function, declare a new public variable called public AudioSource AnimSound.

Figure 12.46: Our new AnimationSounds.cs

Now, inside of our `PlaySound()` function, let's add `AnimSound.Play()`.

Next, in the inspector, we can add the `AudioSource` component to the serialized field in the `AnimationSounds.cs` component and add a footstep sound effect!

Figure 12.47: AnimationSounds.cs script in the inspector

Awesome! Now we can move on to tagging our animation with events.

Tagging animations with events for sound

One big problem that we have with adding animation events is that we can't add events directly through the animation window, so we'll have to open up the FBX file inside of Unity.

The best way to do this is to go into **Assets** > **Animations** and select the `Myvari_Walk_Basic` FBX.

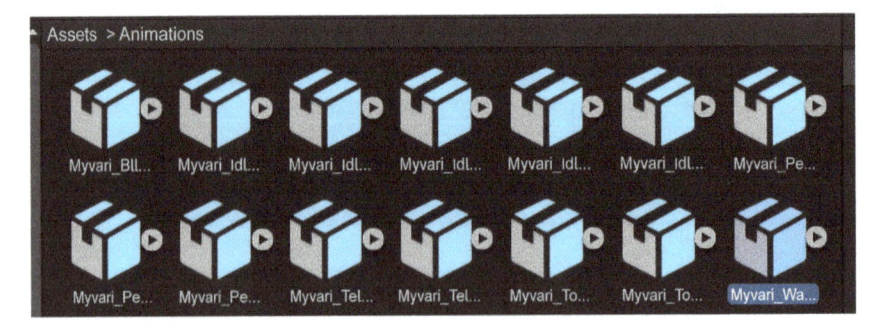

Figure 12.48: The project explorer in Unity in the Assets > Animations folder

Next we'll scroll down on the inspector until we reach the **Events** dropdown.

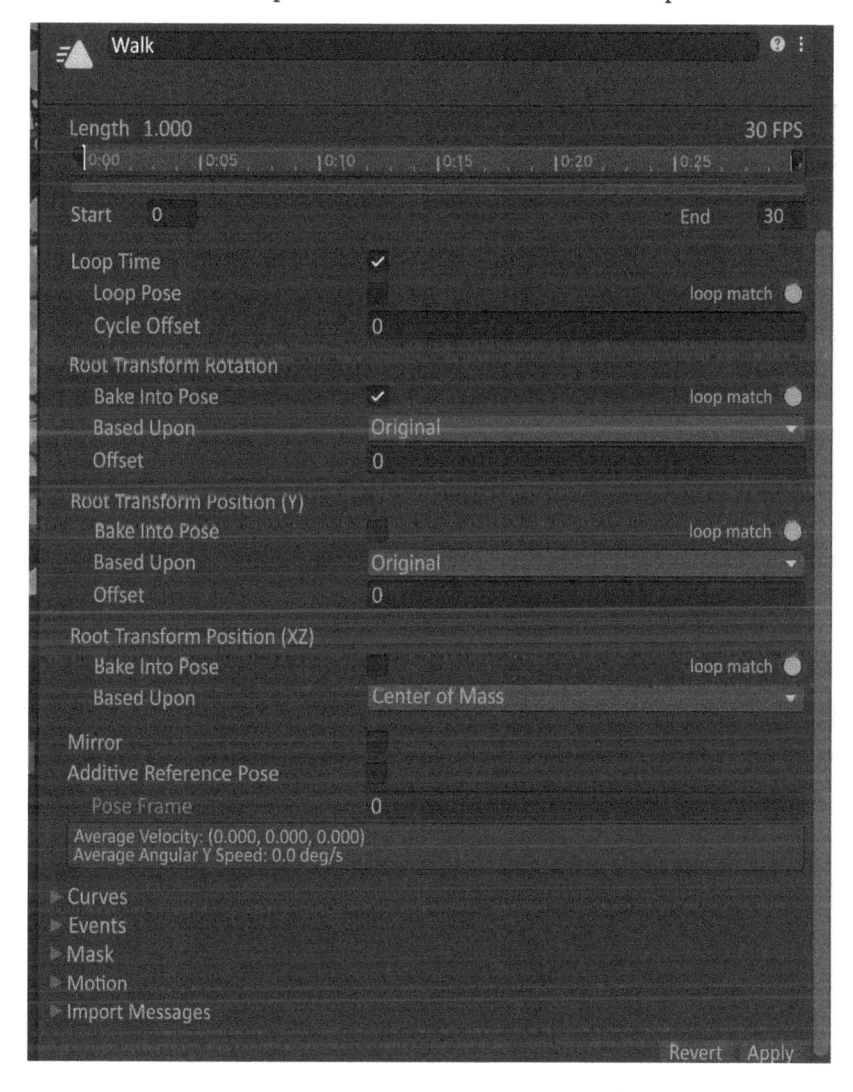

Figure 12.49: Animation clip inspector window

Open up that **Events** dropdown, and also open up the **Preview** window at the bottom of the inspector.

It might be hidden at the bottom of the inspector, but you can click and drag from the bottom to bring it up! It should look something like *Figure 12.50*:

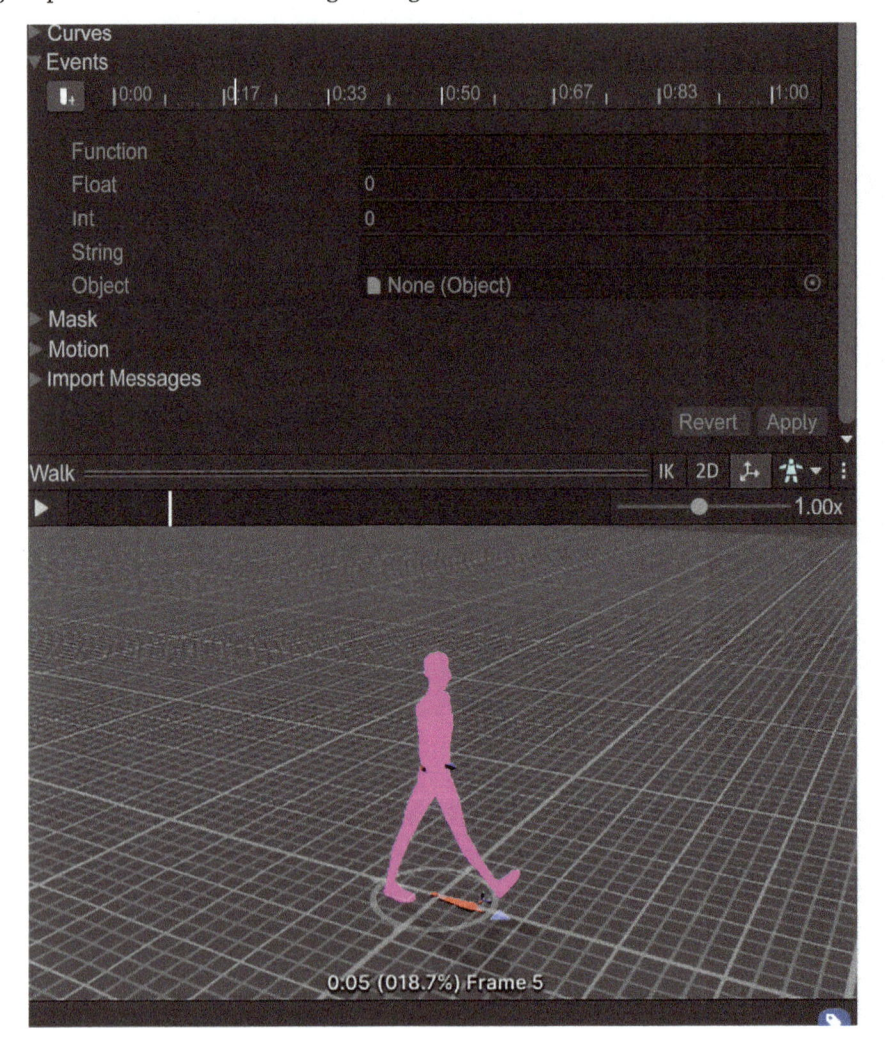

Figure 12.50: Animation Clip inspector window preview

Next, using the timeline above the preview, we can cycle to different parts of the animation. In particular, we are trying to find places for footsteps, so we'll want to find spots like this, where the foot is meeting the ground:

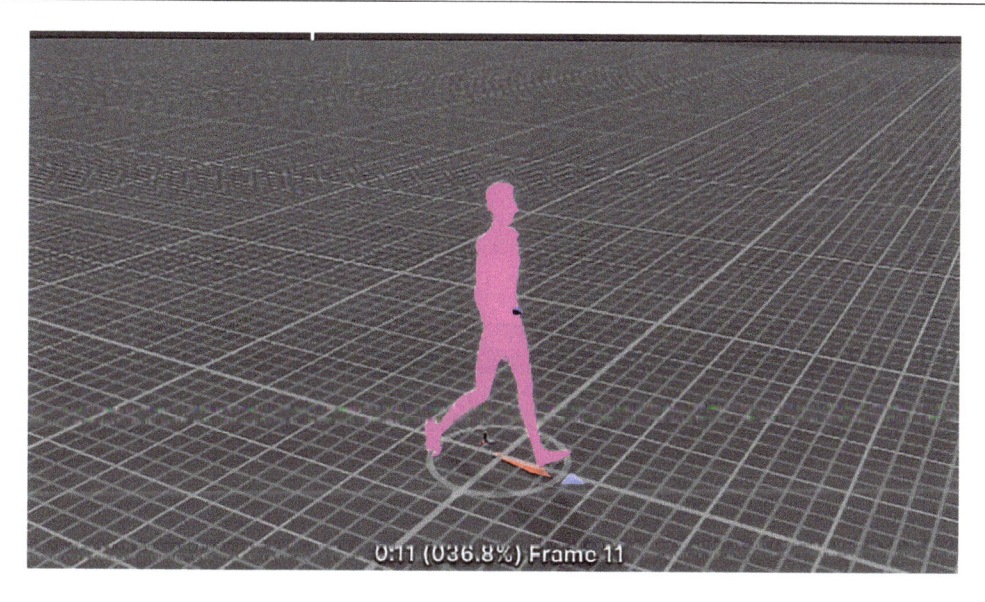

Figure 12.51: Animation Clip inspector window preview

Once your timeline is lined up, go ahead and add an animation event. And in the spot that says **Function**, type in PlaySound — *do not* include the parentheses you've seen previously (in PlaySound())! For some reason, including the parentheses won't trigger our function properly.

Here is where we placed our events.

Figure 12.52: Animation Clip inspector window timeline with events

Now, when you go into the game and walk around, you'll hear sound! Congrats! We now have footstep sounds!

Randomized sounds

You'll probably notice that our footstep sound is fairly repetitive. This is why we often like to add randomized sounds to a game!

This is a process of randomly playing from a pool of sound effects so that sounds will be less repetitive! In this instance, we have five different footstep sound effects to choose from, which can be found in /Assets/Sounds:

MainFS_01.wav – MainFS_05.wav

Next, let's open up our AnimationSounds.cs script and check out how we can add randomized sounds. So in this instance, we're going to use a list of AudioClips, like this:

```
public List<AudioClip> soundPool = new List<AudioClip>();
```

Figure 12.53: Animation.cs public list soundPool

Then, inside of PlaySound we're going to select a random clip from this, and load it into our AudioSource component. We'll use Random.Range to accomplish this:

```
void PlaySound()
{
    AnimSound.clip = soundPool[Random.Range(0, soundPool.Count)];

    AnimSound.Play();
}
```

Figure 12.54: Animation.cs PlaySound() function

Next, let's open up the inspector where our AnimationSounds.cs script lies, highlight all of our MainFS.wav sounds, and click and drag them directly into our sound pool serialized field:

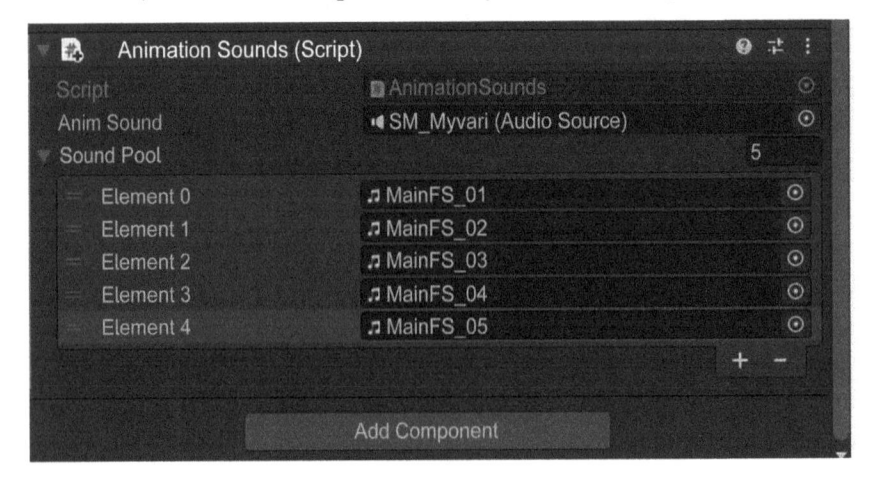

Figure 12.55: Animation.cs in the inspector

And that's all! We now are playing from a pool of random sounds!

Randomized pitch

Sometimes adding even more variation can be accomplished through randomizing the pitch. This is a very simple process as well. The first thing we have to do is define the range of pitch that we will affect.

I like to just play the sound and play around with the pitch to see where it sounds good. Open up the AudioSource component that holds our footstep sound and toggle the **Pitch** slider! This will update in real time.

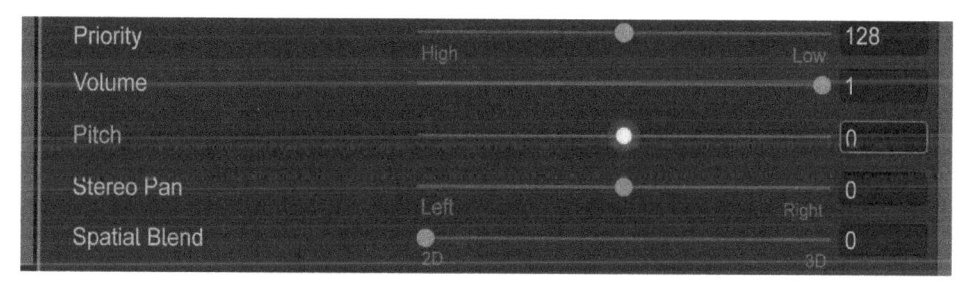

Figure 12.56: AudioSource component

You'll hear that going too high or too low makes a fairly unrealistic sound. So I like to stick to a range of 0.3 and -0.3. In our code, let's just add a simple Random.Range() while targeting the pitch of our AudioSource component.

```
AnimSound.pitch = Random.Range(-0.3f, 0.3f);
```

Figure 12.57: AudioSource component showing how random pitch is achieved

This is all we need! One of the most important ways to create depth in the soundscape of our game is to add as many sources as possible. And adding things like random variation, sound to small details in animations, and dynamic audio can go a long way! Go ahead and play the game to hear your changes.

Summary

This chapter went over many different tools that we have worked through within our project. We took some time to go over our process for finalizing the art and assets. We focused not only on the models and textures but also on checking in on the design to make sure that each asset fits within the world as expected. Within this, we also went over adding effects from the Shuriken and VFX Graph particle systems. This included the implementation of effects to show telekinesis.

We then went over the lighting design. We broke down Unity lighting with lightmaps, reflection, light probes, and baking. Lighting can add so much to a game, so this part shouldn't be taken lightly!

Then to round up our game polish we went through sound polishing to trigger sounds through animations and add randomness to the sounds to bring more life to the gameplay.

This is it for the book! Thank you so much for reading all the way through and we hope it provided you with lots of knowledge. Please consider joining the Discord server, where we will be able to answer questions and go over the project in more detail.

There is a bonus chapter after this that goes over some more Unity tools that can be used for different projects as well as some products that Unity has to offer for multiplayer, XR, and visual scripting. Let us know if you would like a book on those topics as well!

13

Bonus: Other Unity Tools!

Across this book, we have gone through a third-person environmental puzzle vertical slice. This is a specific genre of game with its own unique problems in development, and this does mean that a lot of Unity's great tools weren't mentioned, so we wanted to take a small section and write about what other offerings Unity could provide for your next project. We will cover an introductory-level understanding of the following:

- Multiplayer
- XR
- Machine Learning Agents
- Bolt visual scripting

Unity Gaming Services

We've explored a group of tools named Unity Gaming Services, or UGS. These tools are designed to provide solutions that would take a significant amount of time to develop and can be integrated into your project in much less time. These tools can help directly with setting up multiplayer, XR (which is a mixture of virtual reality and augmented reality), visual scripting (known as Bolt), and finally a group of creative workflow tools. Let's first look into the multiplayer tools available.

Multiplayer tools

Unity provides a surplus of services, ranging from pivotal tools and education to successfully implementing that multiplayer factor into your project. Breaking down the category of multiplayer, Unity divides the focus into three pillars: **Creation**, **Connection**, and **Communication**.

Creation

Unity considers this the foundation of your game and introduces the options of Netcode for GameObjects and Netcode for Entities. Netcode for GameObjects is a new networking library built for the Unity game engine that contains libraries, tutorials, and samples that are customizable and extensible to meet the needs of your next multiplayer project.

Netcode for Entities takes advantage of Unity's new Data-Oriented Technology Stack (DOTS). This new, high-performance, multithreaded DOTS allows you to take full advantage of multicore processors to create richer user experiences and iterate faster with C# code that's easier to read and reuse across other projects. DOTS provides an intuitive sandbox for programmers to create safe, multithreaded code for an array of multiplayer development advantages.

Focusing on streamable data, DOTS allows for the flexibility of reusing code, helps others to understand it, and improves collaboration. Having these various capabilities, DOTS transforms pre-existing workflows into the conversion workflow. This workflow converts your GameObjects to entities with a single click. At runtime, the Entity Preview Inspector visualizes how DOTS transforms your GameObjects into entities. In tandem, using the Unity Live Link feature will allow you to iterate instantly in Play Mode without creating a new build every time. Harnessing a faster iteration without having to create a new build every time allows you and your team to test game experiences on target devices in real time.

Unity has created DOTS packages for use with their stack of usable assets. They highly recommend that you use preview packages for testing and pre-production phases of your projects at this time as they verify packages to become production-ready.

Connection

User experiences in multiplayer gameplay are often associated with matchmaking, pre-and post-game lobbies, and queue times. Unity has developed services to complement these cooperative engagements through Lobby, Relay, Multiplay, and Matchmaker.

Unity Lobby grants players the ability to connect before or during a game session. Public lobbies can be created by the players using simple game attributes. These lobbies can be searched, discovered, and joined by other players. Private lobbies can allow players to create exclusive spaces for invite-only guests.

Relay is a service-to-service tool offered by Unity that pairs well with Lobby. When a player disconnects from a game, Relay will automatically remove the disconnected players and will notify you of the unexpected disconnects. In addition, you can access a reliable foundation for your cooperative game with Netcode for GameObjects.

Multiplay offers a resilient, multi-cloud hybrid game server through Unity. This service allows you to access server hosting and matching without having to build and maintain your own backend infrastructure. Focused on delivering smoother player experiences, Unity has invested in the creation of over 190 data centers that are designed for resilience and performance at scale. These servers operate across the globe, upholding a standard of Quality of Service (QoS). The QoS locates the optimum region for match connectivity, giving your players the most stable connection wherever they're playing from, thereby maximizing player engagement, reducing downtime, and delivering new content to your players regardless of platform.

Matchmaker is created through an open source collaboration with Google called Open Match. Matchmaker is also part of Unity's dedicated game server hosting solution, Multiplay, offering out-of-the-box integration for Unity's Enterprise customers that can scale to various player base capacities. Matchmaker contains developer-configured match logic, a customizable evaluator, and a matchmaking loop with scheduled match function execution as its hosting solutions to match your players in the right place, at the right time.

Communication

Player engagement and retention happens when experiences are healthy, immersive, and have a solid quality of interaction with each other. Unity offers player engagement tools to support positive social experiences through Vivox and Community and Safety.

Vivox is an easy-to-implement and dependable feature that supports a feature-rich voice and text chat service for your game. Trusted by industry-leading titles such as Valorant, League of Legends, Rainbow Six Siege, and PUBG, Vivox delivers the best comms service to their players. Operational with any platform, around the globe, and on any game engine, Vivox can be integrated in less than two days and scaled to millions of players.

Coming soon is Unity's latest addition to its communication arsenal, Community and Safety. Unity's focus with this platform is player safety analysis and game management.

XR plugin

XR is an umbrella term that encompasses the following applications: Virtual Reality (VR) and Augmented Reality (AR). VR creates a unique environment completely around its user. AR overlays digital content over the real world through the lenses of technical devices. XR applies a combination of both environments of the user's real world and the digital world to interact with one another.

Unity has developed a new plugin framework called XR SDK. This framework enables XR providers to successfully integrate with the Unity engine and all its features for optimization of each application mentioned previously.

Unity supports these platforms for XR:

- ARKit
- ARCore
- Microsoft HoloLens
- Windows Mixed Reality
- Magic Leap
- Oculus
- OpenXR
- PlayStation VR

Unity does not currently support XR on WebGL.

This plugin-based approach allows Unity to adapt with quick bug fixes, distribute SDK updates from platform partners, and support new XR devices without having to modify the core engine.

Machine Learning Agents

Unity understands that the advancement of Artificial Intelligence (AI) research depends on resolving tough problems in existing environments using current benchmarks for training AI models. When a game becomes complex, developers will need to create intelligent behaviors, which may lead to writing tons of code with highly specialized tools.

Unity has created a Machine Learning Agents (ML-Agents) toolkit that means that you no longer need to "code" emergent behaviors, but instead teach intelligent agents to "learn" through a combination of deep reinforcement and imitation learning.

Therefore, this allows developers to create AI environments that are more physically, visually, and cognitively rich, along with more compelling gameplay and enhanced game experiences.

Bolt visual scripting

Develop gameplay mechanics with interaction logic visually. Bolt allows you to create visual, graph-based systems, instead of writing out traditional lines of code. Through visual scripting, Bolt promotes seamless collaboration between teams of designers, artists, and programmers for faster prototyping and iteration.

More technical team members can empower non-programmers with custom nodes to encourage productivity regardless of the level of programming knowledge. Bolt offers Flow Graphs, State Graphs, Live Editing, Debugging and Analysis, Codebase Compatibility, and Ease of Use, which we will describe below.

Flow Graphs

Flow Graphs will be the main tool for interaction in your projects. Using node-based actions and values, these graphs will let you dictate logic in any order you specify.

State Graphs

State Graphs allow you to create self-contained behaviors that command objects what actions to execute when they achieve a particular state. State Graphs are compatible with high-level logic such as AI behaviors, scene or level structure, or any behaviors to transition between states.

Live Editing

Live Editing can be done in real time to graphs in Play Mode. Quickly iterate and test ideas without needing to recompile project changes.

Debugging and Analysis

Debugging and Analysis can be found during Play Mode across the visual scripted graph. Bolt will highlight which nodes are being executed and then, if an error is to occur, the node will be easily identifiable.

Codebase Compatibility

Codebase Compatibility allows for any third-party plugin or custom scripts to be used within your graphs. Visual scripting accesses your code base directly via reflection and is always up to date, irrespective of whether it is a method, field, property, or event from Unity.

Ease of Use

Ease of Use visual scripting is designed to be accessible by less technical creators through user-friendly features, commenting, and searchable capabilities.

Summary

This chapter's purpose was to show some of the capabilities that Unity can offer you on your next game design ventures. They weren't used in our project, which is why we left them to a bonus chapter. The multiplayer tools are an incredible source to have for making multiplayer games. By bringing together the plugins from AR and VR into an XR plugin, we now have a nice, centralized plugin for all of the altered realities regardless of the hardware you are using. Then, to conclude this book, we talked about Bolt's visual scripting. If programming isn't easy for you to work with, consider checking that out.

We hope you learned some things from this book and had a good time while doing so. We mentioned at the beginning and throughout the book that the community on Discord is a good place to be if you want to engage with others who have purchased this book or other Packt-published, Unity-centric books. We would love to see you there and help with your next great idea.

packt.com

Subscribe to our online digital library for full access to over 7,000 books and videos, as well as industry leading tools to help you plan your personal development and advance your career. For more information, please visit our website.

Why subscribe?

- Spend less time learning and more time coding with practical eBooks and Videos from over 4,000 industry professionals
- Improve your learning with Skill Plans built especially for you
- Get a free eBook or video every month
- Fully searchable for easy access to vital information
- Copy and paste, print, and bookmark content

At www.packt.com, you can also read a collection of free technical articles, sign up for a range of free newsletters, and receive exclusive discounts and offers on Packt books and eBooks.

Other Books You May Enjoy

If you enjoyed this book, you may be interested in these other books by Packt:

Coding Roblox Games Made Easy, Second Edition

Zander Brumbaugh

ISBN: 9781803234670

- Use Roblox Studio and other free resources
- Learn coding in Luau: basics, game systems, physics manipulation, etc
- Test, evaluate, and redesign to create bug-free and engaging games
- Use Roblox programming and rewards to make your first game
- Move from lobby to battleground, build avatars, locate weapons to fight
- Character selection, countdown timers, locate escape items, assign rewards
- Master the 3 Ms: Mechanics, Monetization, Marketing (and Metaverse)
- 50 cool things to do in Roblox

Game Development Patterns with Unity 2021, Second Edition

David Baron

ISBN: 9781800200814

- Structure professional Unity code using industry-standard development patterns
- Identify the right patterns for implementing specific game mechanics or features
- Develop configurable core game mechanics and ingredients that can be modified without writing a single line of code
- Review practical object-oriented programming (OOP) techniques and learn how they're used in the context of a Unity project
- Build unique game development systems such as a level editor
- Explore ways to adapt traditional design patterns for use with the Unity API

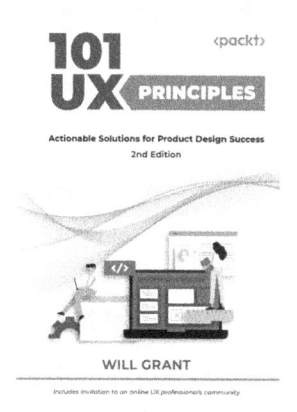

101 UX Principles, Second Edition

Will Grant

ISBN: 9781803234885

- Work with user expectations, not against them
- Make interactive elements obvious and discoverable
- Optimize your interface for mobile
- Streamline creating and entering passwords
- Use animation with care in user interfaces
- How to handle destructive user actions

Packt is searching for authors like you

If you're interested in becoming an author for Packt, please visit authors.packtpub.com and apply today. We have worked with thousands of developers and tech professionals, just like you, to help them share their insight with the global tech community. You can make a general application, apply for a specific hot topic that we are recruiting an author for, or submit your own idea.

Share your thoughts

Now you've finished *Unity 3D Game Development*, we'd love to hear your thoughts! Scan the QR code below to go straight to the Amazon review page for this book and share your feedback or leave a review on the site that you purchased it from.

https://packt.link/r/1801076146

Your review is important to us and the tech community and will help us make sure we're delivering excellent quality content.

Index

Symbols

2D sounds 241, 242

3D game development, components
  cameras 6
  collision detection 10
  coordinate systems 4
  edges 6
  faces 6
  local space versus world space 5, 6
  materials 7-9
  meshes 6
  rigid body physics 9, 10
  shaders 7-9
  textures 7-9
  vectors 6
  vertices 6

3D Geometry 104

3D puzzle adventure game
  game loop 125
  interaction 126
  interactive volumes 142
  rings 132
  stairs interaction 126
  tight spaces 140

3D sounds 242
  2D ambience 251
  ambient sounds, adding to game 249, 250
  ambient sounds, filling out 251
  audio listener part I 243
  audio listener part II 246-249

  settings 243-245
  using 242

A

Action Maps 74

Add node 218

Alpha version 28

Ambient Occlusion (AO) 213

analysis tools
  Frame debugger 267
  Memory profiler 265, 266
  Physics debugger 267-269
  Profiler module 267
  Unity profiler 264, 265

Andrewvscott
  reference link 233

Angular Drag 146

animation
  tagging, with events for sound 316-319

animation events
  sound, triggering through 314-316

asset 18

asset finalization 278, 279
  architecture cleanup 283
  cinematics 304
  detail meshes 287
  detail normal 280-282
  environment clutter 286, 287
  polishing effects 287
  secondary animation 305

stylized pass on assets 279
texture blending 284-286

B

backface culling 283

Beat Saber 151

Beta version 28

Blackboard 213, 214

Blipsounds
  reference link 233

blocking-out phase 90

bolt visual scripting 327
  Codebase Compatibility 327
  Debugging and Analysis 327
  Ease of Use 328
  Flow Graphs 327
  Live Editing 327
  State Graphs 327

broken pedestal 153
  design 154
  implementation 154

Build settings 258
  architecture 259
  autoconnect profiler 260
  compression method 261
  create Visual Studio solution 259
  deep profiling support 260
  development build 259
  Scenes In Build block 258, 259
  script debugging 260
  scripts only build 261
  server build 259
  target platform 259

built-in rendering 30

C

cameras 6

canvas component 182
  Additional Shader Channel 184
  Render Mode options 184
  render modes 183

Canvas Scaler 185
  Constant Pixel Size 185-187
  Scale With Screen Size 185, 186

center attribute 72

channel packing 221

character
  concept 54-58
  designing 54
  movement, scripting 68
  need for 54

character controllers 67
  built-in 68
  Rigidbody 68

character rigging 58
  animation 66, 67
  animation-first thinking 58
  bones and joints 61
  constraints 62, 63
  controls 64
  deformation 59
  deformers 64
  Forward Kinematics (FK) 62
  hierarchy 60, 61
  Human Inverse Kinematics (HIK) system 66
  Inverse Kinematics (IK) 62
  physics-based animation 66

Index

character script, for movement and rotations 68
   code entry point 77
   code, updating 78-80
   idling 75, 76
   methods 80-82
   RequireComponent 78
   Unity, initial setup 69-75
cinematics 304
Codebase Compatibility 327
collection 123
collision detection 10, 149
   Continuous 150
   Continuous Dynamic 150
   Continuous Speculative 151
   Discrete 149, 150
Color node 218
compression method, Build settings
   default 261
   LZ4 261
   LZ4HC 261
constraints, character rigging 62, 63
Constraints, Rigidbody component 151
control rig 61
controls, character 64

D

data types 41
   bool 42
   float 43
   GameObject 44
   integer/int 42
   strings 43
Dead Space 170
Debugging and Analysis visual scripting 327

debug log 47
decrementer 47
deformers 64
detail normal 280, 281
   Boolean keyword 283
   Combine node 281
   Multiply node 281
   Normal Reconstruct Z node 281
   Normal Strength node 282
   Sample Texture 2D node 281
   Scale and Bias nodes 281
   Swizzle node 281
   UV node 281
Diegetic UI form 169, 170
Digital Content Creation (DCC) 58, 220
doom-style controller 68
Drag, Rigidbody component 146
dynamic lighting 308-310

E

Ease of Use visual scripting 328
edge flow 59
edges 6
elements, sound design
   envelope 233, 234
   frequency 236, 237
   layering 238
   pitch 235
   source 232, 233
emissive map 210
envelope, sound design elements 233
   attack sound 234
   release sound 235
escape menu 177, 178

events for sound
  used, for tagging animation 316-319
Extrude tool 113
extrusions 114

F

faces 6
facial deformation 59
final puzzle 154
  coroutine 161, 162
  design 155
  execution order 155-157
  implementation 155
  project code 162-165
  static method 158
  UnityActions 159, 160
first-person shooters (FPSs) 124
Flow Graphs 327
for loop 47
  versus while loop 48
Forward Kinematics (FK) 62
four-way tiling texture 290
Fragment Nodes 206
frame debugger 267
frequency, sound design elements 236, 237
functional testing 262
  examples 262, 263

G

game design document 22, 23
game design fundamentals 21
  concepting 26-28
  deliberate decisions 23, 24
  iterative production 24-26

game loop 119-121
game mechanics 121
  collection 123
  design and implementation 124, 125
  limitations 123
  research 123
  resource management 122
  risk versus reward 122
  spatial awareness 122
GameObject (GO) 18, 44
game view 15, 16
generic type 136
gimbal locking 82
Graphic Raycaster Component 187, 188
Graph Inspector 214, 215
grayboxing 32

H

heads-up display (HUD) 171
heuristic design 22
hierarchy 11, 12
High-Definition Rendering Pipeline (HDRP) 29-31
High-Level Shader Language (HLSL) 201
Human Inverse Kinematics (HIK) system 66

I

idle break animation 54
if statements 45
indirect baked lighting 306, 307
infinite loop 46
Info block, Rigidbody component 151, 152
insets 114
inspector 13, 14

Integrated Development Environment (IDE) 37
interaction 121
 design and implementation 124, 125
interaction UI implementation 195-197
interactive Unity UI Objects 188
interactive volumes 142
 design 142
 implementation 142, 143
Internal UI 168
Interpolate 148
inventory systems 174
Inverse Kinematics (IK) 62
Is Kinematic boolean 147
item interaction system 175
iteration 116
iterative design or production 24

J

journal implementation 194, 195

L

Label 189
layering, sound design elements 238
Lerp node 219
lighting 305
 overview 278
lighting, purpose
 3D form 305
 gameplay design 305
 mood, providing 305
 Unity lighting 306
light probes 310-312
Lit Shader Graph 203

Live Editing 327
localization testing 270
local space
 versus world space 5, 6
Long-Term Support (LTS) release 28, 29
low barrier of entry 174

M

Machine Learning Agents (ML Agents) 326
main menu 174-176
 implementation 192-194
Main Preview 215
Mass property, Rigidbody 146
Master Stack 205-208
 Ambient Occlusion (AO) 213
 base color 208
 emissive 210-213
 metallic 209
 normal 209
 smoothness 210
Master Stack sections
 Fragment 205
 Vertex 205
Matchmaker 325
materials 7-9
memory leak 270
Memory profiler 265, 266
meshes 6
meta-progression 120
meta UI 172, 173
method 48-50
Minecraft
 game loop 120
Minimum Viable Product (MVP) 24, 34

mood board 88
  examples 88, 89
movement-related scripts 69
multiplayer tools 323
multiplayer tools pillars
  communication 325
  connection 324, 325
  creation 324
Multiply node 219, 220

N

Narrative 168
nodes 216, 217
  Add node 218
  Color node 218
  Lerp node 219
  Multiply node 219, 220
  Sample Texture 2D node 220
  Saturate node 221
  Split node 221
  UV node 222
  Vector node 222, 223
non-diegetic UI form 171
null 45, 163

O

Object Oriented Programing 41
official release version 28
order of execution, for event functions
  reference link 155

P

package manager 16, 17
packages 20
paint holes tool 95

painting
  details 104
Paint Terrain tool 94
paint textures tool 97-99
Paint Trees tool 102, 103
parenting 63
Particle Systems 223
  Shuriken 223, 224
  VFX Graph 224-228
performance testing 263
Physically Based Rendering (PBR) 203
physics-based animation 66
physics debugger 267-269
physics interaction 152
pitch, sound design elements 235
plane 7
PlayerInput 72
playtesting 269, 270
polishing effects 287
  Shuriken system 292-296
  stair blocker 287-292
  VFX Graph 296-304
Positional anchoring 182
Prefab 20, 71
premade shapes 115
ProBuilder 105, 106
  installing 106
  Object mode 108
  shapes, creating 109, 110
  shapes, editing 111
  tools 112-115
  Window path 107
Profiler module 267
programming logic 44

project window 14, 15
Proof of Concept (PoC) 33, 34
prototyping 31
  graybowing 32
  Minimum Viable Product (MVP) 34
  vertical slice 34
  wireframing or paper creation 31
puzzle sound
  adding 254, 255
  tree puzzle sound 255

R

Raising or Lowering Terrain brush 95
randomized pitch 321
randomized sounds
  adding 319
real-time lighting 308
real-time strategy (RTS) games 122
Rect transform 180-182
refactoring 137
render mode options
  Pixel Perfect 184
  Sort Order 184
  Target Display 184
render modes 183
  Screen Space, camera option 183
  Screen Space, overlay option 183
  World Space canvas 184
research 123
resource management 122
ribbon rig 64
Rigidbody
  design and implementation considerations 152

Rigidbody component 145, 146
  Angular Drag 146
  Collision Detection 149
  Constraints 151
  Drag 146
  Info 151, 152
  Interpolate 148
  Is Kinematic boolean 147
  Mass 146
  Use Gravity boolean 147
Rigidbody physics 9, 10
Rings puzzle 133
  control 139, 140
  design 133, 134
  implementation 134
  puzzle pieces 135-139
  puzzle trigger volumes 134, 135
risk
  versus reward 122
rocks falling 153
  design 153
  implementation 153

S

Sample Texture 2D node 220
Saturate node 221
scale 57
scenes 18
scene view 11, 12
scriptable rendering pipeline (SRP) 30
  built-in rendering 30
  culling 30
  High-Definition Rendering Pipeline (HDRP) 31
  post-processing 30

rendering 30
  Universal Rendering Pipeline (URP) 30
scroll view 190
sculpting tool 56
Shader Graph 201
  creating 202, 203
  Lit Shader Graph 203
  setup 201, 202
  Sprite Lit Shader Graph 204
  Sprite Unlit Shader Graph 204
  Unlit Shader Graph 204
Shader Graph interface 204
  Blackboard 213
  Graph Inspector 214, 215
  Main Preview 215
  Master Stack 205-208
  node 216, 217
shaders 7-9
Shuriken system 223, 224, 292-296
sketches
  examples 87, 88
sketching 86
SKYES Audio
  reference link 233
smoothing 100, 101
soak testing 270
sound 231
  designing, for scale 238
  making, for game 239
  overview 278
  puzzle sound, rotating 254, 255
  tree puzzle sound, adding 255
  triggering, through player interaction 251
  triggering, through Unity events 252, 253
sound design 232
  elements 232

implementing, for project 239
sound design, for project
  2D sound 241, 242
  3D sounds 242
  music 240, 241
  organizing 240
  sound, playing 239
sound polish 314
  animation, tagging with events 316-319
  sound, triggering through animation events 314-316
source, sound design elements 232, 233
spatial awareness 122
spatial tooltip 178
spatial UI 171
Split node 221
Sprite Lit Shader Graph 204
Sprite Unlit Shader Graph 204
staging 89
stair blocker 287-292
stairs interaction 126
  design 126-128
  implementation 128
  interaction block 128-131
  interaction manager 131, 132
  stair blocker 131
stamp tool 101
State Graphs 327
static objects 150
Stretched anchoring 182
string interpolation 47

T

telekinesis 152
ternary function 80

Index   343

terrain
   creating 91
   height, setting 99, 100
   height, smoothing 100, 101
   lowering 95
   painting 94
   raising 95
   settings 92, 93
   stamping 101

testing
   functional testing 262, 263
   game testing 261
   localization testing 270
   performance testing 263
   playtesting 269, 270
   soak testing 270

text 189

texture blending 284-286

textures 7-9

tight spaces 140
   design 140
   implementation 141

Tiling And Offset node 289

Time node 289

transform 4

Transform component 18

U

UI elements 173
   health representation 175
   inventory systems 174
   item interaction system 175
   main menu 174

Unity
   building with 257

   fundamentals 40, 41
   initial setup 69-75

Unity canvas system 179, 180
   canvas component 182
   Canvas Scaler 185
   Graphic Raycaster component 187, 188
   Rect transform 180-182

Unity concepts 18
   asset 18
   components 18, 19
   GameObject (GO) 18
   packages 20
   prefabs 20
   scenes 18
   script 19

Unity environment 38-40
   setting up 37

Unity events
   sound, triggering through 252, 253

Unity Gaming Services (UGS)
   bolt visual scripting 327
   Machine Learning Agents (ML-Agents) 326
   multiplayer tools 323
   XR plugin 326

Unity Hub 28

Unity interface 11
   game view 15, 16
   inspector 13, 14
   package manager 16, 17
   Project window 14, 15
   scene view and hierarchy 11, 12

Unity lighting 306
   light probes 310-312
   mixed lighting 306
   reflection probe 312, 313

Unity profiler 264, 265

Unity project 28
  scriptable rendering pipeline (SRP) 30
  template, selecting 29
  Unity Hub 28
  version, selecting 28, 29
Unity Terrain 90
Unity UI 179
  implementation 192
Unity UI objects 188-191
Universal Rendering Pipeline (URP) 7, 29, 30
Unlit Shader Graph 204
Use Gravity boolean 147
user experience (UX) 271
  branding 271
  design 271
  final puzzle 274, 275
  first puzzle 272, 273
  initial problem 272
  secondary mechanic 273, 274
  usability 271
user guidance 56
user interface 168, 169
  Diegetic 169, 170
  in project 175
  meta 172, 173
  non-diegetic 171
  spatial 171
using directive 40
UV node 222

V

variables 41
Vector node 222, 223
vectors 6
vertical slice 34

vertices 6
VFX Graph 224-228, 296-304
  nodes 229
visual effects
  overview 200
visual elements 188
visual Unity UI Objects 188

W

while loop
  debug log 47
  decrementer 47
  string interpolation 47
  versus while loop 48
while loops 46, 47
world space 5
  versus local space 5, 6

X

XR plugin 326

Lightning Source UK Ltd.
Milton Keynes UK
UKHW052137271022
411221UK00006B/45